P9-BYT-127

SIERRA
MADRE

Altadena Dr

New York Dr

Sierra Madre Blvd

Sierra Madre Villa Ave

I-210

Foothill Blvd

Colorado St

San Gabriel Blvd

Altadena Dr

Blvd

ARCADIA

Rosemead Blvd

EAST
PASADENA

California Blvd

Sierra Madre Blvd

Sunset Blvd

EAST
SAN GABRIEL

Huntington Dr

HOMETOWN
PASADENA

2009 • 2010
The San Gabriel Valley Book

Prospect Park Books

PROSPECT
·PARK·
BOOKS

Hometown Pasadena is a trademark of Prospect Park Books.

Published by Prospect Park Books
www.prospectparkbooks.com

Distributed to the trade by
SCB Distributors
www.scbdistributors.com

Special Sales
Bulk purchase (10+ copies) of Hometown Pasadena 2009.2010 is available to companies, colleges, organizations, mail-order catalogs and nonprofits at special discounts, and large orders can be customized to suit individual needs. For more information, go to prospectparkbooks.com.

Library of Congress Control Number: 2008925250
The following is for reference only:
Bates, Colleen Dunn.
        Pasadena / Colleen Dunn Bates
                p.cm.
        Includes index.
        ISBN: 978-0-9753939-4-9
        1. Pasadena (Calif.) – Guidebooks 2. San Gabriel Valley (Calif.) – Guidebooks.
        I. Bates, Colleen Dunn II. Title.

Second Edition, First Printing

Production in the United States of America. Cover art by R. Kenton Nelson.
Design by James Barkley. Production graphics by Kate Hillseth.
Printed by Four Colour Imports, China.

This book was printed on paper that was certified as sustainably produced by the Forest Stewardship Council.

HOMETOWN
PASADENA

2 0 0 9 • 2 0 1 0
The San Gabriel Valley Book

Editor
Colleen Dunn Bates

Writers
Colleen Dunn Bates
Jill Alison Ganon
Sandy Gillis
Mary Jane Horton
Melody Malmberg

Prospect Park Books

Contents

But First, a Word from Two Guys Named Larry   6
Larry Mantle, host of KPCC's *AirTalk*, and Larry Wilson, an editor
of the *Pasadena Star-News*, talk about their hometown.

About *Hometown Pasadena*   8
Round two for the book the San Gabriel Valley has come to
rely on.

Pasadena is...

16 Towns in One   9
From Sierra Madre to San Gabriel, La Cañada to Eagle Rock,
Pasadena is the hub of many remarkable communities.

Historic   27
What stories. What people. What a history.

Smart   41
Caltech, JPL, Art Center, Occidental, PCC, Idealab, Parsons... you
want smart, we've got smart. Einstein lived here. Enough said.

Literary   57
From the early days of Lummis and Gilman to the modern era of
Salzman and Kaufman, this is a writers' – and readers' – haven.

Architectural   67
Pilgrims come from around the world to see the buildings by
Greene & Greene, Wright, Neff, Marston and Neutra, as well as
the "ordinary" Craftsman bungalows, midcentury moderns and
Spanish-style cottages.

Horticultural   89
From the famed grounds of the Huntington to the secret gardens
of Caltech, the San Gabriel Valley is a garden-lover's paradise.

Famous   105
It may not have the bling of Beverly Hills, but Pasadena is
internationally famous – for its parade, its people and its
locations for movies and TV shows.

Artistic   113
World-class museums, dynamic galleries, engaging classes...
it's a right-brainer's heaven.

Reaching Out — 125

Pasadena is one of the do-good capitals of California, and here's how to get involved.

Hungry & Thirsty — 133

A diverse, food-savvy population means we get everything from the best Chinese-food community in the U.S. to terrific wine bars, steakhouses, taco joints and coffeehouses. And don't forget the farmer's markets, takeout places, gourmet stores, bakeries…

Entertaining — 177

There's theater. And music. And dance. And movies. And festivals. And laughs.

Outdoorsy — 189

Whether they're biking the Rose Bowl or skiing Mountain High, walking the Arroyo or hiking the San Gabriels, Pasadenans get outside and move.

Athletic — 203

Spectators have Rose Bowl football, horse racing, baseball and diving. Participants have it all – from swimming, golf and tennis to archery, lawn bowling and disc golf.

Materialistic — 215

The flea markets are legendary. The antiques stores are superb. The old-fashioned shopping districts are charming. In short, it's a shopper's dream.

Childlike — 237

People settle here to raise their kids, so it's no wonder there's so much going on for children.

On the Train — 253

Hop on the Gold Line to wonderful L.A. destinations, from Olvera Street to Disney Hall.

Home Away from Home — 263

Pasadena was settled by teetotaling Protestants, so by nature it's a practical place. Need a hotel, B&B, spa, pharmacy, post office, salon, florist, ER or calendar of events? You'll find it here.

Index — 275

Photo Credits — 281

Acknowledgements & Further Reading — 282

But First, a Word from Two Guys Named Larry

My Hometown
By Larry Wilson

Oft-told hometown story:

So I'm walking down 5th Avenue circa 1983 in the most fabulous metropolis in the world with Eliza Wing, the gorgeous assistant to the managing editor of *Rolling Stone*. I am a lowly fact-checker. We are on a lunch break, and she wants to buy lingerie. I'm not quite sure why I'm along for the errand.

I'm regaling her with fascinating stories of my life. As we stroll past the glittering Manhattan store windows, I'm not paying much attention to my subject matter, figuring, I don't know, that it's the singer, not the song.

She halts suddenly. Holds up her hand. I stop speaking.

"You sure talk about Pasadena a lot," says Eliza, not sounding amused.

"I do?" We resume walking and I awkwardly lurch toward a new subject.

Within a few months, I have returned to the city to which my great-grandparents moved in the late 19th century, and I get a job at the upstart *Pasadena Weekly*. I buy my first house. I have traveled and lived around the world, and yet I came back, and I've stayed back.

So what was the attraction?

First, there was a there there. And I was connected to that there. Also, a great renaissance was about to hit Pasadena. The air, choked with smog for decades, was getting markedly better. Historic preservationists were rediscovering the remarkable buildings that so contribute to the sense of place. Houses were still relatively cheap. Old Pasadena was turning the corner from skid row to major attraction. Westsiders who had turned up their noses at anything east of Fairfax took a look and liked what they saw: less traffic, bigger lots, realer people.

They saw what many of us had always seen: The greatest residential architecture in Southern California. Racial diversity the suburbs can't match. The genius of Caltech. The artistic and literary heritage of the Arroyo culture. Old money, new money, no money, all living in close quarters.

It was a wonderful city with more than its share of problems – problems that, because of Pasadena's medium scale, at least seemed to be solvable. People of goodwill joined to create more nonprofits per capita than perhaps anywhere else on Earth.

And now, nearly a quarter-century into its rebirth, Pasadena remains an enormously attractive place, a place more and more people from around the world want to be. Including me.

Larry Wilson is the public editor of the *San Gabriel Valley Tribune* papers and a columnist for the *Pasadena Star-News*

No, It's My Hometown
By Larry Mantle

I can think of no better city from which to host my daily interview/call-in program, and no better place to live, than Pasadena. In my travels across the country, I have never encountered another city that combines and balances so many desirable features. I have become a booster of the Crown City.

As a fourth-generation Southern Californian, I grew up deeply appreciating our region. The array of places to visit and fascinating people to meet will keep anyone who is open to new experiences from being bored. But it's Pasadena that brings what I like best about the Southland into a crisp and contained focus.

Here you will find an unmatched intersection of educational, cultural and spiritual institutions, great local history, remarkable architecture, natural and landscaped beauty, several superb shopping districts and a dynamic mix of residents, workers and visitors.

There are abundant challenges, to be sure. Among them are how, despite high housing costs, the city can keep such a diverse mix of residents; how to improve the achievement of students in the public schools; and how to keep traffic from strangling the city's vitality. Nevertheless, this is a community that works hard to address its shortcomings – on a per-capita basis, I don't think there is another city of this size that boasts such a huge corps of volunteers serving hundreds of valuable causes.

Pasadenans care passionately about their quality of life. Visitors pick up on this civic cohesion and express surprise that a Southern California community can feel more like a Midwestern college town than part of a sprawling megalopolis.

We who live and work here need to keep that visitor perspective in mind. Both Pasadena and the larger San Gabriel Valley offer a unique combination of assets that are worth protecting. The challenge is in balancing the effort to preserve what we have without shutting out the changes sure to come our way. This city has succeeded by not flinching from its future. And that is a legacy to preserve, too.

Larry Mantle is the host of KPCC's acclaimed *AirTalk* and the author of *This Is Airtalk: 20 Years of Conversation on 89.3 KPCC* (Angel City Press)

About *Hometown Pasadena 2009.2010*

Here we go again! In 2006, I got together a group of smart, funny, connected pals and set out to create a book about Pasadena and her sister towns. Only this wouldn't be a conventional guidebook, designed to steer tourists through a quick weekend of amusements. It was going to be a new kind of city book, in which locals wrote for locals, digging deep to reflect the place that we found so special.

All longtime residents, my friends and I spent a year learning, eating, interviewing, hiking, drinking, exploring, writing and editing. Our friend Kenton Nelson provided us with the cover painting of our dreams, and our friend Paul Click (and I) took a lot of photos. The resulting book, *Hometown Pasadena*, became the talk of the town. And now, two years and four printings later, it's time for a new edition.

What could possibly be new in just two years, you ask? Plenty. City Hall is now renovated and owns LEED Gold certification for its environmental sustainability. The Huntington finished its renovation and built a spectacular new Chinese garden. Mt. Waterman came back from the dead and is again our favorite local ski mountain. A bevy of midcentury antiques stores appeared on East Colorado. A remarkable new public garden took root on a weedy old Caltrans lot. New galleries, bookstores and boutiques sprung up. South Pasadena has become a foodie haven, Eagle Rock keeps getting hipper, and now Highland Park is reaching for its moment in the gentrification spotlight. And as for food and drink – well, let's just say there are enough new restaurants, cafés, bars, food shops and coffeehouses to fill up a small town.

So welcome to *Hometown Pasadena 2009.2010: The San Gabriel Valley Book*. Whether you're a fifth-generation native or a Rose Parade–attending visitor, I hope you'll join me, Sandy, Jill, Mel and Mary Jane in exploring, celebrating, enjoying and learning about Pasadena and her neighbors. From Sierra Madre to San Gabriel, Eagle Rock to La Cañada, San Marino to Altadena, this is a community of communities, each of which has heart, history, character, beauty, intelligence and a really good appetite.

Colleen Dunn Bates
Editor

P.S. The More Things Change...

Please forgive us if a business has closed, if prices have been raised, or if your experience does not match ours. We labored mightily to verify every scrap of information in this book, but some places will close, change or misbehave, and we can't do a thing about it.

But we can keep you more current online: Go to hometown-pasadena.com for the latest news and views on Pasadena and the San Gabriel Valley.

Pasadena is...
16 Towns in Search of One

From Sierra Madre to San Gabriel, La Cañada to Eagle Rock, Pasadena is the hub of many remarkable communities. In this chapter you'll get to know each of these towns: their founders, hangouts, dog parks, libraries, famous residents and strange laws. And, yes, even in these proper towns, their embarrassing facts.

But first, a word about the history of each community. We introduce a few people and events that helped shape each place, but we rarely mention the early days, because the story was pretty much the same everywhere. The valley's first people, the peaceful, sophisticated Tongva, were ultimately overwhelmed by the arrival of Spanish missionaries, whose Mission San Gabriel covered almost the entire valley. The Spanish were in turn displaced by Mexican secular rule, which scattered the wealthy mission's land holdings to ranchers and farmers, more of whom arrived with the onset of American rule. Both Mexican and American descendants of these early settlers played a significant role in California's future as an agricultural Eden. The local Tongva, however, were wiped out by European diseases within a couple of generations.

Please explore the Historic chapter to learn more about early life and changes in the valley, from the days of the First People to the present.

Pasadena   10

Around the Valley: Alhambra to South Pasadena   12

Pasadena

Crown of the Valley, Rose of the Southland

The Facts
What It Is: A 22.5-mile city ten miles northeast of downtown L.A.
Population: 146,166
Sister Cities: Mishima, Japan; Beijing, China; Ludwigshafen am Rhein, Germany; Vanadzor, Armenia; and Jarvenpaa, Finland
Ethnic Diversity: 53.4% Caucasian, 14.4% African-American, 10% Asian and 17% other ethnicities; within those groupings, 33% are Hispanic (don't ask – the U.S. Census follows its own bizarre logic)
Median Household Income: $46,012

Key Players
Led by brothers-in-law Dr. Thomas Balch Elliott and Daniel Berry, Pasadena's first American settlers were some 100 Indiana families fleeing the Midwest's nasty winters. Called the Indiana Colony, they bought a 4,000-acre hunk of the San Pasqual Ranch and began building a town and wooing newcomers. The early arrivals were conservative Christian folk, who in 1886 incorporated the city mostly so they could outlaw the sale of alcohol.

The Name
"Pasadena" is a Chippewa word for "valley," although it was interpreted to mean "Crown of the Valley" – hence the nickname "The Crown City." (It's sometimes also referred to as "The Rose City," thanks to a certain parade and football stadium.)

Telling Moments
The new city became a wintertime haven for wealthy Eastern industrialists, and its arts, schools, churches, gardens and architecture thrived. The Valley Hunt Club, founded by fox hunters, began the Rose Parade as a booster activity in 1890; Throop Polytechnic Institute (later Caltech) was founded in 1891; resort hotels and health sanitariums in the San Gabriel Mountains and foothills thrived; and the Rose Bowl came along in 1922, replacing a dump in the Arroyo Seco, the ancient river canyon that runs through Pasadena's west side.

In 1970, Pasadena won national fame for something other than the Rose Parade: It was the first non-Southern city ordered by the feds to desegregate its schools. The decade that followed was one of bitter battles within the community, and the effects are still felt today – including the fact that nearly a third of Pasadena's children attend private schools, the highest percentage in the nation.

Then & Now
Pasadena lost its once-glamorous resort luster during the Depression and gradually morphed into a city known for its scientific and technical businesses and education, its high society, its do-gooderism and its handsome neighborhoods. With the 1940 opening of the west's first freeway, the Arroyo Seco Parkway (now called the Pasadena Freeway), it also became home to many L.A. commuters. The city's last renaissance began in the mid-'80s with the restoration of once-squalid Old Pasadena, now a glossy outdoor mall. Pasadena has boomed in the last decade, with offices, condos, apartments and the Gold Line light-rail train all being built. (It takes a lot longer to drive across town, but, boy, have our property values soared…)

Our Favorite…
Library: Pasadena Central Library, a grand and lovely 1927 Mediterranean-style building; don't miss the Peter Pan fireplace, created by Pasadena artist Maud Daggett in the '20s
Park: Lower Arroyo Seco, home to a casting pond, archery range and miles of trails
Dog Park: Alice Frost Kennedy Off-Leash Dog Area in Eaton Wash Park, on Orange Grove just west of Sierra Madre Villa
Farmer's Markets: Victory Park, on Sierra Madre Villa, Saturday 8:30 a.m.-12:30 p.m.; and Villa Park, Villa Street at Garfield, Tuesday from 8:30 a.m.-12:30 p.m.; pasadenafarmersmarket.org
Arts Organization: Pasadena Art Alliance, a venerable group that combines blue-blood credentials with a cutting-edge sensibility
Parade: Gee, does Pasadena have a parade?
Radio Station: KPCC, 89.3 FM, a National Public Radio station
Newspaper: *Pasadena Star-News* and *Pasadena Weekly*
Hospital: Huntington Hospital, with complete ER, 626.397.5000
Web Sites: pasadenacal.com; cityofpasadena.net

Don't Be a Lawbreaker!

Noah, you'd better find another place for the ark!
No person shall keep or maintain any hog or hogs within the city of Pasadena.

Other ordinances forbid feeding pigeons, letting pet monkeys run free within the city limits, and low-altitude formation flying before sunrise.

What She/He Said

"Suburbs, developments and intersections, and here we are in Pasadena. Softly sloping avenues loll between orange trees and thickset palms."
— *Simone de Beauvoir*

"Come to think of it, Pasadena's as good a place to die as any."
— *from the 1993 film* The Player, *directed by Robert Altman*

"I once witnessed more ardent emotions between men at an Elks' Rally in Pasadena than they could ever have felt for the type of woman available to an Elk."
— *Anita Loos*

"In addition to everything, you have those mountains."
— *Doris Lessing*

Best Hangouts

Vroman's Bookstore; Peet's Coffee & Tea; Old Town for teens and young adults; the excellent Senior Center for the over-65ers; and Tournament and Singer parks for the under-8 set.

The Smart Set

Since its early days, Pasadena has been a haven for education, science, the arts and intellectual pursuits. Today it is home to the following institutions of higher learning:

Art Center College of Design, famed for its automotive-design program but also highly regarded for its photography, graphic design, fine arts and product design programs

The California Institute of Technology (Caltech), a world-renowned center for undergrads, graduate students and researchers in science, math and engineering

California School of Culinary Arts, offering AA degrees and culinary training

Fuller Theological Seminary, a Christian graduate school for future ministers, therapists, psychologists and theologians

Occidental College, an excellent liberal-arts college (okay, it's really next door in Eagle Rock)

Pacific Oaks College, a nationally known college for teachers and counselors

Pasadena City College, a highly rated community college offering AA degrees and continuing and vocational education

Born in Pasadena

Octavia Butler

Julia Child

Sally Field

Harry Hamlin

Jackie Robinson

Jet Propulsion Laboratory

John Singleton graduated from Blair High School

Eddie & Alex Van Halen were born in Holland but raised in Pasadena

Embarrassing Fact

The Human Betterment Foundation (HBF), which advocated eugenics – the compulsory sterilization of the mentally ill and mentally retarded – was founded in Pasadena in 1928 by citrus magnate Ezra Seymour Gosney. Inspired by the eugenics program practiced in Nazi Germany, the HBF boasted such luminaries as the president of Caltech and the chancellor of Stanford as members.

OLD PASADENA
Is Listed In
THE NATIONAL
REGISTER OF
HISTORIC PLACES
By the United States
Department of the Interior
September 15, 1983

Alhambra
Gateway to the San Gabriel Valley

The Facts
What It Is: A 7.5-square-mile city eight miles east of downtown L.A.; the San Bernardino Freeway (I-10) runs through the south end of town, and the 710 Freeway ends at Valley Blvd.
Population: 85,804
Ethnic Diversity: 47% Asian, 35% Hispanic, 30% Caucasian, 2% black or African-American
Median Household Income: $44,513

Key Players
During the era of Mexican rule, Ramona Yorba of the Rancho de Santa Ana clan married rich trapper Benjamin ("Don Benito") Wilson, bringing him large land tracts, which he skillfully added to, and which included what is now Alhambra. (Ramona died young, and Wilson later remarried.)

The Name
Wilson named his town for the book about the Moorish-Spanish palace, *Tales from the Alhambra,* because his 10-year-old daughter Ruth (who became the mother of Gen. George S. Patton) was reading it.

Telling Moment
Don Benito Wilson's son-in-law, an engineer named James de Barth Shorb, mastered iron plumbing for the new town of Alhambra and cleverly sited plumbed lots near the new transcontinental railway (mail delivery daily – not weekly, as in Pasadena!). And so the new town prospered.

Then & Now
After World War II, Alhambra became a destination for upwardly mobile Latinos; in the '50s, many Italian-Americans discovered these pretty neighborhoods. White flight in the '70s made way for émigrés from Taiwan, Vietnam, Hong Kong and mainland China. The more recent immigrants have been less affluent than in neighboring Monterey Park and San Gabriel, and the community has had to deal with some crime issues. But this is an energetic and pleasant Asian-majority town with an appealing Old Town and lots of good Chinese restaurants.

Our Favorite...
Library: The new, even busier 45,000-square-foot Civic Center Library houses wings for children's, adult nonfiction and reference – and there's two floors of garage parking, too!
Farmer's Market: On Monterey St., Sunday 8:30 a.m.-1 p.m.
Park: Massive Almansor Park, home to a highly regarded 18-hole golf course, large soccer fields, playgrounds, tennis, a gymnasium and more
Hospital: Alhambra Hospital Medical Center, with 24-hour emergency service, 626.570.1606
Web Site: cityofalhambra.org

Don't Be a Lawbreaker!
Did you feel that?
It shall be unlawful for any person to create, maintain or cause any ground vibration that is perceptible without instruments.

Best Hangout
The small Old Town-style district centered around Main and Garfield, where people gather at Starbucks, Angelena's soul-food café, a good internet café and Bluecherry, a yogurt spot that's not at all a ripoff of a certain pink spot!

Slept in Alhambra
Swashbuckling star Tyrone Power lived here in the early '20s – he was a sickly child, and his parents thought the climate would help. But when they divorced, it was back to Cincinnati for the family.

Embarrassing Fact
Famed record producer Phil Spector (that's Mr. Wall of Sound to you), who once claimed his parents were first cousins, lives here, in a double-gated hilltop fortress, where B actress Lana Clarkson was found shot dead, with Spector and his gun present. The first murder case ended in a mistrial; at press time he was holed up awaiting a retrial. Maybe his parents really were first cousins. It would explain a lot.

Altadena

Upper Pasadena (or *Altadinky*)

The Facts

What It Is: An 8.7-square-mile area in unincorporated L.A. County, located between the San Gabriels and Pasadena, seventeen miles northeast of downtown L.A.

Elevation: 1,342 feet

Population: 42,610

Ethnic Diversity: 39% Caucasian, 31% African-American, 20% Hispanic, 3% Asian, 2% American Indian

Median Household Income: $60,549

Key Players

In 1882, brothers John and Frederick Woodbury bought 937 acres from the Indiana Colony (which founded Pasadena) and began planning a residential development called the Highlands, which they later named Altadena. This subdivision of Pasadena promised health and wealth, attracting Midwestern tycoons and farmers to build mansions and ranches. Sanitariums were numerous, as were olive and citrus orchards and vineyards.

Telling Moments

While the conservative neighborhoods of 19th-century Pasadena were dry, Altadena took pride in its vineyards and its variety of locally produced wines (some of which managed to find their way down the hill into Pasadena's hotels). Despite its disapproval of its wanton neighbor, Pasadena chipped away at Altadena's borders, subsuming property for the increased tax base. In 1950, Altadena put a stop to takeover efforts, but it never incorporated as a city.

Then & Now

Starting with former slave Robert Owens, an entrepreneur who became L.A.'s richest black man in the 1850s, Altadena has been home to one of the largest, most thriving African-American populations in Southern California. And it is the fictional home of Marty Culp and Bobbi Moughan-Culp (aka *SNL's* Will Ferrell and Ana Gasteyer), music teachers at Altadena Middle School (which doesn't actually exist).

Our Favorite...

Library: 600 E. Mariposa; don't miss preschool story time

Park: Loma Alta Park, atop Lincoln – little used, with great tennis courts, playing fields and even equestrian facilities

Theater: Farnsworth Park's old-timey amphitheater (summer concerts) and WPA-built Davies Memorial Building, on the National Register of Historic Places

Parade: February's Black History Parade, down Fair Oaks

View: Take the 2.5-mile hike up Echo Mountain (trailhead atop Lake Ave.)

Hospital: Down the hill to Huntington Hospital, with complete ER, 626.397.5000

Web Site: altadenatowncouncil.org

R.I.P.

At Mountain View Cemetery on Fair Oaks, actor George Reeves, TV's Superman, slumbers near black activist Eldridge Cleaver, architect Wallace Neff and John Ransom (author of *Andersonville Diary,* the 1881 book about a notorious Civil War POW camp). *Seinfeld's* funeral episode for Susan, George's fiancé who died from a wedding-invitation paper cut, was filmed here.

Best Hangout

Under Christmas Tree Lane's 140-year-old deodars, on Santa Rosa south of Altadena Dr.

What He Said

"That first spring, we marveled to see the slope ablaze with poppies and were told that ships steered their course by the bright color."
— *Rufus Fiske Bishop, recalling his first sights of Altadena, in 1858*

Born in Altadena

California's Boy Scout Troop #1, in 1919

Slept in Altadena (But Not Together)

Painter Charles White, actors Ivan Dixon, Sidney Poitier and Claude Akins, pulp-Western writer Zane Grey and Keystone Cop Fatty Arbuckle

Arcadia
Home of... Homes

The Facts
What It Is: An eleven-square-mile city due east of Pasadena
Population: 55,992
Ethnic Diversity: 46% Caucasian, 45% Asian, 11% Hispanic, 1% African-American
Median Household Income: $56,100

Key Player
During American statehood, Elias J. "Lucky" Baldwin began developing the area as an agricultural paradise, building himself a Queen Anne mansion and a stable to house his race-winning thoroughbred horses; when settlers started pouring into California, he built houses for them to buy. Baldwin was a legendary ladies' man who faced many a lawsuit from former wives and mistresses, one of whom was only 16. The Arboretum is what's left today, after his once-vast fortunes dwindled, which forced Mr. B. to rethink his nickname.

Then & Now
Long after Baldwin's bust, Arcadia enjoyed a midcentury boom; the suburban architecture of the 1940s and '50s still dominates, even in the many (near-empty) bars along Huntington Dr. for the party-till-you're-paunchy set. Preservationists are scarce, bowing to commerce and the development of a grand new Grove-style shopping mall right next to the Westfield shopping mall. This industrious, upscale bedroom community throws itself into its excellent public school system and many hours of private tutoring.

Our Favorite...
Library: The beautifully equipped Arcadia Public Library, on W. Duarte Rd., is jumping at 3 p.m.

daily. Kids working, or workin' it – mondo cell phone usage. Can you say "Shhh"?
Dog Park: Eisenhower Park, 2nd & Colorado
Park: Arcadia Park, a huge county facility with tennis courts, baseball diamonds, an Olympic pool, violin lessons and caper dancing, whatever that is
Skate Park: Bonita, on 2nd Ave. just southeast of Huntington; helmets required, citations happen
Breakfast: Watching the horses work out at Santa Anita Racetrack's Clockers' Corner, weekdays in season (Dec.-Apr.) from 7:30 a.m.
Hospital: Arcadia Methodist, with a full ER, 626.445.4441
Web Site: ci.arcadia.ca.us

Don't Be a Lawbreaker!
Say, can you direct me to the nearest house of ill repute?
Immorality prohibited. No person shall… suffer or permit any portion thereof to be used as a house of ill fame… nor direct persons thereto or elsewhere for immoral purposes.

What He Said
"By gads! This is paradise!"
"By gads! I'm not licked yet!"
> – *Lucky Baldwin, upon arrival and at various intervals*

Look Fast!
The Santa Anita Racetrack is a magnificent art deco jewel, designed by Gordon Kauffman (who also did Hoover Dam).

Best Hangout
The Arboretum in the summer; come for the California Philharmonic's evening music series on the great lawn.

Arcadia Notables
Athletes love Arcadia: Brad Bedell (Green Bay Packers), John Grabow (Pittsburgh Pirates), Scott Peters (San Francisco 49ers). Seabiscuit raced here, and, bucking the athletic trend, Hunter S. Thompson wrote much of *Fear and Loathing in Las Vegas* in a motel across from the racetrack

Embarrassing Fact
During World War II Santa Anita Racetrack was used as an "assembly center" for more than 20,000 good and loyal Japanese-American citizens, who lived here before U.S. government relocation to internment camps. Actor George Takei, *Star Trek's* beloved Mr. Sulu, slept here.

Eagle Rock

"That's Right, You Heard Me: Eagle Rock Is Hip!"

The Facts
What It Is: An L.A. community bordered by Pasadena to the west, Glendale to the east and north, and Highland Park to the south
Population: 17,763
Ethnic Diversity: 47% Caucasian, 39% Hispanic, 25% Asian (including a significant Filipino population), 2% African-American
Median Household Income: $47,488

Key Players
Occidental College moved here from Highland Park in 1914; the three original buildings designed by famed architect Myron Hunt stand today, and the college is one of the finest liberal-arts schools in the West.

The Name
The huge boulder on the northeast end of town, looming over the 134 Freeway, has a natural bas-relief that looks like an eagle.

Telling Moments
In the late 19th century, America's westward expansion saw settlers flourishing here. By 1909 one could ride the #5 streetcar from Eagle Rock all the way to the Pacific coast. Eagle Rock was incorporated in 1911, but became annexed to L.A. in 1923 – a decision linked to its need for water and the arrival of Owens Valley water to L.A.'s aqueduct. Ironically, the famous Sparkletts Drinking Water Corporation was founded in 1925 on Eagle Rock's York Boulevard, atop three wells that contained plenty of water.

Then & Now
For many decades, Eagle Rock was an ordinary, middle-class place with a plethora of auto-repair shops. Now real estate values are soaring and destination coffeehouses and restaurants have arrived. But the community has retained its one-of-a-kind, still-funky character. It's a little gem – an eccentric one, but a sparkler nonetheless.

Our Favorite...
Library: Eagle Rock Branch Library, on Caspar Ave.
Farmer's Market: Friday evenings, 5-8:30 p.m., at 2100 Merton Ave.

Arts Organization: The Center for the Arts, Eagle Rock; says executive director Jenny Krusoe, "We treat this place like the mother ship, supporting great collaborative satellite sites for artists and arts education throughout northeast L.A."
Parade: The Northeast Christmas Parade & Winter Fest is going strong for over 60 years
Newspaper: *Boulevard Sentinel;* its motto is "To comfort the afflicted and afflict the comfortable"; boulevardsentinel.com
Hospital: Glendale Adventist in Glendale with complete ER, 818.409.8000
Web Site: eaglerocknet.com

What He Said
"Eagle Rock: Where land use and planning is a contact sport."
— *The Eagle Rock Association e-newsletter*

Best Hangout
Love, love, love Swork, at the corner of Colorado and Eagle Rock, for great coffee, free WiFi and a toddler play area (don't come here if you hate kids); command central for modern Eagle Rock life is Auntie Em's, the hippest café/bakery/gourmet shop on the eastside.

Born in Eagle Rock
Madeleine Stowe

The Writers' Life
In 1930, John Steinbeck wrote an early novel, *To an Unknown God,* in a $15-a-month house here, and Ben and Matt wrote *Good Will Hunting* in a back house on Hill Drive.

Little-Known Fact
Officers of the Chinese revolutionary army that overthrew the Manchu Dynasty in 1911 trained in the Eagle Rock hills, led by Oxy alum Homer Lea.

Glendale
The Valley Valley

The Facts
What It Is: A 30.6-square-mile city west of Pasadena and seven miles north of L.A.
Population: 201,326
Ethnic Diversity: 66% Caucasian (including 30% Armenian and 20% Hispanic), 16% Asian, 1% African-American
Sister Cities: several, including Hiroshima, Japan, and Kapan, Armenia
Median Household Income: $41,805

Key Players
In 1784, a corporal in the Spanish Army from Baja named Jose Maria Verdugo started ranching cattle in the area, and in 1798 he was granted a massive tract called Rancho San Rafael. He eventually went bankrupt, and his children and grandchildren sold off hunks of the ranch over time, some of which became Glendale, Eagle Rock and Highland Park.

The Name
The community was named in 1884. "Glendale" is nonsensical, meaning "valley valley." Rejected choices included Minneapolis and Etheldean.

Then & Now
For decades Glendale was known as a suburb for conservative white people. Today it is a diverse, bustling metropolis that is home to, among others, a large and vibrant Armenian community. It is blessed with lovely parks, handsome older homes, the grand old Alex Theatre and the gorgeous Brand Library, home to the world's largest collection of books on cats.

Our Favorite…
Library: Brand Library, in a 1904 Moorish mansion in Brand Park; excellent art and music program
Farmer's Market: Thursday morning on Brand Blvd., in front of the Exchange
Park: Verdugo Park, alongside Cañada Blvd., a huge, green oasis with everything from a volleyball court to a way cool skate park
Arts Organization: The Alex Film Society, alexfilmsociety.org, hosts great classic-movie screenings

Parade: Glendale-Montrose Christmas Parade, first Saturday in December
Newspaper: *Glendale News-Press*
Hospital: Glendale Adventist, with complete ER, 818.409.8000
Web Site: ci.glendale.ca.us

Don't Be a Lawbreaker!
Every party has a pooper, that's why we invited you!
Don't pull a rabbit out of your hat in Glendale – magic is banned. Also illegal are fortune-telling, sand gazing, mental telepathy, spirit writing, palmistry, astrology and, of course, trumpet séances.

What He Said
"Glendale… a high-class, positively restricted development for discriminating people that run filling stations, and furniture factories, and markets, and pie wagons. The garden spot of the world – in the pig's eye."
– from *Mildred Pierce, by James M. Cain*

Best Hangout
Forest Lawn Memorial Park is final home to locals and celebrities alike, including W.C. Fields, Walt Disney, Casey Stengel, Bette Davis, Karen Carpenter, Nat King Cole and Chico Marx. Forest Lawn was the model for Evelyn Waugh's great satirical novel *The Loved One.*

Born in Glendale
Bob's Big Boy

Baskin-Robbins 31 Flavors

John Wayne wasn't born here, but he graduated from Glendale High.

Embarrassing Fact
In 1964, George Lincoln Rockwell chose Glendale as the headquarters for the American Nazi Party. The downtown office remained open until the early '80s.

Hermon
The Little Town That Could

The Facts
What It Is: A half-square-mile L.A. community bordered by Highland Park to the north and west, El Sereno to the south and Monterey Hills to the east
Population: 3,327
Ethnic Diversity: No statistics available; presumably the majority groups are Hispanic and Anglo
Number of Homes: 1,100
Number of Grocery Stores: 2

Hermon Who?
Perhaps you're like us – you've lived here your entire life and never once heard of Hermon. Well, we're here to tell you that Hermon's been right under our noses all along – we just didn't know it.

Key Players
In 1902, a group of Free Methodists walked up the Arroyo Seco from L.A. to look for land to build a school, and they found this tidy little valley. The land's owner knew his property's isolation made it a tough sell, so he donated some of it to the Methodists to seal the deal. The new settlers named the town Hermon after the biblical Mount Hermon, and by 1904 they had 50 homes, a church, a private Methodist school and a public school (now the Bushnell School).

Telling Moments
In 1911, the town fathers founded California's first junior college, which went on to become Los Angeles Pacific College (which later merged with Azusa College and left town). In 1912, Hermon became part of the mushrooming city of Los Angeles, but it retained its clean-living Methodist ways. Then in the '60s, when L.A. Pacific College moved, a grocery store bought the land and scored a liquor license. Hermon gradually lost its Methodist soul.

Then & Now
The community's final insult came in 1978, when L.A. councilman Art Snyder renamed Hermon Ave. "Via Marisol" for his 3-year-old daughter, Erin-Marisol. All the street signs and the sign for the Pasadena Freeway exit were changed, leaving locals feeling angry but powerless. Finally, in the late '90s, neighbors banded together to fight a hillside development, and as part of that process they demanded that their community get its name back. Hermon was born again, and the tree-lined streets of modest little frame houses are looking sprightlier.

Our Favorite...
Library: Just across the Pasadena Freeway is the Arroyo Seco Regional Branch Library, on Figueroa St., a very cool stone building
Arts Organization: Art-in-the-Park, which runs art classes, a Day of the Dead festival and the Lalo Guerrero School of Music, named for the "godfather of Chicano music"
Dog Park: Hermon Dog Park, a wonderful doggie playland in Hermon Park, off Via Marisol and Ave. 60
Web Site: hermon.org

Best Hangout
Lovely Ernest Debs Regional Park, which makes up the west border of the community.

Born in Hermon
Claude A. Watson, a prominent Hermon attorney who ran for U.S. president on the Prohibition Party ticket in the 1944 and 1948 elections

Highland Park
Arroyo Arts Haven

The Facts
What It Is: A 3.76-square-mile section of L.A., west of South Pasadena and south of Eagle Rock
Population: 58,051
Ethnic Diversity: 73% Hispanic and/or white, 12% Caucasian and 3% African-American
Median Household Income: $34,000

Key Players
In the early 20th century, Highland Park was a mecca for intellectual practitioners of the Arts & Crafts movement, including painter William Lees Judson and printer/typographer Clyde Browne, who built the now-shabby Arroyo San Encino, a gathering place for artists. It was also the location of many a silent film – one of L.A.'s first movie studios was located next to Sycamore Grove Park.

Telling Moment
One of L.A.'s earliest subdivisions, Highland Park asked to be annexed to the city of Los Angeles in the late 1890s – it needed water and it wanted the bigger city's police force to help control the wild saloons that had sprouted up around what is now Sycamore Grove Park.

Then & Now
Charles F. Lummis settled here after writing about his 1884 walk from Ohio to take a job at the *Los Angeles Times.* His handmade castle, El Alisal ("Place of the Sycamore"), is open to the public, as is the nearby Southwest Museum, L.A.'s first museum and a bounty of Native American photos, art and artifacts. Today, Highland Park isn't as affluent as its hillside neighbors Washington Heights and Monterey Hills, but its increasingly boho-meets-bodega atmosphere is drawing more and more of the Prius-and-chai set.

Our Favorite...
Park: Sycamore Park, with playgrounds and climbing structures, the Hiner Bandstand, tennis courts, families out on Sunday afternoon and multitudinous picnic tables and barbecues shaded by old sycamores; taco trucks park on Figueroa in case you forgot a picnic
Library: Arroyo Seco Regional Branch on Figueroa, whose architecture pays tribute to El Alisal
Arts Organization: The Arroyo Arts Collective, sponsoring art shows, community art projects and an annual tour of artists' homes
Attraction: Heritage Square, a collection of Victorian mansions, some of which were moved here to save them from demolition
Web Sites: historichighlandpark.org, hpht.org

Best Hangouts
Pets with Fez, an incense-filled weaving studio on York (lessons on jumbo looms!); the new gastropub on York called, of course, the York; and, for underage drinkers, Galco's Soda Pop Stop, home to 500 specialty sodas.

What He Said
"This Arroyo would make one of the greatest parks in the world!"
                    – President Teddy Roosevelt
                         to Charles Lummis, 1911
(Twelve years later, Lummis pressed the city into dedicating 60 acres to the Arroyo Seco Park System. Bully for us!)

Born in Highland Park
USC's College of Fine Arts (1901)

Lived in Highland Park
Occidental College (moved from Boyle Heights in 1898)

Jackson & Severin Browne, musicians and grandsons of Clyde Browne

Edward Furlong, actor

Porntip Nakhirunkanok, Miss Universe 1988 (Thailand)

Bobby Riggs, tennis star

Rocky Delgadillo, L.A. City Attorney

La Cañada Flintridge
"We Moved Here for the Schools"

The Facts
What It Is: An 8.5-square-mile city thirteen miles northeast of downtown L.A., stretching along the San Gabriels and bordered by Glendale to the south, La Crescenta to the west, and Altadena and Pasadena to the east
Population: 21,555
Ethnic Diversity: There must be a minority around here somewhere! Actually, as of the 2000 census, La Cañada was 75% Caucasian and 21% Asian, with 73 African-Americans around town, too
Ratio of White-collar to Blue-collar workers: 11 to 1
Median Household Income: $133,754

Key Players
Once part of Mexican rancher Jose Maria Verdugo's vast spread, this land changed hands several times before being bought in 1875 by two Michigan health seekers, Jacob Lanterman and Adolphus Williams. Because there was no water, they got the whole spread for $10,000 and soon subdivided it. La Cañada's early years were hardscrabble, but eventually deep wells – and a road down to L.A. – brought prosperity.

Then & Now
In 1913, the new subdivision of Flintridge was formed, comprising luxury homes on large, secluded hillside lots. For decades La Cañada and Flintridge were part of unincorporated L.A. County, but as Glendale and Pasadena moved to annex these wealthy, conservative 'burbs – and their superb schools – the communities banded together, and in 1976, the city of La Cañada Flintridge was born. Nobody calls it that, though – we just call it La Cañada (and that's "cun-ya-da").

Our Favorite...
Library: La Cañada Flintridge Library, on Oakwood
Farmer's Market: Beulah Drive at Foothill, Saturday 9 a.m.-1 p.m.
Park: 1,300-acre Hahamongna Watershed Park, technically in Pasadena's jurisdiction, but more linked to La Cañada
Arts Organization: Descanso Gardens, where horticulture is indeed an art form; good art gallery on-site
Parade: Fiesta Day Parade, on Memorial Day down Foothill Blvd.
Newspaper: La Cañada Valley Sun, lacanadaonline.com
Hospital: Verdugo Hills Hospital, with limited ER services, 818.952.2222
Web Site: lacanadaflintridge.ca.gov

Don't Be a Lawbreaker!
Frankly, it's that infernal dinging we don't care for.
If you own a business in La Cañada, don't put in a pinball machine – they're illegal!

What She Said
"I found most of the families in the Valley to be interesting, kindly people, some prosperous, but mostly struggling ranchers, for a drought was upon the land, and a threatening depression alarmed everyone."
– *Emily Lanterman, an early La Cañada settler, in 1885*

Best Hangout
The Crescenta-Cañada YMCA on Foothill is the hub of the community, offering everything from bingo to yoga to a superb Youth & Government program; nonmembers pay $15 a day.

Slept in La Cañada
Delta Burke and Gerald McRaney used to be La Cañadans, and actors Haley Joel and Emily Osment went to school here, as did Steven J. Cannell.

Embarrassing Fact
We couldn't find any, but since the *Desperate Housewives'* Wisteria Lane is so very La Cañada-like, the embarrassments are surely of the private kind.

La Crescenta & Montrose
"I Thought This Was Glendale!"

The Facts
What It Is: Sister suburbs at the base of the San Gabriel Mountains, north of Glendale and west of La Cañada, about twelve miles north of downtown L.A.; unincorporated, they are overseen by the L.A. County government
Population: 18,532
Ethnic Diversity: White folks make up a considerable majority, but, move over, it's now about 19% Asian and 10% Hispanic
Median Household Income: $60,089

Key Players
In the early 1880s, an Indiana doctor named Benjamin Briggs discovered the area while seeking a place with an ideal climate for a health resort. Although he didn't live to see his community thrive, it did become a popular locale for clinics and health sanitariums; in the teens and '20s, the Crescenta Valley also became home to orchards, ranches and vacation homes for well-off families way down in Los Angeles.

The Name
Briggs named La Crescenta for the crescent-shaped mountain peaks he saw out his kitchen window.

Telling Moment
When onetime owner Don Jose Maria Verdugo went bankrupt and lost the land, these San Gabriel foothills were populated mostly by bandits, some of whom were Tongva Indians that the rancho had displaced; the bandits became known as "verdugos."

Then & Now
The flash flood on New Year's Day 1934 brought devastation, but by the '40s tract homes arrived, and these towns became the quiet, comfortable bedroom communities they are today, with good schools and friendly mom-n-pop businesses.

Our Favorite…
Library: The Montrose-Crescenta Library on Honolulu, with great programs for kids and teens
Farmer's Market: Honolulu at Ocean Ave. in Montrose, Sundays 9 a.m.-2 p.m.
Park: Two Strike Park on Rosemont, with sports, picnic and play facilities
Arts Organization: The Montrose-Verdugo City Chamber sponsors monthly art walks
Parade: Glendale-Montrose Christmas Parade, 1st Saturday in December
Newspaper: *Glendale News-Press* & the *Crescenta Valley Sun,* crescentavalleyonline.com
Hospital: Glendale Adventist, with complete ER, 818.409.8000
Web Site: yourtowncouncil.org

Don't Be a Lawbreaker!
I know that ruler is around here somewhere. . .
It is illegal for any female waitress or performer in a public place to expose "any portion of either breast below a straight line so drawn that both nipples, and all portions of both breasts which have a different pigmentation than that of the main portion of the breasts, are below such straight line."

What He Said
"When the developers began to sell land up here, many were leery about shady deals. There was a saying: 'The first year you get cheated. The second year you watched others get cheated. And the third you started cheating others.'"

– *Charles Bausback,*
Montrose, California: The First Eighty Years

Best Hangouts
Any of several places along pedestrian-happy Honolulu in Montrose, especially the Star Café, Zeke's Smokehouse and Coffee Bean & Tea Leaf.

Born in La Crescenta
A number of fine, upstanding citizens you've never heard of

Monrovia
Small Town U.S.A.

The Facts
What It Is: A fourteen-square-mile city bordered by the San Gabriel Mountains to the north, Pasadena to the west, Arcadia to the south and Azusa to the east
Population: 37,996
Ethnic Diversity: Primarily Caucasian and Hispanic, but also 9% African-American and 7% Asian, the latter of which is oddly small given the large Asian population in neighboring towns
Median Household Income: $53,322

Key Players
By the 1880s, land that had gone through Spanish ownership was purchased by four men, including railroad builder William N. Monroe, namesake of the growing town. Early in the 20th century, railroad travel made it possible for Monrovians to commute to work in Los Angeles, and for tourists to make their way to Monrovia.

Telling Moments
As you might expect of such a picturesque locale (Victorian cottages, tree-shaded lanes, a vintage Main Street), Hollywood has found its way here – many films have used its fetching small-town locations, *Grosse Pointe Blank* and *Legally Blonde* being two of our favorites.

Then & Now
In 1925, the fabulous Aztec Hotel, designed by architect Robert Stacy-Judd, was built on what we now know as Route 66. It's pretty shabby these days, but now that the Aztec has historic-landmark status, it is slowly being renovated, and it welcomes travelers to stay the night or drop in for a drink at the Brass Elephant.

Our Favorite…
Library: Until the new building opens its doors in lovely Library Park (they say spring 2009, but we all know how these things can drag on), the library is housed at the youth center at 843 N. Olive Ave.
Farmer's Market: Monrovia Farmers' Market & Family Festival, along N. Myrtle on Friday evenings, is quite the shindig

Park: Aptly named Recreation Park, on Shamrock and Lemon, with tennis, baseball, volleyball, basketball and more
Arts Organization: Monrovia's finest art pieces are its older homes; the Monrovia Old House Preservation Group helps save those gems
Parades: Monrovia Days in May, with a parade, soapbox derby and festival; there's usually a Christmas parade, too
Newspapers: *Monrovia Weekly* & *Monrovia Today*, a monthly newsletter
College: Mount Sierra College offers bachelors degrees through on-campus or online programs
Adult Ed: Low-cost Monrovia Community Adult School on Mountain Ave.; classes in workplace Spanish, software, and the famed upholstery workshop, which has a two-year wait list.
Web Site: ci.monrovia.ca.us

Don't Be a Lawbreaker!
All-righty then… that was Mr. and Mrs. Smith, right?
It's against the law to enter a fictitious name onto a hotel register.

Who Knew?
There is a wonderful eight-foot stained-glass window of C.S. Lewis and the characters from *Narnia* in St. Luke's Episcopal Church.

Best Hangout
The aforementioned Farmer's Market & Family Festival, which is the place to be on Friday evenings.

Slept in Monrovia
The great silent-film star Mabel Normand died of tuberculosis at a sanitarium here in 1930; Upton and Mary Sinclair lived in Monrovia, and their former house is now a landmark.

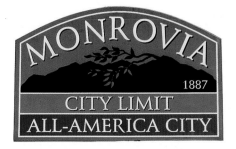

Monterey Park
America's Chinatown

The Facts
What It Is: A 7.7-square-mile city eight miles south of Pasadena and nine miles east of downtown L.A.
Population: 60,051
Ethnic Diversity: 62% Asian, 29% Hispanic and/or Caucasian and darn few African-Americans, Native Americans and Pacific Islanders
Median Household Income: $41,000

Key Players
These pretty hills were originally inhabited by First People Tongva, who, like their Chumash and Shoshone kin, were believed to have used paths alongside nearby waterways as a land route to the ocean. When Spanish explorer Juan Batista de Anza arrived, the green hills of Monterey Park fed his horses, and the Arroyo Seco served as a renewing water source for his famed journey from Mexico to Monterey.

Then & Now
In the 1970s and '80s, affluent Taiwanese professionals immigrated here, and Mandarin became the dominant Chinese language. Mainland Chinese and Vietnamese arrived later, and today Monterey Park is the first American city with a majority Asian-descent population. In 1986, the then-predominantly white city council ruled that all businesses must post business signs and the nature of the business in English. *Capice?*

Our Favorite...
Library: Bruggemeyer Memorial Library on Monterey Pass Rd. has staff members who speak Cantonese, Mandarin, Spanish and Vietnamese
Park: Garvey Ranch Park, on Orange Ave., for the Wednesday-night Astronomical Society talks and the eight-inch refractor telescope
Market: The Hong Kong and Shun Fat supermarkets, both of which have their flagship stores here
Parade: The annual Lantern Parade, held on Garvey Ave. for Chinese New Year
Newspaper: It's a toss-up – both the *Chinese Daily News* and the *International Daily News* are printed here
Hospital: Garfield Medical Center, with full ER, 626.307.2129
Web Site: ci.monterey-park.ca.us

Best Hangouts
The Cascades on Kingston St., a jumbo fountain for 1920s homes that never materialized. Thanks, Depression! Also look for El Encanto garden across the street on Mercado.

Don't Be a Lawbreaker!
Permission in Mandarin and English?
No person shall discharge or explode gunpowder, dynamite, torpedoes… (aw, shucks!) without first having obtained the special permission of the City Council.

Born in Monterey Park
Laura Scudder's potato chips – Mrs. Scudder lived here and began making her chips in her home kitchen in 1926.

San Gabriel
Where It All Started

The Facts
What It Is: A 4.1-square-mile city bordered by San Marino, Temple City, El Monte, Alhambra and South Pasadena
Population: 40,987
Sister City: Celaya, Mexico
Ethnic Diversity: Predominantly Asian, with a 31% Hispanic minority
Family Matters: 76% of residences are family (nonsingle), giving the city a high concentration of family homes
Median Household Income: $49,111

Key Players
Junipero Serra and his fellow missionaries established Mission San Gabriel Arcangel in 1771, making San Gabriel the oldest European settlement in Los Angeles County. San Gabriel's fertile land was the home to North America's first grapevines, in the late 18th century, and in the 19th century, as many as 11,000 gallons of wine were produced annually.

Telling Moment
John Steven McGroarty built the magnificent Mission Playhouse (later renamed the San Gabriel Civic Auditorium) in 1927 just to present his four-and-a-half-hour work, the *Mission Play,* which had already been running for fifteen years in a smaller venue.

Then & Now
The Chinese immigrants who began settling here in the 1970s have prospered, and today San Gabriel has a diverse Asian population and is home to one of the nation's most thriving suburban Chinatowns, anchored by "The Golden Mile," a stretch of Valley Blvd. lined with upscale Chinese restaurants, shops and offices.

Our Favorite...
Library: San Gabriel Library, on S. Del Mar, has a growing collection in Chinese and Vietnamese
Park: Check out the Dinosaur Playground at Vincent Lugo Park on Wells St. before the city demolishes it, although activists are fighting to save the worn but beloved old play structures
Arts Organization: The ornately Spanish San Gabriel Civic hosts everything from high school choirs to experimental theater
Parade: A Lunar New Year parade, complete with floats and dragons

Fiesta:
The Mission Fiesta, on Labor Day weekend, is the town's biggest blowout
Local Newspapers: *San Gabriel Valley Tribune, Sing Tao Daily* and *Chinese Daily News*
Hospital: San Gabriel Valley Medical Center, 626.289.5454
Web Site: sangabrielcity.com

Don't Be a Lawbreaker!
Aw nuts...well, then can I have a puppy?
No person shall have, keep or maintain, or have in possession or under control, any elephant, bear, hippopotamus, rhinoceros, lion, tiger, leopard, wolf, monkey or any poisonous reptile of any kind... without first applying to and receiving from the Council a permit.

What She Said
"...slumped in her new Lexus, blood all over the place, right there in the parking lot of Fabric World in San Gabriel."
— From The Jasmine Trade,
by Denise Hamilton

Best Hangout
San Gabriel Square Mall (aka the Great Mall of China), at the corner of Valley and Del Mar, home to the great 99 Ranch Market and a dazzling array of restaurants.

Born in San Gabriel
Gen. George S. Patton Jr., who grew up in neighboring San Marino

Embarrassing Fact
While Mission San Gabriel brought wealth, wine and Christianity to Southern California, it also set a new standard for the near-slavery of Indians, forcing the Tongva to work on the 1.5 million acres the mission had claimed. The Tongva population eventually declined to just a few hundred.

San Marino

Where Republicans Go to Enjoy Their Lawns

The Facts

What It Is: A four-square-mile city just south of Pasadena and South Pasadena and nine miles northeast of downtown L.A.

Population: 13,665

Ethnic Diversity: Formerly the whitest place on earth, San Marino is now more than half Asian, primarily first- or second-generation Chinese immigrants

Median Household Income: $143,785

Number of Apartment Buildings: 0

Key Players

Railroad tycoon Henry Huntington, who had made his own fortune and inherited another from his uncle Collis, bought the citrus-producing San Marino Ranch in 1903 as an investment. He later built a mansion on the property to house his growing collection of art and rare books, and he established botanical gardens around the mansion. In 1919, he deeded it all to a trust, wanting to "give something to the public" before he died.

Telling Moments

In the last two decades, the high-performing schools started attracting wealthy Chinese immigrant families – including teenagers living alone in sprawling houses while Mom and Dad worked in China. Not long ago, the increase in the number of teen-run households inspired the city to pass an ordinance requiring an adult to live in each house.

Then & Now

San Marino was founded in 1913 as a conservative, wealthy (and dry) residential town with an emphasis on education. It's no longer dry, but the emphasis on education remains – its schools boast the highest SAT 9 scores in L.A. County. And African-American motorists are no longer stopped for being, you know, African-American. (That really was routine practice not so long ago.)

Our Favorite...

Library: The town is justly proud of its brand-new library, nearly double the size of the old one, at 1890 Huntington Dr. (sanmarinopl.org)

Park: Lacy Park, perhaps the prettiest park in the San Gabriel Valley

Arts Organization: The California Art Club, founded in 1906 by plein-air painters; its gallery in the Old Mill building is worth a visit

Parade: A small-town 4th of July parade, followed by fireworks at Lacy Park

Landmark: The Old Mill (Molino Viejo) was the mill for the vast Mission San Gabriel and is the oldest standing commercial building in Southern California

Newspaper: *The San Marino Tribune*

Web Site: ci.san-marino.ca.us

Don't Be a Lawbreaker!

I'm sorry, ma'am, we have to take the lawn in for questioning.

A dead lawn is a crime in San Marino, as are handbill distribution and any visible sign of rubbish. Oh, and by law, every house must have at least a two-car garage and use it for parking cars only.

What He Said

"If you're not sure in San Marino, it's illegal."
– Paul Crowley, San Marino Historical Society

Best Hangout

The shady patio at Julienne, where everyone who's anyone lunches on niçoise salads and roasted chicken with pommes frites.

Slept in San Marino

Gen. George S. Patton Jr. may have been born in San Gabriel, but he grew up in San Marino

Embarrassing Fact

For decades San Marino was best known as the western headquarters for the Red-fearing, ultra-right-wing John Birch Society.

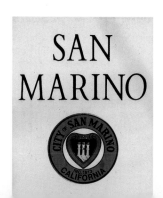

Sierra Madre
Village of the Foothills

The Facts
What It Is: A four-square-mile town bordered by Arcadia, Pasadena and, to the north, the San Gabriel Mountains
Population: 11,146
Ethnic Diversity: 86% Caucasian (including 10% Hispanic), 6% Asian and not very many African-Americans or Native Americans
Median Household Income: $65,900

Key Players
In 1881, Nathaniel Carter bought the 1,103 acres that would become Sierra Madre, most of them from Lucky Baldwin, the impresario of Arcadia; the town began to grow, in part because it was a gateway to Mt. Wilson.

Then & Now
Tucked into Sierra Madre's canyons are waterfalls and old-growth oaks, which supported the Tongva and attracted 19th-century tourists. Today's residents remain fiercely protective of the canyons.

Sierra Madre lacks even one stoplight and is home to the region's only remaining volunteer fire department. It's a favorite spot for such hometown events as the annual Wistaria Festival (March), Mt. Wilson Trail Race (May) and 4th of July Parade (well, July). The Volunteer Fire Department Marching Band leads the parade, then quickly changes costume to reappear later as the Community College Marching Band. Where's the Community College, you ask? "Next to the airport!" they shout.

Our Favorite...
Library: The Sierra Madre Library, on Sierra Madre Blvd.
Building: The Essick House, home to the Sierra Madre Woman's Club
Park: Memorial Park, with its band shell, play structure, newly restored cannon (because you never know...) and good congregation of day laborers

Cemetery: Pioneer, one of the loveliest in the SG Valley
Farmer's Market: Wednesdays from 3 to 7 p.m. in the Mariposa parking lot at Baldwin and Hermosa
Arts Organization: Sierra Madre Playhouse for live theater productions
Hospital: Arcadia Methodist is closest; Sierra Madre is home to many convalescent and assisted-living facilities for seniors on the go-go
Web Site: cityofsierramadre.com

Don't Be a Lawbreaker!
But we draw the line at hugging...
The Englemann Oak, *quercus englemanii,* is designated as the official tree of the city of Sierra Madre... and shall be a preferred replacement tree for mitigation measures, and shall be given special consideration for preservation.

Best Hangouts
The sidewalk cafés on Baldwin at Sierra Madre Blvd.: Bean Town for ice cream and coffee, Village Pizzeria for pizza, and Starbucks (one of only two chains allowed in town) for mocha Frappuccinos.

Born in Sierra Madre
E. Waldo Ward, a local orchardist, started making marmalade in 1917, and it became a big seller. His family still produces his famed wisteria jelly, along with a large line of gourmet preserves.

It's a Classy Town, and Yet...
Dude, Where's My Car? was filmed in part here.

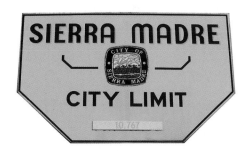

South Pasadena

Mom & Apple Pie... and Sushi & a Latte, Too

The Facts
What It Is: A regular Mayberry of a town, 3.44-square-mile South Pas is bordered by Pasadena to the north, San Marino to the northeast, Alhambra to the south and Highland Park to the west
Population: 24,292
Ethnic Diversity: 51% Caucasian, 16% Hispanic, 27% Asian, 3% African-American
Median Household Income: $65,489

Key Players
During the Mission San Gabriel era, what is now South Pasadena was part of a large Mission ranch called El Rincon de San Pascual. By 1843 that property was owned by Mexican Manuel Garfias, who built South Pasadena's first home, El Adobe Flores, in 1846.

Telling Moment
The Cawston Ostrich Farm opened in 1896 on the Arroyo Seco, and it became a huge tourist destination, as well as a merchant of ostrich-feather boas and hats.

Then & Now
In the late 1800s, American settlers arrived; from 1900 to 1920, trees and Craftsman bungalows grew together on wide, gracious streets. Cited five times by the National Trust for Historic Preservation as one of the nation's "Most Endangered Places," South Pas remains deeply embroiled in a decades-long battle to stave off the extension of the 710 Freeway, which would bisect the picturesque town and destroy many stately homes and mature trees.

Our Favorite...
Library: On El Centro. Why try to resist Pajama Story Time, the art history section or the inviting lawn?
Park: Garfield Park on Mission, home of sycamores, a playground and countless 4-year-old birthday parties

Farmer's Market: A small but great one at El Centro and Meridian, Thursdays 4-8 p.m.
Soda Fountain: Fair Oaks Pharmacy & Soda Fountain has been the corner drug store since 1915, with a turn-of-the-last-century soda fountain and lunch counter
Parade: Everyone who's anyone is at the 4th of July parade down Fair Oaks, followed by fireworks at the high school
Newspaper: *The South Pasadena Review* (since 1888)
Web Site: ci.south-pasadena.ca.us

Don't Be a Lawbreaker!
You, that's right – you on that Schwinn with the banana seat – pull over!
It shall be unlawful for any person to operate or use... any bicycle propelled wholly or in part by muscular power... without first obtaining, from the director of finance, a license.

What He Said
"Sex in South Pasadena was something boys talked about but didn't practice... The most a boy could hope for was heavy kissing with a girl after the third date. Only one or two girls in each class were reputed to allow boys to 'cop a feel.'"
— *From* Golden Boy: The Untold Story of William Holden, *by Bob Thomas*

Best Hangouts
The great Buster's/Kaldi coffeehouse debate; Garfield Park with little kids; the Thursday-evening farmer's market for noshing and socializing with neighbors; Mike & Anne's patio for a sunny-day lunch; Mission Tile West for tileophiles.

Born in South Pasadena
"Steady" Ed Headrick, inventor of both the Frisbee and Frisbee golf

William Holden (moved here when he was 3)

Joel McCrea

Hilary Swank graduated from South Pas High

Trader Joe's (born in 1966 and still standing)

Historic

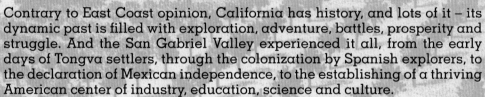

Contrary to East Coast opinion, California has history, and lots of it – its dynamic past is filled with exploration, adventure, battles, prosperity and struggle. And the San Gabriel Valley experienced it all, from the early days of Tongva settlers, through the colonization by Spanish explorers, to the declaration of Mexican independence, to the establishing of a thriving American center of industry, education, science and culture.

The Early Settlers — 28

A City Is Born — 31
    Success & Failure

A Vacation Paradise — 33
    Jeanne Carr & the Horticultural Brigade

They Paved Paradise... — 36
    The Crown City Tarnished

An Incomplete Timeline — 39

History on View — 40

The Early Settlers

The Peaceable Tongva

More than 2,000 years ago, the ancestors of the San Gabriel Valley Tongva settled a 4,000-square-mile area bordered by ocean and mountain. Their lands spanned the coast from Malibu to Laguna, including Catalina and parts of the Channel Islands, and went inland through Riverside and Tujunga. Originally from Southern

This circa 1832 painting of Mission San Gabriel by Ferdinand Deppe depicts a bucolic mingling of Tongva and Spanish cultu

Oregon and Nevada, the Tongva pushed out the Hokan, Chumash and our local clans, the Hahamongna. They were skilled weavers who made vessels for water, acorn gathering and daily living. They husbanded oak groves, which provided food and shelter, and made tools from canyon stone. The Tongva revered protective spirits, shared and traded with their coastal cousins, and redirected lost Spaniards (Doh!) on more than one occasion.

A statue of Junipero Serra at Mission San Gabriel

Spanish with a Mission

By the 18th century, Spain's explorations of the New World showed that Garcia Ordonez de Montalvo's 16th-century novel about the fabulous island of California was, alas, fiction. This gold-drenched isla ruled by Queen Calafia wasn't all it was imagined to be, but nonetheless Spain decided to move in. Father Junipero Serra came through with Gaspar de Portola in 1769 as part of Spain's faith-based initiative, the mission system. In 1771, its first year of operation, Mission San Gabriel de Arcangel baptized 1,300 Tongva and renamed them "Gabrielinos."

Job training was necessito for the Gabrielinos, and 26-year-old Father Zalvedia, the intense head padre from 1806 to 1826, was the go-to guy. Described as "austere," "cruel" and "of great managerial experience," Zalvedia whipped his crew morning, noon and night to make the mission one of the most profitable in the chain. And what's good for the goose made padre take a gander – Zalvedia was an aesthete who practiced self-flagellation and wore an inward-spiked belt to remind him of earthly burdens (but only when he breathed). When Zalvedia was transferred in 1826, he was negotiating a deal to buy enough iron to fence in San Gabriel's entire 16,000 acres – Mexico's threat of forced secularization of the missions had him in a state of near hysteria.

Until secularization, the Gabrielinos learned trades: brick-making, boiling animal tallow for soap and candles, animal husbandry, growing wheat, smithing, tanning hides (a key export product), tending citrus and grapes, and making wine and brandy, from which the mission generated a whopping $12,000 annually in sales. The Gabrielinos also burned lime in pits near what is now South Pasadena to make superior mortar, which was used in missions as far north as Monterey. Under the padres' care, the Gabrielinos built a fortress-like mission with tall walls to keep good Gabrielinos in and bad Tongva out.

When Mexico broke from Spain, it granted eight million acres of former mission property in 500 parcels to Californios. Of the Gabrielinos who were left behind, without resources or education, about half died in the smallpox epidemic of 1862. The few Tongva who survive today are the ancestors of those who fled the missions early on, or those who stayed, quietly protecting traditions and the memory of their antecedents while mixing it up with the passing Euro parade.

El Molino Viejo

Just one of Father Zalvedia's figurative and literal millstones was El Molino Viejo. Designed by the padres and built by the Gabrielinos, the mill never worked right. The meal got so wet that Gabrielinas had to sift it and cart it back to the mission, then sift it again for storage. A labor drain, El Molino Viejo was abandoned after seven years for a new mill on mission grounds. In the 19th century it became a private residence, and in the 20th century it served as the clubhouse for Henry Huntington's golf course. Fully restored and in pristine condition today, this public museum is also headquarters for the California Art Club, which has a fine gallery.

The Rancho Era

Pio Pico, Mexico's last governor of California, sliced two massive tracts from Mission San Gabriel, where he had been born in 1801. He sold one of them, 13,000-acre Rancho Santa Anita, to William Workman and Hugo Reid in the name of Reid's Gabrielina wife, Victoria, and he deeded the other, Rancho San Pascual, to the longstanding manager of the mission, Eulalia Perez. She soon forfeited the rancho to relatives, who in turn gave it up to a series of owners. Skilled on horseback but untrained in accounting, many of these new rancheros didn't hold cash reserves for the maintenance of livestock and property, and they often lost their land.

Mission San Gabriel today

Nicknamed "Don Benito" because of his good relations with Gabrielinos and Californios, Benjamin Davis Wilson thought the Tongva needed protection from the white man. Don Benito served as an Indian agent and the first mayor of Los Angeles.

One example was Manuel Garfias, the third owner of Rancho San Pascual. He borrowed to build a grand $5,000 hacienda with a loan from Benjamin "Don Benito" Wilson, a rich trapper and trader originally from Tennessee. Unable to generate income from his large ranch, Garfias was forced to sell to Wilson at a loss.

In 1845, the Californios proclaimed their independence from Mexico, and the next year the United States declared war on Mexico in a land grab. The Gold Rush began in 1848, cinching statehood in 1850 and forcing all Mexican land claims before the U.S. Land Commission. Under Mexican rule, surveys and written contracts weren't required, so many secularization grants were invalidated. The Land Commission did, however, return to the Catholic Church all church buildings, cemeteries, orchards and priests' dwellings attached to the missions.

By 1847, Hugo Reid had sold Rancho Santa Anita to pay off debts; the one-story adobe he and Victoria built still stands in its original location, at the L.A. County Arboretum. As a widow, Victoria continued to live on her own rancho (which covered what is now San Marino, San Gabriel and Alhambra), eventually selling it to Don Benito Wilson, who renamed it Lake Vineyard; his grandson, George Patton Jr., was born here in 1885.

In 1860 Wilson sold half of Rancho San Pascual for $4,000 to a business associate, Dr. John Griffin, a Confederate army surgeon. Griffin carved out portions of his share for family and friends. Griffin's sister, Elizabeth Johnson, bought 250-plus acres and named the land "Fair Oaks" for her Virginia homestead. She later sold it to Judge Benjamin Eaton, who became a prominent Pasadena citizen, bringing irrigation and new settlers and eventually building the mile-high Mt. Wilson Toll Road in 1891.

Transcontinental Railroad

The transcontinental railroad reached this valley in 1873, and by 1875 40 homes stood in what became Pasadena. James de Barth Shorb, Don Benito's son-in-law and owner of San Marino Winery, America's largest winemaker, persuaded Southern Pacific to make stops at his tracts, delivering daily mail and tourists and carrying wine and citrus to markets back East. By 1885 Southern Pacific was bombarding the Midwest with advertisements for health and wealth in the San Gabriel Valley, and people arrived in droves to see the sunny farms planted with 10,000 orange, lemon and olive trees and 150,000 grape vines. When the Atchison, Topeka and Santa Fe arrived in 1885 as the valley's second transcontinental railroad, one-way fares from Ohio dropped to $1. Travel west peaked in 1887, with 120,000 visiting Pasadena and land prices increasing 500 percent. By 1890, 6,000 claimed residency here.

A City Is Born

The Indiana Colony

In 1873, Eaton hosted Daniel M. Berry, a schoolteacher, journalist and land scout for the California Colony of Indiana, a group of Midwesterners who were sick and tired of being sick and tired and cold. He explored six areas of Southern California and was most charmed with the locale

This shack was reportedly the first house in the new town of Pasadena.

we now call Pasadena – its residents were educated, accomplished professionals, all working the land and breathing clean air. The phlegmatic Berry slept soundly for three nights at Eaton's, then wired for approval to buy land from Don Benito Wilson and John Griffin. Berry wrote of building a health sanitarium, growing fruit to sell across the country, building a polytechnic school and enjoying the natural observatory from the mountains' perch. And in time, it all came true.

But first came a national financial panic, on September 18, 1873, six days after the Indiana Colony entered negotiations with Wilson and Griffin. With the speed of molten molasses, the Indianans replaced their cash-strapped investors and, on November 11th, under the name San Gabriel Orange Grove Association, offered $25,000 for the land they coveted. Wilson, delighted to close the deal, threw in an extra 1,400 acres of "worthless" land east of the Arroyo Seco, an area we fondly call Worthlessland, or Altadena. The final price: $6.31 an acre for about 4,000 acres. Discovery of an underground spring saved the expense of leasing water rights.

The adolescent community applied for a post office branch in 1875; the postmaster rejected the town name "Indiana Colony" but agreed to Pasadena, a

Pasadena in 1885, one year before it incorporated as a city; the buildings in the distance mark the "downtown" intersection of Colorado and Fair Oaks.

faux Chippewa word. It sounded authentic and lyrical, so Pasadena it was. The new post office operated from Hollingworth's General Store at Colorado and Fair Oaks, with the government paying the Hollingworths a handsome 25 cents a week.

Dry & Proud of It

Moderation and hard work were the mainstays of the original colonists, most of whom were Protestant and sensibly Midwestern; churches, numbering eleven by 1888, were the social centers. The temperance movement was gaining ground nationally, and such town leaders as the Hollingworths, Abbot Kinney, Amos Throop, Hiram Reid and Jeanne Carr were all in favor of it. In 1882, townsfolk established the Library and Village Improvement Society for women, children, tourists and, especially, young men who had leisure time, so they wouldn't "drift into resorts of pernicious influence." Meanwhile, businessman Maritz Rosenbaum noticed that working folk enjoyed alcohol and billiards. The landholding citizens protested his whiskey-serving general store at Colorado and Orange Grove, but Rosenbaum insisted that he was within his rights to sell spirits. So in 1886, the temperance folks circulated a petition to incorporate Pasadena with anti-saloon laws. South Pasadena followed suit two years later. Thirty-five years before the rest of the country, Pasadena renounced demon alcohol.

Happy orange pickers gather the valley's bounty.

Sanitariums & Citrus

From the beginning, health sanitariums sprung from the foothills for the consumptive of the land. Private residences set up facilities for croupy patients; and such larger institutions as Las Encinas, Las Casitas, La Viña, Mountain Glen Healthatarium, the Chaney Sanitorium, Pinney House, Esperanza and the Sierra Madre Hotel welcomed respiratory patients, half of whom didn't recover.

Part of the health tonic was citrus. New methods in agriculture made citrus profitable for growers and affordable for buyers. Within twenty years of railroad shipping, growers had organized into sales syndicates to get the best price for their crop, which they shipped out in new refrigerated cars developed in part by local man Thaddeus Lowe. In 1893, East Coast markets bought six million boxes of oranges through growers' co-ops for $6 million, which brought massive profits to local farmers.

Success & Failure

- In the 1880s wool production quickly became a huge industry in the SG Valley. But when drought killed many of the sheep, Australia jumped into the market. Within ten years the local wool market had collapsed.
- The viticulture that the padres brought continued on after the mission era at James de Barth Shorb's San Marino Winery, which was, for a time, the nation's largest. But the fungus that devastated Shorb's crop had no effect on Northern California vines, so the Napa Valley developed as California's wine country.
- Inventor Thaddeus Lowe created hot air balloons for travel and espionage. President Lincoln appointed him Chief of Army Aeronautics in 1861. Lowe and his fleet reported on and photographed 3,000 missions during the Civil War. After the war he moved to Pasadena, where he built the Scenic Mt. Lowe Railway, perfected refrigeration techniques and adapted them for railway cars. He died in poverty and obscurity in 1913.

A Vacation Paradise

Rachael and Hiram Reid and their grandchildren ride early bicycles. Reid wrote a history of Pasadena in 1895.

The Resort Life

Pasadena developed as a tony winter resort complete with rabbit hunting (at Raymond Hill), horse racing and gambling (at Lucky Baldwin's ranch), burrow pack rides and sightseeing from the Mt. Lowe Railway and Eaton Canyon, trout fishing in the Arroyo and strolls through the highland poppy fields, with views of Catalina Island. Bicycles were popular, and in 1900 construction began on the wood-plank Pasadena Cycleway, which was to be a link to Los Angeles via the Arroyo Seco – but it ultimately made it only between the hotels Green and Raymond. Beginning in the 1880s, glittering dance parties and musicales took place at the Green Hotel, the Maryland, the Wentworth (later the Huntington) and the Alhambra. Presidents Benjamin Harrison and Teddy Roosevelt visited, as did tycoons Collis Huntington and Leland Stanford. In the jazz age, daredevils flew their biplanes to the Cecile B. DeMille Airfield before 23-skidooing off to the Vista del Arroyo, the Raymond, the Mt. Lowe Hotel or the Flintridge, which was sold to the Biltmore chain in 1931 and then to the Dominican Sisters of San Jose for their fine Sacred Heart Academy, which still matriculates young women today. Movie stars

The grand Maryland Hotel had cottages for its long-term guests.

Gloria Swanson, Tyrone Power and Gary Cooper played golf at the Midwick Country Club in Alhambra, with its regulation-size polo fields. Of all that glamour, only the Huntington (newly dubbed the Langham Huntington) remains as a hotel; the Green Hotel is now the Castle Green, home to HUD senior housing and swank private co-ops, and the Vista del Arroyo is a federal appeals courthouse. The others all burned down or were torn down after Pasadena's resort glory days ended.

Jeanne Carr & the Horticultural Brigade

Postcards celebrating Pasadena's landscaping attracted émigrés by the thousands.

Ezra Carr, a medical doctor and professor of chemistry, natural history and agriculture at the University of Wisconsin and U.C. Berkeley, and his wife, Jeanne, an amateur botanist, moved to Pasadena in 1876. Both were from Vermont, she a seventh-generation Puritan and early feminist who found housework and fashion a waste of precious time. John Muir had been Ezra's student, and Jeanne became his lifelong mentor, encouraging his writing and his exploration of a personal union with God through nature. The Carrs moved to Pasadena when Ezra became California's superintendent of schools, and they lived on a 46-acre estate, Carmelita, at the current location of the Norton Simon, where they built a lush garden filled with rare plants. Jeanne invited John Muir to visit, and he was impressed by the "literary and scientific tastes displayed" in Pasadena, as well as the rugged San Gabriel Mountains.

Jeanne Carr set the refined green standards for other early residents, encouraging the use of hedges instead of fences and the planting of pepper trees interspersed with Mexican limes, climbing roses and grape vines. Other prominent early horticulturalists included tobacco magnate Albert Kinney, an ardent conservationist and developer of Venice, California, who bought a 500-acre property that he called Kinneloa. Charles H. Hastings, a horticulturalist from Cornell, turned Hastings Ranch into a garden of exotic plants. At Wynyate, the home of Margaret Collier Graham, a fiction writer of the American realist school, John Muir is said to have planted a lemon eucalyptus that still grows.

Selling the Romance

Charles Lummis on his famed journey west

Popular fiction and essays advertised the romance of the San Gabriel Valley. Eccentric journalist Charles Lummis serialized his 1884 adventures during his walk from Cincinnati to L.A. in the *Los Angeles Times*. He settled in Highland Park, the white-hot center of the Arroyo arts culture, and hand-built El Alisal, a river-rock fortress in a sycamore grove. Also in 1884, Helen Hunt Jackson wrote the blockbuster *Ramona* after visiting her Pasadena pal, botanist Jeanne Carr. The public misinterpreted Jackson's bittersweet story of the disappearing American Indian way of life, clutching to the notion of Southern California as exotic wonderland. Early in the 20th century, Pasadena pulp fiction novelist Zane Grey romanticized the west and a semi-civilized path to adventure in the tumbleweeds. During World War I Hollywood began its rise to prominence in film production; such fantastic backdrops as Busch Gardens, Descanso Gardens, the Rose Bowl, Henry Huntington's mansion, the Athenaeum and Lucky Baldwin's lake became favorite filming locations.

The first float winner in the first Rose Parade, organized in 1890 by the Valley Hunt Club as a booster event for the young city of Pasadena

Playground for the Prominent

From the 1890s through the 1920s, Midwestern business magnates built grand winter homes in the greater Pasadena area, including map publisher Andrew McNally; razor monarch King Gillette; plumbing heiress Kate Crane Gartz; patent medicine millionaire Colonel G. G. Green; newspaperman William Scripps; the king and queen of clean, David and

Part of the Red Car system, Scenic Mt. Lowe Railway brought tourists to the resort atop Echo Mountain in what is now Altadena.

Mary Gamble; artist Grace Nicholson; chewing-gum tycoon William Wrigley; Anna Bissell McKay, daughter of the emperor of vacuum cleaners; Lucretia Garfield, widow of President Garfield; Henry and Arabella Huntington; and utopian and sometimes Socialist muckraker Upton Sinclair and his wife, Mary. Private trolley cars connected the outlying areas with the Pacific Electric Red Car system, and after 1910, automobiles further allowed the growing middle class to get to work in Pasadena and Los Angeles.

The African-American Legacy

From the beginning, Pasadena and environs have been home to an illustrious roster of accomplished black residents. Of the first settlers in the pueblo of Los Angeles, more than half were of African descent. Robert Owens, a freeman who settled here in 1850, ran a successful logging business in Altadena's El Prieto Canyon and became a wealthy land developer in Los Angeles, and W.E.B. DuBois extolled the virtues of Pasadena and Los Angeles. Pasadena's earliest African-American neighborhood was around Vernon Avenue between Orange Grove and Fair Oaks, and the region's oldest AME church was founded here in 1888. The three adult children of abolitionist John Brown settled in the Altadena mountains after their father was hanged for storming the arsenal at Harper's Ferry to arm a black uprising. Son Owen Brown, who lived to be an old mountain man, is buried atop Brown's mountain. There is a public right of way to his gravesite, but beware the

The Abolitionist Brown family at their Altadena cabin

unstrung gent who as of press time lives at a neighboring house – he's been known to brandish a pistol at hikers. The author and MacArthur Genius Grant winner Octavia Butler was born in Pasadena in 1947 and died in 2006; her gravesite can be found at Altadena's Mountain View Cemetery. The legendary Robinson brothers grew up here and attended PCC; track star Mack showed beautifully at the 1936 Olympics, and Jackie broke

The Robinson Memorial

the color barrier in baseball in 1947. Although their childhood home is gone, you can visit the Robinson Memorial across the street from Pasadena City Hall. These jumbo busts benefit from an up-close look – in their hair are reliefs and etchings of memorable events and places in their lives. Relevant quotes also were chiseled into nearby stone benches. This monument is lively, compelling and rich in detail.

Henry Huntington Does It Right

As the 20th century dawned, Henry Huntington began his second career as "the man who built Los Angeles." He first worked for his uncle Collis Huntington's Southern Pacific Railway in West Virginia and San Francisco, until retiring a wealthy man in 1900. He purchased the James Shorb estate called San Marino and bought up Southern California land and all of the region's small railway routes, creating a transportation and real estate empire. He then built electric generators to supply power and launched the Pacific Electric Railway, a new, organized grid

Henry Huntington

of electric train cars that united the "Orange Empire" counties in more than 1,000 miles of track. Eventually his Red Car system was the largest in the world, stretching from Newport Beach to Santa Monica, Redlands to Chatsworth. He also purchased the Mt. Lowe Railway, making it a stop on the Red Car line, until fire and rainstorms damaged the tracks beyond repair.

Automobiles dented Huntington's customer base by the 1920s – and that's when he began divesting himself of Pacific Electric and building a collection of rare manuscripts, books and art. He and his second wife, Arabella, built their home intending to repurpose it as a public gallery and library research center, which indeed it became in 1928.

They Paved Paradise...

The Caltech Contribution

The California Institute of Technology began with the benevolence of Amos G. Throop, a self-educated business tycoon, abolitionist, Chicago politician and eventual mayor of Pasadena. In 1891 he rented space in the Wooster Building on Fair Oaks and Green and opened Throop University. He believed in "learning by doing," instead of relying solely on books. The coed student population, elementary through college, got a liberal arts education and vocational training in such skills as bookbinding, tilemaking and typesetting.

Then, in 1907, astronomer George Ellery Hale, who was having much success with the new Mt. Wilson Observatory, turned his contagious energy to creating a serious science and engineering center in Pasadena. He and partners Arthur Noyes and Robert Millikan morphed the school into Throop Polytechnic Institute, then Throop College of Technology and finally, in 1921, the California Institute of Technology. Along the way it spun off an elementary and high school, Polytechnic, which remains one of the finest schools in the state today. Hale and his partners attracted committed administrators and scientists, many of whom they had worked with at the National Research Council during World War I.

L to R: Arthur Noyes, George Ellery Hale and Robert Millikan, Caltech's founding triumvirate, in 1917

By the early '30s many physicists had expatriated from Europe and moored at Caltech, most notably Albert Einstein. Aeronautics joined the curriculum, and the school grew its reputation for having a brain trust in quantum physics, biochemistry and astronomy. During World War II Caltech became a lab for rocketry, which led to the growth of the Jet Propulsion Laboratory, still managed for NASA by Caltech. After the war, the college grew more, adding research in nuclear astrophysics, chemical biology, geochemistry and planetary science. During this phase it built San Diego's Palomar Observatory, whose 200-inch telescope held the distinction of being the world's largest from 1948 to 1988.

Many scientific developments we take for granted today were hammered out here, including the nature of chemical bonds; molecular biology and its relationship to viruses; seismographs and the Richter scale; and the understanding of theoretical physics by Caltech's most loveable legend, the late Richard Feynman.

The Crown City Tarnished

Several racist and nativist campaigns peppered Pasadena's history. Chinese immigrants recruited to build the transcontinental railroad in the 1860s became a cheap and available labor force when the rails were completed. Agriculture absorbed many of them, but their presence still threatened many we-got-here-first working people. National anti-Chinese sentiment culminated in the 1882 Congressional Chinese Exclusion Act. Locally, a race riot broke out in Mills Alley in 1885. A white mob stormed a Chinese-owned laundry, harassing the occupants until a fire erupted; the laundry owners were physically unharmed but were then required by law to live outside city limits. In 1931, once again threatened by a cheaper labor force, California repatriated 12,600 workers from Los Angeles to Mexico. During World War II, Japanese Americans were "processed" through Santa Anita Racetrack; U.S. citizens lived there in primitive conditions for many months before being interned at camps across the country.

In 1970, the feds ordered Pasadena to desegregate its schools, and forced busing began. This led to massive white flight (and multiracial upper-middle-class flight), which was great news for the private schools. Nowadays only two-thirds of Pasadena's children attend public school, even though busing stopped years ago; the good news, however, is that several PUSD schools have improved markedly in recent years.

The Depression Hits

Rose Parade Grand Marshall Shirley Temple cheered Depression-weary Americans in 1939.

During the Depression, the tourist trade dried up, resort hotels closed, businesses folded, and the Colorado Streeet Bridge was nicknamed Suicide Bridge. Upton Sinclair, who lived here with his wife, Mary, from 1915 to 1953, ran unsuccessfully for governor of California as a Socialist in Democrat's clothing in 1934 on the End Poverty in California platform. Terrified Republicans manufactured phony newsreels of Dust Bowl drifters invading California looking for welfare assistance. Sinclair's local supporters included society matrons Kate Crane Gartz and Aline Barnsdall, both of whom were criticized in the 1920s for being "wobblies" and "goo goos" – euphemisms for "good government" espoused by fervent liberals who supported unions and the working class.

During these difficult times, some took relief from hopeful messengers. The most famous was evangelist Aimee Semple McPherson, who capitalized on new radio technology for her weekly Pentecostal sermons that aired from the 1920s until her death in 1944. Although she commanded a huge following, preaching to 5,000 parishioners at her Angelus Temple in Echo Park, she also was controversial, for possibly faking her own kidnapping and having an affair with a married man.

World War II to the New Century

Yep, the loss of tourism during the Depression messed up Pasadena. But all those brainiacs lured to Caltech in the '30s helped create the aerospace industry, the single greatest postwar job producer in Southern California, including at our very own JPL.

From the 1990s into this new century, Pasadena and the San Gabriel Valley have been working to meld two competing goals: development and preservation. The city of Pasadena has seen the economic advantage of preservation – Old Town's huge success, for instance, had a lot to do with Pasadena Heritage's efforts to save its charming, historic buildings. A smart and sophisticated workforce and beautiful residential areas have inspired many companies to headquarter here. And therein lies the challenge. Pasadena and its neighboring towns are thrilled to be home to such employers as Indymac Bank, See Beyond, Idealab, JPL, Parsons, Avery Denison and Caltech. They all need office space, and their employees need housing. But if development leads to intense traffic and the destruction of historic sites and peaceful, neighborhoods, those employers won't want to be here anymore.

The story of the last two decades has been the story of that struggle: South Pasadena's battle to stop the proposed extension of the 710 Freeway through its gorgeous neighborhoods; Alhambra's efforts to get the freeway built, to abate traffic and provide jobs; the construction of the Gold Line and high-density housing near its stations; the increasing success of historic-home tours and festivals; and the building of condos, offices and even some green spaces seemingly everywhere you look. It's a delicate balance that some say is working and some say is not; only time will tell.

An Incomplete Timeline

1771	Mission San Gabriel is founded.
1821	Mexico declares independence from Spain.
1847	The Mexican-American war ends, and the U.S. gets California.
1873	The railroad arrives in the San Gabriel Valley.
1875	Jacob Lanterman and Adolphus Williams buy the land that would become La Cañada.
1881	Nathaniel Carter buys the land that would become Sierra Madre from Lucky Baldwin.
1886	The city of Pasadena incorporates as a dry town. The town of Monrovia is founded. The Raymond Hotel opens.
1888	South Pasadena incorporates.
1890	First Tournament of Roses parade.
1891	Throop University (later Caltech) founded.
1893	Thaddeus Lowe's Echo Mountain Incline Railway begins service.
1896	Cawston Ostrich Farm, a famed tourist attraction, opens in South Pasadena.
1902	First Tournament of Roses football game is Michigan vs. Stanford, 49-0. Henry Huntington begins Pacific Electric Railway, which becomes the world's largest inter-urban rail system by 1910.
1903	George Ellery Hale begins building Mt. Wilson Observatory.
1905	Upton Sinclair's *The Jungle* is published; Upton and Mary Sinclair move to Pasadena in 1915.
1906	California Fruit Growers' Exchange begins marketing oranges to the East.
1908	California bungalows become a popular architectural style, and the Greene brothers complete the Gamble House.
1910	Hiram Johnson is elected governor of California, campaigning against the corrupt influence of the Southern Pacific Railway.
1912	100,000 cars registered in Los Angeles, and gas is 12 cents a gallon.
1913	San Marino incorporates as a dry town.
1914	The Southwest Museum opens in Highland Park. Occidental College moves to Eagle Rock.

1919	The Henry Huntington Library and Art Gallery is founded, opening to the public in 1928. Prohibition becomes law.
1922	Rose Bowl construction completed.
1925	The Pasadena Playhouse opens.
1927-1932	Pasadenca Civic Center is built; the San Gabriel Civic Auditorium is built in 1927.
1931	Albert Einstein arrives at Caltech.
1933	Dustbowl refugees trek to California in search of work, food and a better climate. Prohibition repealed.
1934	Santa Anita Racetrack opens. Upton Sinclair loses his bid for governor of California.
1938	31 inches of rain over five days causes 100 deaths and $65 million in damages in Southern California; La Crescenta is hard hit.
1940	Arroyo Seco Parkway, California's first freeway, opens.
1942	Executive Order 9066 sends Japanese-Americans to Santa Anita and then on to internment camps for the duration of World War II. Mexican laborers arrive to pick crops.
1947	Pasadenan Jackie Robinson becomes the first black athlete on a Major League baseball team. Bullocks opens on South Lake.
1948	Arthur Melin and Richard Knerr start Wham-O in Knerr's parents' Pasadena garage, eventually creating the Hula Hoop, Frisbee, Superball, Slip 'N' Slide and Silly String.
1963	Pacific Electric Red Cars stop running.
1966	The first Trader Joe's opens in South Pasadena.
1969	The Pasadena Museum of Modern Art (now the Norton Simon) opens.
1970	Pasadena begins forced busing.
1976	Art Center moves to Pasadena.
1978	The Hillside Strangler, the Eagle Rock killer of nine women, is arrested. First Doo Dah Parade.
1982	UCLA moves its home football games from the Coliseum to the Rose Bowl.
1992	Developers and the city complete the renovation of Old Pasadena.
1997	JPL's Mars Rover explores the Red Planet.
2003	The Gold Line begins light-rail service.

History on View

The bells of Mission San Gabriel

Casa Adobe San Rafael
1330 Dorothy Dr., Glendale
818.548.2147, 818.854.5400
Open daily
The Casa Adobe, built in 1865, is listed as a California landmark and was saved from the wrecking ball in 1930 by concerned neighbors. Docents lead tours the first Sunday of the month from September through June and every Sunday in July and August, but you can stop by any day for a self-guided tour. Look for the Fiesta de las Luminarias in December.

El Molino Viejo (The Old Mill)
1120 Old Mill Rd., San Marino
626.449.5458, oldmill.info
Open Tues.-Sun. afternoons
This first grist mill for Mission San Gabriel is a two-story adobe made from oven-baked bricks. Completed in 1816 over an underground stream, it operated for seven years before being abandoned as a mill. Today it is a small museum run by the city of San Marino, with a welcoming staff; expert volunteers maintain the grounds. This monument to California history is a gem.

Lummis Home (El Alisal)
200 E. Ave. 43, Highland Park
323.222.0546, socalhistory.org
Open Fri.-Sun. afternoons
Journalist, activist and adventurer Charles Lummis, who founded the Southwest Museum, hand-built this house over a twelve-year period beginning in the late 19th century. He used local materials, most notably Arroyo river rock, and built many of the furnishings, setting the stage for the Arts & Crafts movement that soon took the nation by storm. Low-maintenance native gardens surround the giant sycamore (El Alisal) on the property.

Mission Museum
Mission San Gabriel de Arcangel
427 S. Junipero Serra Dr., San Gabriel
626.457.3048, sangabrielmission.org
Open daily
Within the high walls of Mission San Gabriel are all the signs of 18th-century Spanish life: tanning beds, tallow vats, outdoor kitchen pots, jumbo grape vines climbing the arbor and Gabrielino-painted canvases depicting the Stations of the Cross. Beyond the cool, dark, detail-rich church is the actual Mission Museum, a tidy series of rooms filled to the brim with artifacts, clothing and furniture; it's a lot to take in, so be sure to ask for a tour. Inside the walled garden you'll spy resting places of priests and Indians who labored here, but the official mission cemetery is outside the walls; it cradles both average Joes and such local legends as Don Benito Wilson.

Pasadena Museum of History
470 W. Walnut St., Pasadena
626.577.1660, pasadenahistory.org
Open Wed.-Sun. afternoons
Once the home of Dr. Adalbert and Eva Fenyes, this 1906 Beaux Arts mansion was an early 20th-century salon for the Fenyes's circle of writers, artists, politicos and industrialists. The mansion served as the Finnish Foreign Consulate from 1947 to 1964. It is now part of the Pasadena Museum of History, offering exhibits, mansion tours, a research library and an excellent museum store with Pasadena-specific books. Don't miss the on-site Finnish Folk Art Museum, the only one of its kind in the country.

South Pasadena Historical Museum
913 Meridian Ave., South Pasadena
626.799.9089
Open Thurs. & Sat.; call for times
This totally cute (and free) hometown museum is located in the old Meridian Iron Works building, just off the Mission stop on the Gold Line. The local history includes displays about Cawston Ostrich Farm and the Raymond Hotel.

Verdugo Adobe
2211 Bonita Dr., Glendale
818.244.2841
Grounds open daily
The oldest building in Glendale, this adobe features an actual old-school brick under glass. If that doesn't thrill you, how about a cast-iron bell marked with a sign that says "Bell"? Okay, okay, Verdugo Adobe is on the National Register of Historic Places because in 1847, Mexican Gen. Andres Pico met his brother, U.S. soldier Jesus Pico, right here and agreed to surrender to American troops – so some historians consider Verdugo Adobe to be the birthplace of California. The house is open by appointment only, so call first or you'll have to settle for peeking through the windows.

Smart

Forgive us while we toot our own horn, but this is one smart place. Nobel laureates litter the Caltech campus like palm fronds after a Santa Ana wind. Scientists specializing in interplanetary volcanoes or interferometer systems line up for enchiladas in the JPL cafeteria. Researchers prowl the stacks of our many libraries. Art historians lecture at Occidental College, theologians ponder at Fuller, and designers contemplate vehicles we can't even imagine at Art Center. The town where Einstein and Feynman wandered is every bit as brainy today, as you'll discover in these pages.

6 Caltech Smarty-Pants: The Profs Get Down with the People   42

Where to Hear Geniuses Speak   45

Starstruck: JPL & Mt. Wilson Observatory   46
     E.T., Phone Pasadena!

The College Tour   48
     Einstein in Pasadena, Fun & Games at Caltech,
     On the Outskirts

3 Great Libraries   54
     More to Explore

Q & A: Lucy Jones   56

6 Caltech Smarty-Pants: The Profs Get Down with the People
(Or, Who Says Science Can't Be Fun?)

Here was the challenge: We asked some of Caltech's smartest folks to answer a fundamental question in 150 words or less, in language that regular people can understand. If they succeeded, they got a bonus question. They all succeeded admirably. Read on to learn.

1. Harry B. Gray
Arnold O. Beckman Professor of Chemistry and Founding Director of the Beckman Institute

The legendary Professor Gray came to Caltech in the '60s and is famed as one of the founders of the field of bioinorganic chemistry. He has been fascinated by color since his childhood in Kentucky.

What gives gems their color?
In gemstones, color is all about electrons jumping into higher energy levels in the metal atoms. Certain colors of the spectrum of visible light are selectively absorbed by metals: chromium, iron, manganese and titanium make rubies, tourmalines, sapphires and emeralds much more colorful than diamonds, which are pure carbon and have no metal atoms. Light that is not absorbed is the color that we see – rubies are red because blue light is absorbed, leaving the red light to be displayed by the beautiful gemstone. Chromium electrons in rubies jump to higher levels when excited by blue light, so the blue light is absorbed and as a result rubies are red. Blue gemstones are just the opposite. Find out which metals are in your gemstones to figure out which colors of light are absorbed by their jumping electrons!

The Rubipy
1 oz. vodka
1.5 oz. Watermelon Pucker
.5 oz. orange liqueur (Cointreau or Triple Sec)
Splash of lime juice
Splash of grenadine (optional)

Bonus: I understand the Athenaeum has honored you with a cocktail. How is it?
It is great to have a bright red drink in honor of my work, and the drink is very colorful, but I prefer a simple rum and tonic most of the time, because I get too excited when I drink a Rubipy!

2. Marianne Bronner-Fraser
Albert Billings Ruddock Professor of Biology

Utilizing chicken embryos, Professor Bronner-Fraser studies neural crest cells, migratory cells that are involved in certain birth defects and cancers.

What is a stem cell?
A stem cell is defined by its unique ability to divide and form two types of cells: a cell like itself, plus a cell that can form a differentiated cell type (for example, muscle). There are several flavors of stem cells. Totipotent stem cells give rise to all cell types – these are "embryonic" stem cells that exist in the embryo or that can be grown in cell culture. The best example of a totipotent stem cell is the fertilized egg itself. Other stem cells are multipotent and are able to give rise to only a certain subset of cells comprising the embryo. For example, "blood" stem cells form red blood cells, white blood cells, platelets and several other derivatives, whereas "neural" stem cells form nerve cells and glia. There is much interest in discovering if these stem cells can be used to regenerate missing cell types in adults.

Bonus: Which came first: the chicken or the egg?
*The egg! Both reptiles and amphibians lay eggs and preceded birds. A chicken-like crea-
ture would have laid the first egg containing what we now recognize as a true chicken.*

3. Michael E. Brown

Professor of Planetary Astronomy

Professor Brown was one of the team that discovered a tenth planet,
described as the most distant object ever seen in orbit around the
sun. Prior to the announcement of its discovery, the planet was referred to by such code names as "Santa" and "Easterbunny."

We know we live on a planet, but what makes a planet a planet?
*People all around the planet use the word "planet" every day, so it
comes as a shock to most to realize that scientists have no agreed-upon definition of what
makes a planet a planet. Some define "planet" to mean the few large objects that dominate
the solar system. By this definition Pluto and Eris (the newly discovered object that is bigger
than Pluto) would not be planets. Others define planet to mean anything in the solar system
that is shaped like a sphere (and is not a moon). This definition would include Pluto and Eris,
and perhaps fifteen other new planets. The lack of agreement has caused scientists like me
to adopt a rather arbitrary compromise. Because we have called Pluto a planet for 76 years,
it stays a planet and sets the lower boundary for what we call a planet. Eris, which is just a
bit bigger than Pluto, is the tenth planet by this definition. By whatever definition we use,
there are many new planets awaiting discovery, either in the outer parts of our solar system
or orbiting distant stars.*

A note from your faithful editors: Shortly after this interview, 424 astronomers at a meeting
in Prague stripped Pluto of its long-held status as a planet. Watching a webcast of the vote,
Michael Brown was heard to utter, "Whoa, Pluto's dead. There are finally, officially, eight
planets in the solar system." But hold on there, Professor Brown: Alan Stern, project leader
of NASA's mission to Pluto, begs to differ, citing the fact that less than five percent of the
world's astronomers voted and saying, "Of course Pluto is a planet: It's massive enough to
have its shape controlled by gravity rather than material strength, which is the hallmark of
planethood. I think it's exciting that we're discovering whole new classes of planetary bodies like the ice dwarfs, of which Pluto is the charter member." Egad, how we love scientists.

**Bonus: What mnemonic device did you learn in grade school to memorize the order of
the planets in their orbits around the sun?**
Martha Visiting Every Monday and Just Staying Until Noon.

4. Melany Hunt

Professor of Mechanical Engineering

Professor Hunt studies the flow of particulates and granular
materials. As a mentor with Caltech's Summer Undergraduate
Research Fellowships (SURF) program, she has spent several
summers investigating booming dunes.

**For centuries, desert travelers have described an eerie, yet very pure tone (in the cello
range) emanating from certain sand dunes. Assuming no mind-altering substances
were involved, what makes this happen?**
*The booming of the dunes is unusual in that it is a single frequency, between 70 to 110
hertz, and under the right conditions, it can be heard several miles away. At Caltech, we
hypothesize a resonance mechanism in which the upper layers of the sand are sheared
during avalanching, creating a range of frequencies. The dune, however, amplifies just a
single frequency, which depends on the sound speed within the dune and the thickness of*

a dry loose layer of sand atop a denser layer of sand. Hence, the sound is generated at the surface and reflected by the subsurface.

Booming dunes can be found in about 30 locations around the world. In China at the Hill of the Sounding Sand, ancient villagers celebrated the Dragon Festival by sliding down the dunes. The ancients deified the sand with its perceived supernatural powers.

Bonus: I've seen photos of you and your team sliding down the dunes. Any chance we'll see dune sliding as an Olympic event?
The loudest booms occur in temperatures above 100 degrees. Since there are no chair lifts, the walk up the dune is hot and exhausting. Although Caltechers enjoy the outing, dune sliding will probably remain an obscure sport.

5. Kenneth G. Libbrecht
Professor of Physics

Among Professor Libbrecht's areas of research is the Interferometer Gravitational-wave Observatory (LIGO) Project, which detects and studies gravitational-wave signals from violent astrophysical events such as black holes. A well-known researcher in snow crystals, Professor Libbrecht is the author of several books on snowflakes, but he says that lately he is really interested in computers.

Will the day come when computers are able to think?
I believe computers will someday be capable of creative thought and intelligence. People have been talking about artificial intelligence for decades, but only now are we getting to a point where it begins to be feasible. The human brain contains roughly a trillion neurons, but a modern desktop computer contains roughly a trillion transistors. The interconnections between neurons are much more complex than the wiring between transistors, but transistors operate about a million times faster than neurons. It's not clear which machine – your brain or your computer – has the greatest potential.

Many people believe the brain is somehow special, that thinking and consciousness are uniquely human traits. We also used to believe that Earth was the center of the universe, but we have come to realize that Earth is but one planet, and humans are but one animal species. It will be a while, but someday thinking machines will profoundly impact our lives, our world and even our very sense of self.

Bonus: Might computers also develop the capacity for emotion?
Once computers become intelligent and self-aware, they could direct their own hardware and software evolution to an utterly unprecedented degree. One cannot predict where that might lead.

6. Cindy Weinstein
Professor of English

Professor Weinstein's research focuses on 19th-century literature and culture. She has long been interested in the life and works of Herman Melville.

Author James Frey faced public derision after being outed for having fictionalized his memoir, *A Million Little Pieces*. Would such a thing have happened in 19th-century American publishing?
Oprah Winfrey's outrage at discovering that James Frey's "memoir" had fiction in it resonates with readers of 19th-century American fiction. When Herman Melville published his first book, Typee, in 1846, readers were taken aback. Not only had he savagely critiqued the missionary zeal with which Americans viewed the natives of the South Sea

Islands, but readers didn't believe that a sailor could have possibly written such an erudite and clever book. When it came out that Melville had expanded his month-long adventure on the island of Nukuheva into a four-month journey, readers were incensed. Melville's publisher, John Murray, worried that Typee read like the book of a professional author, and once the smell of fiction was in the air, it never went away. Even though Melville's shipmate, Richard Tobias Greene, who jumped ship when Melville did, swore to the truth of Typee, the book's authenticity has always been in question. As Melville biographer Leon Howard writes, anticipating Frey's dilemma, "Typee was, in fact, neither literal autobiography nor pure fiction." American writers have always torn the facts of their lives into a million little pieces.

Bonus: Name the actors who played Ahab in the three movies made of *Moby Dick*?
John Barrymore was Captain Ahab in the 1930 version; Gregory Peck played the part in John Houston's 1956 remake; and Patrick Stewart, everyone's favorite Trekkie, played Ahab in the 1998 television version.

Where to Hear Geniuses Speak

Besides the series below, check the web sites of Caltech (caltech.edu) and Occidental (oxy.edu) to look for special guest lecturers.

Distinguished Speaker Series
Pasadena Civic Auditorium
300 E. Green St., Pasadena
626.449.7360, 310.546.6222
speakersla.com
Some of the most fascinating people in the world come to Pasadena from October through May as part of the Distinguished Speaker Series of Southern California, which also sponsors talks in Redondo Beach and Thousand Oaks. The speakers range from world leaders like Mikhail Gorbachev, to writers like Tom Wolfe, to journalists like Christiane Amanpour, to all-around fabulous people like Jane Goodall and Maya Angelou. A series season includes seven talks; unfortunately, you cannot buy tickets for individual events (except perhaps on Craigslist).

Earnest C. Watson Lectures.
Beckman Auditorium
Caltech, 332 S. Michigan Ave., Pasadena
626.395.4652, events.caltech.edu
Was your math SAT score a few hundred points too low for Caltech admission? Not to worry: Caltech and JPL brainiacs enlighten all of us at these free and fascinating lectures at Beckman Auditorium. Recent examples include the great physicist Kip Thorne explaining Einstein's theory of relativity and chemical engineering prof Mark Davis on fighting cancer with nanoparticle medicines.

Social Activism Speaker Series
Caltech Y
Bldg. 62, Caltech
1200 California Blvd., Pasadena
626.395.6163, sass.caltech.edu
Intended to engage students who might otherwise be lost in astrophysical space, this lecture series showcases social activists making a difference, such as Peter Cleary, whose company is helping provide clean water to the developing world. All are open to the general public, and every one is free.

Voices of Vision
Beckman Auditorium
Caltech, 332 S. Michigan Ave., Pasadena
626.395.4652, events.caltech.edu
Yet another wonderful – and free – Caltech program, this one brings great thinkers to town. The range is diverse: One month you can hear MIT prof Seth Lloyd discuss "Programming the Universe: A Quantum Computer Scientist Takes on the Cosmos," and another month, Al Franken might riff on politics and humor.

Vroman's Bookstore Author Visits
695 E. Colorado Blvd., Pasadena
626.449.5320, vromansbookstore.com
A dazzling variety of authors stops by throughout the year to talk about their work and sign books. The setting is intimate, allowing you to get up close and personal with your favorite author, whether it's gonzo food writer Anthony Bourdain, thriller queen Mary Higgins Clark, novelist Walter Mosley or journalist Malcolm Gladwell.

Starstruck: JPL & Mt. Wilson Observatory

Jet Propulsion Laboratory (JPL)

Perhaps it is our particular mindset, but we have never been on the JPL campus without imagining it to be a James Bond set: park-like grounds that seem so peaceful... until somebody in there presses the launch button, and then all hell breaks loose. That, of course, is absurd. The truth is that within the confines of this bucolic setting, thousands of scientists and engineers have created robotic craft

JPL's campus at the foot of the San Gabriel Mountains

and probes for NASA that have explored eight of the named planets, all but Pluto and Eris, and peered out at the universe beyond. And in case you think these brainiacs are unlikely to be fun at a picnic, please be informed that JPL mechanical engineer Lonnie Johnson, while working on thermodynamic systems for Galileo and Mars Observer projects, inadvertently invented the SuperSoaker. So not only would he be fun at a picnic, he could afford to bring the champagne – and the good stuff at that!

A federal facility, JPL is managed by Caltech for NASA. Its pedigree can be traced back to the 1930s, with the rocket-propulsion experiments of Caltech physicist and engineer Theodore von Kármán. It would be difficult to overstate the enormity of JPL's contribution to America's space program: Surveyor, Voyager, Galileo and Mars Pathfinder, to name just a few.

JPL offers free tours with advance reservation, and we highly recommend a visit. This is yet another fantastic Pasadena resource. (Okay – technically most of the 170-plus-acre campus is in La Cañada, but a few buildings, as well as the main gate, are in Pasadena, so we claim it for our own.)

JPL's Rover team at work

JPL
4800 Oak Grove Dr.,
Pasadena
Tour reservations
818.354.9314

Mt. Wilson Observatory

The dome holding Mt. Wilson Observatory's 100-inch telescope, not long after it was built in 1917

Mt. Wilson Observatory, founded in 1904 by the Carnegie Institution of Washington (CIW) with astronomer George Ellery Hale, sits atop the 5,715-foot summit of Mt. Wilson in the San Gabriel Mountains. Since the 1980s, when it decided to restrict deep-sky astronomy research to its Las Campañas Observatory in Chile, CIW now partners with the Mt. Wilson Observatory Association (MWOA) to maintain operations. Check out the MWOA web site (mwoa.org) for fantastic photos of the 100-inch telescope mirror being hauled up the mountain in July 1917. Telescopic observations here began with studies of the sun and quickly expanded to include study of the properties and origins of all celestial objects and events. In other words, astrophysics was pretty much invented in the mountains overlooking our fair town.

There are docent-guided tours or you can print out your own self-guided tour, available at mtwilson.edu. About a twenty-mile drive into the rugged and beautiful mountains, a visit to the observatory makes a wonderful half-day trip. Typically, it is open April through November, but weather concerns may force a closure at any time. The CHP designates the Angeles Crest Highway (the road up the mountain) a "special enforcement zone," requiring daylight headlights to be on. Don't ignore the signs, as they have been known to ticket – and the fine can be a whopper! Also, remember your picnic basket, because the picnic tables command an eagle's-eye view of the Los Angeles basin – depending, of course, on the weather.

Mt. Wilson Observatory
Red Box Rd. off Angeles Crest Hwy.
No phone; mtwilson.edu & mwoa.org

E.T., Phone Pasadena!

In an old Craftsman bungalow on a quiet Pasadena side street lurks the Planetary Society, a nonprofit founded in 1980 by three extremely smart people: famed scientist and author Carl Sagan, former JPL chief Bruce Murray and deep-space scientist Louis Friedman, all of whom were fed up with NASA, which they felt had given up on space exploration to be a low-orbit "trucking company." The Planetary Society's mission? To bravely go where no man has gone before... no, wait, that's Star Trek's mission. But the Society's is quite similar: "To inspire the people of Earth through education, research, private ventures and public participation to explore other worlds and seek other life." In other words, they're looking for extra-terrestrials by seeking planets beyond our solar system, developing such technology as the SETI optical telescope and planetary microphones, and encouraging student engagement in such projects as the Mars Rover. For more information or to join the Society, go to planetary.org.

The College Tour

Ah, the lucky students who get to live and learn in Pasadena! They get culture and coffeehouses galore, mountains and trees, bookstores, nightlife, smart people everywhere, and proximity to the L.A. megalopolis. Here's what you need to know about our institutions of higher learning in the Cambridge of the west.

California Institute of Technology
1200 E. California Blvd., Pasadena
626.395.6811, caltech.edu

Sitting and thinking on the Caltech campus

With a faculty and alumni population that includes 31 Nobel laureates, five Crafoord laureates and scientists who have discovered everything from antimatter to the difference between the left brain and the right brain, Caltech is one of the smartest places in the world. But it's not a particularly populous place: It's home to just 896 undergrads and 1,276 grad students. There are almost that many faculty members, as well as another 2,600 non-faculty employees, so students enjoy a remarkable degree of support. As well they should – these are the people most likely to find a cure for cancer, unravel the secrets of the universe and invent something even better than Velcro.

Located in the heart of Pasadena, Caltech's campus is a lovely place, full of gardens (see the Horticultural chapter) and a fine mix of old and new buildings – including Beckman Auditorium, which hosts first-rate public concerts and lectures. Locals know they have truly arrived if they can score a membership to the Athenaeum, a private club for Caltechers, JPL folks, Huntington Library fellows and a lucky few neighbors and community leaders. Funded by a stock gift that was cashed in just before the crash of 1929, the ornate club (including hotel rooms, dining facilities and entertaining spaces) was officially launched in 1931 with a formal dinner welcoming visiting professor Albert Einstein. Guests of Athenaeum members can even stay in the Einstein Suite, which housed the Einsteins for a couple of months.

Besides educating the scientists and visionaries of the future, Caltech is a serious research center, and it also staffs and manages (for the federal government) nearby JPL, with which it collaborates on all sorts of R & D ventures. Its students also work with the Huntington on various research projects.

Einstein in Pasadena

"Here in Pasadena it is like Paradise. Always sunshine and clean air, gardens with palms and pepper trees, and friendly people who smile at one and ask for autographs."

– Albert Einstein

Of the many great thinkers who've lived in the Crown City, none was more famed than Albert Einstein. In 1930, at the peak of his glory, 51-year-old Einstein, apprehensive about the rise of Nazis, decided to leave the University of Berlin, and the world's scientists went bonkers trying to lure him to their towns. The winner was Caltech astronomer Edwin Hubble, whom Einstein admired – and in late 1930, Albert and Elsa Einstein arrived in Pasadena. They wintered here for the next three years, eventually settling in Princeton in 1933.

His time at Caltech was not one of fabulous discoveries; he was beginning to seek a unified field theory, an ultimately unsuccessful quest that occupied him for the rest of his life. But he did make his mark on Pasadena, spending lots of time at the Mt. Wilson Observatory and being feted at dinner parties. He became fast friends with Socialist author and local rabble-rouser Upton Sinclair, an ESP believer who convinced Einstein and two other Caltech scientists to attend a séance. Unfortunately, the seer was unable to conjure any spirits in the presence of such ultra-rational minds, and as far as we know, that was the end of Einstein's dabbling in the paranormal.

Today, Einstein's local legacy lives on: A Tudor house on Hill Avenue across from Caltech is home to the Einstein Papers Project, an international collaboration that is gradually publishing 25 volumes of the great thinker's writing. For information, go to einstein.caltech.edu.

Fun & Games at Caltech

There's more to Caltech than searching for prime numbers and new planets. Its students also are famed for their pranks, or "hacks." Here are a few favorites:

► At the nationally televised halftime show for the 1961 Rose Bowl, hackers replaced the flip cards on the seats of Washington Huskies fans, so instead of seeing an image of the school's mascot, the nation saw a huge buck-toothed beaver, followed by the word CALTECH instead of HUSKIES.

► At the 1984 Rose Bowl game, hackers rewired the scoreboard to say "Caltech 38, MIT 9."

► In 1987, on Hollywood's 100th birthday, hackers doctored the Hollywood sign to spell CALTECH.

► More recently, its rivalry with MIT has been heating up. At a 2005 open house MIT had logo T-shirts for prospective students; not until the students unfolded them and put them on did anyone notice that the back of each shirt read, "Because not everyone can go to Caltech." In 2006, MIT got revenge by stealing the Caltech cannon and carting it across country; four days later, Caltech students flew east and recovered it. In 2007, again during MIT's open house, Caltech distributed a fake edition of "The Tech," complete with lots of digs against its rival.

Art Center College of Design

Hillside Campus, 1700 Lida St., Pasadena
626.396.2200, artcenter.edu
South Campus, 950 S. Raymond Ave., Pasadena
626.396.2319

Under the leadership of dynamo Richard Koshalek, this 75-plus-year-old institution is one of the world's leading schools for product, graphic and transportation design, as well as fine art, advertising and illustration. It's most famed for its automotive program, students of which have gone on to design such cars as the PT Cruiser and the Volkswagen Bug. But Art Center grads are responsible for much more than cars: They've dreamed up everything from R2-D2 in *Star Wars* to Frank Sinatra album covers to Oakley's aerodynamic Zeros sunglasses. Alums say they've never worked harder in their lives – it's a challenging school that pushes students to both develop strong technical skills and think as far outside the box as possible.

Although originally based in L.A., Art Center moved to a Linda Vista hillside in 1976, adding its South Campus (in the former Caltech Wind Tunnel building) in 2004. In a recent development, the Pasadena City Council approved an agreement to lease the Glenarm Power Plant to Art Center to further develop its South Campus Graduate Research facility. Some 1,400 students travel between the two campuses; the South Campus also offers another 5,200 people extracurricular education, from night classes for design professionals to a thriving Saturday high school program. Its plans for the future, and for Pasadena, are grand and modernistic, ranging from sleek new dormitory buildings next to the South Campus to a Frank Gehry–designed library and research center at the Hillside Campus. And it's also involved in the renovation of South Arroyo Parkway.

Both campuses are well worth visiting; make sure to check out the student galleries and the wonderful Williamson Gallery at the Hillside Campus and the public exhibitions in the Wind Tunnel.

Student chefs at CSCA

California School of Culinary Arts

521 E. Green St., Pasadena
626.229.1300, csca.edu

This new college has been growing like chanterelles in a French forest – students in chef's whites are seen all over town, coming in and out of the various buildings the school rents for additional space. The gleaming kitchen classrooms and student-staffed restaurant, 561, are found at the main facility on Green Street in the Playhouse District – young chefs are on display behind the glass walls, working night and day. CSCA offers four Le Cordon Bleu–certified degrees, with specialties in cooking, baking and restaurant management; programs typically last one to two years. It's hard to imagine that there are enough restaurants out there to hire these armies of new chefs, but so far grads seem to be doing just fine.

Fuller Theological Seminary
135 N. Oakland Ave., Pasadena
626.584.5200, fuller.edu

A Christian graduate school with an evangelical bent, Fuller trains ministers, psychologists, therapists and philosophers. The central-Pasadena campus, which comprises lovely old homes and a few modern buildings, is the school's headquarters, but there are many satellites, including in Colorado Springs, Seattle and Sacramento. The student body is remarkably diverse, coming from all over the world. Fuller takes scholarship seriously, and its master's and doctoral programs do a fine job of preparing marriage and family counselors, ministers and psychologists. Everything, however, is cast with an evangelical Christian hue – agnostics, atheists and non-Christians need not apply.

The quad at Occidental College

Occidental College
1600 Campus Rd., Eagle Rock
323.259.2500, oxy.edu

Okay, so it's not actually in Pasadena, but since Oxy is just a few miles west in Eagle Rock, it might as well be. Many of its faculty live in Pasadena, its alums are all over town, and when students want fun on Saturday night, they head for Old Town.

One of Southern California's oldest colleges, Occidental was founded in 1887 and today is one of the finest liberal arts colleges in the west. With just 1,840 undergrads and a nearly ten-to-one student-faculty ratio, it's a small, tightly knit community with a devoted corps of alumni and a top-notch faculty. Unlike some liberal arts colleges, majors go beyond philosophy, comparative lit and women's studies to include geology, cognitive science and geophysics; Oxy is known as an excellent place for premed work. Students also may take classes at Caltech and Art Center. Extras include a well-rounded roster of NCAA Division III sports teams, 100 clubs (the Bad Movie Club, Queer Straight Alliance and Associated Boardriders are just a few); a peaceful hillside campus centered around three Myron Hunt buildings; strong programs in theater, dance, music and visual art; and many junior-year-abroad options.

Notable alums include U.S. Senator Barack Obama, U.S. Congressman Jack Kemp, poet Robinson Jeffers, actor Luke Wilson, movie director and former Python Terry Gilliam and journalist Patt Morrison.

Pacific Oaks College
5 Westmoreland Pl., Pasadena
626.397.1300, pacificoaks.edu

With a Quaker heritage and a Craftsman-era campus next to the famed Gamble House, Pacific Oaks is devoted to the well-being of children and families. It is primarily a teachers' college, offering such upper-division and graduate-level classes as language and literacy, cognitive development in mathematics in a diverse classroom, behavior intervention for children with special needs and all the coursework necessary for getting a teaching credential. There's a particular emphasis on anti-bias curricula and teaching in a diverse environment. Also offered are a B.A. and M.A. in human development and a graduate degree in Marriage, Family and Child Counseling. With just 700 students at the main campus, the atmosphere is warm, nurturing and diverse, and the people here deeply believe in what they do.

Future educators have a wonderful resource in Pacific Oaks Children's School, a prestigious preschool on the edge of the Arroyo, where student teachers get hands-on lessons in early-childhood development.

Pacific Oaks also has satellite campuses in many locations – Oakland, San Diego, Visalia, Palm Springs, Chico – most of which offer B.A. and M.A. degrees in human development.

Pasadena City College
1570 E. Colorado Blvd., Pasadena
626.585.7123, pasadena.edu

Originally called Pasadena Junior College, this exemplary school began in 1924 on the site of the original Pasadena High School, which later moved to East Pasadena. The alum roster is impressive indeed for a junior college, including teacher Jaime Escalante, author Octavia Butler, rock star Eddie Van Halen, filmmaker John Singleton (who took his first film class here), baseball legend Jackie Robinson (who later transferred to UCLA), actor William Holden and fashion designer Bob Mackie.

PCC has something for everyone. It's one of the top transfer colleges in the state, sending many students on to good universities. It offers AA degrees in many majors; pre-college classes for high school students; parent-ed classes; extended-learning programs; and certificates in everything from nursing to welding. It also has a beautiful campus; a pretty good football team; an art gallery; an acclaimed band that performs in the Rose Parade every year; and a superb flea market, held the first Sunday of each month. Oh, and it's responsible for the finest news- and talk-radio station in Southern California, KPCC 89.3 FM.

On the Outskirts

The Claremont Colleges
150 E. Eighth St., Claremont
909.621.8000, claremont.edu

The Oxford of California, Claremont comprises seven highly ranked small colleges in a pretty town 27 miles east of Pasadena: Claremont McKenna, a 1,000-student liberal arts school specializing in business and public affairs; Harvey Mudd, a 700-student undergrad school that's one of the nation's best for math, engineering and science; Pomona, a 1,500-student liberal arts college that now rivals Stanford in its academic prowess; Scripps, a small women's college with strong humanities and cultural studies; Pitzer, a 950-student liberal arts college with a '60s pedigree and progressive approach; Claremont Graduate University, offering 22 doctoral and master's degrees; and Keck Graduate Institute of Applied Life Sciences, a grad school devoted exclusively to a two-year master's program in bioscience. Each school has its own faculty, focus and campus, but all share facilities and programs in one way or another (i.e., Pomona and Pitzer have combined sports teams), and a student in one school can take classes at the others.

Glendale Community College
1500 N. Verdugo Rd., Glendale
818.240.1000, glendale.edu

This fine community college is perched on the San Rafael hills just west of Pasadena, over-looking the city of Glendale. Like PCC, it's an all-around community resource, offering AA degrees, vocational certificates, continuing ed, pre-college classes, clubs and intercollegiate sports.

3 Great Libraries

Here are our three favorite public libraries. The most famous library in town, the Huntington, is discussed in the Artistic chapter. If you're a serious and credentialed scholar, you can apply for the chance to access its world-renowned collection, but otherwise, you'll have to make do with a peek at a few of its most famous pieces in the Library Exhibition Halls.

Brand Library & Art Center
1601 W. Mountain St., Glendale
818.548.2051, library.ci.glendale.ca.us

A Moorish detail at Brand Library

High in the foothills overlooking Glendale, with a design inspired by the East Indian Pavilion of the 1893 Chicago World Columbian Exposition, "El Miradoro" was completed as a home for railroader Leslie C. Brand in 1904. (Since you're at the library anyway, check out *The Devil in the White City* by Erik Larson, an excellent nonfiction telling of the Chicago Exposition and the nefarious goings-on of a serial murderer stalking the city at the same time. But we digress.)

Brand donated the house and grounds to the city with the provision that when it was no longer the residence of his widow, it would become a library and park. And so it is, with the addition of an art gallery and recital hall in 1969. An art- and music-focused library directed at adult usage, Brand houses books, periodicals, videos, CDs, slides and prints. (There's no book drop, so return materials during library hours.) This specialized library also maintains a collection of framed prints, which may be borrowed for 56 days. The art gallery features four shows of California artists each year, and the recital hall is used for music and art events.

Don't forget to ask a librarian about the ghost, thought to be the redoubtable Mr. Brand, who died here in 1925 and is perceived by those who have felt his presence to be of the benevolent and protective order of spirits.

Pasadena Public Library, Central Branch
285 E. Walnut St., Pasadena
626.744.4066, ci.pasadena.ca.us/library

In 1924, Myron Hunt and H.C. Chambers were one of ten architectural firms to submit a design for the Pasadena Public Library. Their Spanish Renaissance structure, with its elegantly scaled entry and patio, was particularly pleasing to the judges, and it fit the tone of the developing Civic Center, so it won. Construction began in 1925, and the library opened to an enthusiastic public in 1927. An extensive, historically sensitive restoration took place from 1984 to 1990, and today, the beautiful and highly functional pride of our library system is on the National Register of Historic Places.

Of 840,000 items (including print, non-print and electronic resources) in Pasadena's ten libraries, 394,800 are at this branch, which is known for its reference, business and local history. Step inside and, we swear, you feel the thrum of inquiry (and, yes, some adorable flirting) from those seated at the solid wooden tables stacked with piles of books. You'll also find people thumbing through the selection of 1,000 magazines, a centrally located reference desk, a wonderful children's collection housed in its own large room – and that's before even making it up to the stacks.

The unflappable reference staff will help you do your own research, or you may ask them to research a particular question via telephone or e-mail. And though it's historic, it has fully embraced the digital era, offering a sizable collection of books and music that can be downloaded for a two-week lending period with a Pasadena or Glendale library card. Extras include children's programs, films and services for the house-bound. This glorious library remains well used and much loved by generations of Pasadenans. If you haven't hung out there, you're missing out, and if you don't have a library card: What the hell are you thinking? Get one – you'll be glad you did.

South Pasadena Public Library

1100 Oxley St., South Pasadena
626.403.7340
ci.south-pasadena.ca.us/library

This library does not retain any of its original 1907 domed, classical-revival design, but its handsome 1930 Mediterranean Revival facade by original architect Norman Marsh faces El Centro Street, while a more modern facade dating from a 1982 addition by Howard Morgridge welcomes patrons to the Oxley Street entrance. With its well-kept lawns and towering shade trees, the South Pas Library welcomes all, including the peripatetic green parrot flock that favors the surrounding trees for more-than-occasional, distinctly non-library-voiced gab sessions.

Being a responsive community resource is at the heart of the library's activities, from the in-library bookstore to the Restoration Concert Series, both sponsored by Friends of the South Pasadena Library. There are workshops for adults (including web site development and business marketing), career counseling and online college-prep support for teens, and cozy storytelling events for the little ones. The pajama storytime evening is a must – be there or be squarepants!

More Libraries to Explore

Altadena Library
600 E. Mariposa St., Altadena
626.798.0833
library.altadena.ca.us
A good small-town library, with an active book club, a community room, computers and a well-rounded collection of books.

Arcadia Public Library
20 W. Duarte Rd., Arcadia
626.821.5567
library.ci.arcadia.ca.us
This modern facility has excellent technology (computers, wireless internet access, learning stations for kids), job-hunting resources and a local-history collection.

La Pintoresca Branch, Pasadena Public Library
1355 N. Raymond Ave., Northwest Pasadena
626.744.7268
ci.pasadena.ca.us/library
One of the prettiest libraries in the SG Valley, this Spanish-style gem sits in a green park complete with a playground. Special features include a collection of African-American history and literature, a community meeting room, storytimes, job-hunting resources and a computer lab.

Sierra Madre Public Library
440 W. Sierra Madre Blvd., Sierra Madre
626.355.7186
cityofsierramadre.com
Part of a consortium of libraries in the small towns surrounding Los Angeles, this one has a great collection of local history, computer classes, story hours, a teen book club and lots of special events, from travel slide shows to writing workshops.

Q & A: Lucy Jones

The face of Dr. Lucy Jones on the network news is beamed across America every time there is a significant seismic event in Southern California – but because she is a fourth-generation daughter of Southern California, we claim her as our own. Lucy has authored more than 80 papers on research seismology and has been with the U.S. Geological Survey since 1983. Jill met with Lucy at her office at Caltech (and yes, the bookshelves are bolted to the wall).

We know you are the earthquake czarina of Southern California, but what is your actual title?
Scientist-in-charge of the USGS Earthquake Program in Southern California.

Yikes! That's saying something.
I know, but don't bother memorizing it, because by next year it is likely to change. I'll be in charge of a multi-hazard project that will work to improve disaster management in Southern California by applying relevant science to all the hazards we face here.

We're at your office on the Caltech campus, but do you work for Caltech?
I know this confuses people, but I've never worked for Caltech. I'm a federal employee of the U.S. Geological Survey. If I did work for Caltech, my job would be creating scientific papers – and I do some of that – but as a fed, my job is to apply the best science to reducing losses from earthquakes in the United States, particularly in Southern California.

You appear to be permanently tethered to your laptop. Have you ever had a serious computer crash?
No…well, I dropped it once – do you know what a laptop screen does when you shatter it? Well, it was interesting, but I couldn't see it anymore. That was traumatic, but fortunately it was pretty easy to recover the hard drive.

If you had one minute to tell Southern Californians what to do about earthquake safety, what would you say?
I would say go online and look at earthquakecountry.info, which is where you'll find the best we have, including Putting Down Roots in Earthquake Country, *a preparedness handbook I wrote. And the one piece of scientific information I'd offer is that the worst earthquake is inevitable – and we haven't seen it yet. I know I'm scaring people, but that is good if it convinces them to take precautions. I'm so impressed with Pasadena for making a huge investment in retrofitting City Hall as a part of its preservation effort. If the levees in Louisiana had been fixed, they would not have had a catastrophe – a disaster, yes, but not a catastrophe.*

Is there any particular scent that evokes Pasadena for you?
There is that scent of jasmine in the spring. Certain places that get you when you walk by. It is in the air right now.

Pasadena is...

Literary

Not only did the visual arts flourish in the Arroyo culture of the 19th and early 20th centuries, but so did the literary arts. Journalists, memoirists, poets and novelists made their mark on the national literary scene then, and today a new wave of writers continues the tradition – as does a thriving community of bookstores and writer-friendly libraries and coffeehouses.

Literary Pasadena   58

The Words   60

Bookstores We Love   62

Where to Write   65

Q & A: Michelle Huneven   66

Literary Pasadena

Charlotte Perkins Gilman

From its earliest settling by Midwesterners, the Arroyo area attracted writers. One of the best known was **Charles Fletcher Lummis**, who in 1884 walked from Cincinnati to L.A. for a job as a reporter at the *Los Angeles Daily Times*. This was a brilliant publicity stunt, of course, and he arrived in town a famous man. He remained famous, writing for the *Times*, fighting for Indian rights, writing editorials and poetry, photographing Native Americans and founding a magazine called *Land of Sunshine* (later *Out West*), for which he recruited such writers as Jack London and Charlotte Perkins Gilman. He also built – by hand – a river-rock house on the Highland Park banks of the Arroyo that is today a cherished landmark.

Charlotte Perkins Gilman came to Pasadena to recover from the emotional stress she felt marriage and motherhood placed upon her and began her lifetime of writing and speaking on woman's issues. Here she penned her most powerful and successful novella, *The Yellow Wallpaper* (1890), a thinly veiled telling of her journey into madness.

Mary Hunter Austin and **Idah Meacham Strobridge** were not only contemporaries but also kindred spirits. They both had lived with the harsh elements of the desert – Austin in the Sierra Nevada and Strobridge in the Nevada Great Basin – and had coped with the sadness of family life (Austin had a disappointing husband and a developmentally delayed daughter, and Strobridge had to bury a husband and three children). Both came to the Arroyo and became a part of Lummis's literary circle. Both found their literary voices in the landscapes of the desert, Austin with *Land of Little Rain* (1903) and Strobridge with *In Miners' Mirage-Land* (1904), illustrated by another local, Maynard Dixon. Strobridge established the Artemisia Bindery on the Arroyo near Abbey San Encino, where Clyde Browne had his printing operation, and there she continued to write, publish and hand-bind books.

Other important local literary figures of that early era included:

▶ **Adam Clark Vroman**, a photographer of Western and Native American culture who founded Vroman's Book and Photographic Supply in what is now Old Pasadena in 1894. Now located a little further east on Colorado, Vroman's Bookstore remains the literary heart of the San Gabriel Valley.

▶ **Olive Percival** was a devotee of gardens and children's books who combined those loves to write the *Children's Garden Book*. She also wrote about gardens, and her library of children's books was one of the best in the country.

▶ Ohio-born **Earl Derr Biggers** was a prolific writer who moved to Pasadena in 1925 and had an office upstairs in the Star-News Building. Although the movie versions displayed negative stereotyping, in Biggers' original novels, protagonist Charlie Chan was a savvy detective who just happened to be Chinese.

▶ **Alice Millard** was a rare book dealer who commissioned Frank Lloyd Wright to design a home in which she could display and sell her wares, as well as host literary salons. The result was Prospect Park's La Miniatura (1923), the first of Wright's block-construction houses in California.

▶ Maryland native **Upton Sinclair** moved to Pasadena in 1915. He was a literary and political celebrity, thanks to the success of *The Jungle* (1906) and his unsuccessful but newsworthy efforts on behalf of the Socialist party. He and his wife, Mary, spent nearly 40 years in Pasadena, during which time he ran for governor of California (as a Socialist candidate), wrote *The Flivver King*, dabbled in telepathy and psychic phenomena and, in the 1940s, found another round of success with the Lanney Budd series of historical novels.

▶ Hugely prolific Western writer **Zane Grey** honeymooned in Altadena in 1906 and returned to settle in 1918. He and his wife, Dolly, lived at 396 Mariposa in Altadena from 1920 until his death in 1939; he was cremated at Mountain View Cemetery.

▶ **Holling Clancy Holling**, a Michigan native and later Pasadena resident, wrote several children's books, notably the 1942 Caldecott winner *Paddle-to-the-Sea*.

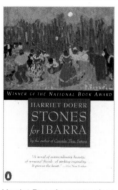
Harriet Doerr's masterpiece

In more modern times, Pasadenan **Harriet Doerr** (a granddaughter of Henry Edwards Huntington) achieved international acclaim in 1984 when she published her first novel, *Stones for Ibarra*, at age 73. It went on to win the National Book Award. She continued to write until her death in 2002. Also in 1984, Caltech professor, physicist and bon vivant **Richard Feynman** found publishing success with *Surely You're Joking, Mr. Feynman!*

Although they didn't necessarily stay in their hometowns, local natives who went on to publishing acclaim have included science fiction master **Octavia Butler** (*Kindred*), who died in Washington in 2006 and is buried at Altadena's Mountain View Cemetery; legendary cookbook author and San Marino native **Julia Child**; *How to Make an American Quilt* author **Whitney Otto**; and *Distant Land of My Father* author **Bo Caldwell**.

Today finds the culture as vibrant as ever. Among the hometown scribblers from Pasadena, Glendale, Altadena, South Pasadena, La Cañada and Eagle Rock are:

▶ Memoirist and novelist **Mark Salzman** (*Lying Awake, Iron & Silk*)

▶ Novelist **Michelle Huneven** (*Jamesland, Round Rock*)

▶ Crime writers **Denise Hamilton** (*Sugar Skull, Los Angeles Noir*) and **Naomi Hirahara** (*Snakeskin Shamisen*)

▶ Children's book author **Eve Bunting** (*Fly Away Home, Smoky Night*) and author/illustrator **Marla Frazee** (*Mrs. Biddlebox, Roller Coaster*)

▶ PEN-award-winning poet and Oxy professor **Martha Ronk** (*Why/Why Not*)

▶ Nonfiction author **Greg Critser** (*Fat Land, Generation Rx*)

▶ Academy Award–winning screenwriter **Charlie Kaufman** (*Being John Malkovich, Adaption*) and screenwriter **Scott Frank** (*Get Shorty, The Lookout, Marley & Me*).

▶ Novelist, poet and teacher **Jim Krusoe** (*Iceland, Blood Lake*)

▶ Memoirist **Wil Wheaton** (*Just a Geek*)

The Words

Writers both famous and undeservedly little-known have lived in, or passed through, Pasadena and her sister towns, and we could fill a book with the words they've written about these towns. But for now we'll fill these two pages.

Now I was truly in "God's country" – the real Southern California which is peerless…. Next day, February 1, 1885, a thirty-mile walk through beautiful towns, past the picturesque old Mission San Gabriel, and down a matchless valley, brought me at midnight to my unknown home in the City of Angels.

– A Tramp Across the Continent
Charles Fletcher Lummis

The house was on Dresden in the Oak Noll section of Pasadena, a big solid cool-looking house with burgundy brick walls, a terra cotta tile roof, and a white stone trim… There was a heavy scent of summer on the morning and everything that grew was perfectly still in the breathless air they get over there on what they call a nice cool day.

– The High Window
Raymond Chandler

Quacks are plentiful in Pasadena, and they are very popular, especially with the wealthy, middle-aged matrons on whose diamond-studded hands time, alas, hangs heavier than a six spade bid doubled and redoubled.

– "Croesus at Home"
Morrow Mayo

Pasadena is a place of gated and walled estates. Cal Tech, and the Norton Simon Museum, and the Huntington Library, with its permanent collection of Gainsboroughs and Romneys, its first folios and Gutenbergs, are all located in Pasadena. More Nobel laureates live in Pasadena than in any other American city. South Pasadena is more… cozy is as good a word as any.

– Smoked
Léon Bing

Pasadena? I've heard that's where very old people live in very big houses with their parents.

– Edith Oliver, former theatre critic
for the New Yorker

To California, in its natural features, I owe much. Its calm sublimity of contour, richness of color, profusion of flowers, fruit and foliage, and the steady peace of its climate were meat and drink to me.

– The Living of Charlotte Perkins Gilman
(about her time in Pasadena)
Charlotte Perkins Gilman

Tiny ramshackle houses gave way to stores, and then again to houses, albeit nicer, as they crossed into Alhambra, and nicer still in South Pasadena. Now the median was lawn and tended bushes. The sign said San Marino and the houses were nicer still…

Suddenly the houses were large and lovely, the dream realized. They sat back on wide lawns; their inner workings were modern American, the latest plumbing, the latest wiring, the latest central air. They were lath and plaster, but their looks were diverse copies of English Tudor and French Provincial, Monterey Colonials, brick Williamsburg, and sprawling modern ranch. Their grounds were manicured and flowers still bloomed despite it being December. A few already had decorated Christmas trees in big front windows framed with lights.

Mad Dog whistled. "This is definitely the high-rent district."

– Dog Eat Dog
Edward Bunker

Monty lay still, and smoked a long time. Then, in a queer, shaky voice he said: "I always said you'd make some guy a fine wife if you didn't live in Glendale."

"Are you asking me to marry you?"

"If you move to Pasadena, yes."

"You mean if I buy this house."

"No – it's about three times as much house as you need, and I don't insist on it. But I will not live in Glendale."

"Then all *right!*"

– Mildred Pierce
James M. Cain

Everywhere there was beauty, and the nerve-rest of steady windless weather.....

This place did not seem like earth, it was paradise. Kind and congenial friends, pleasant society, amusement, out-door sports, the blessed mountains, the long, unbroken sweep of the valley, with snow-peaks at the far eastern end.
> — *The Living of Charlotte Perkins Gilman*
> (about her time in Pasadena)
> Charlotte Perkins Gilman

The name of the Millionaire Town has scared away from Pasadena many respectable middle-class people who have gone to Southern California to make their homes. Once they take a look around the place, see the palatial mansions, note the lack of industry, and hear the fatal words, Millionaire Town, they are on their way to Whittier, Monrovia, Glendale, or some other community of just folks.
> — *"Croesus at Home"*
> Morrow Mayo

Roy knew that people *adored* this town, even the psychos. Homeless people "loved" being homeless in Pasadena. Pasadenans who moved away, for whatever length of time, almost always moved back. What made Pasadena so special? Was the Crown City really that different from any other place?

... Roy was fascinated by the personal lives of Pasadena elites, who always married well. The images of gorgeous, poised, healthy-looking young women dressed up as Rose Princesses and Rose Queens no doubt impressed rich, would-be mothers-in-law with their uxorial qualities. Roy guessed that few of the college-bound members of this royal family finished their education without a diamond ring to go with their degree.
> — *Love, Death, and Other War Stories*
> Victor Cass

When we'd finished downtown, she headed back to Pasadena, which she said was eminently civilized. In a study of 295 American cities, she said proudly, Pasadena has been ranked as America's most desirable city, based on its high ratio of radios, telephones, bathtubs, and dentists to residents. She believed it to be the most beautiful, healthful, cultured, and intelligent community in the West.
> — *The Distant Land of My Father*
> Bo Caldwell

Tibbs shook his head. Before he could speak, Gillespie intervened. "Virgil here is a police investigator out in Beverly Hills, California."

"Pasadena," Tibbs corrected.

"All right then, Pasadena. What difference does it make?"
> — *In The Heat of the Night*
> John Ball

There is a saying in Los Angeles that rich people who move to Southern California do not go to Pasadena to live unless they have had money for at least two decades....

Money does not flash in Pasadena. The community is so modest on the subject of wealth that even the word millionaire is taboo in the local press. In the whole history of the town no movie star has ever lived there.
> — *"Croesus at Home"*
> Morrow Mayo

Bibliography

▶ Ball, John. *In the Heat of the Night*. Center Point Publishing, 2001 (originally published 1965).

▶ Bing, Léon. *Smoked: A True Story About the Kids Next Door*. HarperCollins, 1993.

▶ Bunker, Edward. *Dog Eat Dog*. St. Martin's Press, 1996.

▶ Cain, James M. *Mildred Pierce*. Vintage Books, 1989 (originally published 1941).

▶ Caldwell, Bo. *The Distant Land of My Father*. Harcourt, 2001.

▶ Cass, Victor. *Love, Death, and Other War Stories*. iUniverse Inc., 2005.

▶ Chandler, Raymond. *The High Window*. Random House, 2002 (originally published 1942).

▶ Gilman, Charlotte Perkins. *The Living of Charlotte Perkins Gilman*. University of Wisconsin Press, 1990 (originally published 1935).

▶ Lummis, Charles Fletcher. *A Tramp Across the Continent*. University of Nebraska Press, 1982 (originally published 1892).

▶ Mayo, Morrow. "Croesus At Home." *American Mercury*. 27.106 (1932): 230-6.

Bookstores We Love

Book lovers should also read about our favorite libraries in the Smart chapter; for children's books, see "Shopping Like a Kid" in the Childlike chapter.

Alexandria II Metaphysical Bookstore
567 S. Lake Ave., Pasadena
626.792.7885, alexandria2.com
The aroma of incense lures shoppers strolling between Ann Taylor and Starbucks, tempting them to step into this New Age store to get in touch with their auras or their past lives. You'll find new and used books on everything New Age, as well as crystals, candles, jewelry, videos and music (for massage, yoga, spiritual chanting, guided imagery and more).

The Archives Bookshop
1396 E. Washington Blvd., Pasadena
626.797.4756, archivesbookshop.com
Closed Sun.
Next door to Cook Books by Janet Jarvits and across the street from Mitchell Books (or Crime Time), Archives is a huge, well-lit, thoughtfully displayed used bookstore that is the yin to Crime Time's yang – while murder and mayhem lurk at Mitchell, theology and pastoral counseling fill the pages here. A great resource for those seeking bibles (including collectible bibles) and books on philosophy, ministry, ethics and more, including textbooks used by students at Fuller and Claremont School of Theology.

Barnes & Noble
111 W. Colorado Blvd., Old Pasadena
626.585.0362, bn.com
The Old Pas branch of this nationwide chain has the usual B&N assortment of titles, a solid newsstand and a very nice staff. There's another location in Glendale.

Book Alley
1252 E. Colorado Blvd., Pasadena
626.683.8083, bookalley.com
Whether you're seeking a first edition of *Catcher in the Rye* for $2,100 or a new graphic novel, Book Alley is well worth a prowl. Now in larger quarters farther east from its original location in the Playhouse District, it displays new and used books side by side. Titles on California, photography, history, art, anthropology, poetry and literature are particular strong suits, and it buys and sells textbooks, too.

Book 'Em Mysteries
1118 Mission St., South Pasadena
626.799.9600, bookem.com
Closed Mon. & holidays
If you can't get enough of Inspector Dalgliesh or Kinsey Millhone – and what murder-mystery buff can? – you'll want to haunt Book 'Em, which carries new and used murder mysteries, detective novels and crime fiction. It's quite a bright and cheerful place for such dark subject matter, and the staff members are not at all likely to commit the sort of unspeakable acts they read about all day.

Bookfellows
238 N. Brand Blvd., Glendale
818.545.0121
This is a fun destination for lovers of used and/or rare books. Known for one of the largest sci-fi and horror collections in the region, it also stocks plenty of mysteries, and the lurid, color-saturated covers of its pulp paperbacks make for entertaining grazing. Local author talks and signings add to the neighborhood ambience. You'll also find some fine rare books, and don't miss the excellent poetry collection upstairs.

Just a few of the thousands of used titles at Book Alley

The BookHouse
1026 Fair Oaks Ave., South Pasadena
626.799.0756
They call it Fair Oaks Avenue, but it's really Main Street, U.S.A., and this main street has a swell bookstore housed in a 1905 Greek Revival home. The eclectic and well-ordered collection of used and rare books is a pleasure to peruse. We

A light and airy home for readers at Flintridge Bookstore

walked in to nose around and walked out with a second edition of a beloved book of poems and three paperbacks from the general literature and poetry sections – and still had money left over to shop for dinner at Bristol Farms up the street. Check out the great collections of such children's series as Nancy Drew and the Boxcar Children.

Borders Books

475 S. Lake Ave., Pasadena
626.304.9773, borders.com
A multimedia megastore, with books, a good collection of CDs (including world music, jazz and classical), DVDs, a decent newsstand, a large children's section, lots of greeting cards and a popular café. Other locations in Glendale and in the Santa Anita Mall.

Cliff's Books

630 Colorado Blvd., Pasadena
626.449.9541
Makes one think of the wonderful Arnold Lobel children's poem that begins, "Books to the ceiling, books to the sky. My piles of books are a mile high." One makes one's way gingerly through this cluttered shop of used and rare treasures. Comic and record collectors have made some very special finds here, but mostly it's books (on many topics) that abound. In the world of the book megastore, Cliff's is a welcome anachronism.

Cook Books by Janet Jarvits

1388 E. Washington Blvd., Pasadena
626.296.1638, cookbkjj.com
Closed Sun.-Mon.; hours irregular
Cookbooks upon cookbooks upon cookbooks, all used and sometimes rare, are piled all the

way up to the fifteen-foot ceiling and on every available surface. Chances are good that you'll need help finding what you seek.

Distant Lands

56 S. Raymond Ave., Old Pasadena
626.449.3220, distantlands.com
Oh, the happy hours we have whiled away in Distant Lands, poking through guidebooks to the Swiss Alps, travel memoirs of adventures in Russia and practical phrasebooks for all sorts of languages. And then there are the maps, the wonderful travel-friendly clothing, the luggage, the nifty gadgets.... If you love to travel, or love to dream of traveling, get to Distant Lands, and plan to stay a while. The owners and employees are all dedicated travelers and enthusiastic readers, and they'll point you to just the right title.

Flintridge Bookstore & Coffeehouse

964 Foothill Blvd., La Cañada
818.790,0717, flintridgebooks.com
It seems like anyone who'd open a large independent bookstore in this Amazon era would have to be insane, and yet Lenora and Peter Wannier appear to be completely sane – and smart, too. They've done everything right in their handsome new store: chosen the titles carefully to reflect the interests of locals, created a peaceful café area, worked with the local school district to stock its curricula titles, started a teen advisory board to choose books that teens actually want to read, established a Saturday-morning children's storytime, offered meeting space and discounts to book clubs, and stocked just enough non-book gifts to round out the mix. Even though it looks completely at home in this

high-ceilinged space, the store will be moving two doors west on Foothill sometime in 2009 or 2010, when the Wanniers build a new store on the site of the old flower shop that's been under-used for years.

Architecture books and Craftsman-era replicas are Gamble House specialties.

Gamble House Bookstore

4 Westmoreland Pl., Pasadena
626.449.4178, gamblehouse.org/bookstore
Closed Mon.-Wed.
The former garage for the Gamble House is now jam-packed with enough Arts & Crafts–related books, art and gifts to make an aficionado tremble with joy: limited-edition sets of drawings of Greene & Greene houses; gorgeous books on the Gamble House, the Greene brothers, the Arts & Craft movement, architecture, design and local history; greeting cards; reproduction tiles, lamps and pottery; and much more.

Imix Bookstore

5052 Eagle Rock Blvd., Eagle Rock
323.257.2512, imixbooks.com
Literature from Latin America is the focus at this compact and friendly book/gift store in the heart of Eagle Rock. You'll find titles on politics and culture, English translations of Spanish-language novels, and some fiction and nonfiction in Spanish, too, along with jewelry from Lisa Rocha and Sergio Flores, art from Chicano and Native American artists, and some fun gifts.

Once Upon a Time

2207 Honolulu Ave., Montrose
818.248.9668, onceupona.com.
A true community bookstore, this place is owned by Maureen Palacios, who seems to know every customer personally – and every book, too. Her store isn't large, so she chooses the titles carefully. So even though much of the store is devoted to children's books, adults will find lots of great reads, with particularly good choices in new fiction, politics, culture, humor and nonfiction. Fountain-pen owners (we know you're out there!), take note of the excellent and well-priced selection of inks. The children's events, like the teddy-bear picnic in honor of Corduroy's 40th birthday, are swell.

Sierra Madre Books

18 W. Sierra Madre Blvd., Sierra Madre
626.836.3200, sierramadrebooks.com
Closed Mon.
Small and personable, in the heart of Sierra Madre's impossibly charming downtown, this new shop is part community hub – offering tutoring, poetry readings and a meeting room – and part new and used bookstore. The selection isn't large, but you'll find all the new bestsellers, and well as some terrific used finds.

Vroman's Bookstore

695 E. Colorado Blvd., Pasadena
626.449.5320, vromansbookstore.com
3729 E. Foothill Blvd., East Pasadena
626.351.0828
At the flagship Colorado store you can roam many shelves of books and still have that inner glow of knowing you are supporting a local business – this Pasadena institution is going strong after more than 100 years. In fact, in 2008 *Publishers Weekly* named it Bookseller of the Year. Call ahead and pick something up at Will Call (they gift wrap, too), or browse for hours with help from a great staff that knows and loves books. The children's section upstairs is flush with books and glorious toys. Take a load off at Zeli's, the coffee shop, and browse the excellent news and magazine stand outside. Worthy gifts abound, but books take center stage. Subscribe to the newsletter to stay apprised of the author events, reading groups and children's story times, and note that the big-deal author signings (Jimmy Carter, David Sedaris) can draw huge crowds. The Hastings Ranch branch is smaller but is quite beloved by East Pasadenans.

Bring Your Laptop: Where to Write

The following hangouts all have a writer-friendly vibe and free WiFi:

It feels like home at the Zephyr.

Altadena Public Library
600 E. Mariposa St., Altadena
626.798.0833
Quieter and less crowded than the Pasadena Central Library; reading area with armchairs.

Bean Town
45 N. Baldwin Ave., Sierra Madre
626.355.1596
More convivial than studious, but you can hang out as long as you like.

Café Alibi
84 S. Fair Oaks Ave., Old Pasadena
626.577.5779
A shady patio next to the historic Castle Green.

The Coffee Gallery
2029 N. Lake Ave., Altadena
626.398.7917
The service is often slow, but the atmosphere is relaxed and funky. Private meeting room.

The Coffee Tree
696 E. Colorado Blvd., Pasadena
626.796.8256
Tucked-away location in Arcade Lane across from Vroman's makes this a swell secret spot.

Flintridge Bookstore & Coffeehouse
964 Foothill Blvd., La Cañada
818.790,0717
A peaceful spot that usually has plenty of tables, including out on the terrace.

Jones Coffee
537 S. Raymond Ave., Pasadena
626.564.9291
Great service and coffee, though parking and tables are scarce.

Kaldi
1019 El Centro St., South Pasadena
626.403.5951
Across from the South Pasadena Library, Kaldi has a European-café feel.

Metropolitan
716 E. Colorado Blvd., Pasadena
626.356.2288
Soft classical music and quiet, studious patrons make this an ideal spot for writers.

Pasadena Central Library (and Central Grounds Coffee)
285 E. Walnut St., Pasadena
626.744.4066
Beautiful architecture, an extensive collection of books, and an outdoor café.

Red Door Café
Caltech (next to the bookstore)
1200 E. California Blvd., Pasadena
626.395.6158
This lovely outdoor patio under trees is perfect for students and non-students alike.

South Pasadena Public Library
1100 Oxley St., South Pasadena
626.403.7340
A serene small-town library; consider taking your laptop out on the tree-shaded lawn.

Zephyr Coffee House & Art Gallery
2419 E. Colorado Blvd., East Pasadena
626.793.7330
It's easy to find a spot in one of the nooks and crannies of this handsome Craftsman house.

The WiFi isn't free, but you can't beat the atmosphere:

Café Culture
1359 N. Altadena Dr., Pasadena
626.358.8654
A welcoming neighborhood hangout.

Zona Rosa
15 S. El Molino Ave., Pasadena
626.793.2334
Nice, quiet upstairs area with couches and tables – and it's open late.

Q & A: Michelle Huneven

Writer Michelle Huneven is a native of Altadena; her dad arrived as a boy in 1923. Michelle was on the path to ordination as a minister, having spent two years at Claremont School of Theology, when she wrote her first novel, the tender and funny *Round Rock*; she left the seminary to be a full-time writer. Her second critically acclaimed novel, *Jamesland*, lovingly and hilariously ticks through scenes featuring characters who live in Los Feliz and Silverlake. Her newest book, co-authored with Bridget Murphy, is the *Tao Girls Guide to Real Estate*. Sandy talked to Michelle and whispered to her dog, Piper, in her Altadena home.

You bought a house in Altadena after growing up here, right?
I moved away for a long time. I got my master's at Iowa Writers' Workshop after college. I lived in L.A. for nine years, and then in Pasadena. But you could draw a straight line a mile west of where I live now, and that's right where my dad bought a piece of property when he was 19. Let's see, when you marry inside your tribe, it's endogamy. So, related by property, hmm, I guess that makes me... endogeographic.

What's the silliest misconception you've heard about Pasadena?
That it's smog-socked. That it's nowhere, unappealingly away from the ocean and the center of things.

What's your favorite Pasadena smell?
I love the smell of bay leaves in the Arroyo. And a fresh orange just off the tree has a wonderful vanilla-y smell. And, I shouldn't say this, but you know when you go on a camping trip, and you're on your way home, driving over Angeles Crest Highway, and you finally see our valley, and it's got that brown smudge hanging in the air? I take a deep breath and say, "Ah! Home!"

Where's your favorite place to have breakfast?
Pie 'n Burger.

What do you like to do on Sunday?
Go to the Neighborhood Unitarian Universalist Church. And take my dog up the Arroyo.

How many times have you gone to the Rose Parade?
Oh... ten times as a kid. Once as an adult. Sumi from Europane invited me.

Wow, Sumi from Europane invited you? You are famous.
No, no, she's an old friend. The last time I went before that, Dwight Eisenhower was grand marshal. There were a lot of presidents in the parade back then, but he was the dapperest.

What do you *really* think of the parade?
It's like a big, long commercial break. Except I like the bands. The Mexico City band? The best!

Pasadena is...

Architectural

What Pasadena has always promised – gracious living in a verdant setting and mild climate, with an artistic sensibility and a respect for technological innovation – led to an environment that nurtured architecture from the very beginning. Add a preservationist mind-set and you end up with one of the world's most cherished architectural gems. Here's where to find the best of it, from the shingled bungalows of South Pasadena, to the estates by Neff, Marston and Greene & Greene, to the modernist campuses of Art Center, to the green buildings for the new century.

Architectural Capital of the United States?   68

Going... Going... Green   75

City Hall: Good as Gold   76

9 Great Architectural Walks   77

Sneak a Peek: Home Tours & Festivals   86

Q & A: Robert Winter   88

Architectural Capital of the United States?

The Hotel Green, now the Castle Green apartments, is the only survivor of Pasadena's 19th-century resort-hotel boom.

California Dreaming

First came the entrepreneurial visionaries who cast off the mantle of the long, hard Indiana winters in favor of a bright sun shining down on nascent orange groves and vineyards....

From its beginning, the Indiana Colony, founded by Daniel M. Berry, was meant to be a haven. Berry, an asthmatic, sought refuge from the brutal Midwestern winters for himself and his family and friends from Indiana. So he made his way to California and formed the San Gabriel Orange Grove Association, with the goal of acquiring property along the Arroyo Seco. In 1874, the newcomers incorporated, first as the Indiana Colony, then in 1886, as the city of Pasadena. As was the case with American expansion in the 19th century, the town prospered with the arrival of the railroad; in this case, the Southern Pacific and Santa Fe delivered people, and the allure of orchards, improved health, scenic mountains and financial gain did the rest. A business hub was soon seen at the intersection of Fair Oaks and Colorado, the dining, entertainment and retail center we now call Old Town.

As the 20th century rolled in, tycoons of America's industrialization left their crowded Eastern and Midwestern cities for this newly minted resort town. Here the back-to-nature movement and its intellectual and inventive cousin, the Arts & Crafts movement, also had found a home. They arrived by trains that stopped at such stations as the Oaklawn Waiting Station, and they made their way to the Raymond (long since burned down), the Wentworth (today's Langham Huntington), the Maryland (torn down), the Hotel Green (one section of which still stands), or another of the elegant resorts. That Craftsman architecture took hold here was no accident: Wealth, a dedication to artisanship and an intellectually expressed desire for a simpler way of life rooted here, matured here and remains "Greene" to this day.

Certainly, you can see examples of Victorian architecture in Pasadena, as well as in such neighboring towns as Monrovia and Sierra Madre; we point out several charming Queen Annes in our walking tours. But it was the bungalow – from its loftiest expression, designed for the wealthy, to the inexpensive kit homes from Sears Roebuck and the Ready-Cut Bungalow Company – that provided Pasadena with the mother lode of Craftsman architecture for which it is famed today.

Arts & Crafts Haven

Charles and Henry Greene joined their parents here in 1893 and embarked, first together and then individually, on an architectural odyssey that left a lasting and meaningful imprint on both Pasadena and the larger world of architecture. The scope of their achievements is seen today in a number of refined and relevant homes, from the Blacker House (1907) and the Gamble House (1908), to the cluster of houses on Arroyo

Blacker House, one of Greene & Greene's masterworks

Terrace (1901 to 1907), to many notable, if more modest, structures. These houses, and their influences – from the brothers' commitment to the Arts & Crafts philosophy of building homes that reflected unity with their surroundings, to their fascination with the structural forthrightness of the Japanese Pavilion they viewed at Chicago's World Columbian Exposition just before moving to Pasadena – conspired with the freer

The current owners of the Blacker House restored every detail, including the front door.

thinking of this uncluttered landscape. A sort of alchemy occurred that outpaced the initial desire of Pasadena's wealthy newcomers to simply replicate the mansions they lived in back East. Out here, Frank Lloyd Wright, a founding member of the Chicago Arts & Crafts Society who was famed for his Prairie-style homes, found an environment that was open to his modernism, as seen in Prospect Park's textile-block La Miniatura (1923). (Acclaimed landscape architect Helen Van Pelt designed the gardens, many of

American Bungalow

John Brinkmann is founder and publisher of *American Bungalow* magazine, which sits on many a Pasadena coffee table. Its mission is to preserve and restore "the modest American 20th-century home, the bungalow, and the rich lifestyle that it affords." John spoke with Jill about his magazine's connection to Pasadena.

"One rainy night in 1987, I went to hear Bob Winter lecture on 'the bungalow.' At the time, he was the only one really doing that sort of thing. So there I was at the Edgar Camp House, a Greene & Greene bungalow in Sierra Madre, and it just sort of hit me... that the house I grew up in – the house that that everyone I knew had grown up in here in Southern California – was a bungalow. But somehow I had never made the connection between the houses that were central to my youth and the houses I saw in my frequent drives through Pasadena – the homes by the Heinemans and the Greenes. But Bob made it very clear.

"As the idea for the magazine progressed, the fact that we were so near Pasadena provided the cornerstone for our decision to go forward. In Pasadena, we had it all: the expertise, the architecture. The first bungalow was not built in Pasadena, but the popularization of the bungalow as a home for everyday people did start there. At the Gamble House, the family enjoyed the nice weather and lived the Arts & Crafts life, but it wasn't their main residence. But the fact that you could live that way here created a rage for the lifestyle that spread all over the country and became an everyman's option. We all benefit from the fact that a place like the Gamble House has been preserved – but the real wonder is that so many of those little two-bedroom bungalows all over town have been preserved. Appreciation of the architecture and the lifestyle is a real national movement now, and it all started in Pasadena."

which can be viewed from the Rosemont Avenue side of the house.)

Not only was Pasadena a resort destination for the pedigreed wealthy, but it also served as the locus for the gifted architects who embraced the more humble and humanizing core of the Arts & Crafts movement. Louis Easton, for example, built homes that were more modest than the grander homes of the Greenes. His 1906 bunkhouse in Altadena embodied the Craftsman ideal. Bungalow courts, clusters of cottages with a central courtyard, were built first as vacation spots; the St. Francis Court (1909) was designed by Cornell-educated Sylvanus Marston, who also designed other lovely homes and commercial buildings in different vernaculars throughout the region. Sadly, the bungalows at St. Francis Court were moved in the '20s because of street construction; you can find several of them on South Catalina Street near Polytechnic School.

The Craftsman ideal, with its intellectual and elite beginnings, eventually led to affordable, respectable housing for the "working man" and his family in neighborhoods throughout Pasadena, South Pasadena, Sierra Madre and

Bungalow courts like this one made the Arts & Crafts life accessible for ordinary folks.

Operated by the USC School of Architecture, the Gamble House is a museum open to the public.

Monrovia, where low population density made for a comfortable, relaxed standard of living. Brothers Arthur and Alfred Heineman took the costly bungalow made famous by the Greene brothers and brought it down to earth, creating, among other achievements, Bowen Court (1913), at 539 East Villa Street, and leading the way in the design of affordable homes. From Garfield Heights to Bungalow Heaven, these neighborhoods, with many original homes remaining, are visual reminders of Pasadena's early days. (As to their affordability today… well, you might need to take that up with your accountant.)

Oaklawn Days

Bruce Stratton is the longest-term resident of South Pasadena's historic Oaklawn neighborhood, which has Greene & Greene portals and a host of grand and architecturally diverse houses. In 1940, he celebrated his first birthday in his family's stately 1904 timbered Tudor home, where he lives today with his wife, Connie (his high school sweetheart), their daughter, and the antiques, art and wonderful objects he has found at flea markets and skillfully restored.

"I've lived here long enough to see whole generations come through," he says. "First there were baby carriages, then bicycles, then all the teenage parties, then kids going off to school. Then the parents would have their nice quiet lives for a while until they decided they didn't need to live in such a big house anymore, and before you knew it, we saw young families and baby carriages again."

It is a rare thing these days to find someone living in his childhood home. And such a beautiful home! Standing in the foyer, with its grand staircase and stunning original Judson Glass stained-glass windows of St. George slaying the dragon, we asked Bruce if he slid down the sweeping banister a as kid. "Of course I did! And this was a great house for playing sardines – someone hides, and when you find them, you crawl on in with them." To find hidey-holes in a big old house like this… well, that's a childhood any kid would envy.

A Civic Identity

As the city grew larger, there was greater need for a civic and cultural presence. Massachusetts-born Myron Hunt, who had built his reputation in Chicago with the likes of Louis Sullivan, took on several of these commissions, among them Henry and Arabella Huntington's 1910 home (known today as the Huntington Art Gallery & Library), the original buildings of Caltech and Polytechnic School (1907) and Occidental College (1911 to 1913), all with colleague Elmer Grey. In 1925, Hunt and H. C. Chambers designed the Pasadena Public Library, which opened in 1927 as the northern anchor of Pasadena's Civic Center; the Civic Auditorium (Bergstrom, Bennett and Haskell, 1932) is the southern anchor, and City Hall (Bakewell and Brown, 1925 to 1927) serves as the center.

Pasadena City Hall, the heart of the Civic Center

Like the rest of the nation, the Great Depression hit Pasadena hard. Pasadena's run as a resort center drew to a close. By 1935, the Works Projects Administration (WPA) was providing jobs for unemployed Americans; many of the stone walls and steps around the Arroyo Seco were built as WPA programs. In 1938, the Altadena Library on Lake Avenue was designed by Altadena native son Wallace Neff and built with WPA funding. (The library now resides in a larger and more modern facility on Mariposa, but the original building still stands.)

A New Era

Pasadena's most enduring architectural icon, the Colorado Street Bridge

The invasion of Pearl Harbor carried America into World War II, which lifted us out of the Depression. Pasadena's Vista del Arroyo Hotel was used as a U.S. Army hospital (it's now a federal appeals court), and other resort hotels, bereft of their rich clientele, also were used by the military. Caltech and the Jet Propulsion Lab (JPL) ushered in an era of technology and research, building the framework for Pasadena's reincarnation as a scientific research center. The Arroyo Seco Parkway, California's first freeway (known today as the Pasadena Freeway), connected us to Los Angeles, and we were back in business. In 1947, the architectural firm of Wurdeman and Becket designed the moderne Bullocks Pasadena (now Macy's) on Lake Avenue, giving shoppers a suburban destination with the feel of the great urban department stores.

The postwar economy brought prosperity, and with commuting now a part of life, Pasadena's housing needs skyrocketed; new housing tracts spread eastward, and luxury housing tracts, such as Hastings Ranch, filled up with low-slung California ranch homes. The years from 1945 to1966 saw a large-scale architectural experiment called the Case Study House program, primarily in the L.A. area. John Entenza, editor of *Arts & Architecture*, gathered some of the great modernist architects of the day to design prototype homes with cost-effective materials and construction techniques, in hopes of inspiring the creation of affordable housing. In Pasadena, Kemper Nomland & Son designed Case Study House #10 (1947; 711 South San Rafael Avenue), and in 1958, Buff, Straub and Hensman designed the Saul Bass House (Case Study House #20) at 2275 Santa Rosa Avenue in Altadena. In the same spirit of economy and clean design, architect Gregory Ain created one of the first housing developments in the country in 1945: Park Planned Homes, on Highview between Mariposa and Altadena Drive in Altadena. These houses, some of which have been beautifully restored, exemplify postwar modernism.

The tiny, Richard Neutra–designed Perkins House, high in the San Rafael hills

Austrian modernist Richard Neutra also participated in the Case Study program, though the Perkins House (1955; 1540 Poppy Peak Drive), his only Pasadena house, was not a part of the program. Neither was his Beard House, at 1981 Meadowbrook Road in Altadena. Neutra's seamless merging of house and surrounding landscape was exceptional.

America's buttoned-down '50s gave way to the go-go '60s and '70s, and Pasadena, once famed for its healthful climate, became infamous for its smog. Culturally, the 1969 opening of the Pasadena Museum of Art (now the Norton Simon), designed by Ladd and Kelsey, was a coup for the city; less successful were the many lifeless office buildings that went up in the '60s and '70s. The late 1980s and the '90s brought the much-needed revitalization of Old Town, as well as preservation efforts throughout the valley, from Sierra Madre to Eagle Rock. Fortunately, while interest in preservation grew, the federal government began requiring more stringent automobile emission regulations, and the mountains once again became visible.

The streamline moderne Bullocks in 1947

21st-Century Innovation

Pasadena's interest in architectural innovation can be seen today in such projects as the Tricom Office Building (2003) at 2812 East Walnut Street. Designed by Caldwell Architects, this is a prototype of sustainable building and drought-tolerant landscaping, and most of its construction materials were manufactured locally, thereby supporting our economy and reducing the environmental impact by limiting the need for trucking. Like Tricom, the brand-new NW Innovation Center on Eureka just west of Fair Oaks hews to the stringent LEED (Leadership in Energy and Environmental Design) building standards. In 2002, Caltech's Broad Center for the Biological Sciences, designed by the late James Ingo Freed of Pei Cobb Freed & Partners, opened its doors. With three gleaming sides of stainless steel and one side a facade of travertine, the Broad Center is the gateway to a new North Campus that will develop in the coming decade.

Art Center's South Campus, a dynamic reuse of an old scientific-research building

Having made its way to a new century, Pasadena faces the dual challenges of honoring its past through often-costly preservation, and endowing its future by committing to the architectural visionaries of today. Santa Monica's Daly Genik Architects recently combined sustainable techniques with aesthetic beauty in turning the former Caltech wind tunnel building into Art Center's South Campus. And we eagerly await the sculptural surprise Frank Gehry has in mind for the heart of Art Center's main campus. Also in the early planning stages is a visitors' center at JPL, which is likely to be architecturally significant.

All in all, it's quite an architectural legacy for what began as a pokey little town with a swell view of the mountains.

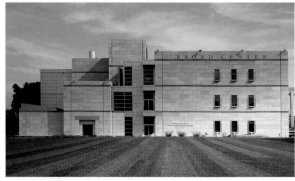

Caltech's Broad Center, designed by James Freed

Going... Going... Green

Okay, so Kermit was right all along: it's not easy being green—but we're working on it, starting at the municipal level, moving on to commercial building and finally greening up residential consciousness with education, programs and rebates.

Green City

Pasadena is a member of Green Cities California (GCC), which was created in late 2007. It joins Los Angeles, San Diego, Sacramento, Santa Monica, Santa Barbara, San Francisco, Oakland and Marin County (well, yeah…) in adopting a five-point action plan to take environmentally meaningful steps toward greening up. These steps are:

▶ Purchasing 100% post-consumer recycled paper for municipal operations.
▶ Prohibiting the purchase of bottled water for municipal operations and government-sponsored events.
▶ Adopting a carbon-offset plan for municipal employee air travel.
▶ Adopting fuel-efficiency standards for the municipal fleet.
▶ Promoting the purchase of California foods for municipal events and operations.

Green Building

Increasingly, the city is tackling some of the tough 21st-century concerns affecting a Pasadena that can no longer in anyone's judgment be considered a pokey little town. In 2006, the city council passed the Green Building Practices Ordinance, which impacts public and private sector buildings falling within certain parameters. LEED – the green-building rating system for the U.S. Green Building Council's Leadership in Energy and Environmental Design – is hot, hot, hot in Pasadena, which is now offering financial incentives for affordable housing in green buildings. The push/pull of development is a big challenge in our fair city; townies and visitors alike can learn about this progressive program at ci.pasadena.ca.us/permitcenter/greencity/building/gbprogram.asp.

Green Housing

Pasadenans can make some green for going green: Pasadena Water and Power has rebates for various water-using products, including high-efficiency washing machines and toilets. It also has incentive programs for the installation of approved energy-efficient home cooling products, from central air and room air conditioners to attic fans and sun/shade screens. (Buy your products from local retailers and your rebate goes up – way to be a hometown booster!) And we love the coolest rebate of all, the Cool Trees Program – a significant rebate for planting one or more of a variety of 37 shade trees. Power (and water) to the people! Check it out: ci.pasadena.ca.us/waterandpower.

City Hall: Good as Gold

Completed in 1927, Pasadena's City Hall, from which one can have a commanding view of the Pasadena Civic Center complex, is a stunning example of the City Beautiful movement: an early 20th-century tool of progressive architectural reform whose goal was to improve the social order through beautiful public buildings.

Eighty-one years later, after a three-year construction project that included seismic retrofitting and tech-savvy infrastructure, this imposing center of government is back in business and as gorgeous as ever. Best of all, it has been awarded LEED (Leadership in Energy and Environmental Design) Gold Certification by the U.S. Green Building Council. We stand inspired by a city hall that leads by example, with energy efficiency that is almost twenty percent above state standards; efficient fixtures that reduce water use by 40 percent; the use of green cleaning products… and the list goes on.

So here's a shout-out to Pasadena's civic leadership for going the distance – the renovation cost $117 million, a huge investment for a smallish city – in bringing this massive project in on time and within budget.

The Longley House

9 Great Architectural Walks

Our town is filled with so much worthy architecture and so many gracious residential neighborhoods that we cannot possibly do it justice. But we can try. In the pages that follow we describe our favorite architectural walks – and in some cases we suggest you hop back in the car and drive, especially in the surprisingly hilly San Rafael area. In each neighborhood we point out a few places worthy of mention, but the great reward is in wandering and experiencing the sights and scents, feeling what it may have been like 100 years ago, and seeing how it has evolved.

We would not have discovered some favorite neighborhoods ourselves if it were not for the bible of all things architectural in these parts: *An Architectural Guidebook to Los Angeles*, by David Gebhard and Robert Winter. It includes many detailed pages about Pasadena and its neighboring communities, and it is the most practical tool you can have along on these walks. And don't forget to bring a bottle of water – it gets hot and dry here in the summer months.

Southwest Pasadena & South Pasadena

Filled with glorious homes both modest and grand, Southwest Pasadena and South Pasadena make for superb strolling territory. The stately trees, street-facing gardens and shaded porches evoke a timeless sense of the American neighborhood. Of particular note are the Oaklawn Portals, designed by Greene & Greene in 1905. Walk through the portals and follow broad Oaklawn Avenue to the Oaklawn Bridge and Waiting Station, another Greene & Greene project – and their only bridge – designed to link the Oaklawn housing development to bustling Fair Oaks Avenue. If you begin this walk on Orange Grove, be sure to wander the side streets, such as Markham and Wigmore.

One of the two Oaklawn Portals

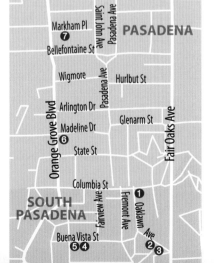

❶ Oaklawn Portals (1905)
❷ Oaklawn Bridge (1906)
❸ Oaklawn Waiting Station
Oaklawn Avenue south of Columbia, South Pasadena
Designed by Charles and Henry Greene, this bridge was one of America's first to be made of reinforced concrete. The Greenes also laid out the street and designed its wall and portal gates.

❹ Longley House (late 1897)
1005 Buena Vista St., South Pasadena
Displaying a mixture of architectural styles, this house is believed to be the earliest standing structure by Greene & Greene.

❺ Garfield House (1904)
1001 Buena Vista St., South Pasadena
Charles and Henry Greene built this house for Lucretia Garfield, the widow of President James Garfield, who served for only four months before he was assassinated.

❻ Westridge School
324 Madeline Dr., Pasadena
You can view this private girls' school campus from its gates on Madeline Drive, and you can also see several of its contemporary and Arts & Crafts–era buildings along Orange Grove or State Street. Sylvanus Marston, Whit Smith and the Greene brothers are represented on the campus.

❼ Blankenhorn Lamphear House (1893)
346 Markham Pl., Pasadena
This house is one of Pasadena's finest examples of the Queen Anne style, the most romantic and fanciful of the Victorian era's architectural idioms.

Oak Knoll

Arthur S. Heineman designed this fanciful Craftsman at 1233 Wentworth Ave.

Pasadena's Oak Knoll began life before the turn of the 20th century as an estate region. Today, many of the original homes remain, though some, such as the Greene & Greene masterpiece the Blacker House, no longer have the extensive grounds they once claimed. Because homes were built in succeeding decades in various revival styles, the neighborhood boasts a wonderful architectural diversity. The world-famous Huntington Hotel, now known as the Langham Huntington Hotel, makes Oak Knoll a destination for many visitors. The brothers Greene, Arthur and Alfred Heineman, Sylvanus Marston and Wallace Neff are all represented in this glorious area, which was designed to showcase its lovely native oaks. If you make your way south and east to Los Robles Avenue, you'll see the experimental, post-war Wallace Neff Dome House, quite unusual for Pasadena.

❶ Langham Huntington Hotel (1906, rebuilt in 1991)
1401 S. Oak Knoll Ave.
Opened as the Hotel Wentworth in 1907, the hotel failed and was purchased by tycoon Henry Huntington, who had it redesigned by Myron Hunt; it reopened as a resort destination in 1914 and came to represent Pasadena's good life.

❷ Blacker House (1907)
1177 Hillcrest Ave.
Considered, along with the Gamble House, to be Greene & Greene's crowning achievement, Blacker House has withstood the ravages of time and inconsistent maintenance and is now in the hands of private owners who have restored it with pristine attention. A treasure.

❸ Freeman House
1330 Hillcrest Ave.
Arthur S. Heineman designed this whimsical Craftsman. The designer of the first motor hotel, he is said to have coined the term "motel" for motor hotel.

❹ Dome House
1097 S. Los Robles Ave.
Wallace Neff began experimenting with concrete structures in 1941. This 1946 example of his "bubble" construction was a part of his ongoing interest in building affordable housing. Another Neff house, done in a much more traditional Spanish Revival style, is at 1290 Hillcrest Avenue.

Prospect Park

This area, designed as a housing development in 1906, boasts Sylvanus Marston clinker-brick portals on Orange Grove at Prospect Boulevard. Mature camphor trees create a shady arch over the wide boulevard as you enter from Orange Grove. You will find Frank Lloyd Wright's La Miniatura in this neighborhood, as well as the extraordinary Gamble House and, on Arroyo Terrace, a plum collection of Greene & Greene houses.

❶ Charles Sumner Greene House (1901)
368 Arroyo Terrace
Amid a cluster of Greene & Greene homes is Charles Greene's own Craftsman dwelling, to which he made several additions over the years. Just next door, at 370 Arroyo Terrace, is the home built for Martha, Violet and Jane White, sisters-in-law to the brothers Greene.

❷ Neighborhood Church (1972)
1 Westmoreland Pl.
Designed by Whitney Smith, this active, community-minded Unitarian church blends seamlessly into the neighborhood; it is a particularly discreet presence near its distinguished neighbor, the Gamble House.

❸ Gamble House (1908)
4 Westmoreland Pl.
Built for David and Mary Gamble of Proctor & Gamble fame, this home by Charles and Henry Greene is as much famed for its perfectly executed functional interiors as its quietly gracious exterior, which is so beautifully sited on the property. The Greene brothers also designed its furnishings. Make sure to take the tour (see "Sneak a Peek").

❹ Cole House (1906)
2 Westmoreland Pl.
This Greene & Greene home was under construction when the Gambles were considering their property purchase, and is thought to have influenced them to buy the neighboring property and hire Charles and Henry Greene to design their home.

❺ Alice Millard House (La Miniatura) (1923)
645 Prospect Crescent
Concrete-block construction (perfected in later Wright projects, such as the Ennis House) distinguishes this home, which was built for Alice Millard after the death of her husband, rare-book dealer George Millard. Alice was a rare repeat customer of the irascible Wright, and though the house was beset with difficulties during construction and remains plagued by problems (like a leaky roof) today, its Mayan-influenced design is acclaimed by many as one of the architect's most interesting residential works.

The Charles Sumner Greene House

❻ Hindry House (1909)
781 Prospect Blvd.
The Heineman brothers, Arthur and Alfred, designed this elaborate home without benefit of formal architectural training. A sketch for the entry hall's fireplace is known to appear in a notebook belonging to Charles Greene, but it was not built to his specifications.

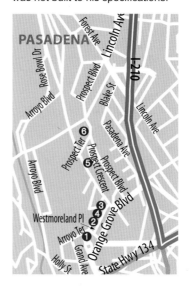

Lower Arroyo Seco & San Rafael

This pastoral residential area has retained many of its lovely homes, though the elaborate Busch Gardens closed in 1937, its 30 acres subdivided and developed with California ranch houses. The famed "Millionaire's Row" on Orange Grove has given way to meticulously maintained condominium complexes, but just to the west, the many stately homes on Grand Avenue are well worth a walk by. Start on the north end of Grand, at Green Street, walk south to Arbor Street, head west down Arbor and then left (south) on Arroyo Boulevard. Arbor is a steep slope, so some may prefer to drive down the hill before getting back on foot to see the many Arts & Crafts homes along the Arroyo. To get to the San Rafael area, drive across the pretty La Loma Bridge at Arroyo and La Loma. Because the grandest of San Rafael's homes are, for the most part, hidden behind gates and long driveways, it's best to drive through the area with occasional stops. The brilliant landscaping visible from the street inspires gardeners. On your way out of San Rafael, go south on Avenue 64 to see the Church of the Angels.

One of three Victorians on Locke Haven, built in 1887

❶ Colorado Street Bridge (1912-1913)

Pasadenans love this graceful, curving bridge made of reinforced concrete, and steadfastly supported its restoration in the 1990s. The nearly 1,500-foot span connects Old Pasadena to the San Rafael hills and Eagle Rock.

❷ Vista del Arroyo Hotel (1920)

125 S. Grand Ave.
In the 1940s, the federal government acquired this Sylvanus Marston–designed resort hotel to use as a military hospital; it is now the Ninth Circuit Court of Appeals.

❸ La Casita del Arroyo (1933)

177 S. Arroyo Blvd.
This modest structure, designed by Myron Hunt at no charge, was built using Arroyo stone and lumber from bicycle tracks built at the Rose Bowl for the 1932 Olympics.

❹ Batchelder House (1909)

626 S. Arroyo Blvd.
Ernest Batchelder was a famed artisan, producing decorative tiles that became emblematic of the Arts & Crafts movement. Batchelder's kiln remains in the backyard of this

lovely home, and the discerning viewer can see examples of his tile work from the street.

❺ Pergola House (1910)

1025 S. Arroyo Blvd.
Remnants of Busch Gardens are incorporated into a home built considerably later.

❻ Wrigley Mansion (1911)

391 S. Orange Grove Ave.
This ornate mansion built for chewing-gum mogul William Wrigley, who controlled the development of Catalina Island, is now home to Pasadena's Tournament of Roses.

❼ Perkins House (1955)

1540 Poppy Peak Dr.
Sited above street level, this small Richard Neutra home is modest, but it's all about the expansive view from inside the house.

❽ Church of the Angels (1889)

1100 Ave. 64
The widow of Alexander Campbell-Johnston, the developer of Rancho San Rafael, commissioned British architect Arthur Edmund Street to design this beautiful church to memorialize her husband.

Old Pasadena Historic District

You'll never stop locals from calling it Old Town, but the powers-that-be tell us the official name is Old Pasadena Historic District – so then, Old Town it is. Pasadena's original business district began at the intersection of Fair Oaks Avenue and Colorado Boulevard. Though a new shopping area developed on South Lake with the opening of Bullocks in the late 1940s, and Old Town languished in the '70s, revitalization turned it into one of Southern California's leading destinations. (They don't readily admit it, but refugees from L.A.'s westside have been known to make the trek east.) The Norton Simon Museum on Colorado at Orange Grove is a great place to start a walk, heading east through Old Town.

Continuing farther east, by foot or by car, you'll find the adjacent Civic Center and Playhouse District, where Pasadena's cultural expansion took hold in the 1920s. And eyes up for the wonderful post-war neon signage for Zinke's Shoe Repair (at 592 East Colorado Boulevard, at least until it's torn down for condos).

❶ Norton Simon Museum (1969)
411 W. Colorado Blvd.
Designed by the architectural firm of Ladd & Kelsey, this acclaimed art museum's interior was renovated by Frank Gehry from 1996 to 1999.

❷ Hotel Green (1898)
99 S. Raymond Ave.
Known today as Castle Green, this was the second building of a lavish 19th-century resort built in the Moorish style for wealthy Easterners who fled their winter homes for a more temperate climate. The enclosed bridge that now ends at a small tower once crossed Raymond to connect with the first building in the hotel's complex. The architect was Frederick Roehrig.

Restored architectural details abound in Old Pasadena.

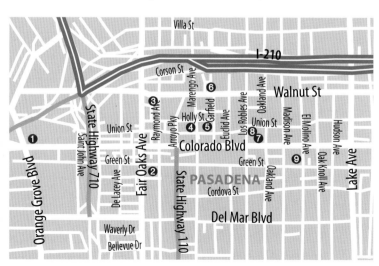

St. Andrew's interior is rich in detail and beauty.

❸ Saint Andrew Catholic Church (1927)
311 N. Raymond Ave.
This exceptionally beautiful church is said to have been modeled on the ancient Basilica of St. Sabina in Rome. Marble pillars – each unique – line the length of the church. The church's modest proportions make its powerful yet tranquil presence all the more noteworthy.

❹ YWCA Building (1920)
Marengo Ave. & Holly St.
This Julia Morgan design was commissioned by Mary Gamble (of the Gamble House) to be emblematic of Pasadena's concern for women in need of shelter and support.

❺ Pasadena City Hall (1927)
100 N. Garfield Ave.
The cornerstone of the Civic Center, this imposing example of the Mediterranean style was translated to fit its California setting by the San Francisco architectural firm of Bakewell and Brown. The impressive circular tower rises six stories and is topped by a dome, which is in turn topped by a cupola that is finally topped by an urn and ball. An extensive seismic retrofitting was completed late in 2007.

❻ Pasadena Public Library (1927)
285 E. Walnut St.
This library, with an interior as rich as its exterior is dignified, was designed in the Spanish Renaissance style by the architectural firm of Myron Hunt and H. C. Chambers.

❼ Linden Optometry (1927)
469-483 E. Colorado Blvd.
The striking green glazed-tile exterior is a glorious expression of art deco in a commercial building. This building originally housed exclusive shops that catered to the wealthy winter resort crowd.

❽ Pacific Asia Museum (1924)
46 N. Los Robles Ave.
Now we have come to the Playhouse District, and one of the first things we find is a Chinese palace designed by Marston, Van Pelt and Maybury, one of the premier Pasadena architectural firms of the day. It served originally as residence and art gallery for Grace Nicholson.

❾ Pasadena Playhouse (1925)
35-39 S. El Molino Ave.
Architect Elmer Grey designed this Spanish Colonial Revival structure, which has had a dramatic life, as befits a theater. It was falling into decrepitude and remained closed from 1969 to 1975, when it was purchased by the city and revived for a successful third act. Bravo!

The YWCA building is vacant and in need of restoration.

The McNally House

Altadena

Wild, wonderful, eccentric and un-incorporated Altadena has it all. As one might anticipate, many of its large estates and ranches have long since been subdivided, and it is almost as though the homes themselves are longing for the wide-open spaces of yore. Nevertheless, it is a very fine place to live in the 21st century, and the tremendous range of architectural styles, from Neutra to Roehrig to Greene, have attracted an equally diverse cast of characters. During the holidays, Christmas Tree Lane, the stretch of Santa Rosa Avenue between Woodbury and Altadena Drive, is a nighttime must-see for children of all ages. Note that while you can walk between some houses (McNally, Woodbury, Case Study House # 20), to see them all you'll need a car.

❶ Beard House (1934)
1981 Meadowbrook Rd.
Built by Richard Neutra for Caltech professor Richard Beard, this small, all-metal house was inspired by Neutra's fascination with the machine as icon. The sliding metal patio doors were an architectural innovation at the time.

❷ Case Study House # 20 (1958)
2275 N. Santa Rosa Ave.
One of the prototype homes built between 1945 and 1966 and photographed by Julius Shulman.

❸ McNally House (1888)
654 E. Mariposa St.
Andrew McNally partnered with William Rand to create Rand-McNally, a successful business that produced maps and globes out of Chicago. As was the case with many of his well-to-do compatriots, McNally staked out his territory in sunny California and had Frederick Roehrig

design this vast Queen Anne house. McNally's grandson, Wallace Neff, would become a highly regarded architect in California.

❹ Williams House (1915)
1145 Sonoma Dr.
Charles and Henry Greene left their mark on Altadena as well as Pasadena. This house, unusual for the Greenes, is covered with gunite, a blown-on cement that also covers the pillars of the rear porch.

❺ Woodbury House (1882)
2606 Madison Ave.
Originally surrounded by 937 open acres, this house was built by Iowa brothers Fred and John Woodbury, who planned the first subdivision here, borrowing the name "Altadena" from Byron Clark's nursery. Fred was the farmer and John the banker; they planted the deodars on Santa Rosa (a.k.a. Christmas Tree Lane).

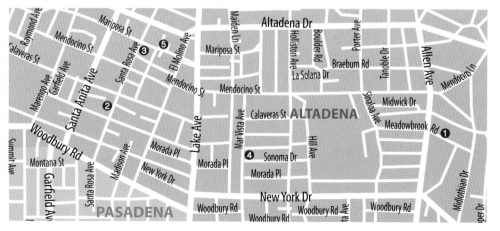

A typical kit house in Bungalow Heaven

Bungalow Heaven

So many Craftsman bungalows distinguish Pasadena's first Landmark District that people sometimes forget there are examples of other architectural styles represented in the neighborhood. But the casual visitor should be forgiven the oversight, because these streets are unabashedly about the tale of the California bungalow from 1900 to 1930.

In the 1980s, several visionary community activists took on the enormous task of raising awareness about how easily their neighborhood could be ravaged by development. Years of hard work from residents, Pasadena Heritage and the city culminated in the 1989 granting of Landmark District status to Bungalow Heaven.

Rather than seeking any specific homes, the great treat is to walk these streets and recognize that many of these bungalows were built from kits – often at a cost of less than $1,000 – and delivered to new Californians eager to build the low-slung, often single-story homes with the deep verandas and overhanging eaves that protected them from California's powerful sunshine. A walk through Bungalow Heaven makes it easy to visualize this neighborhood as a birthplace of the good life for Americans of modest means who came west in the early 20th century.

Garfield Heights

From mansions to Craftsman bungalows to historic two- and four-unit apartments, this neighborhood is remarkably unaffected by the ravages of time. As you stroll these lovely streets, with homes built from the late 19th century to the 1920s, note the distinctive architectural features – pillars, retaining walls, foundations – made of river rock.

❶ The Gilmore House (1891)
1247 N. Garfield Ave.
A Neoclassical house by Roehrig and Locke. Frederick Roehrig was also the architect of Castle Green and many enduring Pasadena homes.

❷ Bates House (1920)
1290 N. Marengo Ave.
This U-shaped house was designed by Glen Elwood Smith, one of Pasadena's highly regarded residential architects of his era.

❸ The Gerlach House (1913)
985 N. Los Robles Ave.
A beautifully sited Sylvanus Marston design. Note the deep shade provided by the graciously proportioned veranda.

Madison Heights

Here we find another Pasadena neighborhood that keeps its eye on historic preservation, thanks to the active Madison Heights Neighborhood Association. It is interesting to note the connection to Pasadena's Eastern roots, with street names such as Euclid Avenue, named by area founder C.M. Skellen for a street in his hometown of Cleveland, Ohio.

❶ E. J. Blacker House (1912)
675 S. Madison Ave.
No, not that Blacker House. This fine Craftsman home was built a few years later than its grander Oak Knoll neighbor to the south.

❷ Heineman-designed House (1911)
885 S. El Molino Ave.
This Craftsman home was designed by Arthur S. Heineman, who famously penned "The Periodic Cottage" in response to an article called "The Bungle-ode"; both were published in 1918 in *Architect and Engineer of California*.

❸ Allendale Branch Library (1920s)
1130 S. Marengo Ave.
At the southern border of Madison Heights, this adobe structure is currently a Pasadena Public Library branch as well as a school library for Allendale Elementary School. Built as an isolation hospital for patients with infectious diseases, it became a library in 1951.

One of many beautiful homes in Madison Heights

Sneak a Peek: Home Tours & Festivals

Altadena Homes Tour
Altadena Guild of Huntington Memorial Hospital
626.304.4678, altadenaguild.org
Tour in spring
Since 1952 this annual tour has benefited
the important work of what is now called the
Huntington Medical Research Institutes. With no
shortage of worthwhile architecture in Altadena,
we know it will be around for another 50 years.

Architectural Tours L.A.
323.464.7868, architecturetoursla.com
Tours twice daily; call for times
You'll take in more than 90 sites on this two-and-
a-half-hour tour of Pasadena. The tour includes
buildings by Greene & Greene and Myron Hunt,
and it encompasses the Civic Center, Caltech
and several lovely Victorians; you'll ride in air-
conditioned vans with leather bucket seats.

Arroyo Arts Collective:
Annual Discovery Tour
323.850.8566, arroyoartscollective.org
Tour in Nov.
Self-guided maps are distributed at the starting
point at this annual opportunity to check out the
studios and homes of Arroyo artists. Stops in
Highland Park, Eagle Rock and Los Angeles
are included.

Bungalow Heaven Home Tour
626.585.2172, bungalowheaven.org
Tour in April
Aficionados turn out in droves for this exploration
of *Sunset* magazine's 2002 "Best Neighborhood
in the West." This charming neighborhood of
modest homes built from the 1900s through the
'30s was Pasadena's first Landmark District;
you can just hear the echoes of a century of
summer-evening front-porch conversations.
The self-guided walking tour includes lectures,
demonstrations, raffles and more.

Caltech Architectural Tours (CATS)
551 S. Hill Ave., Pasadena
626.395.6327, cwclub.caltech.edu/cats.htm
Tours the 4th Thurs. of the month at 11 a.m.;
no tours July, Aug. or Dec.
This 90-minute tour sponsored by the
Caltech Women's Club will familiarize you
with this historic campus. Groups meet at the
Athenaeum; call ahead for reservations.

Castle Green
99 S. Raymond Ave., Old Pasadena
626.577.6765, castlegreen.com
Tours 1st Sun. in June & Dec.
If you're lucky enough to know someone who
lives here, you can spy inside the residential
apartments, but for most of us, attending an
event in the lush public rooms or taking one of
these two annual romps is how we get our fix
of 19th-century Moorish, Turkish and Victorian
splendor. Originally a resort hotel, the Castle
Green is listed on the National Register of
Historic Places.

Eclectic Eagle Rock Home Tour
323.799.1190, TERA90041.org
Tour in fall
An eclectic tour for this eclectic town. It is a
big fund-raiser for the very active Eagle Rock
Association, and it's a great volunteer effort.
Homes may range from turn-of-the-century to
midcentury modern. Tons o' fun.

El Alisal
200 E. Ave. 43, Highland Park
323.222.0546, socalhistory.org
Open Fri.-Sun. afternoons
Charles Fletcher Lummis – journalist,
archaeologist, friend to Teddy Roosevelt and
all-around colorful character – began to build
his home in 1889 from Arroyo rock. A tireless
advocate for the rights of Native Americans,
Lummis founded the nearby Southwest
Museum, and he was famous for his gatherings
of local intelligentsia. The Historical Society of
Southern California (HSSC), founded in 1883, is
now headquartered here.

Fenyes Mansion Tours
Pasadena Museum of History
470 W. Walnut St., Pasadena
626.577.1660, pasadenahistory.org
Tours Wed.-Fri. 1 p.m., Sat.-Sun. 1:30 & 3 p.m.;
call 7 days ahead for reservations in Aug. &
Sept.
The turn-of-the-century home of the museum's
benefactors, Dr. Adalbert and Eva Fenyes, is an
elegant reminder of what life was like in the early
20th century on Millionaire's Row.

Gamble House
4 Westmoreland Pl., Pasadena
626.793.3334, gamblehouse.org
1-hour guided tours Thurs.-Sun. afternoons;
reservations accepted for 2 p.m. tour only
Charles and Henry Greene designed
this celebrated example of Arts & Crafts
architecture (and its furnishings) in 1908 as a
winter residence for David and Mary Gamble.
Nowadays it's a National Historic Landmark,
a museum and a fine example of partnering
for preservation – it is owned by the city of
Pasadena but operated by USC's School of
Architecture. "Behind the Velvet Ropes," a
more personal look at the house, is offered
periodically, or it can be scheduled as a private
event; call 626.395.9783 for details.

Garfield Heights Evening Home Tour
626.388.2174, garfieldheights.org
Tour in Aug.
Garfield Heights Landmark District is located
north of the 210 Freeway between Marengo and
Los Robles. This self-guided tour of its historic
homes may include houses designed by such
noted architects such as Charles and Henry
Greene, Sylvanus Marston and Arthur Benton.

Historic Highlands Home Tour
626.791.8443, historichighlands.org
Tour in May
Several homes representing the diversity of
Pasadena architecture – from Craftsman to
Spanish Colonial Revival to English Tudor –
are open during this worthwhile annual
neighborhood crawl.

Lanterman House
4420 Encinas Dr., La Cañada
818.790.1421, lacañadaflintridge.com
Tours Tues. & Thurs. & 1st & 3rd Sun. 1-4 p.m.
Dr. Roy Lanterman, son of La Cañada's founding
family, commissioned this U-shaped 1915 house.
Architect A. L. Haley took pains to provide access
to the home's interior patio area from all first-floor
rooms. The house's second story is a grand
ballroom, used to great effect for the Lanterman
Ragtime Tea Dance each autumn.

Mother's Day Monrovia Home Tour
626.358.7822
Tour on Mother's Day
From Craftsman and cottage style to Victorian
and American foursquare, Monrovia has it all,
and its annual home tour is certain to please
the architecturally inclined mom. The town
does it up on this self-guided exploration, with
refreshments, entertainment and crafts.

Museums of the Arroyo Day
213.740.8687, museumsofthearroyo.com
Event in May
They call it "MOTA Day," and it comes but once
a year. A consortium of six museums – the
Pasadena Museum of History, the Gamble
House, El Alisal, the Southwest Museum,
Heritage Square and the Los Angeles Police
Historical Society Museum – opens all its
doors to celebrate the history, art, culture and
architecture of the Arroyo Seco, and it's all free!
Shuttles circulate among the museums.

Pasadena Heritage Events
651 S. St. John Ave.
626.441.6333, pasadenaheritage.org
The keeper of the town's architectural flame,
Pasadena Heritage sponsors walks, talks and
events throughout the year, including these:
Craftsman Weekend. One of the country's
most comprehensive Arts & Crafts shows, this
mid-October fest draws enthusiasts from across
the nation. Day and evening activities include
walking and bus tours, dozens of exhibitors and
lectures. Buy tickets early – they do sell out.
Spring Home Tour. Each year, Pasadena
Heritage chooses a theme for its March tromp
through several exceptional houses – perhaps
it's a style of architecture, such as modern or
Victorian, or the work of a particular architect.
Docents are on site at each location.
Old Pasadena Walking Tour. The first Saturday
of each quarter, knowledgeable guides lead
90-minute jaunts through this National Register
Historic District. Reservations required.
Private Walking & Bus Tours. Experienced
docents take guests through historic districts
and/or noteworthy neighborhoods, such as
Old Pasadena, the Civic Center and Bungalow
Heaven. Museum visits and meals can be folded
into the adventures.

Pasadena Showcase House for the Arts
626.578.8500, pasadenashowcase.org
Tours in April-May
Each year, in a Herculean effort that includes
scores of designers, the Pasadena Showcase
House for the Arts (PSHA) chooses an estate,
transforms its interior and grounds in lavish
fashion, and for one glorious spring month,
throws open the doors to an eager public. In
the last 50 years, PSHA has raised $14 million
to support the L.A. Philharmonic and music
education for children. Plan to spend the
day here, exploring the rooms and gardens,
having lunch in the café and shopping in the
Marketplace. It's one of Pasadena's absolute
must-attend annual events.

Bob Winter's Southwest Pasadena home

Q & A: Robert Winter

How's this for a title: Architectural historian and author Robert Winter, Ph.D., is Occidental College's Arthur G. Coons Professor of the History of Ideas Emeritus. But if you should meet him, he's likely to ask that you just call him Bob. This silver-tongued fellow is delighted to wax eloquent on those facets of architecture that please him, and just as quick to skewer any architectural folly that falls under his astute gaze. An internationally recognized scholar of the Arts & Crafts movement, Bob is also the author of many books, including *An Architectural Guidebook to Los Angeles*. Currently in its fifth edition, the guide is essential for architecture buffs. Jill talked with Bob, her former colleague at *American Bungalow*, where he is still a member of the advisory board.

It would seem you were fated to live in Pasadena.
Hugh Morrison taught a class I took in American architectural history at Dartmouth in the 1940s, and he had come out here to do some research and discovered Greene & Greene, and we saw slides in the class. So the first thing I did when I came to UCLA to teach in 1956 was to walk through the Gamble House. You could say I always wanted to live here because of the rich architectural history.

How did you come live in the Batchelder house? (Ernest Batchelder was the famous Arts & Crafts tilemaker whose beautiful home was built in 1909.)
I was teaching at Occidental and living in Eagle Rock. In 1972, I heard the Batchelder house was for sale by Francis Dean (the distinguished landscape architect). He was asking $53,000 for it, and I didn't want to pay more than 40 – so we dickered, and I got it for $46,500. (Bob chortles.) That'll make people mad.

Is there an architect whose local work has not received the attention you think it deserves?
I'd say the Heinemans (Alfred and Arthur S. Heineman, who built the 1913 Bowen Court bungalows, among other fine buildings) deserve more credit. They need a book, but I'm too busy to do it.

How would you grade Pasadena on preservation?
We're way ahead of many places. The great strength of Pasadena architecture has always been in its residences, and it is amazing how well they've been preserved. We know about the attacks on the Blacker House, for instance (ed. note: It was stripped of its fixtures and furnishings by an owner in the '80s), but when a private owner steps up, as is the case there, tremendous work can be done. And it is a remarkable thing to see the partnership between Pasadena Heritage and the city as they have teamed up to actually move endangered buildings. And look at City Hall – there's sensitivity to preservation like almost nowhere else in the world.

So tell me about your most recent book and we'll call it a day.
It is called The Architecture of Entertainment – L.A. in the Twenties. *There's a lot about Pasadena, as you might imagine.*

Horticultural

Since the end of the last Ice Age, the San Gabriel Valley has been a horticultural paradise. It was a bountiful home for the Tongva, a hospitable place for Spanish, Mexican and American ranchers to establish citrus groves and vineyards, and the perfect environment for wealthy, wintering East Coasters to plant kitchen gardens and grand botanical wonders. Today, it is home to acclaimed public gardens, a vast urban forest, roses galore and some of the finest nurseries in the country.

The Urban Forest   90

The Big Three: Descanso, Huntington & the Arboretum   91

Secret Gardens of the San Gabriel Valley   96

Cemeteries We Love   100

Nurseries We Love   102

Q & A: Betty & Charles McKenney   104

The Urban Forest

Yep, we built L.A.'s first freeway – actually, it was called a parkway, and for good reason. And, hey, we've also got bragging rights on being the greenest place in the greater City of Angels. Coincidence? Or providence? We don't like to make judgments here off the 134 and 110. Let's just say Pasadena is more urban forest than asphalt jungle.

The dazzling facts: Pasadena is home to 23 parks and more than 1,000 acres of parkland. Some 60,000 trees shade its streets. Add 25,000 park and wild-growth trees and 123,000 trees on private property, and the Rose City holds an estimated arbor value of $100 million... and that's not in firewood, my friend. And that's not counting such intensely arbored burgs as Altadena, Sierra Madre and South Pasadena.

Is Pasadena's landscape far superior to all others? To attempt to reach an answer, enter the Parrot Project, which began in 1994 to catalog the massive flocks of cackling wild parrots around Pasadena. The Audubon Society lists five or more parrot groups that rely upon our urban forest. Theories on their origin suggest: 1) an escape from an East Pasadena pet store in 1969; 2) migration from Mexico as nonnative plants were introduced here that provided a habitat; or 3) jealous types from El Monte, still mad that they ended up with the Confederates while we got the Union sympathizers, snuck hyperactive, possibly inbred parrots up the 605 Freeway. (This last theory is purely a guess and is not the opinion of Prospect Park Books.) These flying chatterboxes are especially noticeable around Central Park next to the Castle Green and at the South Pasadena Library, and they've made their presence unmistakable in Altadena, Arcadia and Alhambra in recent winters. Two camps line up on the topic: those who think the wild parrots are a delight in their arboreal aviary, and those who consider them noisy pests perfectly suited for the stew pot.

The Rose City's eco-friendliness was codified via the United Nations' Green Cities Declaration and the Green Cities of California initiative. Whether you like your green spaces as cultivated as a meeting of the Junior League or as wild as a bunch of raucous parrots that could go Hitchcock any minute, parks, gardens, trees and the wildlife they support abound in and around Pasadena. Claritin optional.

The Big Three:
Descanso, Huntington & the Arboretum

Descanso Gardens

1418 Descanso Dr., La Cañada
818.949.4200, descansogardens.org
Open daily 9 a.m.-5 p.m. (must arrive by 4:30 p.m.); adults $7, seniors & students $5, kids $2, kids under 5 free; fee for tram tour & weekend kiddie train

A flowering plum tree greets Descanso visitors in spring.

Here's one of the realities of living in Southern California: People want to visit you. In the summer, when the kids are out of school. In the winter, when the snowbirds need someplace warm. People who don't even know your surname will call or write – and call again – asking if they can come visit.

Out-of-town visitors are one of many good reasons to love Descanso Gardens, all 160 acres bursting with seasonal splendor. Not that this is a place to stick the relatives – far from it. This is a place to go together, or to send them and wish you were going, or to sneak off by yourself, to renew your appreciation of the breadth and beauty of Southern California's botanical wealth.

A Los Angeles County park since 1953, the garden was developed as a private residence for E. Manchester Boddy, who moved here in 1921 with his young family and a case of pneumonia. In 1926 he bought the *Los Angeles Daily News*, increased its circulation, and in 1937 settled in the San Rafael hills on 165 acres that he called Rancho del Descanso. To rest and repose he built a Regency-style 22-room manse and set up cattle ranching and camellia growing under his plentiful oaks. (He also wrote the screenplay for the 1949 film *Malaya*, about a newspaperman and World War II rubber plants, starring Spencer Tracy and Jimmy Stewart and filmed on location at... the L.A. County Arboretum. Oh well, you can't have everything.)

Today, one of Descanso's most spectacular attraction was Mr. Boddy's passion: camellias, which he hybridized and propagated for the florist trade to fund his ever-expanding collection. The 34,000 camellias, often more than twenty feet tall,

Under the tabebuia at the entrance to Descanso Gardens.

represent 700 species, many of which were hybridized from twenty Chinese varieties that were previously unknown to the West. This is North America's largest camellia collection, thanks in great part to F.M. Uyematsu, the owner of nearby Star Nursery. At the start of World War II he was forced to sell his entire stock, tens of thousands of camellia plants, before being interned with other Japanese-Americans.

The property opened in 1950. On opening day, 6,000 guests caused traffic jams, which angered neighbors and led to its quick closing. The gardens reopened a year later, charging $1, in part to discourage attendance.

Plan on at least an hour for your visit, which will fly by. Wear walking shoes, as there's plenty to see, starting with the boards near the information window, where you'll find daily cuttings from the gardens. Seasonal highlights are spring-flowering cherry trees and massive tulip displays; specialty lilacs bred for this climate (March); and the insanely fabulous five-acre rosarium (spring through fall), shaded under arbors and tree-lined routes. Extras include an extensive lecture series covering all aspects of horticulture, weekend music events, annual plant sales and, huzzah, early-morning fitness walks and yoga classes! There's a thoughtful selection of horticulture books in the gift shop, and the Patina-run café is good for sandwiches and salads, plus tea service at the Japanese Tea House. Members receive discounts on all purchases.

All aboard the Descanso choo–choo train.

The Huntington Botanical Gardens

The Huntington Library, Art Collections and Botanical Gardens
1151 Oxford Rd., San Marino
626.405.2100, huntington.org
Open Mon., Wed., Thurs., Fri. noon-4:30 p.m., Sat.-Sun. 10:30 a.m.-4:30 p.m.; summer hours extended; adults $15-$20, seniors $12-$15, students $10, kids $6, kids under 5 free; free the 1st Thurs. of the month. It's worth joining if you visit more than twice a year.

The three-acre rose garden is one of the world's finest.

If you have only one day to spend in Pasadena, this is it. The Huntington Botanical Gardens are, in a word, splendid. In each of the eighteen specialty sections, including the new Chinese Garden of Flowing Fragrance, the landscaping is both formal and refreshingly beckoning.

Railroad magnate Henry Edwards (H.E.) Huntington purchased this citrus-ranch property in 1903. Originally 600 acres, today it's a "manageable" 207 acres, 150 of which are planned and open to the public. In 1904 Huntington hired landscape supervisor William Hertrich to begin the botanical collections; H.E. died in 1927, but Hertrich continued on until 1948. Today, their handiwork is the visitor's holiday.

Upon arrival try to snag the free daily garden tour, or go with a self-guided exploration. South of the entrance are four acres of spectacular decorative palms (H.E.'s favorite for public gardens and railway stations), and to the east is the twelve-acre desert garden, which Hertrich convinced his boss, the collector, to build not as a specialty garden but as a noteworthy collection for an area with difficult soil. Today, 5,000 species of exotic xerophytes (aridity-adapted plants) make this a living lab, complete with a conservatory and quite useful to botanical science and education.

Through the main entrance and straight ahead past the Palm and Jungle Gardens, the oldest section is the four-acre lily ponds, finished by Hertrich in 1904; he installed a heated lining to extend the lilies' blooming season. As you walk back through the Jungle and Subtropical gardens, you'll see half of the known species of prehistoric cycads, sort of a cross between a palm and a conifer.

The most heavily planted gardens are those surrounding the Art Collections gallery, formerly H.E.'s private residence. The formal Shakespeare Garden holds plants referenced in the Bard's works, many of whose original manuscripts are in the Huntington Library. The North Vista is woven with palms and antique statuary, terminating with an ornate, oversize fountain. West of the Art Collections, the three-acre historical Rose Garden features more than 1,800 species and cultivars in 40 planted beds. As is true with most Southern California rose gardens, April is the prettiest month (before all that deadheading begins), but blooms occur from March through December. Climbing roses cover pergolas leading to the graceful Japanese

Huntington's Japanese garden, dating to 1912

garden, which was assembled in 1912, when all things Japanese were the rage. The walled Zen garden, with its swath of fine raked gravel, is a copy of a famed temple in Kyoto. Beyond are the extensive camellia groves, grown from seed, propagated and grafted by Hertrich over a 30-year period and cataloged in three volumes. In a northerly section, behind a tall, lacy gate, stands the stately marble Huntington Mausoleum, designed by John Russell Pope of Jefferson Memorial fame.

Huntington was also presciently interested in old trees; it is said that he encouraged all efforts to save endangered trees and that modern tree surgery began here. As for the citrus that once covered this land, a twenty-acre grove remains.

The new feather in the Huntington's chapeau is the amazing Liu Fang Yuan (Garden of Flowing Fragrance), which opened in 2008. Most of the building elements were constructed in Suzhou, China, home of famed gardens from the 16th and 17th centuries, on which this convergence of art, architecture and nature was modeled. Bottlenecks may occur at any of the seven pavilions, but they're worth any minor wait. The lovely Terrace of the Jade Mirror, a reference to the moon, features incredible hand-carved wood panels, whose maintenance in the blistering Southern California sun makes us shudder. If you don't want to reserve a month in advance for a guided tour ($22 on weekdays, $25 on Saturdays), download the free walking-tour podcast in Mandarin, Cantonese or English at huntington.org.

For those not even remotely interested in botany, art or literature (and if that's you, scram, you bum!), happiness also awaits. The darling Tea Room is not nearly as stuffy as it could be. Ham-fisted sandwiches and good salads without the clatter of silverware are served around the corner at the Café, which is less expensive by half than the Tea Room.

Los Angeles County Arboretum & Botanic Garden

301 N. Baldwin Ave., Arcadia
626.821.3222, arboretum.org
Open daily 9 a.m.-5 p.m.; adults $7, seniors & students $5, kids $2.50, kids under 5 free

Founded in 1948, this 127-acre botanical park is a treat for travelers, local botany buffs and bird lovers – countless peacocks and pea hens roam the grounds, a "gift" from La Cañada, which donated some of the imported birds after they'd taken care of the town's rattlesnake problem.

Once part of Mission San Gabriel's vast acreage, this land was deeded during the *Mexicano* period to Hugo Reid, a Scot with Mexican citizenship who was married to Victoria, a Gabrielina. Their sturdy adobe rancho and outdoor kitchen circa 1840 are still here, facing a re-created Tongva tent cluster. The next owner was free-wheeling Southern California real estate baron Lucky Baldwin, and the house he built for his 16-year-old third wife stands across from the Tongva residence. Harry Chandler, former owner of the *Los Angeles Times*, was the land's final owner, before the county purchased it.

The Arboretum is as much about education as it is about pretty grounds. Partnered with *Sunset* magazine and the Cal State system, it has demonstration gardens, including the totally cool Spiny Forest of Madagascar, African and cac-

tus collections, flowering springtime cherries, a horticulture library with 20,000 titles and a knowledgeable and helpful librarian (what a concept!), a comprehensive lecture and continuing-ed series featuring Lili Singer and friends, the Art-in-the-Garden events, a plant hotline and a fabulous web site. And mark your calendar for the ever-expanding L.A. Garden Show each May.

Surrounding Baldwin Lake (the setting for the Tarzan movies and the leeches scene from the *African Queen*) are 90 species of palms, and well-labeled plants fill the desert garden.

Lucky Baldwin built this house for his 16-year-old third bride.

Secret Gardens of the San Gabriel Valley

Throop Pond, on the Caltech campus

Altadena Community Gardens

Loma Alta Park & Community Garden
3330 N. Lincoln Ave., Altadena
This colorful, fenced collection of 63 garden plots on the southwest corner of Loma Alta Park sits on the site of the former Mount Lowe Military Academy, which closed in the 1970s. The citizenry asked the L.A. County Parks Department for a communal garden, so with the help of the California Conservation Corps, walkways and four wheelchair-accessible raised beds were laid, and neighbors were soon growing carrots, tomatoes and beans. Water, tools and fertilizer from local stables are provided for an annual fee, and free workshops are offered on horticultural topics. Spotless restrooms are found in neighboring Loma Alta Park, a lovely and underused county park that also features an equestrian ring, tennis courts, a playground and a jumbo new recreation center.

Arlington Garden

295 Arlington Dr., Pasadena
Surely you've noticed the beautiful phoenix that's risen from the abandoned Caltrans lot along the Pasadena Avenue in Southwest Pasadena? Arlington Garden opened to the public in 2005, after surveys showed the desire for "passive development" on this state-owned, city-leased three-acre property (until the early 1960s, the site of the swell Durand mansion). Dawn-to-dusk foot traffic is encouraged, as are school groups – but come on, the nice signs say "demonstration gardens" (i.e., respeck!). Yes, the amphitheater looks inviting, but it's not a fricking climbing wall. Sorry for the Mrs. Crabapple, but this oasis comes by way of all-volunteer hours and dang, these people have slaved. The California and Mediterranean sections feature native plants; other heat-lovers include olive allée, raised herb beds, spring irises, an orange grove and a new cactus garden. Bright California poppies usually in bloom in March.

Arroyo Seco-South Pasadena Woodland & Wildlife Park

100 block of Pasadena Ave., South Pasadena
This three-acre woodland garden along the L.A. River and the Arroyo Seco demonstrates the power of totally awesome community volunteers. In 1998 they began lobbying the city of South Pas, congressman Adam Schiff, the Santa Monica Mountains Conservancy and the Mountains Recreation & Conservation Authority to transform a nasty illegal dump into easy-access public parkland. Late in 2004 the park opened for dog walkers, horseback riders, day trippers and joggers. It's now home to gorgeous native plants, meandering paths, a lovely view of historic York Boulevard Bridge and Mount Washington, and a name that says

it all. The ASSPWWP features rare California native walnut trees, sycamores, and a savannah grassland. Invasive plants were removed by saintly volunteers who still provide maintenance days. Kindly watch your step in case new native plantings aren't yet labeled. This place is easy to miss, so look for the boulder walls out front.

Caltech Campus

California Institute of Technology
1200 E. California Blvd., Pasadena
626.395.3910

We're particularly fond of two of the many gardens on the mostly lovely 124-acre Caltech campus. Dabney Gardens, designed by landscape architect Beatrix Farrand in 1928, is a secluded and elegant courtyard behind a wrought-iron gate, home to olive trees, stuccoed and tiled walls, sitting and reading spots, climbing roses, a gorgeous wall fountain and a cool pad of grass. An antique bronze statue of a water buffalo bearing Tenjin, a Japanese deity of the arts, sciences and learning, stands in the east corner of this quiet garden. We also love the tranquil, tree-shaded Throop Pond and Gardens, whose winding walkway is hugged by perennials, flowing pools and big boulders. A Cottage Co-op pal and JPL scientist tells us that originally these boulders were Disneyesque fakes, eventually replaced with "geologically significant rocks," so significant they are marked by a plaque. But two fakes remain, listed on the plaque as "pseudoliths: 12+ years." Look for this full disclosure just east of the blue-tiled Milliken reflecting pool, which is neither as large nor splashy (pun intended) as the pool between the Beckman buildings but is an apt prelude for this pretty little route through campus. To find these gardens, stop by the Admissions office (Steele House, 355 South Holliston) to pick up a booklet.

El Molino Viejo (The Old Mill)

1120 Old Mill Rd., San Marino
626.449.5458, oldmill.info
Open daily 1-4 p.m.; closed Mon.
Donation requested

This was the first water-powered mill in California, built in 1816 as part of Mission San Gabriel's vast operations. Father Zalvedia chose this spot because of its water source, and he and his fellow padres then recruited Joseph Chapman, a Yankee and former pirate with keen logging and engineering skills, to handle the monumental construction job. With the help of the kindly Tongva, now renamed the Gabrielinos, trees were cut in Santa Anita and Altadena canyons, about six miles north, and the massive logs were rolled and dragged south to the molino, in the process getting milled by the rocky land; most of these original logs still frame the building's structure. When the mill was completed, several obstacles became apparent. First, the millstones wouldn't turn under the force of the water, due in part to bad spoon-shaped paddles that didn't encourage fast water flow. The Gabrielinos may actually have spent their days pulling the great millstones with leather ropes – in essence, operating the mill with manpower alone. Also, because the mill was built right on top of an underground stream, the floors and walls were continually damp, making it impossible to store the milled flours, so extra manpower was demanded to transport the flours to the mission three miles south.

The mill still stands today thanks to preservation efforts by Henry Huntington, who purchased it in 1902 and later used it for a clubhouse for this hotel's golf course. Maintained by the renowned Diggers Garden Club, the grounds are planted with period specimens (citrus, quince, plum, calla lilies, coral bells) and include pathways, benches and an old fountain. In the summer, the Pomegranate Patio hosts concerts by the California Philharmonic Chamber. You can wander on your own or take a tour with one of the excellent docents. And make sure to venture upstairs to see the plein-air paintings at the California Arts Club gallery. This is one of the prettiest and most serene slices of Euro-California history in the region.

A winding pathway through the Old Mill's walled garden

Sierra Madre's famed wisteria looks like this, only about a million times bigger.

Wisteria Mania
In 1894, Alice Brugman bought a baby wisteria vine in a gallon can for 75 cents and planted it in her Sierra Madre yard. The wisteria thrived beyond her wildest dreams, and when a man named Fennel bought the house from the Brugmans in 1913, he built extra arbors to support the vines. This might not have been such a smart idea – the arbors encouraged the vines to grow over the roof of the house, eventually crushing it in 1931. (The house had to be torn down, and a new one was built a safe distance from the killer vines.) Still in private hands, the wisteria is in the *Guinness Book of World Records* as the largest blossoming plant in the world, more than one acre in size and weighing 250 tons, each spring carrying 1.5 million lavender blossoms. This horticultural wonder is the centerpiece of the annual Wistaria Festival (spelled the old-fashioned way), a shindig marking the one day a year the vine is open for public viewing – typically the second Sunday in March. To see the vine for yourself, call 626.355.5111, or go to sierramadrechamber. com.

Kidspace Children's Museum
480 N. Arroyo Blvd., Pasadena
626.449.9144, kidspacemuseum.org
Gardens open daily June-Aug. 9:30 a.m.-5 p.m.; closed Mon. Jan.-May & Sept.-Dec.
Adults & kids $8
Thanks to its move to Brookside Park, at Kidspace you can now use your outside voice… outside! The museum honors its location at the site of the former Fannie Morrison Horticultural Center with an extensive network of grounds, gardens and "outdoor learning environments." The garden "rooms," designed by landscape artist Nancy Goslee Power, happily engage all the senses – for both kids and adults. Enter through the Wisteria Courtyard's pergola (watch for three-wheeled hot rodders in helmets) and make your way through the oak grove to see native and water-wise plants, feel a tactile garden of soft fuzzies (stay with us, we're still talking horticulture) and visit a really cool scaled-down model of the Arroyo Seco.

Lacy Park
Entrance on Virginia Rd. north of Monterey Rd., San Marino
Open Mon.-Fri. 6:30 a.m.-dusk, Sat.-Sun. 8 a.m.-8 p.m.; nonresidents pay $3 per person to enter on weekends
Originally Wilson Lake in 1875, this 30-acre park was created by the city of San Marino in 1925, when it bought the land and drained the lake. It's one of the prettiest parks in Southern California, landscaped with grand old oaks, sycamores, palm groves (labeled!) and a pristine rose garden and arbor, as well as various memorials: one to World War I vets, one to native son Gen. George S. Patton, one to the Vietnam "conflict" and lots of memorial benches and plaques on walkways and in the rose garden. For the living, there's a baseball diamond, six tennis courts, two walking/cycling paths and plenty of shaded picnic tables. It's also a dog-friendly place, with doggy drinking fountains and poo bags. And for those with less-hairy offspring, there are well-maintained play structures overseen by a mix of nannies (sometimes in actual maid's uniforms, complete with aprons and sensible shoes) and local moms (in five-carat solitaires and impractical shoes). If you don't live in San Marino, it'll cost you $3 a head to use the park on weekends. What, you think paradise is free? Oh, and no loitering near the restrooms, and no smoking within 100 feet of the play structures – yeah, like you'd dare.

Mater Dolorosa Passionist Retreat Center

700 N. Sunnyside Ave., Sierra Madre
626.355.7188

This large retreat center is private property, but a public mass is held every Tuesday at 8:30 a.m., and the grounds are open Monday through Friday from 9 to 5. Buzz if the gate's closed and announce that you've come for personal reflection or prayer. Unless a private function got there first, you'll be welcomed in to wander the Stations of the Cross gardens (ignore the statues if you don't go in for that sort of thing) and visit the succulent garden, the Garden of the Seven Sorrows and the lovely outdoor amphitheater, with its view of the valley.

Norton Simon Museum Garden

411 W. Colorado Blvd., Old Pasadena
626.449.6840, nortonsimon.org
Open Wed.-Mon. noon-6 p.m. (Fri. to 9 p.m.); adults $8, seniors $4, students & kids under 18 free; free to all first Fri. evening of the month
Small enough for a quick stroll but large enough to lose oneself in, this gem is bordered by decomposed granite walkways that get slick when it rains – or so the nervous guards say when they force the grounds into lockdown during a drizzle. (California is not at its best when it rains.) Fragrant patches of lavender, a eucalyptus grove and 180 species of plants composed by landscape designer Nancy Goslee Power mingle with abundant sculpture, a lily pond and a surprise waterfall that almost makes you forget the freeway on-ramp right next door. Lunch at the teak-chic Garden Terrace makes this the perfect antidote to the surrounding asphalt jungle.

Our Lady of Lourdes West Grotto

St. Elizabeth of Hungary Catholic Church
1879 N. Lake Ave., Altadena
626.797.1167, saintelizabethchurch.org
Tucked into the walled northwest corner of the church grounds, this cloister was dedicated in 1939 at a service that drew as many as 10,000 people. (Native son Wallace Neff designed the 1926 church, donating his services and putting him on the architectural map.) It was built by local artist Ryozo Fuso Kado, a fifth-generation stone and rock craftsman, as his 31st and most ambitious sculpture, using 130 tons of Mono

Lake lava rock fortified with 90 tons of concrete and steel. The Carerra marble statues seem to hover over the pools below. The original garden park featured fourteen paintings of the Stations of the Cross (now removed), but it still has the original cement railings shaped like tree branches, a mission-style central fountain, a rustic tile shrine to the Virgin Mary and a curved wrought-iron archway facing Lake Avenue.

Western Asset Plaza Courtyards

385 E. Colorado Blvd., Pasadena
Entering this huge commercial building via a walkway on Colorado, we're aware of the right angles of sidewalk, walls and partitions. And then a chunky fountain set back from the street commands the realization that – ahh! – this is what public landscaping should be. Handsome, with clean lines and a cool gurgle, this glass-and-cement plaza is softened with wonderful gardens, all hidden from the street. Jumbo terra-cotta urns explode with strappy Mediterranean plants, palms and reeds smooth the geometric angles of raised planter beds, and water features abound. In our favorite water feature, a concrete and Mexican-river-rock channel guides the water south, a miniature ode to the Californios' knee-tiled *zanja* (channel) that brought water from the mountains. Here and there are lounge chairs for sunbathing and tables for lunching, and integrated seating is built into walkway planters stuffed with ornamental grasses. What a place to work – or at least to take breaks.

A secret world lies behind the hulking Western Asset Plaza office building.

Cemeteries We Love

A sixteen-foot-tall replica of Michelangelo's David at Forest Lawn

Forest Lawn Memorial Park

1712 S. Glendale Ave., Glendale
800.204.3131

The first in this swank chain of memorial parks (these guys thought up the term "memorial park," because "cemetery" sounded so gloomy), Forest Lawn gives the deceased an upbeat, sun- and light-filled final resting place. So until Angelenos find a Botox-injected cure for death, we can pay our respects in these wide-open spaces – no depressing monuments here! Because it's relatively close to the Hollywood sign, many elements of this 300-acre park are over the top. The wrought-iron gates in front are said to be the world's largest. More than one million visitors pass through them each year, including thousands of schoolchildren on field trips (whaaat?). Some come to visit the 250,000 people interred here, but many come just for the artwork. That's right, hoo boy, the "artwork": a stained-glass "Last Supper," replicas of Michelangelo statuary, a jumbo "Signing of the Declaration of Independence" in 700,000 mosaic tiles, a giant moai carving from Easter Island, an oversize bronze of George Washington that Congress forgot to pay for, so Forest Lawn bought it. It's all big, bigger than life. Oh, now we get it: This is a place to get what you didn't have the first time around. The expanses of lawn are amazing, and the living will earn your next meal walking from Great Mausoleum through the Labyrinth to the English reproduction chapels. You won't get a lot of help from the management in locating your favorite luminaries, armies of whom rest here. Just as you couldn't sit at their table at Chasen's when they were alive. Oh well. This is a cemetery, after all, where reverence and decorum count. Even in Los Angeles.

Mission San Gabriel Cemetery

427 S. Junipero Serra Dr., San Gabriel
626.457.3035

On the north side of the mission, you can't miss the large wrought-iron cemetery gates framed by tiles painted with welcoming skulls. Aside from tombstones and a few elevated monuments, this large, flat, walled block of land isn't very inviting; benches for reflecting are as few as shade trees. The prettier burial grounds are inside the mission's walls ($5 charge). Woven through the courtyards and shaded patios are the final resting places of modern-day priests who served the mission, as well as older graves marked by antique wrought-iron gates framed by giant grapevine trunks. A big marble bench connotes the grave of mission manager Eulalia Perez, the first individual to receive an Alta California land grant from Spain (although she was beset by swindlers and lost nearly all of it). It's definitely worth the $5 to see the mission at final rest. A small sign reports that 6,000 Gabrielinos are buried here, too, which seems yet another insult to the people who were subsumed – and all but forgotten – by California's mission system.

The cemetery inside the old walls of Mission San Gabriel

Mountain View Cemetery in Altadena

Mountain View Cemetery

2400 N. Fair Oaks Ave., Altadena
626.794.7133
Open daily; closes at dusk
Mountain View was created to serve Pasadena as well as the Pasadena Highlands, later known as Altadena. Although located in Altadena, it is Pasadena's major cemetery, outside of some church sites. This stretch of North Fair Oaks is still fairly quiet and isolated, which makes a visit here all the more pleasant, and it's a manageable size, whether you want to take a fifteen-minute look or a three-hour stroll. Approximately 60 acres, with well-spaced trees, Victorian monuments, small headstones, roundabouts and curbs tall enough to comfortably step out of your horse-drawn carriage, Mountain View is home to a couple of cool Civil War sections, as well as the graves of many prominent African-American citizens from the last 160 years, including Thomas Ellsworth, who earned a Congressional Medal of Honor in the Civil War; A.J. Bertonneaux, the Creole business leader who brought football to the Rose Parade celebrations; and Eldridge Cleaver, a founding member of the Black Panther Party. You'll also find such literary pioneers as John Ransom, who wrote the bleak Civil War book *Andersonville Diary;* Earl Derr Biggers, the mystery novelist who created detective Charlie Chan; MacArthur Genius Octavia Butler; and a bunch of regular old geniuses (Richard Feynman, 1965 Nobel Prize winner; Thaddeus Lowe, inventor and railway pioneer; George Reeves, TV's Superman; and Wilbur Hatch, conductor of the Desi Arnaz Orchestra). Hologram biographies of the residents are available on a limited basis. Halloween weekend tours are offered infrequently through local historical societies, and they're well worth attending.

San Gabriel Cemetery

601 W. Rose Rd., San Gabriel
626.282.2764
Open daily 8:00 a.m.-5:00 p.m.
This historic cemetery shares a common driveway with the Church of Our Saviour, home to a life-size bronze statue of Gen. George S. Patton in the church courtyard and a stained-glass window inside the church of a tank (yes, this was Patton's family's church). Take a left at the caretaker's cottage, past the lollipop-sculpted lemon trees, and either walk or drive through the fourteen-acre cemetery. This is one of the coolest cemeteries in the SG Valley, and it's also the ritziest. The celebrities come from California's history pages: Benjamin "Don Benito" Wilson, the Pattons, the potato-chip Scudder family and so forth. The grounds are serene and immaculate, and the tombstones tell lively tales of folks who embraced their work, struggles and families.

Sierra Madre Pioneer Cemetery

553 Sierra Madre Blvd., Sierra Madre
In 1881 the land for this cemetery was purchased, and the first customer arrived in 1884, a Civil War vet who had recently moved to town. This is a lovely, shady, raised burial park with fortified walls and a wrought-iron railing. It also has a new memorial "shed" with touch-screen information on the residents. The curving paths connect the cemetery's 2.5 acres with Sierra Madre's community park, creating a nice flow from this world to the next and back again.

Nurseries We Love

You want azaleas or camellias, Nuccio's has got them.

Burkard's

690 N. Orange Grove Blvd., Pasadena
626.796.4355

Third-generation plantsman Frank Burkard Jr. runs this fine, if not downright posh, nursery. Besides a crack staff, Mr. B. also has an excellent selection of native plants, fruit trees, vegetables and annuals, as well as a riotous selection of hard-to-find tomatoes and an extensive variety of spring bulbs that thrive in this climate. Did we mention seeds, garden ephemera, pots and hand tools? Oh, and the roses... heirlooms, climbers, English and hybrid teas, too! Burkard is a respected horticultural authority and a frequent guest on gardening shows – garden clubs even drive up from San Diego to seek his advice and buy his wares.

California Cactus Center

216 S. Rosemead Blvd., East Pasadena
626.795.2788

On a parched stretch on the east side of town, California Cactus is an oasis of succulents, cacti and tillandsias (that's air plants to the rest of us). This local fixture has been growing prickles for 35 years, and hundreds of its 1,500 rotating species are fantastic show pieces, artfully staged in striking pottery, which is also sold either with or without the plants. The helpful staff answer questions about propagation, transplanting and landscaping. Even if you think you don't like cacti or succulents, this eye-popping place is must-see.

Nuccio's

3555 Chaney Trail Rd. (off Loma Alta), Altadena
626.794.3383

This is the only place in Southern California to shop for camellias and azaleas – and we're not exaggerating. Located at the foot of a great hiking trail, this family operation has six acres covered with thousands of camellias, many of which the Nuccios have hybridized themselves since opening in 1947. Ask for recommendations: Do you like big leaves? Ruffled petals? Variegated? Fragrant? Have a favorite color? These folks are helpful and knowledgeable. The seasonal hours extend in spring and summer, so it's best to call before visiting, and make sure to wear walking shoes.

Burkard's nursery in Pasadena

Persson's

3115 E. Sierra Madre Blvd., East Pasadena
626.792.6073

This mom-and-pop-and-two-daughters-and-son nursery is another local fave. It's a big one, so don't be in a rush. You'll find gaggles of trees, roses, shrubs, vines, natives, annuals and vegetables, as well as a mondo shade garden on the east side of the parking lot. The region's best hydrangeas are here, with giant root stock. Got mulch? They do, and they'll deliver truckloads or less for a modest fee.

San Gabriel Nursery & Florist

632 S. San Gabriel Blvd., San Gabriel
626.286.3782

The granddaddy of local nurseries, this place opened in 1923, and it continues today as a family-owned business, despite threats from encroaching warehouse stores. It carries eye-popping year-round rose selections, bare-root fruit trees (go, dwarfs!), cacti, succulents and orchids, plus tools, pest management and hard-to-find seeds. You'll get a 10% discount if you belong to any of the local botanical gardens.

Acres of blooms at Persson's

So Many Nurseries, So Little Time...

You don't need to go to warehouse garden centers and spend a week's salary on a carload of stuff that will die before you get around to putting it in the ground. Check out these smaller venues for an afternoon's planting project.

Bellefontaine Nursery

838 S. Fair Oaks Ave., Pasadena
626.796.0747
Closed Wed.
A swell, organized place for roses and annuals, as well as fine terra-cotta pots to bring ailing friends at Huntington Hospital across the street.

Kettle's Nursery

1950 Lincoln Ave., Pasadena
626.798.6787
A groovy midcentury building in the Lincoln corridor with a decent selection of annuals, roses and soil amendments.

Lincoln Avenue Nursery

804 Lincoln Ave., Pasadena
626.792.2138
Tucked into a quiet residential stretch of northwest Pasadena, this mom-and-pop place has unusual vegetable and citrus choices. Colorful pottery section, too.

Mission Nursery

2510 Mission St., San Marino
626.799.1689
There's a down-home feeling here, if home is the Hamptons and Mumsy's double-parked out front in the Bentley. A grand neighborhood nursery.

Present Perfect

140 S. Kinneloa, East Pasadena
626.449.6211
With a sometimes-funky plant selection, good fruit trees and expert advice for two decades, this place is known for its pricey and absolutely gorgeous Christmas trees.

San Marino Nursery

2143 Huntington Dr., South Pasadena
626.799.9123
A small-town feel, with a compact, healthy selection of plants, especially for annual color and herbs.

Q & A: Betty & Charles McKenney

Betty and Charlie "Kicker" McKenney are private citizens who serve the public each and every day. How? Well, a few years ago the city approached them to help turn an abandoned Caltrans lot (let's be frank, it was a bleeding eyesore) into a park. Arlington Garden was developed on a minuscule budget, steered by Betty, with support from Kicker. They recruited tireless volunteers to round out assistance from the city and private companies. The results? Some 300 new trees, as well as a cactus garden, a chaparral, a desert section, a meadow and a riparian wash. In the Mediterranean garden "rooms" 3,000 plants thrive, thanks to water conservation. Betty and Kicker talked with Sandy Gillis during the radiant spring poppy season.

If on your 25th birthday, someone predicted that you would eventually be here hand-watering six hours a day, what would you have said?
Kicker: Who are you, and whom are you talking to?

What's your favorite garden chore?
Betty: Finding an area that needs to be worked on and improving it so someone notices that it is now beautiful and wasn't yesterday.

How have your notions about gardening changed since developing this plot?
Betty: Gardening now involves so many things: arranging pots, plants, trees and furniture, planting, pruning, putting up umbrellas, covering strawberries, placing rocks in strategic places, and enjoying others who visit the garden.

What changes – good and ill – have you seen in the Rose City in the last 25 years?
Kicker: It has undergone a serious development boom. This is good, but the size and density of development have changed much of its small-town character. Still, Pasadena has remained a hometown even as it admits to itself that it is an urban city. It has also

maintained itself as a city of volunteers and community involvement.

What's your favorite place for breakfast?
Betty: Our dining room or terrace, with a view of the garden. If we're going out, Julienne's and Marston's are favorites.

Favorite smell in Pasadena? Or would you call it a fragrance?
Kicker: The Arroyo after a rain explodes with a pungent fragrance. And the Arlington Garden has a panoply of fragrances, from oranges to lavender, rosemary and sages.
Betty: The Don Juan rose in the Arlington Garden. The white irises are a close second.

What do you *really* think of the Rose Parade?
Kicker: I have attended nearly every parade and crashed one in 1956 in a Model A Ford with a bunch of friends, when the engine overheated. I love the parade for what it provides for Pasadenans and people from all over the world. What would Pasadena be without the Rose Parade?

Famous

We may not have the bling of Beverly Hills, but Pasadena has fame. The whole world watches our parade and football games, we're Hollywood's favorite backlot, and our neighbors are as likely to be famous for a Nobel Prize in Chemistry as for an Academy Award.

The Rose Parade   106

The Doo Dah Parade   108

Pasadena 90210: We Have Famous People, Too   109

Hollywood East: Movie & TV Locations   110

Q & A: Gale Anne Hurd   112

The LAUSD Marching Band is a Rose Parade regular.

The Rose Parade

It's pretty much impossible to envision life in Pasadena without the Rose Parade. Even parade-hating grinches have to deal with it, because the hullabaloo is so pervasive. Construction begins on the grandstands in the fall, and you can't get into the Old Town Ralphs without negotiating the risers. Local high-school girls swarm the Rose Queen tryouts in September, RVs start appearing

Viva La Familia
EXPERIENCE THE GOOD LIFE

after Christmas, and everywhere you look, there's a white car with a ToR (Tournament of Roses) vanity plate. That car is probably being driven by a normally staid local businessman or woman who has spent the last 30 years putting on a goofy white suit and volunteering in hopes of gaining a spot on the fourteen-member Executive Committee, the grandest of the Grand Poobahs in town.

As the 40 million Americans (and millions more around the world) who watch the parade on TV are told ad nauseum, the Tournament of Roses parade first took place on January 1, 1890; the posh Valley Hunt Club created it as a booster event – and, no doubt, to thumb their sunburned patrician noses at the snowbound East and Midwest. It was a modest spectacle at first, just a few horse-drawn carriages covered in flowers, but it quickly grew to include marching bands, motorized floats and such sporting events as ostrich races. Parade organizers added a college football game in 1902, but when the University of Michigan humiliated Stanford that year, they went back to showcasing chariot races for another fourteen years. Football returned for good in 1916, becoming so popular that a new stadium, dubbed the Rose Bowl, was built in 1922.

We longtime locals have our own Rose Parade traditions. On New Year's Eve, some of us walk over to Rosemont or Orange Grove to see the floats get into position; it's fun to see the flowers up close on a misty night. Others sleep in a little, then head out around 8:30 and find a tippy-toe spot on the sidewalk on the route's east end, where the floats don't arrive until about 9:30 or so. Or, if we're lucky, a friend with an office along the parade route will host a party. As teenagers, we did the rite-of-passage overnight campout and we discovered just how cold Pasadena

The armies of parade volunteers are called the White Suiters.

can get at 3 a.m.; now our teenagers are learning the same lesson. Some of us just stay in our jammies and watch it on TV like the rest of the world.

Here's our advice for visitors: Plan as far in advance as possible. Book your hotel room first, then order grandstand seats from Sharp Seating (see sidebar); these go on sale February 1, eleven months before the parade, but they're usually available into the fall. Consider the excellent packages offered by the Tournament of Roses, which include hotel rooms, parade and football tickets, float viewing, a New Year's Eve celebration and more.

If you want to camp out on Colorado for free seats, have your beach chairs, hibachi and sleeping bags ready to go at noon the day before, and be prepared for cold – this may be California, but it's still the dead of winter. (And don't expect to sleep, because you won't.) If you have neither seats nor a campout spot, look for a parking space that morning in the neighborhoods between Allen and Sierra Madre Boulevard north of Colorado, and try to find an open few inches on the sidewalk to stand.

If all of the above sounds like too much trouble, go out and see the floats the night before (our personal favorite activity), have a fun New Year's Eve, and watch the parade on TV in your hotel room. If you stay at one of the Colorado-adjacent places, like the Marriott or Westin, you're likely to hear the marching bands from the comfort of your room.

Rose Parade Facts

Date: New Year's Day, unless it falls on a Sunday, then January 2

Starting time: 8 a.m.; parade usually lasts 2.5 hours

Route: Orange Grove at Ellis Street, north to Colorado Boulevard, right onto Colorado (TV cameras are at this corner), across town on Colorado, north on Sierra Madre Boulevard, ending at Paloma Street; route is 5.5 miles

Grandstand tickets: $40-$90; Sharp Seating, 626.795.4171, sharpseating.com

Package tickets (parade, hotel, football): Tournament of Roses, 626.449.9550, tournamentofroses.com

Sidewalk viewing: Free; spots are easier to find that morning on the east end of Colorado, between Allen and Sierra Madre Blvd.

Camping: Overnight sidewalk camping allowed on New Year's Eve only; campers can set up at noon on December 31

RV parking: Sharp Seating, 626.795.4171; Easy Parking, 626.286.7576; Brookside Park, 626.577.3100

Car parking: At many structures and lots across town; expect to pay dearly

General information: 626.449.4100, tournamentofroses.com

The Doo Dah Parade

Light Bringer Project
64 N. Raymond Ave., Old Pasadena
626.205.4029, pasadenadoodahparade.info

Wacky, irreverent, weird, silly, anarchistic… is that not how you'd describe Pasadena? No, it's not, and that's the whole point of our "other" parade, the Doo Dah, the rebellious stepsister and antidote to the Rose Parade. As an all-city goof, it's so successful that other towns

The Royal Pains

around the country have started their own Doo Dah Parades. And we're flattered.

The Doo Dah is always on a Sunday (the Rose Parade, never!) – typically, the

Sunday before Thanksgiving, unless they don't feel like doing it then, in which case it might be a month or three later. It starts at, oh, 11:30ish, leading one to assume that the Doo Dah was hatched by some guys who had too many Saturday-night drinks back in 1976, when Pasadena was Funky Town.

Sometimes disorganized, usually raucous, occasionally political, the parade takes about two hours to see all 1,500 to 2,000 participants who walk the 1.25-mile route from Raymond and Holly south to Colorado, then west over to Pasadena Avenue. Of the 45,000 or so people who usually come out to view, some are snowbirds in RVs, but most are locals. Past parade favorites include the Synchronized Briefcase Marching Drill Team, the Dead Rose Queens, Claude Rains and the 20-Member (we think) Invisible Man Marching Drill Team, the BBQ

Count Smokula, one of countless Doo Dah characters

& Hibachi Marching Grillers (who send projectile cooked hot dogs into the crowd), the Men of Leisure Synchronized Nap Team, Tequila Mockingbird, the Howdy Krishnas, the Spawn of Captain James T. Kirk, the Toast Masters (who throw toast), the Grand Old Hags and Linoleum Bonaparte.

Is it open to every Joan and Joe with a T-bone steak hat and the $10 participant's fee? Why yes it is, as long as their float isn't motorized or horse-driven. There are no themes and no commercials (because it's not televised), and the only judging is to select a Doo Dah Queen. The Light Bringer Project, which has been running the parade since 1994, says the queen must be "pretty audacious to stand out" in this group of revelers. Belly dancing and fire spewing are a good start. But she's got to be funny, too. After all, this is the Doo Dah Parade.

The Motorized Couch Brigade

Pasadena 90210: We Have Famous People, Too

Seen at the Grocery & at Flea Markets

If they don't live here, they've hung out here…

Jennifer Lopez

Dennis Haysbert

Diane Keaton

Hector Elizondo

Marlee Matlin

Sidney Poitier

Bill Plaschke

Markie Post

John C. Reilly

Tim Roth

Jane Kaczmarek

Bradley Whitford

The specter of Phil Spector

Judge Lance Ito

Dallas Raines

Nora Dunn

Kevin Dunn

Oscar de la Hoya

Charlie Kaufman

Ben Harper

Madeline Stowe

Johnny Mountain

Elvis

Who Went to School Here

William Holden & Hilary Swank, South Pas High

Steven J. Cannell, La Cañada schools

Gen. George S. Patton, San Marino schools

Phil Hendrie (talk radio host), Eddie Van Halen & John Singleton went to PCC

Julia Child & author Harriet Huntington Doerr went to Polytechnic School

Cheryl Tiegs, Kenny Loggins and Duane Allen went to Alhambra High

Hayley Joel Osment and sis Emily Osment went to Flintridge Preparatory School

Pay Your Respects

Glendale's Forest Lawn is jam-packed with famous folks. We eschew the movie stars and look for the graves of the musicians we love:

LaVerne & Maxene Andrews, two of the Andrews Sisters

Nat King Cole, jazz singer

Sam Cooke, R&B legend

Sammy Davis Jr., Rat Packer

Art Tatum, jazz pianist

Ethel Waters, jazz singer & movie star

Johnny "Guitar" Watson, R&B musician

Mary Wells, Motown singer

Thespians of the Pasadena Playhouse

Just a few of the people who studied at the former Pasadena Academy of Dramatic Arts, which was part of the Pasadena Playhouse:

Gig Young, Eve Arden, Margaret O'Brien, John Barrymore Jr., Raymond Burr, Dustin Hoffman, Elaine May, Mare Winningham, Diahann Carroll, Gene Hackman

And the Award Goes to…

The Emmys and the People's Choice Awards were long held at the Pasadena Civic Auditorium and will hopefully return after the remodel is done, allegedly in 2010.

Locals Who Did Cool Stuff:

Charles Richter, inventor of the Richter Scale

Upton Sinclair novelist, author of *The Jungle* and Pasadena resident from 1915 to 1953

Jackie Robinson, first black baseball player in the Major Leagues

Richard Knerr and "Spud" Melin, who created the Hula Hoop, Frisbee and Super Ball

James Jannard, founder of Oakley Eyewear

PCC grad Verne Winchell, the doughnut guy

Bobby Driscoll (1937–1968), child actor who was the model for the cartoon drawing of *Peter Pan*

Well, Define "Cool"…

Bobby Fischer, chess champ and nut job, claims to have been tortured in a Pasadena jail.

Aimee Semple McPherson, sensational evangelist from 1912 until her death in 1944, pioneered radio ministry, built L.A.'s Angelus Temple and had floats in the Rose Parade.

Jack Parsons, the rocket-inventing genius and co-founder of JPL, was also a way-out-there occultist (he called himself the Antichrist) and sexual free spirit. He and L. Ron Hubbard squabbled over Sarah Northrup, who became Mrs. L. Ron #2. Parsons died in an explosion in his home lab in 1952, and JPL prefers not to mention its notorious founding father too often.

Reportedly Did Time in Local Rehab

Robert Downey Jr.

Rush Limbaugh, OxyContin addict

Jack Osbourne, son of Ozzy & Sharon

Kelly Osbourne, daughter of Ozzy & Sharon

Sharon Osbourne, mom of Jack & Kelly

Tom Sizemore, angry actor

One Final Note

W.C. Fields died in Pasadena in 1946 of complications from alcoholism.

Celebrities frequent rehab at Las Encinas.

Hollywood East: Movie & TV Locations

Something is filming almost every day in Pasadena and environs, from a commercial to a big-budget feature film. See those hand-lettered cardboard signs taped to lampposts, with such cryptic messages as "Fish" or "Wagon"? That's code for the crew, and the arrow on the sign is pointing toward the filming location.

Here are some of the most famed locations around town. Most are public places and/or

This Altadena house starred in "Beverly Hills, 90210."

businesses, but a few are private homes. Please do not trespass on private property or disrupt businesses.

Pasadena

380 S. San Rafael. You can't see it very well from the street, but this was Wayne Manor in the TV show "Batman." The nearby brick mansion that burned down in 2005 was often erroneously called "The Batman House." This is the real Batman house.

843 S. El Molino Ave. This colonial was Steve Martin and Diane Keaton's house in both *Father of the Bride* movies.

All Saints Church, 132 N. Euclid St. It was the Harvard quad in *Legally Blonde* and is one of the most popular locations in town; *Cruel Intentions, The Other Sister* and many other movies have been set here.

Caltech campus, 1200 California Blvd. *Legally Blonde* was shot here, and the Athenaeum served as the posh club in the funniest scene in *Beverly Hills Cop.* The Athenaeum is also seen in *The Wedding Planner, Orange County* and "The West Wing."

Castle Green, 99 S. Raymond. Scenes from *Bugsy* were shot here (and see if you can find the house on Grand Ave. that was his house). *The Man with Two Brains, The Sting* and many episodes of "Murder She Wrote" were also filmed here.

Church of the Angels, 1100 Ave. 64. Aston Kutcher got married here in *Just Married,* and it was the location for the "Hellbound" episode of "The X-Files."

City Hall, 100 N. Garfield Ave. This landmark is a notable character in *Beverly Hills Cop,* Charlie Chaplin's *The Great Dictator* (it is Hynkel's Palace), *A Walk in the Clouds* and *Butterfield 8.*

Colorado Street Bridge (Suicide Bridge). Watch closely and you'll see this bridge often in movies, TV shows and commercials. It appeared in one of our faves, *Being John Malkovich;* in Charlie Chaplin's 1921 film *The Kid,* the Little Tramp stops a suicidal young woman from jumping off the bridge.

Cravens Estate, 430 Madeline Dr. This grand brick estate, now the headquarters of the American Red Cross, is the "J.A.G." headquarters and has been in many movies, including *Enemy of the State* and *Traffic.*

Fenyes Mansion, 470 W. Walnut. This was the White House in *Eleanor & Franklin* and was a key location for *Being There.* Now run by the Pasadena Museum of History, it is open for public tours.

The Gamble House, 3 Westmoreland Ave. This was Doc Brown's house in *Back to the Future.*

Kendall Alley. Scenes from *Pulp Fiction, The Sting, Paper Moon* and many others have been shot in this atmospheric Old Town alley.

Mayfield Senior School, 500 Bellefontaine. Scenes in *Devil in a Blue Dress, The Nutty Professor* and *Lost World: Jurassic Park* were shot here, and it served as the hospital in which Roald Dahl's Matilda was born.

Pasadena Central Library, 285 E. Walnut St. This was the law library in *Legally Blonde.*

Prospect Blvd., Pasadena. Many houses on this street have "worked" as film locations, and the tree-lined street is beloved by directors of car commercials.

The Raymond Theatre, 129 N. Raymond Ave. This now-shuttered theater has been the setting for many movies, from *This is Spinal Tap* to *Pulp Fiction.*

The once-world-famous **Busch Gardens** (a 30-acre garden in the **lower Arroyo Seco** developed by beer tycoon Adolphus Busch) was a public attraction from 1905 to 1937; among the many movies filmed there were *Adventures of Robin Hood* and *Gone with the Wind.*

Altadena

1675 E. Altadena Dr. The Walsh family of "Beverly Hills, 90210" lived in this house in the 91001 zip code.

The Altadena Town & Country Club, at Mendocino and Holliston, is a popular filming location. Our favorites are the country-club scenes from HBO's "Curb Your Enthusiasm."

The house on **Rubio Canyon at Maiden Lane** was Tom Cruise's house in *Risky Business.* It's one of the most popular locations in town, having also appeared in *Can't Hardly Wait, The Babysitter's Club, How Stella Got Her Groove Back* and many others.

Arcadia

L.A. County Arboretum. The Arboretum has provided jungles for countless films and TV shows, including *The African Queen,* lots of Tarzan movies (including old Johnny Weissmuller ones), the classic TV show "Fantasy Island," the modern TV show "Invasion" and, of course, 1960's *Attack of the Giant Leeches. Meet the Fockers* also used it as a location.

Santa Anita Racetrack. Much of *Seabiscuit* was shot at this historic racetrack, as were the Marx Brothers' *A Day at the Races* and the great Hitchcock film *Notorious,* starring Cary Grant, Ingrid Bergman and Claude Rains.

Eagle Rock

Occidental College, 1600 Campus Rd. Films shot here include *Jurassic Park III* and the Marx Brothers' *Horse Feathers;* it also served as the college in "Beverly Hills, 90210" and the high school in *Clueless.*

Monrovia

329 Melrose Ave. This was the house in the movie The *House. Mask* also was filmed in Monrovia.

San Marino

Huntington Library, Art Gallery & Gardens, 1151 Oxford Rd. Robert Redford lived here in *Indecent Proposal.* It also was used for the prom scene in *The Hot Chick.*

Sierra Madre

Sierra Madre's town square, at Baldwin and Sierra Madre, was the town square in the 1956 classic *Invasion of the Body Snatchers.*

South Pasadena

1727 Bushnell Ave. This was Michael J. Fox's house in *Teen Wolf* and Marty's mom's house in *Back to the Future.* Bushnell Ave. has been a location for many productions.

1848 Oxley St. Pee-wee lived here in *Pee-wee's Big Adventure;* the neighborhood was his movie neighborhood, too.

The Rialto Theatre, 1023 S. Fair Oaks. This was the murder site in *The Player.*

The horror classic *Halloween* was filmed all around town in 1978 – the Myers house was moved and sits behind Buster's (on Mission), South Pas High served as Haddonfield High, and the Strode House is at 1115 Oxley.

Pee-wee's house

Q & A: Gale Anne Hurd

Movie producer Gale Anne Hurd (the *Terminator* movies, *Aliens* and many other boffo hits) grew up in Beverly Hills and Palm Springs and has lived all over L.A. But when the time came to settle, she and her husband, screenwriter/director Jonathan Hensleigh, chose Pasadena: first a grand villa on San Rafael (the 2003 Showcase House), and now a less-overwhelming-to-maintain 1930s Spanish Revival near the Huntington Hotel. A restaurateur as well as a Hollywood titan, Gale is the proprietor of Old Pasadena's Vertical Wine Bistro, a chic boîte featuring 100 wines by the glass. Colleen talked with Gale over a glass of Syrah in one of Vertical's sleek booths.

What brought you to the San Gabriel Valley?
Westridge School. I was a product of westside schools, and I wasn't eager to have my daughter repeat my experience. We looked at a lot of schools and loved Westridge.

What do you like about living here?
It's such a good family place. And I love the five-minute drive to my daughter's school, as well as the five-minute drive to Vertical. Also, my husband loves that he can be on the slopes at Mountain High in 45 minutes, and be back at work in the afternoon.

You're used to thinking in big-screen, cinematic ways. Do you see Pasadena as cinematic?
Yes, incredibly so. When you enter town from the west and look across the Arroyo, taking in the sweep of the mountains... it's as beautiful a vista as any I've seen in the world.

How is running a restaurant like producing a movie?
The two careers have a lot in common. They both start with a creative vision, and then both the producer and the restaurateur have to assemble a great team, work within budget parameters, and deliver a terrific experience to the customers or audience.

What do you like to do on the weekends?
On Saturdays my daughter takes a golf lesson at Brookside, and I stay to watch – I never get over how beautiful it is. Sometimes we'll go to Huntington Gardens or the Norton Simon, and we like to try different places for Sunday brunch: the Huntington, Villa Sorriso, Holly Street Bar & Grill. And my husband really likes us to go to Dish in La Cañada for breakfast.

Do you have a favorite smell?
Yes – the jasmine, honeysuckle and yellow trumpet flower that's all around my neighborhood. I'd go for walks and just loved those aromas, so now I've planted all of them at my house.

What do you *really* think of the Rose Parade?
We're usually out of town. But I did ride my horse in the parade several years ago, when I was a member of the California Paso Fino Horse Association. I was dressed as a member of Queen Isabella's court, because our horses are descended from the Spanish horses of that time. It was a lot of fun, and my daughter got to watch me in the parade.

Gale Anne Hurd

Pasadena is...

Artistic

From its earliest days, the arts mattered to Pasadena. The Arroyo culture nurtured painters and craftspeople, the colleges fostered a salon society, and wealthy residents – like Henry Huntington, Grace Nicholson, Norton Simon and Arlene and Robert Oltman, founders of the new Pasadena Museum of California Art – gifted us with world-class art and venues in which to view it. In these pages you'll discover our favorite museums, galleries, art classes and local talents. For the musical and theatrical arts, see the Entertaining chapter; for the literary arts, see the Literary chapter.

4 Museums & Why to See 'Em   114

Art Along the Arroyo   118

Rebels with a Cause: 3 Arts Organizations on the Edge   119

Galleries to Visit   120
    Highland Park Art

Art Your Way   123

Q & A: R. Kenton Nelson   124

4 Museums & Why to See 'Em

This 1897 Mary Cassatt painting, *Breakfast in Bed*, is one of many treasures at the Huntington.

The Huntington Library, Art Collections and Botanical Gardens

1151 Oxford Rd., San Marino
626.405.2100, huntington.org
Open Mon. & Wed.-Fri. noon-4:30 p.m., Sat.-Sun. 10:30 a.m.-4:30 p.m.; summer hours extended; adults $15, seniors $12, students $10, kids $6, kids under 5 free

Where to begin? The gardens are discussed in the Horticultural chapter, but upon arriving here, even if your intent is to see only the art collection, you cannot help but take in at least a few of the 150 acres of sloping lawns, vistas and statuary in Henry Huntington's botanical gardens.

The art collections cannot be separated from their three specialized settings. Gleaming from a just-completed $20-million renovation and expansion, the Huntington Gallery is the original home of tycoon Henry Huntington and his wife, Arabella, and was designed by Los Angeles architects Myron Hunt and Elmer Grey from 1909 to 1911. It is resplendent with many, many things of beauty, including a famed collection of 18th-century British art (with Gainsborough's *Blue Boy* among the pieces), lavish French tapestries, Renaissance-era paintings and sculpture, rugs from Louis XIV's redecoration of the Louvre palace, and, in a new display hall, a fifteen-foot-tall stained-glass work created in 1898 by the firm of Morris & Co., formerly housed in a Unitarian chapel in Lancashire, England.

The Virginia Steele Scott Gallery of American Art is a frequent destination for the many fans of the Arts & Crafts era, because it holds a permanent installation (organized in collaboration with the Gamble House) of work by architects Charles and Henry Greene, in addition to three centuries of American art, artifacts and sculpture.

The Erburu Gallery, which opened in 2005, displays the Huntington's recently expanded collection of American art, includ-

Henry and Arabella Huntington's home is now the Huntington Gallery.

ing works by Edward Hopper, Mary Cassatt, Robert Motherwell and John Singer Sargent.

Finally, there is the Huntington Library, which is vast, comprehensive and considered one of the country's finest in each of its specialty fields, including botany, American history, women's studies, science and civil engineering. The five million research items include books, rare books and manuscript collections of such literary notables as Christopher Isherwood and Jack London. The library itself is not open to the public, but qualified scholars may apply for reading privileges, and the Library Exhibition Halls display some of the most precious pieces in the collection, including a copy of the *Gutenberg Bible* and the double-elephant folio edition of *Audubon's Birds of America*.

To do a day at the Huntington right, splurge on tea in the adorable Tea Room. But if time and money are an object, a quick lunch at the Café will make you happy, too.

The Ellesmere Manuscript of Chaucer's *The Canterbury Tales*, circa 1410, at the Huntington Library

Left: *Pinkie*, by Sir Thomas Lawrence, 1794

Norton Simon Museum

411 W. Colorado Blvd., Old Pasadena
626.449.6840, nortonsimon.org
Open Mon., Wed. & Thurs. noon-6 p.m.,
Fri. noon-9 p.m.; adults $8, seniors $4,
students & kids free

Masterpieces by Degas, Monet and Pissarro at the Norton Simon

As many native New Yorkers will tell you, unless it was for a field trip, they never went to the Statue of Liberty until visiting friends dragged them there. Pity the Pasadenan who has missed visiting the Norton Simon Museum because of that same sad civic naiveté (or procrastination). This museum is a rare jewel – it's unpretentious enough in size to walk it in its entirety in a single visit, yet the collection is a world-class dazzler by any standard. The building that houses this extraordinary private collection was designed by architects Thornton Ladd and John Kelsey and opened to the public in November of 1969. Nearly 30 years later, Simon's widow, the Oscar-winning actress Jennifer Jones Simon, charged famed architect Frank Gehry to undertake an interior renovation. He improved the setting for viewing the collection, raised the ceilings, modified the dramatic curved staircase and added the powerful Asian galleries. The very lovely garden was conceived by landscape designer Nancy Goslee Power, who drew inspiration from Monet's gardens at Giverny.

That this museum houses one man's private collection is a fact that should not be lost on visitors while they view 2,000 years of western and Asian art. In an art market where a single Impressionist painting, Vincent Van Gogh's *Portrait of Dr. Gachet*, was purchased in 1990 for $82 million by a Japanese investor, not even Bill

Rodin's *Bergers of Calais* outside the Norton Simon

Gates's money could assemble a collection like this today. From Europe in the 14th century, to the 19th-century Impressionists, to the west's 20th century, to the art of India and Southeast Asia – to see the scope of this collection is to see the world in your backyard.

Note that the simple order-at-the-counter lunch café is blessed with large, umbrella-shaded teak tables on the edge of the fabulous gardens, and you don't have to pay admission just to come for lunch and stroll the grounds. And don't miss the Museum Store, a terrific source for gifts.

Pacific Asia Museum

46 N. Los Robles Ave., Pasadena
626.449.2742, pacificasiamuseum.org
Open Wed.-Sun. 10 a.m.-6 p.m.; adults $7,
students & seniors $5

You know you are close when you see the distinctly Chinese silhouette of the roofline in Pasadena's Playhouse District. This beautiful site – a replica of a building in Beijing's Forbidden City – offers up 5,000 years of art and

Grace Nicholson's former home is now the Pacific Asia Museum.

artifacts from Asia and the Pacific Islands, and it is the only museum in Southern California with such a specialized collection. Commissioned by Grace Nicholson in 1924, the home was built to provide her with a living space upstairs and galleries downstairs for her Asian and Native American art. Longtime Pasadenans will recall that in the 1950s and '60s, this building was the home of the Pasadena Museum of Art, which would later become the Norton Simon.

Today, Pacific Asia sponsors a broad range of changing exhibits: One might see contemporary Korean ceramics, Tibetan secular and religious furniture, *bijinga* (Japanese paintings of beautiful women) or a display of iconography of Buddha.

With its commitment to community relevance, the museum services as many as 10,000 schoolchildren each year and invites hands-on participation in classes ranging from tai ch'i to mah-jongg to Chinese brush painting. And the lovely courtyard and garden with a carp pond is available for rental.

The dynamic modernism of the PMCA

Pasadena Museum of California Art

490 E. Union St., Pasadena
626.568.3665, pmcaonline.org
Open Wed.-Sun. noon-5 p.m.; adults $6, students & seniors $4

First, may we say, three cheers for the on-site free parking – and that is before we even get to the crux of the biscuit: Before PMCA opened in 2002, not one museum in the Golden State was devoted solely to the display of California art. Now we have a dedicated space to showcase the art, architecture and design of California artists from 1850 to the present.

And what a showcase. Founded by Pasadena collectors Bob and Arlene Oltman, this ultra-modern 30,000-square-foot museum was designed by MDA Johnson Favaro Architecture and Urban Design to include gallery space, a community room and bookstore, a rooftop terrace with a dramatic view of Pasadena's domed City Hall and the San Gabriel Mountains – subject of never-ending interest to California's fine plein-air painters. This relatively new addition to Pasadena's historic Playhouse District is a neighbor to the Pacific Asia Museum, and the ambitious art lover might enjoy both museums in one art-filled afternoon.

Art Along the Arroyo

This Joyous World, one of the acclaimed color-block prints by Pasadena artist Frances Gearhart.

Artists came to Pasadena in the nineteenth and early twentieth centuries because of the light and the mountains and the light on the mountains. They were drawn to the area along the Arroyo Seco, with its natural creeks, light filtered through the trees and the amazing purple San Gabriel Mountains in the distance. This was the Land of Sunshine, where poppy and lupine fields abounded, eucalyptus swayed, and brooks meandered through wooded glens. Year-round, artists could set up their easels and paint by the natural light of the sun until it settled beyond the Verdugos. Southern California was home to Impressionism's Indian summer, the last place it flourished, and the artists who settled here developed a kind of California Impressionism, focusing on defined landscapes, capturing light on the canvas using pure colors, and choosing to paint distinctly California subjects.

These artists established a community. Together they trekked to the High Sierras, the beaches and the desert to paint. They formed clubs, such as the California Art Club, or met on a Sunday morning at Benjamin Brown's Pasadena home studio just to talk about art. Some came because of failing health, such as William Lees Judson, the founder of the Judson Studios, who lived to paint for many years. Many of these artists taught at the schools that were being established to serve the growing arts scene: Otis, Chouinard, Los Angeles Art Students League and the Stickley Memorial School of Art in Pasadena.

Among the Pasadena artists, Guy Rose was one of the few who was born locally – on Sunny Slope, the family ranch. (Rosemead was the name of a second Rose family ranch.) The most illustrious of the California Impressionists, Rose studied and lived in Paris and Giverny but eventually returned to paint, exhibit and teach at the Stickley art school. Alson Clark and Jean Mannheim located their home studios on the banks of the Arroyo Seco, where they could start and end each day with the splendor of nature out their doorstep. Both these structures exist today.

Women artists were prominent in the Pasadena art scene. Frances Gearhart became the leading color-block printer of the American West. She depicted stunning landscapes of majestic mountains and vistas with billowy clouds blowing in the skies. Her home and gallery, at the corner of California and Fair Oaks, became a regional meeting place for other printmakers. Ellen Farr favored oils of pepper-tree branches and was a favorite of Colonel Green of the Green Hotel, where she had a gallery. One of her pepper-tree paintings hangs in the lobby of the Castle Green today. Marion Watchel was unparalleled in her ability to create a dreamy mood and tell a story with the fluid sweep of her watercolors.

It was the impressions of light on the California landscape that captivated all these artists and held them here.

– *Susan Futterman*

Rebels with a Cause:
3 Arts Organizations on the Edge

Center for the Arts, Eagle Rock

2225 Colorado Blvd., Eagle Rock
323.226.1617,
centerartseaglerock.org
This joint is jumpin'. A hub of community activity, the Center for the Arts is located in a 1914 building that was once the town's library and is on the National Register of Historic Places. Today, this arts mecca is making its own history, with unbridled dedication and a commitment to partnering with other arts organizations. Multicultural programming is central to

Center for the Arts, Eagle Rock

this fearless and peerless group, and children's classes in arts, music, dance and media arts are a priority. The center produces the excellent annual Route 66 Art Auction, various free festivals, curated shows at its on-site gallery and such temporary public art as "The ROCK Is Art," an installation at the Eagle Rock monument that was seen by more than 200,000 commuters on the 134 Freeway. To our neighbors to the west we say, Rock On!

NewTown

2259 Country Club Dr., Altadena
626.398.9278, newtownarts.org
Founded in 1993, NewTown is an artist-run organization dedicated to taking art to the streets – as well as to the "alleyways, plazas, storefronts, parking lots, a hiking trail in the San Gabriel Mountains, a swimming pool and even a church basement." NewTown has successfully sought grants to endow the work of visionary artists; a good example was "Trail Markers (I & II): What Desert?" in 2001 and 2002, which supported the work of as many as twenty artists at site-specific installations, each with a different water theme. This committed group of artists from diverse fields, including dance, music, painting, video and film, has reached more than 100,000 people, leading the way in a nonprofit resurgence of support for community arts. You gotta love a place that calls itself "a persistent weed in the garden of art."

Pasadena Art Alliance

464 E. Walnut St., Pasadena
626.795.9276, pasadenaartalliance.org
The Pasadena Art Alliance is the gift that keeps on giving to L.A.'s contemporary artists. Haven't heard of it? Don't believe us? Well, how do more than $300,000 in Pasadena Art Alliance grants since 1976 sound? Yep, we were impressed, too. And that number increases to some $3 million when you include funding for exhibitions. They may prefer to shun publicity (they only recently got a web site), but these ladies are no shrinking violets. They first removed the white gloves and dished up the moxie when they started in 1955 to support and raise funds for the cutting-edge Pasadena Art Museum, then housed in today's Pacific Asia Museum. There was no endowment to get them going, just plenty of hard work, dedication and what have long been the grooviest treasure sales and swingingest fund-raisers Pasadena has ever seen or is likely to see.

Once the Pasadena Art Museum became the Norton Simon, the Alliance reinvented itself as a major funder of contemporary visual art in Southern California, from events at the Art Center College of Design, to Projections at AMC theaters, to artrave 9, to establishing the Pasadena Art Alliance Endowment Fund with the Pasadena Community Foundation in honor of its 50th anniversary. We are all the beneficiaries of the vision and dedication shared by these powerhouse women. Long may they reign.

Galleries to Visit

Galleries come in many forms, looking like curated museum exhibits or shops jumbled with canvases; lots of them do double duty as framers, restorers, appraisers and advisors. Ask your dealer about her/his training and interests and what services they provide at what cost. And if you're considering an expensive piece ("expensive" being subjective, of course), ask for a certificate of authenticity. Lots of good art is out there, created by both the schooled and the self-taught, and you need not pay a fortune to acquire a worthy piece – in fact, great finds (again, define "great") are to be had at art schools, yard sales, flea markets and antiques stores.

The best way to educate yourself is to get out and see art, wherever it may be; museums are often free on Friday nights, and galleries are free all the time. Seeing art falls under the category of "stopping to smell the roses." And, ooh, it's so fragrant here in the Rose City.

Please note that we have not listed gallery hours, because they are notoriously fickle; make sure to call before visiting.

A gallery in the Armory

Aarnun Gallery
603 E. Green St., Pasadena
626.793.4805
A fabulous Arts & Crafts stained-glass door leads into this gallery, which is both small and grand. Marcia Nunnery opened Aarnun 30 years ago, and with help from her sister, Barbara Pinna, created a style that is low-key but resplendent with modern California plein-air paintings, detailed woodcut prints from the 1920s and tony antique plates. Marcia reps several fine artists whose pieces are worth a gander even if you're not in the mood to purchase. You can snazz up family photos or flea-market finds with curatorial framing, featuring a handsome selection of woods and Italian tile frames.

The Armory Center for the Arts
145 N. Raymond Ave., Old Pasadena
626.792.5101, armoryarts.org
We remember the Armory as a raucous theater of operations for kiddie classes and birthday parties. It's still that, but it's really much more: a fortress of quality gallery spaces upstairs and down, as well as a magazine casing for fine and manual arts classes for all ages. The three display spaces are the Community Room Gallery, used by local and emerging artists; the Mezzanine Gallery, a misnomer, as it occupies the second and top floor of the building; and the spacious main-floor Caldwell Gallery. Multimedia exhibits rotate in the Caldwell, and a good show is always mounted for Pasadena's semiannual ArtNight series. The interior hub is dedicated

to class and studio space, and the healthy art library upstairs is fitted with overstuffed couches, which simply demand that you sit, relax and read. The Armory also shows art in a jumbo warehouse space at its Armory Northwest branch (965 North Fair Oaks Avenue). And watch for the digital-art forum called Armory at One Colorado, an occasional series featuring videos projected onto an outdoor screen in Old Town's One Colorado courtyard.

Frederic Stern Gallery

Artworks Gallery
59 W. Del Mar Blvd., Pasadena
626.229.0700, artworksinc.com
Clean lines inside this light-filled showroom make for vivid displays of brand-name modern artists. The pop collections do just that and more – they snap, crackle and pop with big, noisy lithographs and etchings, including lots of lithographs by the big boys (Warhol, Lichtenstein, Hockney, etc.). There's an extensive online catalog for your winnowing pleasure.

California Art Club Gallery
The Old Mill, 1120 Old Mill Rd., San Marino
626.449.5458, californiaartclub.org
The historic Old Mill is cool inside, an inviting backdrop for the warm subjects chosen by many of the 300 members of this arts collective. Traditional, representational painting, drawing and sculpting is what they do, with an emphasis on California plein-air painting. The gallery mounts quarterly shows; some pieces are pricey, but good values exist if you act fast. Bonus: Stroll the gardens and peek downstairs to imagine the mill wheel grinding during Mission days. Members have access to the place for receptions.

curve line space
1577 W. Colorado Blvd., Eagle Rock
323.478.9874
This gallery is too sexy for its space, as it morphs from hip gallery to fab scene – pumping up the neighborhood's ever-increasing cool quotient at its openings, which include DJs and bands. The gallery features the graphite drawings so loved by owner Tim Yalda, as well as other comtemporary art, including etchings and monoprints. The back room offers the swanky framing services for which Tim is known.

Frederic Stern Gallery
55 W. Del Mar Blvd., Pasadena
626.792.3320, fredericsterngallery.com
Frederic Stern comes by his interest in art honestly, as the son of prominent L.A. art dealer George Stern and the nephew of dealer

Louis Stern and Irvine Museum director Jean Stern. One could say he went into the family business, and he did so with obvious pleasure and interest. The gallery is a bright, airy space with an emphasis on artists painting in California from the plein-air and postwar periods to the present – Edgar Payne, Conrad Buff, Sam Hyde Harris, Robert Frame, Raimonds Staprans, Shirley Pettibone and Oren Cooper are among the featured artists.

Galerie Gabrie
597 E. Green St., Pasadena
626.577.1223, gabrie.com
Intimate Galerie Gabrie represents European and American painters from the 19th and 20th centuries, as well as representational modern painters, in rotating shows. It hosts lively receptions for international artists, art walks and art lectures. The storefront is deceptively small, and the collections are tasteful and rich.

Haus Gallery
517 S. Sierra Madre Blvd., East Pasadena
626.356.2408, hausgallery.com
Come on-a their haus for modern canvases; on our last visit, we saw geometric shapes in wild blues and purples, unframed and displayed on white walls. This tidy little cottage is located just south of the upscale, traditional furniture store Feddes – but who needs furniture if you can have art?

The Judson Studios
200 S. Ave. 66, Highland Park
323.255.0131, judsonstudios.com
The Judson Studios has been making sacred and traditional stained glass for five generations. Patriarch William Lees Judson, a plein-air painter and early dean of USC's School of Fine Arts, settled in the Arroyo Seco in 1893 and helped found the Arroyo Guild of artists. (Judson expressed the Guild's credo as "simple living, high thinking, pure democracy, genuine art, honest craftsmanship, natural inspiration and exalted aspiration.") The Arroyo Guild did not survive, but the stained glass remains, an example of how the arts collective introduced

beauty through such daily-use objects as windows and doors.

SoPas Gallery
1121 Mission St., South Pasadena
626.441.2339
The South Pasadena Chamber of Commerce was looking to move to a new space and found it on Mission Street. But to be in compliance with the Mission Street Specific Plan, they needed to add a retail component, and the happy result is the SoPas Gallery. A lovely, light-filled space features the work of talented South Pasadena artists in group and individual shows that are curated by neighboring antiques dealer Thomas Field. Artists and patrons, stay tuned, as the gallery anticipates expanding its focus to include artists from the greater San Gabriel Valley.

Tirage Art Gallery
1 W. California Blvd., Pasadena
626.405.1020, tirageart.com
The gallery fronts California, but you enter through the rear parking lot, and from this vantage it looks less like a gallery and more like a cluttered antiques store. But down the stairs it gets busy with stacks and stacks of landscapes, portraits and representational paintings, ranging from the conventional to the adventurous; there's some good stuff here. Check out the bathroom – paintings are everywhere, the way the Barnes Foundation used to display work. Not all prices are listed, so ask.

Underground Arts Society
2475 N. Lake Ave., Altadena
626.794.8779, undergroundartssociety.com
This place is jam-packed with so much local art your head might spin. Hey, is that a painting of my head spinning? Wow, this place is up-to-the-minute. Acrylic and oil paintings, chain-mail and garden sculpture and art furniture are all displayed in a welcoming, "Hey, fire up a fatty and let's put on an art show!" atmosphere. Wander through the kitchen and back garden to see it all, in living color.

Williamson Gallery
Art Center College of Design, 1700 Lida St., Pasadena
626.396.2200, artcenter.edu/williamson
The winding drive up Linda Vista offers grand views of the city as you approach the woods-shrouded campus. Pass under the bridge, and inside a charcoal-glass building you'll find the impressive Alyce de Roulet Williamson Gallery, which displays works by international artists, many of them Art Center alums. Also check out the main student gallery, home to fine student projects, like traditional paintings on canvas and, hooray, lots of experimental art: zippy futuristic cars, kooky board games, toys and funny dinnerware. Much of the undergrads' material embraces the joy and good humor of Art Center's smart students.

Highland Park Art

Exploring the Northeast Los Angeles Arts (NELA), a collective of 22 galleries in Highland Park, makes us feel like we're in New York in the '80s again. Do not miss the second Saturday night of each month, when gallery doors are thrown wide. Especially fantasmic is MorYork, a converted gym that holds massive collections: buttons, pull tops, board games and such, many converted into sculpture or furniture. Future Studio is home to Chicken Boy, with a line of kitschy merch for your gift-giving pleasure. Note that most galleries are not walking distance from each other, and parking can be a challenge. Here are some current faves.

Avenue 50 Studio
131 N. Ave. 50, 323.258.1435, avenue50studio.com

Cactus Gallery
4534 Eagle Rock Blvd., 323.256.6117, eclecticcactus.com

Future Studio
5558 N. Figueroa St., 323.254.4565, futurestudio.com

Kristi Engle Gallery
5002 York Blvd., 323.472.6237, kristienglegallery.com

MorYork Gallery
4959 York Blvd., claregraham.com/MorYork.html

Outpost for Contemporary Art
6375 N. Figueroa St., 323.982.9461, outpost-art.org

Sea and Space Explorations
4755 York Blvd., 323.445.4015, seaandspace.org

Toros Pottery
4962 Eagle Rock Blvd., 323.344.8330, torospottery.com

Young Art
747 N. Ave. 50, 323.344.1322, youngartgallery.com

Art Your Way

The Armory Center for the Arts
145 N. Raymond Ave., Old Pasadena
626.792.5101, armoryarts.org
Part gallery, part community center, the Armory is perhaps best known as a venue for art classes for preschoolers to seniors. The class schedule is both creative and comprehensive. Teens and adults can explore drawing and painting, pottery at the wheel, letterpress typesetting, architectural study, videography and Photoshop. The younger set gets such age-appropriate classes as "Things with Wings," comic-book writing, pop-up book art, building bridges, designing board games and city planning. There's a 10% discount for members (memberships start at $60), plus tuition assistance for those who qualify. Street parking is limited, but you can get a free permit for the lot at the corner of Walnut and Raymond at St. Andrew Church.

Art Center, South Campus
950 S. Raymond Ave., Pasadena
626.396.2319, artcenter.edu
Opened in 2004, Art Center South, located in Caltech's former wind-tunnel research lab, is a generous venue for the public to study design and visual arts. Children through lifelong learners are welcome to sample a gaggle of offerings, including Art Center at Night (adult classes with open enrollment) and Saturday High (the foundations of design for high school students). Sunday afternoon classes develop visual literacy for kids from 4th to 8th grade, and programs for K-12 teachers help them advance the visual arts in the classroom. The campus buildings are a clever compilation of repurposed materials, and the stepped rooftop garden makes for a tranquil perch from which to survey your registration materials.

Farrin O'Connor Design Studio
146 W. Bellevue Dr., Pasadena
626.796.5300, farrinoconnordesign.com
The jewelry-making classes and studio workshops here emphasize the art of hand fabrication. Wax modeling for metal casting is artist Margo Farrin's specialty (look for her intricate bead and brooch designs, on display and for purchase). The teaching staff are exceptional metal artists who show at national galleries, and here they cover a broad range of smithing, wire works, precious-metal clay design, forging, soldering, tool making, bezel settings, stamping methods and more. The

quarterly class schedule has something for all levels; open studio space is available for enrolled students.

Foothill Creative Arts Group
108 N. Baldwin Ave., Sierra Madre
626.355.8350, creativeartsgroup.org
Since 1960, this not-for-profit cooperative group of rotating artists has taught a variety of ten-week classes for adults and kids in drawing, painting, ceramics, sculpture, polymer clay design, paper works, enameling, knitting, jewelry wire wrapping… and since you have to eat, they teach cooking, too. Artists' works for sale are displayed in the gallery.

Xi'em Clay Center
1563 N. Lake Ave., Pasadena
626.794.5833, xiemclaycenter.com
Industrial designer and Art Center grad Kevin Xi'em Nguyen opened shop in 2003 and found an immediate and devout following. Professional ceramics artists teach six-week classes for absolute beginners through advanced potters, in wheel work, tile making and glaze formulation. The new, state-of-the-art building offers members 24/7 access to studio space; there's also a serene gallery with regular exhibitions and openings. Nguyen's own fine work is shown here and at a variety of Los Angeles galleries, and if you're lucky, you can grab one of his pieces at Xi'em's annual studio sale in June.

A student piece outside Xi'em Clay Center

Q & A: R. Kenton Nelson

Artist R. Kenton Nelson paints a regional America in which the ideal is the subject, as in the exaggerated realism of WPA posters (made when real life in America couldn't get much worse). Nelson's vibrant colors, and his shadows that make the light brighter, show off right angles of buildings, or neat folds in the coats and gloves and dungarees of sturdy and invigorated folk who enjoy chores, eat an apple a day, care about penmanship and think Betty Grable is swell. Nelson's scapes, from a perfect Washington Square to the promise that is Bungalow Heaven, are represented by galleries and museums from Salzburg to New York to Los Angeles. Kenton spoke with Sandy in his Pasadena studio.

Have you always been artistic? Composing tableaux while other kids were drawing stick-figure doodles?
In the sixth grade, at Don Benito, a fellow student paid me 50 cents to draw a Coors logo on his notebook, and that was the beginning of my career in art. That summer I made money painting numbers on curbs.

How did you develop your distinct artistic style and sensibility?
Much to my chagrin, in seventh-grade homeroom at John Marshall Junior High here in Pasadena, my teacher found a drawing that I had done of a robust gal in fishnet stockings in my math book. He pulled me aside and asked me to draw one for him. I've spent my life redrawing her.

How has Pasadena changed since you were a kid?
In the '90s, the L.A. Times printed an article "Pasadena – Southern California's Best-Kept Secret." Since then, Pasadena has been "discovered." It's now full of fabulous people with free-range children. It was better when Jan & Dean sang about it.

Say, I've heard of ghosts at the Castle Green – one in the upstairs ballroom, and a lady who walks the hallways. Does your studio have a ghost?
I'll often leave at the end of the day thinking that what I just painted looks good. When I arrive at work the next day, the ghosts have been in my studio and completely ruined what I did the day before.

Which is your favorite arts venue?
The Pasadena Art Museum, now known as the Norton Simon. Grandma took me there to see Warhol's Brillo Boxes in the '60s.

What would you do if you were mayor?
Put that darn train underground, and lose the diagonal cross-walks in Old Town. Also, we're the only city in the world that has roundabouts with stop signs.

What do you *really* think of the Rose Parade?
A wonderful tradition. Wake up at 5:30, hung over or not, bundle up, get a cup of joe, go see the floats and the horses in line on Orange Grove (this is how I was able to meet Bozo the Clown), then go home and watch the parade on TV.

Pasadena is…

Reaching Out

From such grand philanthropists as Arnold and Mabel Beckman to the get-the-job-done volunteers at local churches, Pasadenans have long strived to make the world a better place. To help people both look within and reach out, this community is home to a remarkable range of organizations – churches, shelters, tutoring centers, temples, clinics, senior centers and nonprofits – that do everything from improve the environment to provide eyeglasses for low-income kids.

Nonprofits That Matter   126

13 Spiritual Centers to Know   130

Q & A: Jaylene Moseley   132

Nonprofits That Matter

One of the best reasons to love Pasadena is for the number and reach of its philanthropic organizations, far more than in most other cities of this size. The community has always had challenges to face, from poverty and segregation to abused children and a neglected natural world, and these challenges are met daily by the organizations that follow. If you're a local, consider choosing one to support with your time and/or money; if you're a visitor, please consider contributing to one of the organizations that have helped make the San Gabriel Valley such a green, educated, historically preserved and aesthetically beautiful destination.

AIDS Service Center
909 S. Fair Oaks Ave., Pasadena
626.441.8495, aidsservicecenter.org
First started in the basement of All Saints Church in the '80s, this center is now independent. It is best known for its Posada, a lovely candelit procession that goes from Old Pasadena to City Hall every holiday season. It operates a food pantry, provides case management and HIV testing and offers counseling, transportation and legal services. Volunteers are always needed.

Altadena Foothills Conservancy
altadenafoothills.org
As development has encroached upon the foothills, this conservancy was born to help preserve open land and historic structures, as well as fight for access to long-established hiking trails. It helped a neighborhood create a "pocket oak" area, it's been restoring the Altadena Crest Trail, and at this writing it is almost finished with creating a pocket park at Woodbury and Marengo.

The Arroyo Seco Foundation's Stream Team gets ready for a day of cleanup work in the Arroyo.

Altadena Guild of the Huntington Memorial Hospital
626.304.4678, altadenaguild.org
Since 1951, this group of smart women has raised money to support the research clinics at Huntington Hospital. Its big affair is the annual Altadena Home Tour, attended by everyone who's anyone in Altadena.

Arroyo Seco Foundation
626.304.3417, arroyoseco.org
Founded by Charles Lummis in the 19th century, ASF languished for decades and was reborn in 1989. Today it is a vital organization that has spearheaded efforts to restore the Arroyo watershed, replant native trees and educate the public about the benefits and history of the Arroyo; it also helps with such celebratory events as Lummis Day. Restoration of the Central Arroyo Stream and of Hahamongna Watershed Park are current priorities.

Convalescent Aid Society
3255 E. Foothill Blvd., East Pasadena
626.793.1696, cas1.org
This wonderful group has been laboring in relative obscurity since 1923, and it's trying to get the word out so more people will take advantage of its services. Its mission is to help people recover from illness and surgery in the comfort of their own homes, by providing the free loan of medical equipment: wheelchairs, hospital beds, IV poles, toilet-seat risers, you name it. You can be any age, and you can be rich, poor or in between – as long as you live in the SG Valley the lovely people here will get you everything you need for free. CAS also sponsors nursing scholarships at local colleges, to help improve the quality of health care in the community.

CORAL Pasadena

2750 E. New York Dr., Pasadena
626.808.1770, coralcenter.org
Short for Communities Organizing Resources to Advance Learning, and originally founded by All Saints, CORAL is devoted to educating Pasadena's low-income youth through after-school tutoring, literacy programs and engaging parents in their children's education. It's a great place for high school and college students to volunteer, especially if they hope to become teachers.

El Centro de Accion Social sits in the green space of Pasadena's Central Park.

El Centro de Accion Social

37 E. Del Mar Blvd., Pasadena
626.792.3148, elcentropasadena.org
Another fine organization dedicated to educating low-income kids, via after-school tutoring (held at La Pintoresca Library, Jefferson Elementary and its colorful center in Central Park, right), youth groups and summer school; it also trains kids to run the L.A. Marathon. And it runs a terrific program for the elderly poor, Villa Parke Senior Network. It always needs kind and patient volunteers.

Five Acres

760 W. Mountain View St., Altadena
626.798.6793, 5acres.org
Founded as an orphanage in 1888, Five Acres now focuses on preventing child abuse and helping victims of abuse. Many of the children it helps live and attend school on the pretty, green Altadena campus; others are placed in foster homes or are guided through the adoption process. Because of the abuse and/or neglect they've suffered, some of these kids are severely disturbed, but Five Acres takes pride in its success rate with both emotional recovery and academic education. It's one of the most worthy organizations in the region, and its needs are many, from foster parents and tutors to financial donations and "angels" – people who provide birthday parties and other fun extras for these kids.

Flintridge Foundation

1040 Lincoln Ave., Pasadena
626.449.0839, flintridgefoundation.org
This local foundation was created via the estate of Francis and Louisa Moseley, longtime residents of Pasadena and La Cañada. Although it funds an array of wonderful things, with an overall mission of encouraging individualism, diversity, creativity, a sustainable earth and social justice, it is best known for helping nonprofits help themselves. Flintridge runs a free staffed library to help groups conduct grant research and seek support, and it provides such resources as grant-seeking classes, consulting and meeting space for local nonprofits.

Foothill Family Service

2500 Foothill Blvd., Ste. 300, Pasadena
626.564.1613, foothillfamily.org
Child, teen and family mental health is the mission of this well-established nonprofit, which serves some 18,000 individuals and families at its centers and at 83 schools in the greater San Gabriel Valley area. Understanding and respecting cultural diversity is key to the work here, and counselors speak a dozen languages. Its work is supported by Friends of Foothill Family, a great group of women who raise money, provide filled back-to-school backpacks and organize a holiday season Adopt-a-Family program.

Grace Center

626.355.4545, grace-center.org
A homegrown organization founded in 1996, Grace Center provides shelter, food, legal services and other (bilingual) aid to abused women and children in the San Gabriel Valley. It needs lots of volunteer aid, from courtroom translators to gardeners who can help with its lovely garden. Grace recently merged with Five Acres.

Habitat for Humanity
770 N. Fair Oaks Ave., Pasadena
626.792.3838, sgvhabitat.org
Our very own Extreme Home Makeover, this
affiliate of the international organization has built
36 homes for more-than-deserving families right
here in the SG Valley. And it's also helped build
houses from Mexico to Sri Lanka. Volunteer aid
of every kind is put to excellent use, from making
lunch for the construction crews to helping build
a house yourself (no experience needed).

Moms learn while the kids play at Mothers' Club.

Hathaway-Sycamores
626.395.7100, hathaway-sycamores.org
Both Hathaway and the Sycamores were
orphanages, and now the two have merged to
further their mission of improving the mental
health of children in the San Gabriel Valley,
offering everything from residential treatment
and foster care to in-home therapy and after-
school enrichment classes. It provides services
at several locations, including the Sycamores'
five-acre, tree-shaded campus in Altadena.
Volunteers help with mentoring, tutoring and
office work.

Hillsides
940 Ave. 64, Pasadena
323.254.2274, hillsides.org
A safe and nurturing haven for children from
dangerous and/or troubled homes, Hillsides is
a peaceful seventeen-acre residential facility,
school and resource center. Its specialty is
helping emotionally disturbed children improve
their coping, social and academic skills, and it's
one of few places that help find housing, work
and schooling for newly emancipated foster kids
who are kicked out of the foster-care system
at 18, typically with few skills to take care of
themselves.

Junior League of Pasadena
149 S. Madison Ave., Pasadena
626.796.0244, jrleaguepasadena.org
This has been Pasadena's blue-blood
philanthropic organization since its founding in
1926 – but it ain't your mother's Junior League.
While today's group still has plenty of country-
club gals as members, it also has working
women, and Junior Leaguers are increasingly
diverse. Famed for its cookbooks (like the new
California Mosaic), this group also raises money
through a couple of social fundraising events
each year, and it trains volunteers to go out into
the community and make a difference. In recent
years it has been focusing on programs for
middle-school girls in the San Gabriel Valley, as
well as the intensive and rewarding Done in a
Day community-service projects.

Mothers' Club Family Learning Center
980 N. Fair Oaks Ave., Pasadena
626.792.2687, mothersclub.org
Established by a retired teacher and Quaker
who saw the challenges faced by young, poor,
isolated mothers in Northwest Pasadena,
Mother's Club is a lifeline for many local women.
It combines a quality preschool for children with
education and support for the mostly Latina
moms, with classes in English, parenting skills,
career planning and more. The volunteer needs
are many, from computer tutors for the moms to
teacher's assistants in the preschool.

National Charity League San Marino
nclsanmarino.org
"Mothers and daughters serving communities
together" is this high-society group's mission
statement, and indeed, the group accomplishes
a lot more than just the famous debutante ball.
Via fund-raisers and hands-on volunteerism,
these teenage girls and middle-aged moms
provide scholarships for young women and help
a variety of SG Valley nonprofits, from Union
Station to Huntington Hospital.

Night Basketball & Books
626.304.0141, nbab.org
Originally run by All Saints Church, NBAB is
now an independent operation. What started
as a few adults shooting hoops with kids whose
other recreational options were gangs and drugs
has grown into a vibrant program that combines
tutoring, mentoring and sports. It's made a real
difference in a lot of lives. NBAB needs volunteer
tutors, coaches, grant writers and more.

Pasadena Heritage

Pasadena Educational Foundation
351 S. Hudson Ave., Pasadena
626.795.6981, x 595, pusd.us
Supporting public education in Pasadena is the
mission of this group, whose board comprises
some of Pasadena's best and brightest. It raises
a good amount of money to support the schools,
and it acts as a portal for volunteers and for
businesses looking to "adopt" a neighborhood
school.

Pasadena Heritage
651 S. St. John Ave., Pasadena
626.441.6333, pasadenaheritage.org
The second largest preservation group in
California, Pasadena Heritage has played a big
part in saving and showcasing the city's best
assets, from Old Town to the Colorado Street
Bridge to the Huntington Hotel. It sponsors two
outstanding events, the nationally renowned
Craftsman Heritage Weekend in October and
the Celebration on the Colorado Street Bridge
in July, and it organizes all sorts of architectural
tours. It always needs volunteers to be event
workers, home-tour docents and, for its newest
and most wonderful of programs, interviewers
for its Oral History Project.

Pasadena Humane Society
361 S. Raymond Ave., Pasadena
626.792.7151, phsspca.org
Created in 1903 to care for animals, this
remarkable organization serves several cities
in the west San Gabriel Valley, offering animal
control, pet adoption and training classes, all
through a beautiful facility just south of Old
Town. Its September Wiggle Waggle Walk is a
local highlight. Volunteer opportunites include
making pet beds and helping with the animals
on-site; the volunteer programs for teenagers
are terrific.

Pasadena Showcase House for the Arts
626.578.8500, pasadenashowcase.org
Every year, a swarm of designers transforms
an already-fabulous Pasadena mansion into
an interior- and landscape-design showpiece,
and thousands of house junkies pony up
good money to tour the property. The money
raised supports 40-plus music education and
appreciation programs, from band instruments
for Pasadena High to music-therapy classes
at Five Acres. The causes are worthy, and the
houses are always great fun to explore.

Union Station Foundation
626.240.4550, unionstationfoundation.org
Union Station serves Pasadena's homeless,
providing food, shelter, counseling, job-seeking
help and much more. It runs several facilities,
including the Adult Center on Raymond near
Central Park; the Family Center, which serves
homeless children and their parents; and Euclid
Villa, a transitional facility for families striving
to achieve stability. It has a pressing need for
volunteers, especially to help cook meals; lots of
locals help with the Thanksgiving and Christmas
Dinner-in-the-Park events.

Young & Healthy
37 N. Holliston Ave., Pasadena
626.795.5166, youngandhealthy-pas.org
Health care for uninsured and under-insured
children is the mission of this terrific group. It
convinces physicians, optometrists, dentists
and therapists to donate their time, and local
pharmacists donate medications; Y&H even gets
free eyeglasses for kids who need them. It also
offers parent-ed classes in nutrition and health.
Volunteer medical professionals are in demand,
as are people to help with both transportation
and translation.

One of many residents looking for a friend at the
Pasadena Humane Society

13 Spiritual Centers to Know

This is by no means a comprehensive list of churches, temples and mosques; we can't possibly mention every worthwhile house of worship. But we felt compelled (by some unknown force!) to introduce you to some of the spiritual leaders in our part of the world.

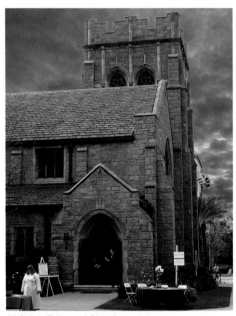

All Saints Episcopal Church

All Saints Episcopal Church
132 N. Euclid Ave., Pasadena
626.796.1172, allsaints-pas.org
Combining high-church Episcopalian pomp with liberal social activism, All Saints draws occasional national attention, like its run-in with the IRS over its tax-exempt status. It's been a longtime leader in Pasadena, starting and then spinning off a number of excellent nonprofits, from Union Station to Young & Healthy. Offerings include frequent services, a fantastic children's choir program, Sunday-school classes, adult education that brings in speakers from all walks of life, youth activities, social-justice programs and ministries for all sorts of groups, from gays and lesbians to diabetics to seniors.

First Congregational Church of Pasadena
464 E. Walnut St., Pasadena
626.795.0696, uccpasadena.org
A member of the United Church of Christ, this grand and beautiful church is home to a liberal Christian congregation that meets on Sundays

for worship services. It also hosts classes and a choir for children, a Lambda group for gay and lesbian congregants and a Justice and Peace outreach ministry.

Holy Family Church
1527 Fremont Ave., South Pasadena
626.799.8908, holyfamily.org
A huge and vibrant Catholic community, Holy Family attracts parishioners from well outside its parish boundaries, thanks in no small part to the dynamic leadership of Monsignor Clem Connolly. The church runs a highly regarded parochial school, a bookstore, lots of outreach programs (food for the homeless, fair-trade merchandise, social-justice activism and a commitment to a community in Haiti), bible study, social events and, of course, plenty of masses.

La Cañada Presbyterian
626 Foothill Blvd., La Cañada
818.790.6708, laCañadapc.org
There's never a dull moment at this big, bustling church, which hews to mainstream Presbyterian doctrine. It sponsors an exceptional roster of outreach programs, from house building in Tijuana to feeding homeless folks locally, and its social and volunteer programs for kids and teens are terrific. The parent-ed classes are also a big draw.

Lake Avenue Church
393 N. Lake Ave., Pasadena
626.844.4700; lakeavefamily.org
Pasadena's Christian megachurch occupies almost an entire city block just north of the 210 Freeway, and something is always going on here, from community meetings to huge worship services to lively teen gatherings. A theologically conservative place, it offers a lot of local and international outreach programs, which emphasize evangelicalism as much as helping the needy.

Masjid Gibrael
1301 E. Las Tunas Dr., San Gabriel
626.285.2573, masjidgibrael.org
This growing Islamic mosque has been

improving itself, adding a minaret, classroom space and a larger prayer room. Besides providing a venue for daily prayer, it offers children's Arabic classes and such special events as post-Ramadan potlucks.

Neighborhood Unitarian-Universalist Church

301 N. Orange Grove Blvd., Pasadena
626.449.3470, uuneighborhood.org
A place of peace and thoughtfulness, this longtime Unitarian church occupies a beautiful campus next door to the Gamble House. In Unitarian fashion, the services draw on many traditions, from Christianity to Buddhism. Neighborhood sponsors excellent music, youth education and social-justice programs, and it also serves as the home for Pasadena Pro Musica. The adult-education classes (ranging from sustainable living to a survey of world religions) are often worthwhile.

Pasadena Buddhist Church

1993 Glen Ave., Pasadena
626.798.4781, janet.org
Established in 1948, this Buddhist temple, complete with a serene teahouse in the garden, has Sunday-morning services in English, followed by classes in both English and Japanese. It sponsors a lovely Obon Festival every summer to honor the memories of the deceased.

Pasadena Church of God

404 E. Washington Blvd., Pasadena
626.794.2951, pasadenachurch.com
This predominately African-American church has a more modern vibe than the old-line AME and Baptist churches – it's made a commitment, for instance, to the American Cancer Society's Body & Soul campaign aimed at black churches, so fruit and granola bars are served after Sunday school instead of doughnuts. Sunday services are held at Pasadena High School (2925 East Sierra Madre Boulevard, East Pasadena), but smaller-group activities, from teen nights to bible study, take place at the offices.

Pasadena Jewish Temple & Center

1434 N. Altadena Dr., Pasadena
626.798.1161, pjtc.net
Although this temple is technically allied with the conservative movement, it honors a diverse range of Jewish belief and practices and has a hip young rabbi. It's a busy and engaged community, with a strong adult-education schedule, events for young families, a full roster of Shabbat and holiday services and good community-service groups, from the Green Committee to the United Synagogue Youth program for high school kids.

Saint Anthony's Greek Orthodox Church

778 S. Rosemead Blvd., East Pasadena
626.449.6943, saint-anthonys.org
A community center as much as a church, Saint Anthony's offers everything from Greek folk dance and Greek school to youth groups and traditional bible study. Liturgies are held weekdays and Sundays. Its fall Greek Fest is a great party for the whole town, with Greek food, music and dance.

Self-Realization Fellowship Temple

150 N. El Molino Ave., Pasadena
626.683.3963
Meditation, prayer and yogic concentration are at the center of this spiritual practice, which helps people find a direct and personal experience of God. Meditations, lecture services and Sunday school for children are hosted on Sundays, with prayer and meditation services on Thursdays and Fridays, too. This is a kind and gentle place.

Temple Sinai of Glendale

1212 N. Pacific Ave., Glendale
818.246.8101, temple-sinai.net
This welcoming Reform temple draws people from all over Pasadena and Altadena as well as Glendale and Eagle Rock. It's home to Shabbat services, lots of bar and bat mitzvahs on Saturdays, Hebrew school and good opportunities for community service, from Habitat for Humanity homebuilding to holiday toy drives.

Neighborhood Church

Q & A: Jaylene Moseley

Pasadena has more philanthropists than you can shake a rose bush at, but few who combine their business with their commitment to doing the right thing as seamlessly as Jaylene Moseley. Jaylene is both president of the JL Moseley Company, a real estate development firm working to revitalize Northwest Pasadena and Altadena, and director of the Flintridge Foundation, which helps community-based nonprofits. Her latest for-profit venture, the NW Innovation Center, turned a shabby old concrete tilt-up into a state-of-the-art, environmentally friendly office building. Colleen talked to Jaylene in the Flintridge Foundation's Philanthropy Resource Library.

Where did you grow up, and how did you end up in Pasadena?

I grew up in Big Timber, Montana, which had 1,000 residents. I didn't leave Montana until I was 20, when I decided to see all 50 states. I worked when I needed money; I made it to 45 states in five years. But then I ended up staying in California, because I like its diversity and its progressive and creative people. I was just lucky in picking Pasadena.

Why do you think your real estate developments have been successful?

I walk door to door to talk to everyone about what they want in their neighborhoods – I've spent a lot of time sitting on front porches! My goal is to develop real estate in order to develop community. We make money, but I also tell my investors that part of the return is a social return.

And your philosophy of philanthropy – how would you sum that up?

People know what they need, so you have to respect them and hear them. When we were planning the Lincoln development, I asked a group of Muir High students to come in and tell me what was wrong with Lincoln Avenue and what would improve it. One of the girls said, "Who cares? No one wants us anyway," and all the other kids nodded in agreement. They felt abandoned by their own neighborhood. I was just stunned. So I helped them start a group called Mustangs on the Move, and they've set up after-school enrichment, tutoring and college-prep programs and made the campus more accessible. The kids did it, and it cost the school nothing; the Flintridge Foundation helped pull together other nonprofits to help, and we provide funding.

What would you do if you were mayor?

I would love to be mayor. It must be an incredibly demanding role. My number-one priority would be to establish an agenda that promotes using the city's resources to bring everyone up to an equal standard.

What do you *really* think of the Rose Parade?

The last time I went to the Rose Parade was the same year I went to the parade in Big Timber, when I was visiting my grandmother. That parade is mostly tractors, combines and all the kids in town waving to their parents. The contrast between that and the Rose Parade was really something. But the enthusiasm was exactly the same in both towns.

Pasadena is...

Hungry & Thirsty

From Chinese Islamic restaurants to Oaxacan cafés, steakhouses to sushi bars, the San Gabriel Valley is a gourmand's paradise.

A User's Guide to Food & Drink   134

Our Favorite Restaurants   135

World Cuisine in the SG Valley   146

Breakfast & Lunch Cafés   149

Best Barbecue   153

Exploring America's Great Chinatown   154

    A Dumpling Lunch with Carl Chu   156

Eat 'n' Run: Fast Food, Pizza, Tacos & Takeout   157

Good Eats: Bakeries & Markets   162

Party Time   166

Farmer's Markets   167

14 Coffeehouses that Aren't Starbucks   168

Tea Time   170

The Drinking Life   171

    5 Great Happy Hours   173

Wine Shops We've Known & Loved   174

Q & A: Nicole Grandjean   176

A User's Guide to Food & Drink

Price Chart
Price symbols are based on the range of most dinner entrees, as follows (for one dinner main dish, or lunch if dinner isn't offered):

$	Less than $12
$$	$13-18
$$$	$19-27
$$$$	$28-up

A Note About Chains
With a few exceptions, we don't tell you about the chains, because chances are you already know them. Just be aware that if you're craving Baja Fresh, California Pizza Kitchen, Cheesecake Factory, Islands, Outback Steakhouse, P.F. Chang's or Ruth's Chris, we've got 'em all. And if it's Starbucks you want, just throw a rock and you'll hit one. (But please try one of our fine independent coffeehouses.)

Good Values
The following give good bang for the buck in their category.

Café Bizou, pg. 136
Daisy Mint, pg. 146
Dish, pg. 138, 149
Dumpling Master, pg. 154
Lebanese Kitchen, pg. 147
Los Gringos Locos, pg. 141
Mei Long Village, pg. 155
Pho 79, pg. 148
Saladang, pg. 143
Song, pg. 144
Taylor's Steakhouse, pg. 144
Tonny's, pg. 144
Zankou Chicken, pg. 161

Open Late
Unless noted, the following are open until at least midnight, often later on weekends. You also can get late-night food at many bars and coffeehouses.

Casa Bianca, pg. 158
Crepe Vine, pg. 137
Doña Rosa, pg. 149
In-N-Out, pg. 157
King Taco, pg. 159
La Estrella, pg. 159
Los Tacos, pg. 160
Lucky Boy, pg. 157
Puebla Tacos, pg. 160
Rick's Drive-In, pg. 158
Taco trucks, pg. 160
The York, pg. 173

The Greatest Hits
Every place in this chapter is recommended, but if you don't have time to try them all, here are our don't-miss favorites in all sorts of categories:

Atmosphere: Parkway Grill, pg. 142
Bakery: Euro Pane, pg. 149, 162
Barbecue: Zeke's, pg. 153
Breakfast: Dish, pg. 138, 149
Breakfast burrito: Lucky Boy, pg. 157
Burger: Tops, pg. 158
Caterer: Auntie Em's, pg. 166
Chinese dumplings: Din Tai Fung, pg. 154
Chinese gourmet: Yujean Kang's, pg. 145
Chinese seafood: Ocean Star, pg. 155
Coffeehouse: Zephyr, pg. 169
Coffee-to-go: Jones Coffee Co., pg. 168
Fine dining: Derek's Bistro, pg. 137
French: Maison Akira, pg. 141
Gastropub: The York, pg. 173
Happy hour: Twin Palms, 173
Ice cream: Bulgarini Gelato, pg. 162
Lunch: Julienne, pg. 150
Lunch (secret spot): Norton Simon, pg. 151
Italian: Celestino, pg. 137
Market: 99 Ranch Market, pg. 165
Mexican: La Cabanita, pg. 140
Mexican gourmet: Babita Mexicuisine, pg. 135
Newcomer: Palate Food & Wine, pg. 142
Pizza: Casa Bianca, pg. 158
Pasadena charm: The Raymond, pg. 143
Romantic: Amori, pg. 135 & Derek's, pg. 137
Salad: Green Street, pg. 150
Sandwiches: Lovebirds, pg. 150
Soul food: Angelena's, pg. 135
Special occasion: The Dining Room, pg. 138
Steakhouse: Arroyo Chop House, pg. 135 & Taylor's, pg. 144
Sushi: Oba Sushi Izakaya, pg. 142
Taco joint: Señor Fish, pg. 160
Tapas: Three Drunken Goats, pg. 144
Thai: Song, pg. 144
Unusual ethnic: Tibet Nepal House, pg. 148
Vegetarian/vegan: Fatty's, pg. 138
Wine shop: Mission Wines, pg. 174

Our Favorite Restaurants

The restaurants that follow range from the modest to the opulent, the cutting-edge to the comforting, and we love 'em all.

Amori
110 E. Lemon Dr., Monrovia
626.358.1908
French/Californian. L Tues.-Fri., D Tues.-Sun. Beer & wine. $$-$$$
This aptly named place is intimate and warm, with mustard-colored walls, a long banquette and soft lighting. Chef/owner Pedro Simental cooked for Shiro, which explains his Asian-French fusion style. He also ran the kitchen across the street at Devon, so he knows what the serious diners in this neighborhood want. He particularly shines with seafood: penne with shrimp and a light smoked-salmon sauce, sea scallops with a lemon-garlic-butter sauce, and the whole deep-fried catfish with ponzu sauce that put Shiro on the map. A superb place for a romantic, memorable meal.

Angelena's Signature Southern Cuisine
33 W. Main St., Alhambra
626.284.7685
Southern. B, L & D daily (Fri.-Sat. to 1 a.m.). No booze. $
Once you pass by the diners outside and through the big glass door, the aroma of serious soul food grabs and won't let go: the steaming vegetables, the scent of hot cornbread, the fragrance of crisping chicken, the tang of barbecue. The ambience is sleek and welcoming, too, with R&B, blues and Motown piped in to keep things lively. What's to eat? Cornbread that resembles a buttermilk cake, butter beans that melt in your mouth and the absolute best collard greens we've ever tasted – not bitter, almost sweet. Our only regret: We couldn't possibly save room for the red velvet cake. But we're going back soon for the catfish special, and the yams, and the black-eyed peas, and the hush puppies...

Arroyo Chop House
536 S. Arroyo Pkwy., Pasadena
626.577.7463
American/steakhouse. D nightly. Full bar. $$$$
Captains-of-industry comfort food is served in a modern setting that would have put Henry Huntington at ease: white linens, etched glass, rich mahogany, Craftsman-influenced chairs and light fixtures, a discreet pianist. Prime steak is the specialty, and most of the time it is cooked as ordered; the New York strip is particularly good. Sides are simple and carefully prepared (asparagus, spinach with caramelized sweet onions, garlic mashed potatoes), drinks are mixed well, and if you have room for dessert (we never do), get the chocolate soufflé.

Babita Mexicuisine
1823 S. San Gabriel Blvd., San Gabriel
626.288.7265
Mexican. L Tues.-Fri., D Tues.-Sun. Beer & wine. $$-$$$
It looks like a dive from the outside, but inside Babita is inviting, with crisp white linens and romantic charm. But no one comes for the setting – they come for owner/chef Roberto Berrelleza's regional Mexican cooking with a Oaxacan focus. He is a serious chef who makes seriously good Yucatecan cochinita pibil, filet mignon with a pimenta-mint sauce, habanera-blazed camarones topolobampo (he'll tone down the heat if you ask) and perhaps the best flan anywhere. Regulars often drive across town just for his chiles en nogada, a fall-only specialty of pork with dried fruit, pecans, roasted chile, cream sauce and pomegranate seeds. The food is sometimes slow to appear, because of Berrelleza's personal attention to every dish.

Bahooka
4501 N. Rosemead Blvd., Rosemead
626.285.1241, geocities.com/bahookarestaurant
Polynesian. L & D daily. Full bar. $$
Release your inner tiki god with a vat-sized flaming tropical cocktail and a pupu platter at this Gilligan's Island of a restaurant. Kids love it, too.

Bashan
3459 N. Verdugo Rd., Glendale
818.541.1532, bashanrestaurant.com
French. D Tues.-Sun. Beer & wine. $$$-$$$$
The space that held Bistro Verdu now holds Bashan, which doesn't look anything like its predecessor; it's sleekly modern, with concrete floors and make-a-statement hanging fixtures. Owner/chef Nadav Bashan cooked at Michael's and Providence, and though his eponymous new spot is more modest in setting, his cooking remains every bit as ambitious. He does remarkable things with farmers' market produce and is also a master of fish dishes – if a barramundi preparation is on the menu, try it. This is destination cooking in an unlikely

destination, with the warmth and (slightly) lower prices of a neighborhood restaurant. The wine list is good, but there are lots more to choose from at neighboring shop Rosso, and corkage is just $5 for Rosso wines. It can be uncomfortably noisy on busy weekends but is usually quiet on weeknights.

Bistro 45's grilled Kurobuta pork tenderloin in a blood-orange marinade, with glazed carrots, Dijon potatoes and grilled balsamic onions

Bistro de la Gare

921 Meridian Ave., South Pasadena
626.799.8828
French. B Sat.-Sun., L Wed.-Sun., D Wed.-Sun. Beer & wine. $$-$$$
We really want to like this new place – it's got a wonderful bistro decor, a traditional French-bistro menu, a mostly French staff, a hip South Pas location and rooms filled with well-dressed locals. But as of this writing, it's not quite right. The fries are undercooked, the entrecôte is overcooked, and the service is inauthentically slapdash (no Parisian bistro waiter would ask, "Who gets the fish?"). But we'll hold out hope for improvement, because the potential is terrific.

Bistro 45

45 S. Mentor Ave., Pasadena
626.795.2478, bistro45.com
French/modern American. L Tues.-Fri., D Tues.-Sun. Full bar. $$$$
Bistro 45, Derek's Bistro and the Dining Room at the Huntington are currently duking it out for the title of Best Upscale Restaurant in the San Gabriel Valley. If you want a livelier buzz and a (just slightly) lower tab, pick Bistro 45, where Pasadena's beautiful people congregate, either on the patio for lunch or in the suavely modern dining rooms (polished wood floors, white linens, fresh flowers) for dinner. Owner and man-about-town Robert Simon takes great pride in his wine list, which is exemplary, if short on less-expensive choices. The cooking of chef Damon Brady, who has run this kitchen

for nearly a decade, is creative and confident: braised veal short ribs with Asian five spice; grilled lamb salad with fingerling potatoes, roquefort, watercress and a Provençal dressing; a superb grouper served bouillabaisse style. If the pastry chef is making the chocolate brioche bread pudding with red currant ice cream, by all means order it.

Briganti

1423 Mission St., South Pasadena
626.441.4664, brigantisouthpas.com
Italian. L Mon.-Fri., D nightly. Beer & wine. $$-$$$
Sleepy South Pasadena is at last becoming a food-lover's town, and the latest of its new restaurants is one of its best. Briganti is the sort of lively Tuscan trattoria that's common on the westside but rare on the eastside, and locals can't get enough of its seafood salad, burrata with pesto and roasted tomatoes, ethereal thin-crust pizzas, classic pastas, excellent fresh-fish specials, and a lovely flourless chocolate cake. The joint is always jumping, with noise bouncing off the brick walls and handsome waiters dashing hither and thither, and everyone seems to be having a great time.

Café Beaujolais

1712 Colorado Blvd., Eagle Rock
323.255.5111
French. D Tues.-Sun. Beer & wine. $$-$$$
A traditional French bistro with Eagle Rock flair – the slogan is "Everything French, even the attitude." Except the only attitude we've seen from the black-T-shirted French waiters is an informal, witty warmth. They deliver green salads topped with goat cheese croutons, crocks of onion soup, escargots, steak frites with some of the best fries in the region, heavenly apple and banana tarte tatins, and affordable bottles of Côtes du Rhône. The good cooking, moderate prices and relaxed charm keep the place packed with a wonderfully diverse crowd. Local jazz musicians play on Wednesday nights.

Café Bizou

91 N. Raymond Ave., Old Pasadena
626.792.9923, cafebizou.com
Modern American. L Tues.-Fri., D nightly, brunch Sun. Full bar. $$-$$$
Upscale style at a moderate price keeps this Old Town place packed. Many non-seafood entrees are less than $18, and salad or soup (try the carrot-rosemary) is just $1 with any entree. We always get the monkfish on saffron-shrimp risotto with a lobster sauce, but the roast chicken with fries, the seafood with black tagliolini, and the pepper steak are all good.

Celestino

141 S. Lake Ave., Pasadena
626.795.4006
Italian. L Mon.-Fri., D Mon.-Sat. Beer & wine.
$$-$$$
The SG Valley's most consistently excellent
Italian restaurant, Celestino combines warm
service and a serious wine list with downright
delicious food. Don't miss the baby lettuces with
roasted peppers, eggplant and goat cheese;
the black and white tagliolini with scallops and
saffron sauce; the gnocchi quattro formaggi; and
the whole grilled branzino. The pastas are terrific.

L to R: Salvatorre Attanasio, owner Calagero Drago
and Mario Tello of Celestino

Columbo's

1833 Colorado Blvd., Eagle Rock
323. 254.9138
Italian/American. B Sat.-Sun., L & D daily.
Full bar. $$-$$$
Columbo's is an Eagle Rock institution, a 1950s
Italian steakhouse where fans of time travel
worship red-checkered tablecloths, padded
booths and slow service. Do yourself a solid
and just relax (and remember the bar's motto,
"Our standard drink is a double.") The matriarch
occupies the back booth most nights, sipping
her gimlet and listening to the terrific old-school
jazz duos and soloists, playing chill Rat Pack
and Cole Porter tunes. When it's time to stop
drinking and eat, order the garlic bread, the good
calamari and tasty handmade pastas (try the
pesto), but beware the steaks. Wine lovers note
that there's no corkage for bottles brought in
from nearby Colorado Wine Company.

Crepe Vine Bistro & Wine Bar

36 W. Colorado Blvd., Old Pasadena
626.796.7250, thecrepevine.com
French. L & D Tues.-Sun. Beer & wine. $$
Tasty, moderately priced wine by the glass,
onion soup, fondue, crepes both savory and
sweet . . . ooh la la, it's the French bistro Old
Town's been waiting for. Both the service and
the atmosphere are *très charmant.*

Crocodile Café

140 S. Lake Ave., Pasadena
626.449.9900
American. L & D daily. Beer & wine. $-$$
It seems like only yesterday that the bright,
casual Crocodile was fresh and hip. Now it's
become an old standby, but it still satisfies. Best
bets are the big salads, the California pizzas,
the grilled flank steak and the easygoing,
inexpensive wines. Good kids' menu.

Derek's Bistro

181 E. Glenarm Ave., Pasadena
626.799.5252, dickensonwest.com
Modern American. D Tues.-Sat. Full bar. $$$$
Hidden in a strip mall that looks like it would
house a taco joint, Derek's is Pasadena's swank
secret. Intimate nooks, luxe table settings and
lovely flowers make this one of the most romantic
restaurants in town. Irish-born
Derek Dickenson, who's
also an acclaimed
caterer, knows what
Pasadenans like
to eat after a hard
day of insider trading, and
he delivers the goods: seared foie gras with
a kumquat marmalade, fresh oysters, beef
Wellington, wild salmon with lentils, bacon and
a mustard beurre blanc, and rich, chocolaty
desserts. Excellent, if pricey, wine list, with a
great choice of beers, too. The private room is a
swell place for a dinner party.

Devon

109 E. Lemon Ave., Monrovia
626.305.0013
Modern American. L Tues.-Fri., D Tues.-Sun.
Full bar. $$$
Old Town Monrovia became a foodie destination
with the arrival of this serious restaurant in a
former carriage house, furnished with high-
backed black-lacquered chairs and a dynamic
bent-copper-tube lighting sculpture. Wild game
is a specialty – perhaps caribou with morel
sauce or quail stuffed with a lamb mousse –
but it doesn't have to be wild to be good, as
evidenced by the artichoke salad with French
feta and the dry-aged rib-eye with a port sauce.
Desserts are challenging, often featuring herbs
and unusual combinations, and the wine list is
very good, if pricey. Worth a trip to Monrovia.

Devon's interior sets the stage for a seriously good meal.

The Dining Room

Langham Huntington Hotel
1401 S. Oak Knoll Ave., Pasadena
626.568.3900
Modern American/French. D Tues.-Sat. Full bar.
$$$$

When handsome young chef Craig Strong took control of this special-occasion dining room, the food went from being fine to being exceptional – which is a darn good thing, given the exceptional prices. The setting may be conservative, but Strong's food isn't – he takes risks in such dishes as strawberry gazpacho with shellfish, and the risks pay off handsomely. But he doesn't always push the envelope so intensely; we won't soon forget his classic grilled lamb chops and lamb loin roulade with basil-infused cannellini beans and marinated tomatoes. Strong started his culinary life as a pastry chef, and his love of sweet things shows in the dessert menu, which emphasizes comfort (warm bread pudding, warm chocolate cake). All the details are perfect, from the amuse-bouches and cheese selection to the chilled glasses of champagne and the light from the crystal chandeliers. Note that even though the Langham has taken over management of the former Ritz-Carlton, Strong remains, and we're glad for that.

Dish

734 Foothill Blvd., La Cañada
818.790.5355
American. B, L & D daily. Full bar. $-$$
A friendly neighborhood restaurant, Dish combines a charming farmhouse decor with an inexpensive menu of American comfort food. It's a good place for breakfast: omelets, robust coffee and booths big enough to hold the Sunday paper. Lunch brings appealing soups, salads and sandwiches; at dinner, we like the brisket and the slow-roasted ham with great mac & cheese. You often see three generations dining together (thanks in part to the excellent kids' menu). Good cocktails and wines by the glass, and a good-value happy hour.

El Portal

695 E. Green St., Pasadena
626.795.8553, elportalrestaurant.com
Mexican. L daily, D Tues.-Sun. Full bar. $
Many's the time we've ended up here unannounced with a large group after a movie at the Laemmle or before a Pasadena Playhouse performance, and the kind, hard-working people have always accommodated us. The large and charming brick patio can always handle another table, so on warm evenings, the margaritas and chips flow freely. They are good margaritas, and if you focus on the delicious Yucatecan dishes – panuchos, cochinita pibil, Yucatan tamales, pumpkin soup – in favor of the average Mexican standards, you will be very happy.

Fatty's

1627 Colorado Blvd., Eagle Rock
323.254.8804, fattyscafe.com
Modern American/vegetarian. D Wed.-Sun. Beer & wine. $$
If you never trust a skinny cook, you'll be drawn to this gem for the name alone. It's a post-ironic title for a sensual vegetarian/vegan restaurant that cooks some seriously delicious food and has fun doing it. This is the place to bring your friends who distrust vegetarian cooking; Fatty's specializes in the rich, eclectic, exotic and elegant, and the kitchen delights in witty juxtapositions. The staff is attentive and knowledgeable, the wine is well selected and priced, available in flights or "glass-and-a-half's," and they make some yummy sake-based cocktails. The tightly composed menu is a feast for the senses that includes tapas, salads, pizza, entrees and fondues. Especially good: vegetarian dumplings, huge homemade potato chips with two kinds of dip, and the sticky and decadent pinky cake.

Firefly Bistro

1009 El Centro St., South Pasadena
626.441.2443, eatatfirefly.com
Modern American. L Tues.-Fri., D Tues.-Sun., brunch Sat.-Sun. Beer & wine. $$-$$$
South Pasadena's newfound hipness is epitomized by this tented bistro, which is bright by day and romantic by night. Owners/chefs/spouses Monique King and Paul Rosenbluh turn out an always-interesting and usually wonderful menu of multiethnic offerings, from five-spice

pork egg rolls to warm spinach salad, braised lamb shank with creamy polenta to grilled rare ahi with vegetable chilequiles. The lunchtime salads are excellent, the desserts comforting, and the wine list creative and affordable.

Fu-Shing

2960 E. Colorado Blvd., East Pasadena
626.792.8898, fu-shing.com
Sichuan/Chinese. L & D daily. Full bar. $$
The only Pasadena Chinese restaurant that could hold its own in Chinese-majority Monterey Park, Fu-Shing specializes in fire-breathing dishes from the Sichuan region, like cold spicy beef tendon, firecracker lamb and "supreme Szechwan" fire pot. It also does a fine job on such Chinese classics as pan-fried noodles, kung pao scallops or chicken, tangerine beef and salt-and-pepper shrimp. Upscale dining room, snappy service and a proper bar.

Gale's Restaurant

452 S. Fair Oaks Ave., Pasadena
626.432.6705, galesrestaurant.com
Italian. L Tues.-Sat., D Tues.-Sun.
Full bar. $$
Hometown girl Gale Kohl and her husband, Rene Chila, know how to run a restaurant. Their waiters are pros, their Italian chef is talented, and their atmosphere is warm. We have many favorites here, including mussels with white wine and garlic, caprese salad, Caesar salad and rosemary lamb chops, but the best eating is typically done off the specials menu. Because Gale's brother, Jerry Kohl, owns the fabulously successful Brighton Collectibles, you get to drink your Barbera out of his silver-encrusted goblets.

Gaucho's Village

411 N. Brand Blvd., Glendale
818.550.1430, gauchosvillage.com
Brazilian/steakhouse. L & D daily. Full bar. $$$
Southern California may have more vegetarians per square inch than the rest of the country, but people are crazy about meat, too, as evidenced by the proliferation of Brazilian churrascarias, all-you-can-eat celebrations of beef, lamb, pork and chicken. This place is one of the best-value churrascarias around, at about $27 per person during the week and $35 on weekends, when sassy dancers entertain the crowds. We prefer the quieter nights, which are still not quiet. The salad/buffet bar is fine but unremarkable, with all the usual beans/rice/roasted vegetables/plaintain sides and salads; the meats and sausages, served tableside from huge skewers, are savory and tasty.

Green Street Tavern

169 W. Green St., Old Pasadena
626.229.9961, greenstreettavern.net
Modern American. L Mon.-Fri., D nightly, brunch Sat.-Sun. Beer & wine. $$-$$$
Not to be confused with Green Street Restaurant (why, oh why do restaurants do this to us?), Green Street Tavern is cozy, upscale, and located on relatively quiet Green Street in Old Town. The space is sculpted with art nouveau curves and consists of a couple of booths, a few tables and a small backlit bar. Service is attentive; ingredients are quality, and often local and organic. Lunch is inventive (three kinds of high-end hamburgers, great salads and entrees), and dinner is deluxe, with excellent rotating specials. The space can get surprisingly noisy, so if it's nice opt for the sidewalk terrace.

Houston's

320 S. Arroyo Pkwy., Pasadena
626.577.6001
American. L & D daily. Full bar. $$$
Just try to drive by this upscale chain without having the aroma of pork products force you to pull into the parking lot, zombie-like, and head for one of the roomy booths. Pass on the bland chicken and so-so seafood in favor of the excellent (if pricey) meat: baby-back ribs, steaks, chops and burgers. No reservations, and there's always a wait for dinner.

Firefly's indoor-outdoor setting – both relaxed and romantic

Any time is margarita time at La Cabanita.

Il Fornaio

One Colorado, 24 W. Union St., Old Pasadena
626.683.9797, ilfornaio.com
Italian. L & D daily, brunch Sun. Full bar. $$-$$$
This California-based chain is one of Old Town's better restaurants. In a bright, modern, noisy setting (complete with a good bar), white-aproned waiters ferry satisfying wines by the glass, savory pastas (the seafood linguine and meat lasagnas are particularly good), thin-crusted pizzas and tasty salads; we avoid the chicken dishes, which tend to be dry. Sunday brunch is lovely.

Japon Bistro

927 E. Colorado Blvd., Pasadena
626.744.1751, japonbistro-pasadena.com
Japanese. L Mon.-Fri., D Tues.-Sun. Beer & wine. $$-$$$
Don't let the home-lettered signs and rather uninviting, tunnel-like space dissuade you from a unique take on sushi and all things Japanese. The knowledgeable young staff can't wait to introduce you to live sea urchin, exotic sake or the izakaya menu, the Japanese equivalent of tapas. The sushi bar is lively, the tables are filled with Caltech foodies discussing nano-technology and black holes, and it's a great place to go that's out of Old Town – sophisticated and delicious, with lots of good things to eat.

La Cabanita

3447 N. Verdugo Rd., Montrose
818.957.2711
Mexican. B Sat.-Sun., L & D daily. Full bar. $-$$
We have friends who drive here from Echo Park just to get salsa to go. Some oldtimers grouse that now that it's twice its original size, this cheerful, crowded neighborhood café isn't as consistent as it once was. But we've never had anything but superb food, especially the beans, the green mole, the sopes compuestos and the chicken soup. Watch out for the margaritas – they're yummy but strong.

La Grande Orange

260 S. Raymond Ave., Pasadena
626.356.4444, lgohospitality.com
Modern American. L Mon.-Fri., D nightly.
Full bar. $$-$$$
The owners of this new restaurant/bar in the handsomely restored 1925 Santa Fe Depot at Del Mar Station have thought of everything. Good-value happy hour? Check. Retro-hip mac 'n' cheese? Check. Grilled ahi tacos? Check. It's got it all, from name-dropping martinis to a thoughtful kids' menu, and at this writing, all of Pasadena was there – early-bird seniors on the enclosed patio, a diverse mix of families and friends in the beamed dining room, and a lively young after-work gang filling the bar. Although it's the kind of restaurant that MBAs, not chefs, create, we admit to totally liking the place, especially the bar, the Caesar salad, the burgers and the fried chicken, a yuppie twist on Roscoe's, with pan-fried boneless breasts atop a bed of mashed potatoes, with a palmier-like cinnamon roll for good measure. Well-poured drinks, charming and hospitable service.

La Maschera

82 N. Fair Oaks Ave., Old Pasadena
626.304.0004
Italian. L & D Mon.-Sat. Full bar. $$
Oozing cool style, this Italian is quiet at lunch and early weeknights but busy on weekend nights – a DJ brings in a young crowd. The look is dark, almost Moorish, with heavy wooden tables and candlelight. Diners (older couples to bachelorette parties) give each other tastes of the bruschetta assortment, the light wild-mushroom gnocchi with scampi, the perfectly cooked risotto of the day and the aromatic Adriatic fish soup. Good service and good-value prices, given the quality of the food and the romance of the setting.

Larkin's

1496 Colorado Blvd., Eagle Rock
323.254.0934, larkinsjoint.com
Southern/soul food. L & D Tues.-Sat., brunch Sun. BYOB. $-$$
One of Eagle Rock's new hot spots, Larkin's occupies a restored Craftsman house with a wrap-around front porch and a convivial living room and parlor. Hipster families and Eagle Rock oldtimers alike come for the casual, friendly vibe and traditional Southern cooking with a bit of Mexican and California flair. Best bets include the wonderfully rich mac 'n' cheese, Mexican-style chile verde soup, skillet-fried chicken, really spicy greens, garlicky roast corn and such smooth, delicious desserts as banana pudding and sweet potato pie. Prices are modest, but so are portion sizes.

Los Gringos Locos

464 Foothill Blvd., La Cañada
818.790.2696
Mexican. L & D daily; Full bar. $
What looks like a strip-mall fast-food joint is in fact a cheerful, cozy sit-down restaurant that's packed with families every night, and for good reason. What meatloaf and mashed potatoes are to Midwesterners, enchiladas and guacamole are to Californians, and this place makes them very well. Try the enchiladas suizas, stuffed with chicken and vegetables and topped with a subtle green chile sauce. Also delicious are the fajitas, which seemingly half the place orders every night; the carne asada and carnitas; the Caesar salad; and the various camarones (shrimp) dishes. Generous, reasonably priced margaritas.

Chef Akira Hirose of Maison Akira

Maison Akira

713 E. Green St., Pasadena
626.796.9501, maisonakira.com
French/Japanese. L Tues.-Fri., D Tues.-Sun., brunch Sun. Beer & wine. $$$$
This quiet, opulent place, decorated like the home of a well-bred Upper East Side matron, doesn't have the flash and buzz of L.A.'s foodie hot spots, but you'll eat as well here as you will anywhere. Chef Akira Hirose knows his way around a kitchen, having trained with Joel Robuchon and cooked for such places as Citrus and L'Orangerie. Some of his simplest dishes are the most dazzling, like the grilled Chilean sea bass with a miso marinade (a dish he made for the Emperor of Japan), or the rack of lamb with rosemary sauce and potato mousseline. He stretches a little more with the starters, like the warm smoked salmon with lentils and micro greens in a ponzu-pesto vinaigrette. The kitchen sometimes falters and overcooks things a little, but otherwise this is exceptional cooking, rivaled only by Craig Strong's over at the Huntington. The Sunday brunch is spectacular.

Melody

755 E. Washington Blvd., Pasadena
626.797.7800, melodysoulfood.com
Southern/Mediterranean. B, L & D daily.
No booze. $-$$
In the spot formerly known as M & M Soul Food, Melody has been reinventing itself. At first this clean, sparely decorated place tried being Mediterranean, but as a waiter said, "That didn't work out." So hooray, it's back to tasty soul food with a smattering of hummus. The short ribs are sweet and fall-off-the-bone tender, the smothered chicken is moist and not too heavy nor salty, the collard greens are a wee bit bitter, just the way we like 'em, the black-eyed peas are buttery and substantial, and the cornbread muffins are served crisp and hot with butter and honey. Good lunch specials.

Mijares

145 Palmetto Dr., Pasadena
626.792.2763
1806 E. Washington Blvd., Pasadena
626.794.6674
Mexican. L & D daily. Full bar. $
A sprawling landmark Pasadena Mexican with basic Cal-Mex comfort food, a family-friendly vibe, good margaritas and a terrific happy hour. The Washington branch is a smaller café with a more limited menu and beer and wine only.

Mike & Anne's

1040 Mission St., South Pasadena
626.799.7199, mikeandannes.com
Modern American. B, L & D Tues.-Sun. Full bar.
$-$$$
We're fans of this friendly modern-American bistro, which opened among Mission Street's antique stores just after the first *Hometown Pasadena* went to press. Everyone wants to sit out on the twinkle-lit patio, not just because

On the patio at Mike & Anne's

it's so pleasant, but because on busy nights, the rafter-ceilinged indoor space roils with noise. Still, it's worth a little shouting to enjoy the zucchini fritter salad with red-pepper coulis; flatiron steak with fingerling potatoes, trumpet mushrooms, green apples and violet mustard bordelaise; and homemade caramel ice cream with warm madelines. Lunchtime brings terrific sandwiches: grilled cheese with melted sweet onions; a yummy eggplant, pesto and roasted pepper; and a good burger.

Oba Sushi Izakaya
181 E. Glenarm St., Pasadena
626.799.8543
Japanese. L Mon.-Fri., D nightly. Beer & wine. $$-$$$
Pasadena's newest Japanese is also its best – and with a Mexican sushi chef, no less. The strip-mall space has held a few Japanese places, but none that looked this good, and certainly none that tasted this good. You can sit at the sake/wine bar, the small sushi bar or in one of two dining areas, and you'll be well served by very nice people; try the fish cake tempura, the incredible poke salad, the organic farm-raised hamachi and the Oba roll, with cucumber, avocado, jalapeño and wafer-thin beef. Lunchtime bento boxes are a good value.

Palate Food & Wine
933 S. Brand Blvd., Glendale
818.662.9463, palatefoodwine.com
Modern American/French. D Mon.-Sat. Beer & wine. $$-$$$
Chez Panisse in Glendale? Before you laugh, get over to Octavio Becerra's place in the site of the former Cinnabar and prepare to get caught up in his joy in robust, simple, reasonably priced small plates served with exuberant wines. Everything either comes from a local farmers' market (or an organic backyard garden) or a small-scale artisanal craftsman (as with the cheeses) or is made in-house: house-churned butter, handmade pasta, house-cured prosciutto. Make sure to try the "porkfolio," a charcuterie plate including a suave pork pâté, the gorgeous cheeses, the sous vide–cooked steak of astonishing flavor and the Valrhona chocolate pudding. In back is a retail wine store, a gorgeous oversize table for parties and a culinary library to browse. After years of working with Joachim Splichal, Becerra is ready to fly on his own, and he's already soaring in L.A.'s culinary stratosphere.

Panda Inn
3488 E. Foothill Blvd., East Pasadena
626.793.7300
Chinese. L & D daily. Full bar. $$
Okay, so the food is phony by San Gabriel Chinese standards, and it's a chain, if a local one. But we love Panda Inn anyway. The vegetables are fresh, the flavors are good, and the service is excellent. It's the sort of place that non-Chinese families bring Grandma for a special occasion, and there's not a darn thing wrong with that. We like the crispy calamari, minced chicken with lettuce cups and kung pao shrimp, and our kids actually eat all the broccoli in the beef with broccoli.

Parkway Grill
510 S. Arroyo Pkwy., Pasadena
626.795.1001
Modern American. L Mon.-Fri., D nightly. Full bar. $$$-$$$$
The Spago of Pasadena, Parkway Grill made a big splash when it opened in 1985, bringing California pizzas and organic vegetables to then-stodgy Crown City. Today the concept is less fresh, and the kitchen execution isn't as crisp as it once was, but we still love the casually elegant space – soaring wood rafters, exposed brick, massive flower arrangements, open kitchen – and the classic dishes are still tasty, especially the ones that aren't too fussy. Try the lobster-filled cocoa crepes, ahi niçoise salad, grilled lamb chops with port-rosemary reduction, and seasonal fruit crisps. Sharp service, good wine list and a great bar, particularly on weekends, when the live jazz cooks.

The Parkway Grill grows its own produce in an urban garden on Marengo.

Porto Alegre
Paseo Colorado, 260 E. Colorado Blvd., Pasadena
626.744.0555, portoalegrebrazilbbq.com
Brazilian. L & D daily. Full bar. $$$-$$$$
Churrascarias are the fad du jour, which isn't hard to understand—handsome men carving unlimited quantities of sizzling meat tableside

is a powerful American fantasy. This vast place, little-noticed on the second floor of the Paseo, is actually one of the best around, more subdued than the wacky Gaucho's Village in Glendale and with better food than Picanha in Burbank. It's expensive – about $35 for the prix-fixe meal – but if you arrive hungry and choose well (i.e. tender lamb chops over the ordinary filet mignon), it's worth it. The buffet is generous (salads, roasted vegetables, prosciutti, cheeses, garlic rice, bananas fritas), and trust us, you won't have room for dessert.

The Raymond
1250 S. Fair Oaks Ave., Pasadena
626.441.3136, theraymond.com
Modern American. L & D Tues.-Sun., tea Tues.-Sun. $$$
Newish owners and an ambitious young chef have breathed new life into this 1901 Craftsman bungalow. It is the epitome of Pasadena charm, with gleaming wood floors, leaded glass, flower-filled patios and an air of tranquility. Pasadena's movers and shakers, along with anniversary-celebrating couples and Craftsman-loving visitors, come here for lunchtime salads, sophisticated Sunday brunches, proper afternoon tea or candlelit dinners. The upscale California cooking isn't always flawless – the roasted bruschetta was bitter on our last visit – but it's elegant in conception and generally very good. Try the crab cakes; endive and baby frisee salad; roast salmon with asparagus, potato risotto and wild thyme; and the hot-fudge sundae.

Saladang
363 S. Fair Oaks Ave., Pasadena
626.793.8123
Thai. L & D daily. Beer & wine. $-$$
Count us among the legion who are addicted to Saladang's yellow curry, light fried calamari, spinach-and-duck salad, beef satay and rad na noodles. The best Thai food in the SG Valley is served by a quick-moving staff in a chic modern room with exposed ducts, colorful table settings and handsome rattan chairs. The lunch specials are bargains.

750ml
966 Mission St., South Pasadena
626.799.0711
Modern American. D nightly. Beer & wine. $$$
Steven Arroyo, the smart guy behind Cobras & Matadors, has done it again with this noisy but *charmant* wine bar/bistro in the heart of old South Pasadena, a cork's throw from the Metro station, for those who want to sample that third glass of wine and not drive home. Our complaints in the first year were the sometimes-

poor service and the high prices. But now the service is better, and to celebrate its first anniversary, Arroyo's kitchen team lowered prices and added more substantial entrees, like the lovely roast young chicken for two with braised peas, chanterelles and truffle butter. The classic steak frites is still there, as are the delicious breadsticks and the good Spanish and French wines by the glass.

Shiro
1505 Mission St., South Pasadena
626.799.4774, restaurantshiro.com
French-Japanese. D Wed.-Sun. Beer & wine. $$$
For years this was *the* restaurant in South Pas – heck, in the whole San Gabriel Valley, with the possible exception of Parkway Grill. Now the competition is stiffer, especially in the immediate neighborhood. For a while chef Hideo Yamashiro seemed to have lost his focus, as he worked on his swell westside spot, Orris, but lately Shiro has been as good as ever, a showcase of elegant French-Japanese fusion cooking. At least half the patrons in this elegantly spare place get the famed whole sizzling catfish with ponzu sauce, and they're always happy.

Smitty's Grill
110 S. Lake Ave., Pasadena
626.792.9999, smittysgrill.com
American. L Mon.-Fri., D nightly. Full bar. $$$-$$$$
We go to this handsome bar and grill now and then and each time are pleasantly surprised at how good it is. It's not as fancy as siblings Parkway Grill or Arroyo Chop House, but it's a bit of a better value, because with each entree you get a side dish, instead of having to order them faux family style ("family style,"

This 1901 bungalow was originally the caretaker's cottage of the long-gone Raymond Hotel.

yeah, if your family's the Windsors and you eat off of pewter platters). The menu changes seasonally, but certain dishes are regulars, like the tangy beet salad, unremarkable meatloaf, excellent petite filet and melt-in-your-mouth sautéed mushrooms. The creamed spinach with bacon transported us to Intensive Care for an angioplasty, but we didn't even care. Maybe because the wine list was so approachable. The interior is sleek, except for the clutter of photos blocking the view of the Kenton Nelson mural.

Song

383 S. Fair Oaks Ave., Pasadena
626.793.5200
Thai. L & D daily. Beer & wine. $-$$
This architecturally dramatic space – a small glass-walled dining room and larger open-air patio set off by fifteen-foot-tall laser-cut steel panels modeled on Thai fabrics – is perfectly suited to the wonderful Thai street food, which is, after all, intended to be eaten outdoors. You'll find dishes you won't find elsewhere in town, like the crispy, addictive corn cakes, fish balls with curry, salad of asparagus and chicken, and skewers of marinated pork. The sister restaurant to neighboring Saladang, this is a romantic spot popular for date nights.

Song's walled patio is one of Pasadena's most inviting spots on a summer evening.

Sushi Roku

One Colorado, 24 W. Union St., Old Pasadena
626.683.3000, sushiroku.com
Japanese/sushi. L & D daily. Full bar. $$$
Sure, it's pretentious, yuppie and overpriced, but it's the best sushi in Old Town, and you could do worse than the fatty tuna sashimi and crab dynamite roll, especially if you've just come out of a movie at the neighboring Laemmle. A sleek design, trendy cocktails and model-pretty hostesses complete the illusion that you're in West Hollywood instead of boring old Pasadena.

Taylor's Steakhouse

901 Foothill Blvd., La Cañada
818.790.7668
Steak/American. L & D daily. Full bar. $$$
Wedges of iceberg lettuce drenched with blue cheese, cold martinis, red Naugahyde booths and generous, perfectly cooked prime steaks for less than $30… forget all those new poseur steakhouses, because Taylor's is the real thing. The only branch of the beloved 1953 L.A. mothership, this clubby, windowless joint is packed every night, so reservations are essential. The bar is La Cañada's hot spot, if La Cañada can have such a thing.

Three Drunken Goats

2256 Honolulu Ave., Montrose
818.249.9950,
Spanish. L & D daily. Beer & wine. $$
Same space, same owners, wildly different vibe: The former deli/shop/wasteland of Goudas & Vines has been transformed into a lively tapas restaurant. Within days of opening it developed a following for its a huge menu of delicious, light small bites (bacon-wrapped dates, croquettes and mushrooms of many kinds, grilled octopus, steamed clams, roasted veggies, small and complex salads), its larger grilled dishes (New York steak with bleu cheese butter), its fun selection of wines and its occasional live gypsy music. Order a bottle of wine or a carafe of sangria, and linger over a parade of interesting dishes while taking in the scene that fills this warm, high-ceilinged, barn-like space. Keep ordering until you are nearly full, saving room for the churros with chocolate dipping sauce – you will never eat churros anywhere else again, ever, because these are the most sublime on earth.

Tonny's

843 E. Orange Grove Blvd., Pasadena
626.797.0866
Mexican. B, L & D daily. No booze. $
Warm and welcoming, this little family restaurant has an open kitchen, a tiny patio out back, about eight tables – and some of the most delicious guacamole ever, chunky and fragrant with

Just a few of the good things to eat at Three Drunken Goats.

cilantro and limes. Fresh-squeezed juices of all kinds – check out the carrots in the fridge! – accompany meals. The Vampiro (a Mexican interpretation of the stateside "suicide" combo of all fountain drinks) is red-tinted (of course) and combines both fruit and veggie juices. Homemade tortillas wrap *delicioso* burritos and seafood tacos, and the chile verde is heavenly. A small but sparkling gem.

Tre Venezia
119 W. Green St., Old Pasadena
626.795.4455
Italian. L Fri., D Tues.-Sun. Full bar. $$$
Italian restaurants litter Old Town, but for the real thing, step off Colorado to find this romantic little cottage on Green Street – and bring a Gold Card. In a dining room decorated like someone's (tasteful) home, a kind Italian staff serves often-extraordinary dishes from Venice, Friuli and the rest of northeastern Italy: beet salad, a superb caprese made with house-smoked buffalo mozzarella, exquisite handmade pastas, fresh fish cooked simply with olive oil, garlic and a splash of vinegar, and the almond-scented crema del gondolier. Acclaimed grappas and a fine list of wines at gasp-inducing prices.

Twin Palms
101 W. Green St., Old Pasadena
626.577.2567
Californian. L & D daily, brunch Sun. Full bar.
$$-$$$
Locals love to bring houseguests from Minnesota here – it's a California fantasy of whitewashed woodwork, palm trees, outdoor stage and open-air seating. The kitchen calls the food "California Coastal," but it's really not as pretentious as it sounds: ahi salad with cucumber and radish, sea bass Veracruz, tasty wood-fired pizzas, a classic filet mignon, a delish chocolate soufflé cake. It's all well prepared and not too expensive, given the festive atmosphere and good service. Weekend nights bring a party crowd for the after-10 p.m. dance music; Sundays feature a terrific brunch with New Orleans jazz.

Vertical Wine Bistro
70 N. Raymond Ave., 2nd Floor, Old Pasadena
626.795.3999, verticalwinebistro.com
Modern American. L Tues.-Fri., D Tues.-Sun.
Full bar. $$$
New York style and a semi-celebrity owner (A-list movie producer Gale Anne Hurd) give this upstairs wine bar and bistro a panache not often seen on the eastside. But it's not an annoying scene – it's the kind of place that you see both good-looking 26-year-olds and your been-around-the-block stockbroker. Some 100 wines are poured by the glass or flight, and dishes are small and designed to share. People complain about the prices, but we find the $7 and $8 wines by the glass always delicious, and if you order food carefully (mini grilled cheeses, a salad of arugula, pear and goat cheese, fantastic wild salmon with lentils and bacon), it's quite fair given the setting and quality. The three-course lunch for $18 is a lovely treat.

Yang Chow
3777 E. Colorado Blvd., East Pasadena
626.432.6868, yangchow.com
Chinese. L & D daily. Beer & wine. $
A branch of the Chinatown classic, this place has a huge and devoted clientele, proving that Yang Chow's famed slippery shrimp is indeed as addictive as cocaine. Twice-cooked and bathed in a subtly sweet, mildly hot sauce, it is impossible to stop eating. Also good are the cashew chicken, fiery Szechwan wonton soup, pan-fried dumplings and dry-sautéed asparagus and green beans. Good service.

Yujean Kang's
67 N. Raymond Ave., Old Pasadena
626.585.0855
Chinese. L & D daily. Beer & wine. $$-$$$
Chef Kang's sophisticated dishes, prepared with a French chef's elegance and a Chinese gourmand's sense of robust flavor, attract food lovers from all over Southern California, and beyond. Don't miss the wonton soup, duck salad with black-bean sauce, tea-smoked duck, Chinese "polenta" with shrimp, mushrooms and scallions, and stir-fried Blue Lake green beans. Kang is an oenophile, and the wine list complements the menu, but it ain't cheap. The prix-fixe lunch, however, is a terrific deal.

Z Sushi
1132 N. Garfield Ave., Alhambra
626.282.5636
Japanese/sushi. L Mon.-Sat., D nightly.
Full bar. $-$$$
This spacious restaurant is one of the best places for sushi east of the 5 Freeway. Inside are knotty-pine walls, a large drinking bar (try the plum martini), a long sushi bar and tables set with black linens. How much you spend depends on whether you order a bargain non-sushi dinner (like chicken teriyaki, barbecued beef or tempura, all less than $12.95) or get carried away with sushi. (Prices are reasonable, but sushi and sashimi can add up.) The extensive menu showcases fresh sashimi, good salads, creative rolls and such appealing cooked dishes as salmon and baby lobster with a subtle wasabi cream sauce.

World Cuisine in the SG Valley

All India Café
39 S. Fair Oaks Ave., Old Pasadena
626.440.0309, allindiacafe.com
Indian. L & D daily. Beer & wine. $-$$
The aptly named All India Café features dishes from many regions of the Subcontinent. Masala dosa, a rich eggplant salad with tomato sauce and ginger yogurt, tandoori fish, lamb frankie and lentil soup are all standouts. Thalis, the tastes served in sets of stainless-steel bowls, are a good way to begin or renew your acquaintance with this rich cuisine. Sidewalk tables and great cooking draw an eclectic crowd.

Azeen's Afghani Restaurant
110 E. Union St., Old Pasadena
626.683.3310
Afghani. L Mon.-Fri., D daily. Beer & wine. $$
Azeen's is an elegant white-tablecloth restaurant with a restful, welcoming atmosphere. Squint at the menu and you'll recognize derivatives (or ancestors) of such Indian, Pakistani, Persian and Chinese dishes as pakoras, curries, dumplings, kebabs and pilafs. Share a sampler plate of appetizers, then try tender beef kebabs or quabili pallaw (lamb with carrots and raisins). Sweet, translucent butternut squash (kadu) is a delicious side.

Blue Hen
1743 Colorado Blvd., Eagle Rock
323.982.9900, eatatbluehen.com
Vietnamese. L Mon.-Fri., D nightly.
No booze. $
For proof of Eagle Rock's ascent into hipdom, look no further than this mini-mall organic Vietnamese place, where the music on the stereo is as cool as the art on the wall. Try the baguette-based Vietnamese sandwiches, the crisp spring rolls, the steaming bowls of pho (noodle soup) and the iced coffee with sweet condensed milk.

Cuban Bistro
28 W. Main St., Alhambra
626.308.3350, cubanbistro.com
Cuban. L & D Tues.-Sun. Full bar. $$
With an ebullient atmosphere (read noisy), this place is popular for its extensive selection of mojitos, which are a bit too sweet, but hey, we're in the magical land of rum and sugar cane. It fairly shouts Cuba, with Caribbean-blue walls and framed reminders of hot Havana nights before that Commie coot barged in. The embarrassingly large serving of plantain chips would be better warm, but the cilantro and lime salsa has a good bite. Lots of pork on the menu, as you'd expect, but you'll also find a crisply grilled, if too salty, mahi mahi, and plates are nicely balanced with sweet (candy-like fried plantains, mango salsa) and savory (salted fish, red rice).

Daisy Mint
1218 E. Colorado Blvd., Pasadena
626.792.2992, daisymint.com
Asian. L & D daily. BYOB. $$
Pasadena's latest darling is a simple storefront restaurant decorated with empty flea-market frames and vintage chandeliers; larger groups get to sit at the fetching family table made from an old door. This is a husband-and-wife operation, and because he's Korean and she's Thai, they decided to serve a pan-Asian menu with something for everyone, including vegetarians, and the result is that (almost) everyone loves it – and almost everyone can afford it, too. The Korean ribeye is sometimes too fatty but mostly delectable; the dumplings are all dreamy (get the Shanghai soup dumplings); and the noodle dishes are interesting and tasty. Desserts aren't worth the calories, except perhaps the fried ice cream just for fun. By the time you read this the wine license should be in place, but the owners promise to have a very low corkage.

Golden Deli
815 W. Las Tunas Dr., San Gabriel
626.308.0803
Vietnamese. L & D daily.
No booze. Cash only. $
Spring rolls are the golden ticket here – fabulously crisp spring rolls that you can eat as is or roll up in a lettuce leaf with basil, mint and/or cilantro, marinated vegetables and chile paste. There's a reason why every single table gets at least one order of them. That's just the beginning of the good eating: rich, oniony pho broth, shrimp paste on sugar cane, myriad and wonderful noodle dishes. If the wait for a table is too long, head across the street to Vietnam House, which also has good food.

Kansai

36 S. Fair Oaks Ave., Old Pasadena
626.564.1560
Japanese. L & D Tues.-Sun.Beer & wine. $
The nice people in this cheerful, open café serve a variety of Japanese dishes (tempura, sushi, gyoza), but the noodles are the thing to get – homemade udon and soba served in a variety of styles and temperatures. (Vegetarians, take note of the hard-to-find vegetarian broth for the noodles.) There's nothing like cold soba on a hot day or steaming udon on a cold day.

Ka-San Restaurant

3115 Foothill Blvd., La Crescenta
818.249.5500
Korean. L & D daily. No booze. $-$$
Delicious Korean barbecue and other specials (hot pots, stews and tang), served by a friendly staff who will help you cook at your gas-fired tabletop grill. Classic marinated beef (kalbi and bulgogi) is tender; kim chi and other side dishes are abundant, delicious and not too spicy for the uninitiated; and the grilled mackerel is perfectly done. You won't mind the lack of beer when you taste the ginger tea, and the Korean tea that's served after dinner – a cool, sweet concoction of ginger and cinnamon – takes the place of dessert and a brandy.

La Caravana

1306 N. Lake Ave., Pasadena
626.791.7378
Salvadoran. L & D daily. No booze. $
Hearty, tasty Salvadoran specialties – pupusas, meat-filled pepitos (like empanadas), savory chicken sautéed with onions and potatoes, carne asada – are served in a handsome room decorated with plush booths and Central American art and woodwork.

Lebanese Kitchen

1384 E. Washington Blvd., Pasadena
626.296.9010
Lebanese/Armenian. L & D Mon.-Sat. No booze. $
It could not have a more bland interior, but the warmth of the people and the quality of the food make up for it. (Besides, we usually take out.) Along with delicious kebabs (the lamb is excellent), falafel and a tasty, smoky baba ganoush, we like such harder-to-find specialties as foul (a ground mixture of fava and garbanzo beans with spices and olive oil), barbecued quail and marinated frogs' legs. As an accompaniment, you can choose traditional tabbouleh or cabbage slaw, and you are gifted with an entire bag of pita with your takeout order.

Mamita

714 S. Brand Blvd., Glendale
818.243.5121
Peruvian. L & D daily. Beer & wine. $
A tiny place tucked among car dealerships and done in early-'80s coffee shop (augmented by murals of Machu Picchu and Andean natives), Mamita serves 107 Peruvian dishes. Most everything but the ceviche comes with potatoes – which, after all, the Incas invented. Lomito Mamitas (beef with french fries, eggs, onions and tomatoes) is a delicious South American take on corned beef hash. Spicy shrimp in a cream sauce with peanuts and yucca strips in garlic and cheese sauce are other standouts. Besides the cinnamon-scented purple soft drink called Chicha Morada, there's Peruvian beer and Chilean wine. The prices seem high at first, but portions are large – one entree and an appetizer are more than enough for two.

Mandaloun

141 S. Maryland Ave., Glendale
818.507.1900
Lebanese. L & D Tues.-Sun. Full bar. $$$
If you haven't been to a wedding or bar mitzvah in a while, head to Mandaloun on a weekend night, and you'll experience the next best thing, Middle Eastern–style. Three-generation family groups (all dressed up) and large tables of friends come for a night of dancing to the band (it's loud – don't plan on having meaningful conversations), festive toasting and watching the impressive late-night belly-dancing show. Hookahs are even available out on the terrace. The prix-fixe menu (mandatory on weekends) features a parade of delicious, carefully prepared Lebanese specialties – light, unusual and beautifully composed – that will leave you happily sated for days. During the week and for lunch, you can choose your own dishes and enjoy a quieter atmosphere. Service is elegant, professional and cool.

Mezbaan Indian

80 N. Fair Oaks Ave., Old Pasadena
626.405.9060, mezbaan.net
Indian. L Mon.-Fri., D nightly, brunch Sun. Beer & wine. $-$$
One of the original Old Town eateries, Mezbaan has live Indian music on Friday and Saturday nights and a great buffet at lunch. The regular menu offers individually prepared dishes including tandoori, benghan bharta and palak paneer, distinctive curries that you can spice from 1 to 10, and Hyderabad specialties (lamb pasinda is delicious).

Mojito's

69 N. Raymond Ave., Old Pasadena
626.796.2520, mojitosrestaurant.com
Cuban. L Mon.-Fri., D nightly. Full bar. $-$$$
The chic, elegant interior whispers upscale –
but more than once we've found ourselves in
convivial shouts to talk above the pumping Latin
musica. The mojitos are good – not too sweet,
with a rummy kick. The irresistible toasted bread
starter comes with a yummy black-bean spread,
so leave the carbohydrate counter at home. We
love the soul-warming black bean soup topped
with ripe cherry tomatoes and avocado, the
citrus-pungent ceviche, the huge bowl of good
paella and the churrasco plate of tender, thin-
sliced skirt steak atop of mountain of mashed
potatoes. Coffee comes with warmed milk, a
nice touch. We've had both good and poor
service, but so it goes in Old Town restaurants.

Pho 79

29 S. Garfield Ave., Alhambra
626.289.0239
Vietnamese. B, L & D daily. Beer & wine. $
In this big room full of round tables, you'll hear
much contented slurping of pho, the great
Vietnamese beef soup. You make each bowl
your own by adding some of the various sides.
The waiters will help you decide among the
nearly 200 menu offerings (pho accounts for
just ten or so); they've been known to prescribe
chicken porridge for a sore throat (and it works!).
Everything is very fresh; also delicious are the
sandwiches served on baguettes – we'll call 'em
pho-boys, if you can excuse the pun. Tropical
sodas and Vietnamese coffee round out the
menu.

Shamshiri

122 W. Stocker St., Glendale
818.246.9541
Persian. L & D daily. No booze. $-$$
Though the kindly service can be erratic, the
food is abundant, interesting and delicious. The
prices are amazing – no dinner entree is over
$15, and the lunch dishes ($6.50 to $8) are
large enough for leftovers. Kebabs are tasty
and tender, and the stews, especially fesenjon,
a sort of Persian mole with pomegranate and
walnuts, are rich and complex. Dill, mint and
saffron garnishes keep the plates beautiful and
the palate refreshed. The rosewater-scented
desserts are evocative of starry nights in Kahlil
Gibran's garden.

Chef Karma Bhotia at the Tibet Nepal House

Tibet Nepal House

36 E. Holly St., Old Pasadena
626.585.0955, tibetnepalhouse.com
Himalayan. L & D Tues.-Sun. Beer & wine. $-$$
Mountaineer and photographer Karma Tenzing
Bhotia trained in Austria as a chef, and he brings
a gourmet sensibility (rich cream sauces, lovely
presentation) to Tibetan and Nepali cuisine.
Reminiscent of both Chinese and Indian food,
but with more subtle flavors, the menu spans
the Himalayas, from lowland curries and dals to
highland yak, noodles and momos (dumplings).
The award-winning buffet lunch is inexpensive
and wonderful. Make sure to try Tibetan butter
tea – it is savory rather than sweet, more like a
soup to the American palate.

Wahib's Middle Eastern Restaurant & Bakery

910 E. Main St., Alhambra
626.281.1006, wahibsmiddleeast.com
Middle Eastern. B, L & D daily. Beer & wine. $$
A big room with banquet-style tables and murals
on the wall, Wahib's is a workaday warehouse
of Lebanese and Armenian food. It's open for
breakfast, has a bakery, and offers daily specials
that are off the beaten kebab-and-falafel path.
Outstanding crunchy frogs' legs fried with garlic
and lemon are served on top of french fries;
also tasty are the cucumber salad, tender lamb
dishes, roast chicken specials, Greek-style
moussaka and great hummus. The baklava is
fresh. Prices are slightly lower for takeout.

Breakfast & Lunch Cafés

Aun Deli Café
40 N. Mentor Ave., Pasadena
626.568.4959
Japanese. L Mon.-Sat., D Mon.-Fri. Beer &
wine. $
In a colorful storefront next to the Ice House is
a Japanese café that's easy to miss but worth
seeking out. The ingredients are mostly organic,
the flavors are bright and fresh, and the prices
are modest. Try the grilled herb salmon with
brown rice, the four-color bowl and the incredible
burger-like tofu patty. The deli case holds salads
and sides, which are great to take home or back
to the office.

Auntie Em's Kitchen
4616 Eagle Rock Blvd., Eagle Rock
323.255.0800
American. B & L daily; L Mon.-Fri. to 7 p.m.,
Sat.-Sun. to 4 p.m. No booze. $
A funky and fetching retro-American diner with
delicious modern-diner cooking. For breakfast,
try an open-faced egg sandwich topped with
bacon, Cajun turkey sausage or portobello
mushroom and roasted red peppers; for lunch,
have the turkey meatloaf sandwich, soup of
the day or grilled-steak salad. The homemade
baked goods are all fab, especially the huge
chocolate cupcakes.

Billy's Deli
216 N. Orange St., Glendale
818.246.1689, billysdeli.com
American/deli. B, L & D daily. Beer & wine. $-$$
Established in 1949, this institution runs on
homemade pickles, towers of lox and pastrami
and lots of rye bread. Deli and bakery cases
complement a dining room hung with huge sepia
photos of a Glendale with Red Cars. The bill
will be on the expensive side, but the selection
is excellent, and everything is high quality.
Straight out of central casting, the waitresses
pamper their customers. Don't miss the food
wall outside– tiles cast from real deli meats and
breads – who knew? Billy's does great platters
for parties or, God forbid, memorials.

Central Park
219 S. Fair Oaks Ave., Pasadena
626.449.4499, centralparkrestaurant.net
American. B, L & D daily. Beer & wine. $-$$$
Run by the folks behind the upscale coffee
shops Shakers and Wild Thyme, the brick-
walled, high-ceilinged dining room and glass-
enclosed patio are comfortable spots to have a
peaceful breakfast, conduct a low-key business
lunch or meet friends for dinner. Prices are
modest for the quality; we're particularly fond
of the Caesar salad, thin-crust pizzas and ahi
niçoise salad. It has all the charm of an Old
Town spot, but because it's a few blocks south of
Colorado, parking is much easier.

Central Park occupies the former Soda Jerks building.

Dish
734 Foothill Blvd., La Cañada
818.790.5355
American. B, L & D daily. Full bar. $
The best spot around for an all-American
breakfast: cornmeal johnnycakes, applewood-
smoked bacon, kids' pancakes and the usual
egg dishes. Lunch brings simple sandwiches,
soups and salads. This is no-frills home cooking,
maybe not better than you can make – but
you're not making it, you're not cleaning up, and
you're not paying too much for it, either.

Dona Rosa Bakery & Taqueria
577 S. Arroyo Pkwy., Pasadena
626.449.2999, dona-rosa.com
Mexican. B, L & D daily (to midnight). Full bar. $
The taqueria is taken to a new level here – you
can have a great and cheap margarita while
you wait, the setting is upscale, and the food
is mysteriously much better than at its fancier
parent, El Cholo. Excellent breakfast pastries,
hearty burritos and tasty tostadas.

Euro Pane
950 E. Colorado Blvd., Pasadena
626.577.1828
American/French. B & L daily. No booze. $
Sumi Chang is a foodie rock star on the

casual-café interior or, as so many locals do, in a to-go version at a board meeting. A version of a Chinese chicken salad, it is simply impossible to stop eating (order the "dinner" size – the full size is ginormous). The rest of the Cal-American menu is just fine, but it's the Dianne that makes Green Street memorable.

Heirloom Bakery & Café
807 Meridian Ave., South Pasadena
626.441.0042
Bakery. B & L Tues.-Sun. No booze. $

South Pasadena's new foodie hot spot is the place to get a scone and latte for breakfast or a sandwich, strada (layered cheesy casserole) or little hand-thrown pizza for lunch. It's primarily a bakery, and it's damn near impossible to leave without ordering a brownie or an entire blueberry pie to have "for later." Toddlerphobes beware: This place has been discovered by hip moms 'n' dads, who discuss preschool options while their colorfully clad offspring vocalize and wander.

Julienne
2649 Mission St., San Marino
626.441.2299, juliennetogo.com
Californian/French. B & L Mon.-Sat. Beer & wine. $-$$
Nothing could be finer than lunch on the shaded sidewalk terrace fronting this impossibly charming café and gourmet-to-go store. The chopped salad with grilled chicken, roasted vegetables and pesto, the lamb sandwich with caramelized onions on rosemary bread, the brownies…we get hungry just thinking about it. Breakfast is swell, too: dreamy bread-pudding french toast, a wonderful salmon hash, perfectly cooked omelets.

Lovebirds
921 E. Colorado Blvd., Pasadena
626.583.8888, lovebirdscafe.com
10 S. First St., Alhambra
626.281.9999
Bakery. B & L Mon.-Sat. No booze. $
Part bakery, part coffeehouse, part lunch purveyor to the many office workers in

eastside, worshipped for her baked goods. But her bakery is also a simple café, and it's a terrific place for breakfast or lunch. Order your coffee, breakfast croissant, incredible egg salad sandwich or ham-and-cheese panini at the counter, snag one of the small tables and read your *New York Times* like everyone else. The food's so good that you will forgive any less-than-pleasant service.

The Fox's
2352 Lake Ave., Altadena
626.797.9430
American. B & L Tues.-Sun. Beer & wine. $
There's never less than a 30-minute wait on the weekends at this old-school diner, and that's for good reason. What's not to like about the hearty omelets, rich French toast, burgers, sandwiches, fresh OJ, bottomless cups of coffee and folksy, woodsy, 1950s setting? And when you consider all the stuffed rodents – er, foxes – you can admire in plexiglass cases… well, it's just too much. During the week, it's a hangout for Altadena ministers, realtors and town council folk, who chew and chat at the red-checkered tables. One of the many reasons to love Altadena.

Green Street
146 S. Shoppers Lane (off Green St.), Pasadena
626.577.7170, greenstreetrestaurant.com
American. B, L & D daily. Beer & wine. $
You cannot call yourself a true Pasadenan until you have had a Dianne salad, whether you eat it on the popular outdoor patio, in the bright,

downtown Pasadena and Alhambra, these spacious, friendly, order-at-the-counter cafés are fine places for lunchtime sandwiches. Generous and made on homemade bread, they are simple and very satisfying.

Marston's
151 E. Walnut St., Pasadena
626.796.2459, marstonsrestaurant.com
American. B & L Tues.-Sun., D Wed.-Sat. Beer & wine. $-$$
The cornflake-coated French toast is tasty and the omelets are generous, but we don't wait an hour on the sidewalk for breakfast, no matter how good it is. We go elsewhere on weekends and come to this fetching old bungalow midweek, when the wait might be just ten minutes and the food is just as good.

Mary's Market & Café
561 Woodland Dr., Sierra Madre
626.355.4534
American. B & L Tues.-Sun., D Tues.-Sat. No booze. $
This rustic little cottage near the base of the Mt. Wilson Trail is rather tired and dusty these days, which is too bad. But it's still open for breakfast, lunch and early dinner, with mondo-good oatmeal cookies for pre- or post-hike energy. It's a handy stop deep in Sierra Madre for locals

who love Taco Tuesday and having a peek back in time at the town's funkier, hippier days.

Nicole's Gourmet Foods
921 Meridian Ave., South Pasadena
626.403.5751, nicolesgourmetfoods.com
French. L Mon.-Sat. No booze. $
Our little corner of Paris by the Gold Line, Nicole's is a regular pit stop for lovers of all foods French, from cheeses and pâtés to truffles and wines. Nicole Grandjean and her lovely staff make delicious baguette sandwiches, salads and quiches, which you can eat on the flower-lined sidewalk patio or in the store.

Norton Simon Museum Garden Café
411 W. Colorado Blvd., Old Pasadena
626.449.6840, nortonsimon.org
American. L Wed.-Mon. Beer & wine. $
The food (by the swank Patina Group) is pre-packaged at this order-at-the-counter café, but with the exception of the sometimes-soggy wraps, it's tasty and inexpensive, and you get to eat at umbrella-shaded teak tables in the Norton Simon's lovely rear garden. It might get noisy if a school group troops through, but otherwise, this is a well-kept secret spot to meet friends or read a book while you have a salad or sandwich.

A sunny day at Nicole's

Penelope's Café, Books & Gallery

1029 Foothill Blvd., La Cañada
818.790.4386, penelopescafe.com
American. B & L Mon.-Sat. No booze. $
The incarnation of the word "cozy," Penelope's is warmed by wooden tables, a fireplace, a patio and book-lined shelves. This café-cum-shop features great food, unusual gifts, paintings, jewelry and pottery for sale, and an eclectic selection of new and used books. You line up, create a sandwich (vegetarian on olive bread, tuna on sun-dried tomato) or order soup or salad, then choose a table or a comfy chair and settle in. Mornings are quieter, with a small selection of coffees, teas and pastries (weekends the menu expands a bit).

Le Petit Beaujolais

1661 Colorado Blvd., Eagle Rock
323.255.5133
French. B & L Tues.-Sun. Beer & wine. $
Ooh la la, we love the quiet charms of this simple French café run by the folks at Café Beaujolais across the street. Bring your newspaper and relax over a morning café au lait and excellent croissant or eggs benedict; at lunch, meet a friend for a salad or croque monsieur and quiet conversation. The sidewalk tables are the most coveted, but inside has a woodsy 1970s charm that we quite like.

Pie 'n Burger

913 E. California Blvd., Pasadena
626.795.1123, pienburger.com
American. B, L & D daily. No booze. Cash only. $
The name pretty much sums it up, although we have a friend who comes here just for the toast, and we've been known to visit just for the bacon. A no-frills diner with a long counter and small tables, it serves very good short-order breakfasts, great burgers and excellent house-made pies of every kind. One of Pasadena's most popular budget caterers.

Porta Via

1 W. California Blvd., Pasadena
626.793.9000, portaviafoods.com
Italian. B Mon.-Sat., L daily. No booze. $-$$
Two longtime Pasadenans who used to run Twin Palms opened this white-tiled, high-ceilinged Italian deli in 2007, immediately filling the need for upscale Italian takeout and café food with easy parking in Southwest Pasadena. Order your custom salad or superb panini and snag a tall table inside or a quieter table on the covered patio, and if you've lived in Pasadena for a while, be prepared to run into people you know. After lunch, clever people with deep pockets (the food ain't cheap) pick up some lasagne, grilled lamb chops and roasted vegetables for dinner later.

The Terrace

Langham Huntington Hotel
1401 S. Oak Knoll Ave., Pasadena
626.568.3900
American/Californian. B, L & D daily. Full bar. $$
Ah, the good life! At your large umbrella-shaded table overlooking the pool, with an iced tea or chardonnay in hand, it's easy to forget about the troubles beyond the walls of the grand old Huntington. The ladies who lunch and the business folk who meet chat quietly over flawless chicken Caesars, gorgeous Cobb salads and a yummy chicken pesto panini. It's a California dream here – only it's no dream. New owners the Langham are threatening to turn this place into a French bistro in 2009, so be prepared for a change.

Ugo's Italian Deli

74 W. Sierra Madre Blvd., Sierra Madre
626.836.5700, ugoscafe.com
Italian. B, L & D Tues.-Sun. No booze. $
The Hamptons have arrived in Sierra Madre, thanks to this upscale foodie spot, where the owner is friendly enough to accept marriage proposals. (We asked her to marry us after tasting her baked goods.) She does all her own baking, so you might as well just give in and order the treats first. We may never forget a recent vanilla cupcake – it was still warm, not to mention moist, buttery and pretty. Aside from sweets, there are great paninis, a fantastic green salad with semi-dried pear tomatoes, sublime cheese-filled risotto cakes, and crunchy cold broccollini peppered with garlic slices. Ugo's is a small spot, with railcar-style seating for twelve inside and umbrella-shaded tables on the sidewalk. It's also a good place to pick up a fancy takeout dinner. Everything is weighed, so your check depends upon how much you buy.

Slinging hash at the Pie 'n Burger

Best Barbecue

The Barbecue Man
Lake Ave. & Morada Pl., Altadena
No phone
Open Sat. only. No booze. Cash only. $
The Barbecue Man, who also answers to the name Marshall, parks his big smoker grill in this service-station lot every Saturday and commences to dish out bargain barbecue. There's nothing special about the bread (plain white or wheat) or the potato salad (Smart & Final), but his meats are expertly smoked, his portions are generous, and the Chris & Pitts sauce is tasty. The tri-tip sandwich, heaped with lean, savory-tangy beef, is a steal for $5; the excellent full slab of ribs is $22. A local lady makes the cobblers and cookies.

Big Mama's Rib Shack
1453 N. Lake Ave., Pasadena
626.797.1792, bigmamas-ribshack.com
L & D Tues.-Sun. Beer & wine. $
A fine neighborhood soul food place, with satisfying ribs, corn muffins, filé gumbo, fried chicken and peach cobbler. The interior is nicer than the exterior would suggest, with polished wood tables and jazz on the stereo.

Gus's BBQ
808 Fair Oaks Ave., South Pasadena
626.799.3251, gussbbq.com
L & D daily. Full bar. $$-$$$
For years people came here just for the 1940s neon sign outside, and now that it's under new management, Gus's is actually worth visiting. It's great looking, with dark-wood floors, an old-school diner kitchen, padded booths and a proper bar (rare in South Pas) in back. The brothers who overhauled the place are the sons of the founder of the original Tops in east Pasadena, and they learned well at their daddy's knee: focus on good, unfussy food that makes people, if not their cardiologists, happy. Nothing is mind-blowing, and it's on the pricey side, especially at lunch. But you'll have a great time eating the dry-rub ribs, brick-flattened chicken, fresh Southern greens, sweet baked beans and tender, salty pulled pork.

Digging into a meaty rib at Robin's

Robin's Wood-Fire BBQ
395 N. Rosemead Blvd., East Pasadena
626.351.8885, robinsbbq.com
L & D Tues.-Sun. Full bar. $$
Blues on the stereo, wood smoke in the air, ribs on the table . . . this is living. Barbecue zealots (and there are many) argue ceaselessly on web sites like Chowhound.com about which places are best in Southern California; Robin's usually rates highly, and it deserves to. The meats are smoked over mesquite and hickory, and they're appropriately tender and soaked with flavor. A swell kids' menu (kids eat free on Wednesday night!), good sides (blueberry cornbread, pecan cole slaw, baked beans), fun retro sodas and beer (Pabst Blue Ribbon on tap!), a kitschy Americana decor and friendly waiters make the wait for a table seem well worth it. Sunday night is all-you-can-eat night.

Zeke's Smokehouse
2209 Honolulu Ave., Montrose
818.957.7045, zekessmokehouse.com
L & D daily. Beer & wine. $-$$
The ribs are very good, a close competitor to the ones at Robin's, but we come back to Zeke's for the Texas beef brisket and the Carolina pulled pork, both of which are first rate. The best sides are the heavenly mashed potatoes, the coleslaw and the sweet-potato fries. The simple, bright café on Montrose's charming main street is pleasant enough, but we usually order our brisket to go.

Shrimp paste atop mushroom caps at 888 Seafood

Exploring America's Great Chinatown

Forget those charming Chinatowns in the old parts of L.A., San Francisco and New York. The best Chinese food in America is now found in the country's great Chinatown: the San Gabriel Valley towns of San Gabriel, Alhambra, Monterey Park, Rosemead and Rowland Heights, home to a huge influx of immigrants from every region in China. Here are our current favorites, as well as a few favorites from Chinese-food guru Carl Chu, but we also encourage you to wander and explore – new places are always opening.

Chung King
206 S. Garfield Ave., Monterey Park
626.280.7430
Sichuan. L & D daily. No booze. Cash only. $
A plain little café with food so hot it'll make your ears turn red and your hair turn white. Avoid the clichés, like the kung pao chicken, and go to the Sichuan standards: beef hot pots, spareribs with Sichuan peppercorns, fried chicken with hot peppers, and chewy dried beef with hot peppers. A little less fiery, but still delicious, are the dry-fried soybeans and the fried potato shreds. Don't forget to do what Sichuan natives do and try a few of the cold dishes from the buffet.

Crown Café
1000 S. San Gabriel Blvd., San Gabriel
626.286.0298
Hunan. L & D daily. Beer. Cash only. $
This friendly café specializes in the spicy, smoky, strongly flavored food of the Hunan province: pungent smoked duck; diced chicken with chiles, red bell pepper and fried garlic; and, most challenging of all, the dish translated simply as "spicy on spicy" – a stir-fry of chiles with ground pork as flavoring, instead of the usual meat with chiles as flavoring. If you can take the heat, it's fabulous.

Din Tai Fung
1108 S. Baldwin Ave., Duarte
626.574.7068
Shanghai/dumplings. L & D Tues.-Sun. No booze. $
Devotees wait at the door for the 11 a.m. opening on Saturdays and Sundays, the only days this famed dumpling house makes the soup dumplings called xiao long bao, amazing broth-and-pork-filled creations that always sell out fast. But those are by no means the only good things

to eat in this cheerful, always-crowded café. We swoon over the juicy Shanghai pork dumplings, the shrimp wonton and the soups. Service is of the eat-and-get-out variety.

Dumpling Master
423 N. Atlantic Blvd., Monterey Park
626.458.8689
Dumplings/noodles. L & D Wed.-Mon. No booze. $
This Formica-clad café is aptly named – come here for dumplings (and noodles), or don't come at all. We particularly love the hand-cut noodles with chicken and chives, as well as all the dumplings: steamed, boiled or pan-fried, filled with pork, veggies, lamb, fish or chicken. The scallion "pie," however, is too thin and oily. Party-throwers take note: All the dumplings are sold in large quantities for takeout.

888 Seafood
8450 Valley Blvd., Rosemead
626.573.1888
Chiu Chow/dim sum. L & D daily. Full bar. $-$$
Famed for its range of quality dim sum – some 60 choices most weekdays and 80 on weekends – this vast and grand restaurant also specializes in seafood and dishes from the Chiu Chow region, like the whole perch poached in broth or the succulent braised goose. For dim sum, don't miss the taro and the exceptionally juicy siu mai.

Green Village Shanghai
250 W. Valley Blvd., San Gabriel
626.576.2228
Shanghai. L & D daily. Beer & wine. $-$$
A loyal crowd has followed Green Village to several locations, and now it's in a huge

space with room for all. It serves "pork pump" even better than Lake Spring's, and a range of Shanghai dishes with more refinement and flavor than most. Try the cold wine-marinated crab, juicy dumplings (listed under desserts), ten-ingredient pan-fried noodles, Shanghai sautéed shrimp and Wuxi crispy eels.

Lake Spring
219 E. Garvey Ave., Monterey Park
626.280.3571
Shanghai. L daily, D Wed.-Mon. Beer & wine.
$-$$
One of the advance wave of regional-Chinese restaurants in the SG Valley, Lake Spring combines a pleasant dining experience – two stylish black-and-pink dining rooms, good service – with first-rate interpretations of Shanghai classics. It's famed for its "noisette pork pump," which sounds faintly obscene but is just a misspelling of "pork rump," a completely irresistible slow-braised dish steeped in rock sugar, soy and star anise, served on a bed of steamed greens. Start with the juicy Shanghai steamed pork dumplings, add a vegetable (try snow cabbage with hot bean sauce), and you'll have a meal to remember.

Mandarin Noodle House
701 W. Garvey Ave., Monterey Park
626.570.9795
Dumplings/noodles. L & D daily. No booze.
Cash only. $
You won't take much comfort in the setting – harsh light, less-than-nurturing service – but you'll get all the comfort you could hope for from the steaming bowl of Family Handmade Noodle Soup, with hand-cut noodles and lots of yummy stuff. We also love the pan-fried dumplings, pork or shrimp soup noodle and our kids' favorite, the "thin onion pancake" – they love these scallion-laced layered pancakes so much they call this place the Crunchy Pancake Restaurant.

Mei Long Village
301 W. Valley Blvd., San Gabriel
626.284.4769
Shanghai/Jiangzhe. L & D daily. Beer. $
In a quiet dining room with mirrored walls and lots of greenery, regulars put away steamed Shanghai-style dumplings filled with crab and pork; light pastry-style dumplings filled with sautéed leeks; Shanghai spareribs; and jade shrimp with a spinach purée. It's all terrific, but it's the dumplings we most crave.

Mission 261
261 S. Mission Dr., San Gabriel
626.588.1666
Cantonese/dim sum. L & D daily, brunch Sat.-Sun. Full bar. $$
A sign of the times that have a' changed in San Gabriel, this extraordinary Chinese restaurant occupies the century-old adobe building that once housed City Hall. It's a vast place – pretty much every weekend you'll find a wedding or other huge celebratory party in one of the seemingly endless rooms; we prefer to sit outside in the pretty, grapevine-shaded courtyard. The ambitious and accomplished kitchen turns out a peaceful, first-rate dim sum that's ordered off a menu; try the juicy pork buns and the spinach and scallop dumplings (if you're vegetarian, you'll have many more choices than at most dim sum places). Dinner brings such specialties as steamed rock cod, which we could happily eat every day for eternity. The service doesn't always live up to the caliber of the food.

Ocean Star Seafood
145 N. Atlantic Blvd., Monterey Park
626.308.2128
Hong Kong seafood/dim sum. L & D daily.
Full bar. $$
Vast and glossy, this reliable Cantonese restaurant is chaotic for dim sum and a bit more refined at dinner; we've had several memorable dinner parties in one of its private rooms. The dim sum, served in the usual way on rolling carts, is fresh and varied, and the seafood is consistently excellent; don't miss the salt-and-pepper shrimp, the whole steamed fish and the crab in black bean sauce.

Triumphal Palace
500 W. Main St. #8, Alhambra
626.308.3222
Cantonese/dim sum. L & D daily.
Beer & wine. $$
It's clear from the minute you enter this palace that you're here to feast, not merely eat. It's more sleek and modern than the typical upscale Chinese place, with cream-colored draperies, relatively soft lighting and comfy upholstered chairs. If you can round up nine friends, order the whole roast suckling pig (served like Peking duck) and get ready for a meal you'll never forget. Smaller groups can try the crispy deep-fried squab, salt-and-pepper crab and baby lamb chops in honey sauce; the dim sum is also excellent. Our only concern is that chef turnover has made the food sometimes inconsistent – but when it's good, it's really good. Wine buffs and alcoholics take note that corkage is just $10 for the table, no matter how many bottles you drink.

A Dumpling Lunch with Carl Chu

Carl Chu

In 1980, young Carl Chu and his family moved from Taiwan to Los Angeles, and they had a terrible time finding anything good to eat. "The food in those days was all Cantonese, and we hated it," he says. This was before the great 1990s emigration of Chinese people to the San Gabriel Valley, before it was easy to find authentic cooking from such regions as Sichuan, Jiangzhe and northern China.

After that great emigration, Carl became an avid student of Chinese cooking, writing and publishing Chinese Food Finder: Los Angeles and the San Gabriel Valley, which has become the essential guide to the food in San Gabriel, Rosemead and beyond. We met Carl for Shanghai dumplings at Mei Long Village in San Gabriel, to talk about eating well in the new Chinatown.

"Most of these mainland Chinese people have been here only a few years," says Carl, "and they're doing it their way – they're not interested in Americanizing their cooking." His book travels the regions of China, explaining how the cuisines vary, describing the staple ingredients and dishes, and leading readers to the best examples of each cuisine. Read it and you'll learn, for instance, what authentic Islamic Chinese cooking is and where to find dabing (sesame pancakes) and flash-fried lamb with leeks.

Carl's foray into cuisine and publishing changed his life. He's given up his first career as an engineer to eat, write and publish books; his latest is The Search for Sushi: A Gastronomic Guide, a primer about the art of preparing and eating sushi.

Here are a few of Carl's favorites:

Lu Din Gee
1039 E. Valley Blvd., San Gabriel
626.288.0588
Beijing. L & D daily.
Beer & wine. $-$$
"Lu Din Gee is really the only authentic Beijing duck restaurant left in Los Angeles," says Carl. It's a fairly swank place, with jazz on the stereo and a hip waitstaff. Although there's other good stuff to eat – scallion pancakes, beef with garlic, the mountain-yam jelly called konnyaku – you come here for the three-course duck dinner. First comes a platter of crisp, salty-sweet skin and moist meat, which you arrange on a pancake, top with a bit of scallion and dash of bean paste, and eat while trying not to groan too loudly with pleasure. The next course is duck stir-fried with bean sprouts; finally comes an aromatic and wonderful duck soup. It's a great feast to share with friends.

Phoenix Inn
208 E. Valley Blvd., Alhambra
626.299.1238
Guangdong/Cantonese. L & D daily.
Beer & wine. $
"This is the best place for hearty Cantonese food," says Carl. "The cooking is consistent, and the ingredients are very good." Don't miss the boneless chicken, a simple but fabulous chicken-soy stir-fry, the spareribs with salt and pepper, the lo mein… in fact, all the Cantonese classics are delicious. Local legend says this place is haunted by a woman ghost who sits at various tables and admires everyone's meals.

Sea Harbour
3939 N. Rosemead Blvd., Rosemead
626.288.3939
Hong Kong seafood/dim sum. L & D daily.
Beer & wine. $-$$$
When he has a hankering for either dim sum or Hong Kong-style seafood, Carl heads to Sea Harbour. "It's a little more expensive than some of the other places, but the quality is very good," he says. A posh branch of a chain in China, Sea Harbour is best known for its ultra-creative dim sum: sui mai topped with flying-fish roe; baozi tinted green by spinach juice; yummy shrimp dumplings with peas; the amazing special soup dumpling, filled with pork and seafood and topped with a shaving of shark's fin.

Eat 'n' Run: Fast Food, Pizza, Tacos & Takeout

Fast Food

Bill's Chicken
1280 N. Lake Ave., Pasadena
626.797.4119
Open daily to 11 p.m. Cash only.
The lack of décor and the troublesome parking (you must approach going north to turn right into the little lot) might deter you, but the fried chicken by-the-bag is upright, the dark meat being moister than the white. Beef ribs are tender, and the barbecue sauce on the sweet side (diabetics beware). Save room for sweet potato pie. A good spot for takeout party food.

Connal's
1505 E. Washington Blvd., Pasadena
626.794.5018, connals.com
Open daily to 10 p.m. Cash only.
We love Connal's burgers, even if they're a bit salty. The buns are warmed on the griddle so they're a little bit shined and fragrant with grease. And we love the old-fashioned tiny crushed ice for the fountain drinks, which are carbonated just right. All in all, this is a fine example of a hometown burger joint. Order your burger, sub or sandwich at the inside counter if you're going to sit at one of the Formica tables, or at the outside window if you're taking out.

Fredo's Phillys
720 N. Lake Ave., Pasadena
626.798.9905, fredosphillys.com
Open daily to 8 p.m.
Authentic Philly cheese steak sandwiches are the stock in trade at this storefront joint, and our Pennsylvania native friends say they are indeed the real deal, made on Amoroso rolls imported from Philadelphia. We like the thinly sliced chicken sandwiches just as much. Snag a sidewalk table if you can, and order a Hank's root beer with your sandwich.

The Hat World Famous Pastrami
491 N. Lake Ave., Pasadena
626.449.1844, thehat.com
Open daily to 10 p.m.
Sparkling clean, featuring retro graphics and a constant background chant of "pastrami burger, pastrami burger," the Hat is an SGV favorite for lovers of (you guessed it!) pastrami and burgers. Since 1951, this cute little checkerboard place with a grandiose name has preserved the stripped-down ethos of fast food and the SoCal car culture that spawned it, while serving up really good, salty pastrami, long, thick fries and soft drinks. Want something light? Fuggedaboudit – even the avocado sandwich is bathed in mayo.

Hi-Life Burgers
1326 Fair Oaks Ave., South Pasadena
626.799.5401
Open daily to 10 p.m. Cash only.
This classic burger joint is the home-away-from-home for kids from nearby South Pas Middle School and South Pas High. They get hopped up on the Suicide (a blend of every soda in the soda machine) and plates of cheese fries before heading out to skateboard and do homework. Good cheeseburgers, chili burgers and burritos.

In-N-Out Burger
2114 E. Foothill Blvd., East Pasadena
310 N. Harvey Dr., Glendale
420 N. Santa Anita Ave., Arcadia
Open Sun.-Thurs. to 1 a.m., Fri.-Sat. to 1:30 a.m. Cash only.
If you're a local, you don't need to be told about In-N-Out. If you're a visitor, hie thyself to one of these red-and-white burger joints to find out why they've become as essential to the California experience as surf shops and Rose Parades. Hand-cut fries, freshly grilled burgers, real milkshakes and unbelievably low prices make this the best fast-food chain in the state.

Lucky Boy
640 S. Arroyo Pkwy., Pasadena
626.793.0120
Open daily to 2 a.m. Cash only.
Everything you could ever want in a fast-food joint: vinyl booths, grungy concrete outdoor tables, messy chili fries, huge burgers and its

claim to fame, a stupendous breakfast burrito, stuffed with more bacon than your cardiologist wants you to eat in a lifetime.

Oinkster
2005 Colorado Blvd., Eagle Rock
323.255.OINK
oinkster.com
American. B Sat.-Sun; L & D daily. Beer & wine. $
It used to be a drive-through; with a near-complete minimalist makeover that preserved the red A-frame roof and spiffed up the patio, Oinkster is making a noise on the north side of busy Colorado Boulevard in Eagle Rock, with pork, burgers, rotisserie chicken, fries and sides (they've even tossed the salad eaters a bone), monster cupcakes and good drinks. It's "slow fast food" that is tasty and complex, while still being convenient, inexpensive and satisfyingly high in calories. Throw out the diet and pig out on a home-cured pastrami sandwich, Belgian fries, shake and a lemon bar.

Rick's Drive-In
680 E. Walnut St., Pasadena
626.449.4842
Open daily to midnight. Cash only.
Oh, sure, Rick's has good burgers, tasty tacos and decadent milkshakes, but you can't call yourself a regular unless you try the spuderito, a burrito filled with french fries, cheese and salsa – it's a staple for countless Pasadena high school boys. If you can't handle that carbfest, try the taco burger, which tastes like the old Tommy's burgers of the '60s. Seating is outdoor only, and there's always a crowd.
Note: For the last two years, Rick's has been looking for a new home, because the landlord is planning to build (what else?) condos, but it hasn't happened yet. Still, call before visiting.

Top's Burger
3838 E. Colorado Blvd., East Pasadena
626.449.4412
Open Sun.-Thurs. to 11 p.m., Fri.-Sat. to midnight.
This born-in-1952 fast-food institution has been spiffed up for a new era, with gleaming tile, shiny laminated tables and modern lighting. The care in the front of the house is also evident in the kitchen,

which turns out large burgers (the Kobe burger is legendary) with lots of crisp lettuce and good tomatoes; tasty turkey and veggie burgers; a full roster of breakfast dishes; sandwiches heaped with pastrami, turkey, roast beef or tuna; hand-cut fries; and generous Mexican classics (tostadas, burritos, tortilla soup). Quality fast food at a Pasadena landmark. Drive-through window, too.

Wolfe Burgers
46 N. Lake Ave., Pasadena
626.792.7292, wolfeburgers.com
Open daily to 10 p.m.
Good char-grilled burgers, perfect beer-battered onion rings, tasty breakfast burritos, a savory turkey-sausage sandwich with grilled onions, homemade guacamole and thick shakes keep this place packed every lunch hour with office workers and every evening with families. It has a nicer atmosphere than the other burger joints in town, and you can get a beer with your burrito.

Pizza

Brownstone Pizza
2108 Colorado Blvd., Eagle Rock
323.257.4992
L & D daily. No delivery. BYOB. Cash only. $
You're best off eating this ultra-thin-crust pizza in the barren café, because by the time you get it home, it'll be soggy. When they're fresh from the oven, though, the large pies or individual slices are absolutely delicious, with a subtly sweet sauce and just enough good cheese. If you want to really live large, wash it down with a bottle of wine from Colorado Wine Company next door.

Casa Bianca Pizza Pie
1650 Colorado Blvd., Eagle Rock
323.256.9617, casabiancapizza.com
D Tues.-Sat. No delivery. Beer & wine. Cash only. $
Widely considered to make the best pizza in the greater Los Angeles area, this funky Eagle Rock landmark is no place for a quick bite – the waits are usually fearsome, and even ordering a to-go pizza can take an hour. The payoff is a thin-crust, New York-style pizza with a flavor that usually makes you forget the hour of misery you just endured. Smart regulars put in their order when they put their name on the list for a table, so the pizza's ready by the time they're seated. The rest of the basic Italian food is fine but forgettable.

Domenico's

2411 E. Washington Blvd., East Pasadena
626.797.6459
236 W. Huntington Dr., Monrovia
626.357.7975
L & D Tues.-Sun. No delivery. Beer & wine. $
The best pizza in the city of Pasadena is found
at this busy, friendly local chain. It's most famed
for its loaded Big D pizza, but we prefer the
simpler sausage pie with the thin crust. If it only
delivered, life would be perfect.

Tarantino's Pizzeria

784 E. Green St., Pasadena
626.796.7836
L & D daily. No delivery. Beer & wine.
Cash only. $
A little and lively family restaurant with low
prices, an annoying cash-only policy and saucy,
thick-crust pizzas, as well as addictive garlic rolls
and the good Pepe's salad. The best pizza by
far is the "white" Florentine. If it's too crowded,
get your pizza to go; at lunchtime you can order
by the slice.

Village Pizzeria

41 N. Baldwin Ave., Sierra Madre
626.355.8817
L & D daily. Local delivery. No booze. $
A hub of Sierra Madre life, Village Pizzeria
features outstanding and creative toppings –
unfortunately they're put on a crust of curious
flavorlessness. But the toppings (like the one
with fresh mozzarella, cherry tomatoes and
a basil chiffonade) are worth a trip here, and
the by-the-slice selection goes well beyond
pepperoni. Bring your dog and your newspaper
and sit out on the sidewalk like everyone else.

Zelo Cornmeal Crust Pizzas

328 E. Foothill Blvd., Arcadia
626.358.8298
L Tues.-Sat., D Tues.-Sun. No delivery.
Beer & wine. $
This tiny, cheerful café is flagged with market
umbrellas and small outdoor tables. Inside,
refrigerated display cases are stacked with
beaucoup beverages and a bowl of tempting
(yes, tempting) chilled beets. The cornmeal crust
is distinct, like a good hush puppy, made with
coarse meal so it crunches with each bite. Corn
pizza on cornmeal crust might sound awful, but
the corn kernels snap and the pancetta is lightly
salted. The eggplant pizza is tender, not greasy.
And don't forget that beet salad with gorgonzola
and walnuts. Pizza is sold by the slice, too.

Chile verde burrito at El Metate

Taquerias

El Metate

12 N. Mentor Ave., Pasadena
626.229.0706
B & L daily, D Mon.-Sat.
"The richest Mexican food in town" is the
slogan here, so dieters beware. The burritos
are massive, the soups robust, and the huevos
rancheros delicious. A real find.

El Taquito Mexicano #2

467 N. Fair Oaks Ave., Pasadena
626.577.3918
B, L & D daily
The women behind the big stove in this cheerful
hole-in-the-wall make classics that are delicious
and dirt cheap. Our current addiction is the
sopes al pollo, a fat, cornbread-like tortilla
heaped with saucy chicken, beans, lettuce,
tomato and cojito cheese. Great $1 tacos.

King Taco

45 N. Arroyo Pkwy., Old Pasadena
626.792-0405
B, L & D daily (until midnight; Fri.-Sat. to 1 a.m.)
Three things make King Taco notable. First,
the incredible juiciness of the meats in its tacos
and burritos. Second, the late hours. Finally,
it's in Old Pasadena, so you can stop by after
shopping, moviegoing or bar-hopping.

La Estrella

502 N. Fair Oaks Ave., Pasadena
626.792.8559
B, L & D daily (until midnight; Fri.-Sat. to 2 a.m.)
This vividly colorful little building looks like it
belongs in a beach town in Mexico. The $1 tacos
are juicy and more seasoned than most, with a
subtle salsa kick. Particularly addictive is the al
pastor, either in taco or burrito form; also terrific
are the Baja-style fish tacos (fried, with cabbage
and white sauce), ceviche and shrimp cocktails.

Los Tacos

1 W. California Blvd., Pasadena
626.795-9291
L & D daily (until midnight; Fri.-Sat. to 1 a.m.)
A reliable Pasadena haven, Los Tacos makes
a tasty soft taco, a hearty menudo and all the
taco-joint classics. The fish tacos (sautéed, not
fried) are particularly noteworthy. The salsa bar
includes an excellent verde that pairs beautifully
with the carnitas. Note to locals: Los Tacos is a
fine and affordable caterer.

Puebla Tacos

#1: 700 N. Lake Ave., Pasadena
626.797.6884
#2: 1819 E. Villa St., Pasadena
626.793.1083
#3: 2067 N. Los Robles Ave.,
Northwest Pasadena
626.296.3390
B, L & D daily (Lake branch until 4 a.m.)
Many people swear by Puebla, but we've had
better. Our main beef: The tortillas used for
the soft tacos are too large, throwing off the
critical meat-tortilla ratio. And lately the cooking
seems lifeless. But the original Lake location,
in a grungy 7-Eleven strip mall with the worst
parking lot in Pasadena, must be commended
for staying open until 4 a.m.

Señor Fish

618 Mission St., South
Pasadena
626.403.0145
L & D daily, B Fri.-Sun.
4803 Eagle Rock Blvd.,
Eagle Rock
323.257.7167
B, L & D daily
The L.A.-area destination
for fish tacos and all manner
of Mexican seafood,
Señor Fish is justly famed
for its cooking, from the
homemade salsas to the
savory beans to the scallop
enchiladas. We're partial
to the seafood quesadilla, a diet-busting dream
of tortillas, cheese, shrimp and scallops, but the
lighter fish tacos are just as good. The Eagle
Rock branch, in an old bungalow with a stone
fireplace and tree-shaded patios, is charming to
boot and is an Occidental College hangout.

Taco Trucks

Two trucks are worth going out of your way
for. In Pasadena at night, go to the truck in the
Nishikawa Auto Service parking lot on Fair Oaks
north of California. It's run by the people at **El**

Taquito Mexicano, so the food is fabulous, and
it's open until 1 a.m. during the week and 3 a.m.
on Friday and Saturday. In Eagle Rock, also in
the evening hours, head for **Leo's Tacos,** which
parks on Eagle Rock Boulevard at Avenue 43
every night until 4 a.m. It's gotta be the only
taco truck with its own web site (leostacos.com)
and a short film made about it (by devoted Oxy
students).

Takeout

Egg Roll Express

2397 E. Washington Blvd., Pasadena
626.791.5336
The name might suggest a greasy spoon, but
the food here is fresh and healthy, made without
MSG and with good ingredients. We love the
sesame chicken, dumplings, wonton soup, string
beans and Sichuan dishes. Lots of vegetarian
options, low prices and free delivery in the East
Pasadena/Altadena area.

Gerlach's Grill

1075 S. Fair Oaks Ave., Pasadena
626.799.7575
You might expect a takeout window next to a
liquor store to be a chili-fries kind of place, but
you would be wrong. Gerlach's has an unusual
Middle Eastern–Mexican menu, so burritos are
filled with saffron-tinged rice. We're sorry that
the menu recently shrunk (we miss the lamb
tacos!), but it still makes excellent grilled fresh
fish (salmon, shark, tuna) at low prices. There's
nowhere to eat, so take it home, to work or a few
blocks east to Allendale Park for a picnic.

Julienne Fine Food

2649 Mission St., San Marino
626.441.2299, juliennetogo.com
Closed Sun.
Sue and Julie Campoy no longer cater
Pasadena's poshest parties – instead they fill
Pasadena's Sub-Zeros with Tuscan meatloaf,
red-onion-crusted salmon, turkey and black bean
chili and spicy Thai beef salad. This spectacular
gourmet-to-go shop has a freezer full of dinner-
for-two entrees; a deli case lined with salads,
quiches, cheeses and entrees; a refrigerator
stocked with soups, sauces and dips; and
platters of brownies, cookies and sweets.

The Kitchen for Exploring Foods

1434 W. Colorado Blvd., Pasadena
626.793.7234, thekitchen.net
Closed Sun.-Mon.
This hugely successful caterer offers a small but

Gourmet-to-go at Julienne

excellent roster of daily-changing to-go food, from soups to vegetarian lasagna to a delicious beef bourguignonne. If you don't have time to make appetizers for that potluck, you can usually pick up a dozen mini Caesar salad cups or zucchini-wrapped shrimp.

Lola's Peruvian
230 N. Brand Blvd., Glendale
818.956.5888
Perhaps the best to-go chicken in the region – okay, in the world – is found at this Peruvian café. The birds are marinated in citrus juice, garlic and chiles and spit-roasted over a wood fire until crisp-skinned and incredibly juicy. Pair them with the homemade French fries (the Peruvians know their potatoes), and you will be deliriously happy. Eat in or take out.

Pasadena Sandwich Co.
259 N. Sierra Madre Villa, Pasadena
626.578.1616
Closed Sun.
Huge sandwiches, low prices and folksy charm keep this long-established spot packed every lunchtime with local working folk, from cops to office toilers to clerks at the mall next door. Split a sandwich with a friend, or get the soup and half sandwich.

Porta Via
1 W. California Blvd., Pasadena
626.793.9000, portaviafoods.com
Long glass cases hold Italian foods that look almost too pretty to eat, but when you take them home, you find they taste as good as they look. Try the Chianti-braised short ribs, chicken parmigiana, fabulous grilled scampi with garlic and chiles and delicious orecchiette with broccoletti. Just be warned that none of

this good stuff comes cheap, but it makes for a great, no-fuss dinner party.

Soumarelo
1090 N. Allen Ave., Pasadena
626.791.0999
Don't tell Zankou, but this may actually be the best takeout chicken in town. The catch is that they don't always have a lot of it ready when you show up – it's not a chicken-producing machine like Zankou – so be smart and call first. Good garlic paste, great lentil soup and such sides as hummus and a delicious Armenian salad.

Teri & Yaki
319 S. Arroyo Pkwy., Pasadena
626.683.9865
229 N. Lake Ave., Pasadena
626.844.4554
106 S. Myrtle, Monrovia
626.256.6705
Closed Sun.
Also known as Himeko Chicken, these three cafés make an addictive teriyaki chicken served with chow mein and rice. The sides (sprout salad, seasoned spinach, garlic noodles) are tasty. You can eat here, but we usually get it to go; it's good party chow, too.

Zankou Chicken
1296 E. Colorado Blvd., Pasadena
626.405.1502
1415 E. Colorado Blvd., Glendale
818.244.2237
The aroma of this Lebanese rotisserie chicken drives our kids mad with hunger. You tear the salty meat and skin off the bird, stuff it into a pita, add garlic sauce, and you're in poultry heaven. Good schwarmas and wraps, but the chicken's the thing here.

Good Eats: Bakeries & Markets

Bakeries & Confections

Berolina Bakery & Café
3421 Ocean View Blvd., Glendale
818.249.6506, berolinabakery.com
Closed Sun.-Mon.
A toe over the Montrose line, this shop has baked tasty northern European and Scandinavian goods for eighteen years. Limpa, anyone? Or how about poppy, Black Forest, rye currant or 28 other varieties on the shelf depending upon the day of the week? You'll also find buttery cookies, cakes and tortes, as well as espresso drinks, juices and a few salads and sandwiches.

Bristol Farms
606 Fair Oaks Ave., South Pasadena
626.441.5450
Our favorite bakery in town for cookies: chocolate chunk, oatmeal, peanut butter and the best chocolate-dipped macaroons anywhere. All the baked goods are tasty, but it's the cookies we drive out of our way for.

Bulgarini Gelato
749 E. Altadena Dr., Altadena
626.791.6174, bulgarinigelato.com
Closed Mon.
Fans from as far away as Santa Monica make the trek to this gelateria in a run-down shopping center at the top of Lake. With rich cream-based flavors (pistachio, from Sicilian nuts; zabaglione; stracciatella; seasonal fruits; chocolate of many kinds) and the intense sorbetti and rough-textured granitas (blood orange, strawberry, kiwi, lemon, pear, pomegranate, espresso), it can be hard to choose your three to five flavors in the small to large cups ($4 to $7). That is no

Bulgarini Gelato

matter – you can get it to go in quantities of up to a couple of kilos for $30. Watch for every-other-Friday night outdoor movies in *italiano*.

Chocolate Box Café
714 Foothill Blvd., La Canada
818.790.7918
This fantastic neighborhood find is packed with decadent handmade Belgian chocolates. (The chili-powder truffle is simply divine.) The coffee bar offers a mocha, and we nearly fainted when the efficient barista hauled out a giant plastic box of chocolate shavings from which to scoop a heap of black gold flakes into the cup. But it's really not a mocha, just a great grownup's hot chocolate with a smoky whisper of espresso.

Dots Cupcakes
400 S. Arroyo Pkwy., Pasadena
626.568.3687, dotscupcakes.com
Closed Sun.
In case you've been living on the planet Zoltran, cupcakes are all the rage, and Dots is the place to get 'em in Pasadena. Although they're not cheap, they're a lot less than at the famous westside Sprinkles, and they're very good; we're partial to the chocolate mint and the pumpkin pie. The mini cupcakes are fun for a party.

Euro Pane
950 E. Colorado Blvd., Pasadena
626.577.1828
Pasadena's version of La Brea Bakery is run by Sumi Chang, who trained at the

Just try to leave Europane without buying something chocolate

mothership and now has a rabid following for her croissants (which sell out quickly every morning), breads, scones, dense chocolate cakes and generous pressed sandwiches. Order ahead if you want to get your heart's desire – nothing lasts long here.

Goldstein's Bagel Bakery
1939 Verdugo Blvd., La Cañada
818.952.2457
412 N. Santa Anita Ave., Arcadia
626.447.2457
It was a sad, sad day when the Goldstein's in Old Town gave way for a chain store – the canary in the coal mine warning that Colorado

Colorful goodies at Little Flower Candy Co.

Boulevard would soon be stripped of all local personality. Thankfully, you can still get its chewy, boiled-then-baked bagels in La Cañada and Arcadia – and both have drive-through service. Delicious turkey bagel wraps.

Gourmet Cobbler Factory

33 N. Catalina Ave., Pasadena
626.795.1005, thegourmetcobblerfactory.com
Closed Mon.
It doesn't look like a gourmet place from the outside, and it's not really about being gourmet anyway – it's about small, family-size or party-size cobblers that will have you returning the next day for more. Mixed-berry, peach and blueberry are our favorites, and all are made with fresh fruit and not too much sugar. Top with vanilla-bean or cinnamon ice cream and prepare to swoon. Call ahead for larger sizes.

Heirloom Bakery & Café

807 Meridian Ave., South Pasadena
626.441.0042
Part of South Pas's oh-so-hip foodie community, Heirloom specializes in pretty American desserts and breakfast pastries: cinnamon rolls, shiny fruit tarts, chocolate cakes and fat cookies. Take 'em home or eat 'em in the bakery or out on a sidewalk table, where you'll likely be surrounded by carefully underdressed parents and their adorable toddlers.

Little Flower Candy Co.

1422 W. Colorado Blvd., Pasadena
626.304.4800, littleflowercandyco.com
Closed Sun.
Christine Moore's famed sea-salt caramels and other remarkable candies are sold at chic food and gift shops all over, and now she has her own shop, complete with a bakery, simple lunch service and good espresso. Her bran muffins are the best in town; cakes and tarts made to order are gorgeous; and the scones are heaven.

Patticakes

1900 Allen Ave., Altadena
626.794.1128, patticakesdesserts.com
The east Altadena stop for a treat (a slice of chocolate truffle cake, a cup of coffee), Patticakes is famed for its special-occasion, made-to-order cakes. They are spectacular, and they taste every bit as good as they look.

Porto's Bakery

315 N. Brand Blvd., Glendale
818.956.5996, portosbakery.com
Founded by Cuban immigrants in the '60s, this huge, gleaming café and bakery displays a gorgeous and staggeringly diverse collection of goods, from the guava and cheese strudel called refugiado to Cuban bread to all-American cheesecake. Its ornate tiered wedding cakes are award-winners. Terrific Cuban sandwiches.

Wildflour Baking Co.

328 W. Sierra Madre Blvd., Sierra Madre
626.355.9000
Closed Sun.
This very fine bakery makes superb wedding, birthday and holiday cakes; walk-ins can usually count on dreamy mini-cakes, lemon bars, cherry bars, muffins and fresh bread. It also makes very fine sandwiches with its own breads (herbes de provence, sourdough, garlic and more), which are as good as Sumi Chang's at Euro Pane. The seating is just okay.

Specialty & Gourmet Markets

Carniceria La Gardenia

123 E. Angeleno Ave., San Gabriel
626.287.0389
An excellent source for carne asada, fajitas, bistec al pollo and other tasty Mexican meats.

Fish King

722 N. Glendale Ave., Glendale
818.244.2161
For some people Sunday morning is about slippers and the newspaper; for others it's about going to Fish King to get something delicious for Sunday dinner. These people know their seafood, and they come here for wild salmon and sushi-grade ahi to opah, ono and other Pacific fish. Don't miss the refrigerator and freezer cases filled with seafood gumbo, fresh mango salsa and lobster bisque.

Sweet treats, French-style, at Nicole's Gourmet Foods

Famima

25 N. Raymond Ave., Pasadena
626.578.0545
621 E. Colorado Blvd., Pasadena
626.304.0500, famima-usa.com
A fast-growing Japan-based chain, Famima was an immediate hit in Pasadena, with two branches serving students, office workers and condo dwellers. It has all sorts of upscale snacks and drinks, as well as steamers and cases of tasty prepared food: Chinese dumplings, pork buns, turkey-cranberry sandwiches, sushi, crème brûlées, cookies and more.

Good Foods Market

1864 E. Washington Blvd., Pasadena
626.794.5367
It's shabby looking on the outside, but this Armenian market is full of very good things to eat: the creamiest hummus on the planet, the softest pita in town, paper-thin cold cuts, feta cheeses and good olives. And it holds Hindoyan Meat Market, which has fantastic marinated chicken kebabs. Do not take offense if they allow line cuts for Armenian speakers. Yes, it happens.

Harmony Farms

2824 Foothill Blvd., La Crescenta
818.248.3069
Run by a goofy and gregarious bunch of guys in butcher's whites, Harmony specializes in wild game and organic, free-range, sustainably produced lamb, turkey, beef and chicken. It's a great place to find buffalo burgers, superb lamb chops and first-rate Thanksgiving turkeys – which you need to order in advance.

Howie's Ranch Market

6580 N. San Gabriel Blvd., San Gabriel
626.286.8871
A trip to Howie's is a trip back to a happier time, when grocers were grocers and service always came with a smile. This compact, all-purpose market is justly famed for three things: Alexander's Meats, with Harris Ranch beef, dry-aged prime cuts, excellent marinated poultry and meat (great asada); a fine and classic American bakery; and the aforementioned service. Also worth noting are the locally made empanadas and tamales. Worth driving out of your way for.

Jones Coffee Company

537 S. Raymond Ave., Pasadena
626.564.9291, thebestcoffee.com
A globe-hopping selection of coffee (including organic choices) is found in a warehouse space filled with giant roasters. The prices can't be beat – the weekly special is just $6.50 a pound. Extras include an on-site café, a home-delivery coffee club and a terrific office coffee program.

Nicole's Gourmet Foods

921 Meridian Ave., South Pasadena
626.403.5751, nicolesgourmetfoods.com
Closed Sun.
If it's French, Nicole carries it: pâtés, cheeses, confit, truffles, chocolates, wines, pastry-making ingredients, pastry shells, puff pastry, French butter, olives, foie gras, sauce bases, frozen quiches, soups, fantastic frozen croissants . . . whether you want to cook a French meal or get a to-go French picnic, you'll find it at Nicole's.

99 Ranch Market

140 W. Valley Blvd., San Gabriel
626.307.8899
1300 S. Golden West Ave., Arcadia
626.445.7899
The Gelson's of Chinese supermarkets, except instead of having 60 kinds of breakfast cereal, it has 60 kinds of fish sauce. An absolute must-visit, with a dazzling array of Chinese produce, sauces, noodles, kitchenware and ingredients, as well as terrific (and terrifically cheap) live seafood. More branches around the SG Valley.

Roma Deli

918 N. Lake Ave., Pasadena
626.797.7748
Roma's fans are so passionate they are almost a cult, and their leader is Rosario, who gives tastes of everything and confidently proclaims his sandwiches, prosciutti and cheeses to be the best in the world. We're not sure about that, but they're certainly outstanding. So are the olive oils, sausages, salamis, gnocchi and imported Italian goodies, all at low prices. Some swear by the inexpensive produce, but we don't.

Schreiner's Fine Sausages

3417 Ocean View Blvd., Glendale
818.244.4735
Closed Sun. Cash only.
This place is a throwback – we're pretty sure we saw Rod Serling musing in the parking lot. It's been here for 50 years, and in Burbank for ten years before that. So says the helpful *frau* behind the counter in the Bavarian dirndl. The

butcher case displays endless foods made of ground-up animals: bratwurst, knackwurst, spicy sausage, bockwurst, caraway-flecked landjaeger, chewy salami. You'll also find chops, rumps and tongues that have been smoked, boiled, preserved, frozen or aged. Shelves of German condiments await your slathering needs, and a fridge is loaded with German beers and American sodas. Order your sausages or sandwich, check out the German sundries in case you're fresh out of *zahnpasta* or *handsalbe*, then zip next door to Berolina for dessert.

Taylor's Ol' Fashion Meats

14 E. Sierra Madre Blvd., Sierra Madre
626.355.8267
Closed Sun.
High-quality marinated meats are the specialty at the former Howie's Ranch Market (only Taylor's survived when it closed): tri-tips, carne asada, pollo asada, butterflied legs of lamb. It's also great for ordering a prime rib, organic turkey or other special-occasion product. Beautiful produce, too.

Trader Joe's

345 S. Lake Ave. (enter on Del Mar), Pasadena
626.395.9553, traderjoes.com
Many other locations
Reason enough to live in California, Trader Joe's is the local's lifeline for affordable foodie staples. Friends visit from out of state and fill a suitcase with TJ's nuts, vitamins, cookies, soups, cheese and wine. And our teenagers would starve if it weren't for our freezers full of TJ's pizzas, taquitos, dumplings and french fries.

Whole Foods

465 S. Arroyo Pkwy., Pasadena
626.204.2266, wholefoodsmarket.com
Normally we eschew chain markets, but the new Whole Foods can't *not* be mentioned. It's an orgo-foodie Disneyland, complete with an actual ride (an escalator that carries up shopping carts) and the most dazzling food court you've ever seen: Korean barbecue, pizza, sushi, a Mediterranean bar, a wine bar, an entire wall of chocolate complete with a chocolate fountain... it's astonishing. It's also terribly expensive, but you will find tons of great food to eat there or take home to prepare later. It all makes you feel kind of sorry for the other branch on Foothill, which is posh by any normal standards.

Rafael the coffee maestro prepares beans to roast at Jones Coffee.

Party Time

Caterers

Auntie Em's Kitchen
4616 Eagle Rock Blvd., Eagle Rock
323.255.0800
This café is also a caterer, known for doing the hippest weddings (gay and straight), milestone birthdays and book parties on the eastside. Great modern American comfort food, fair prices.

Mary Pat Brandmeyer Catering
1860 N. Allen Ave., Pasadena
626.791.5400
Reasonably priced, people-pleasing modern American food – the kind of food you should be able to make yourself but can't – is Brandmeyer's specialty; she's particularly adept at dinner parties and smaller cocktail parties.

Dickenson West Caterers
181 E. Glenarm St., Pasadena
626.799.5252, dickensonwest.com
Pasadena's leading high-end caterer, DW does the finest weddings, benefit dinners and 50th birthday parties, and runs a romantic restaurant.

Elements Kitchen
107 S. Fair Oaks Ave., Old Pasadena
626.440.0100, elementskitchen.com
A lovely new Old Town spot specializing in small parties and dinners to go, featuring elegant but hearty American food. Tiny sidewalk café, too.

Happy Trails
207 S. Fair Oaks Ave., Old Pasadena
626.796.9526, happytrailscatering.com
Closed Sun.
Hidden behind the old brick storefront kitchen is a large, tree-shaded garden that's used for many local weddings and garden parties. Happy Trails also provides hearty, homey American and Mediterranean food off-site for everything from corporate meetings to funerals.

The Kitchen for Exploring Foods
1434 W. Colorado Blvd., Pasadena
626.793.7234, thekitchen.net
Closed Sun.-Mon.
Peggy Dark's bustling company has fed pretty much everyone in town at one function or another: weddings, bar mitzvahs, anniversaries, you name it. Her food is always delicious and fairly priced, and her service is professional. The gourmet-to-go products are great, too.

Party Rooms

Here are some good private dining rooms and party spaces in town. For large groups, also check out the Altadena Town & Country Club, the Langham Huntington, the Castle Green and the Pasadena University Club.

Café Santorini
164 W. Union St., Old Pasadena
626.564.4200, cafesantorini.nett
This fine and charming Mediterranean restaurant has three options for private parties: the Rococco Room, a large facility for up to 170 and a popular wedding spot; a room for up to 30; and the terrace overlooking One Colorado, which can be taken over for events.

Celestino
141 S. Lake Ave., Pasadena
626.768.3269
Warm and snappy service and delicious Italian food make this place a winner for any occasion; it has a private dining room and a potentially private enclosed rear patio.

Derek's Bistro
181 E. Glenarm St., Pasadena
626.799.5252, dickensonwest.com
If you don't mind spending for a swank dinner party for twelve, you won't do better than in the beautiful glass-walled private dining room. Other rooms can handle groups from six to 24.

La Casita del Arroyo
177 S. Arroyo Blvd., Pasadena
626.744.7275, ci.pasadena.ca.us
You can seat up to 80 in this fabulous, fireplace-warmed stone house on the banks of the Arroyo. It's run by the city; rates are reasonable, and you can use any caterer you like.

redwhite + bluezz
70 S. Raymond Ave., Old Pasadena
626.792.4441, redwhitebluezz.com
Hidden behind this small-seeming wine bar, bistro and jazz club are two rooms and a patio, which you can book in various combinations. This is a great spot for private parties for 30 to 200; the patio has a view of the Castle Green.

Farmer's Markets

Alhambra Farmer's Market
Monterey & E. Bay State St., Alhambra
626.570.5081
Sun. 8:30 a.m.-1 p.m.
A well-established market with a good selection of produce, food products and flowers.

Eagle Rock Farmer's Market
2100 Merton Ave., Eagle Rock
323.225.5466
Fri. 5-8:30 p.m.
A fun evening market with live music, kids' activities, a food court and the usual produce, flowers and food products.

Glendale Farmer's Market
N. Brand Blvd. between Broadway & Wilson, Glendale
818.548.3155
Thurs. 9:30 a.m.-1:30 p.m.
This certified farmer's market showcases organic and small-farm produce, flowers and foodstuffs.

La Cañada Flintridge Farmer's Market
Beulah & Houseman Ave., La Cañada
818.591.8161
Sat. 9 a.m.-1 p.m.
A compact weekend market with fresh and organic produce, flowers, prepared foods (nuts, oils) and a few crafts vendors.

Apple season at the La Cañada Farmer's Market

Monrovia Farmer's Market & Food Festival
Myrtle Ave. between Olive & Colorado, Monrovia
866.440.3374
Fri. from March-Dec. 5-9 p.m.
A lively weekly happening that combines a farmer's market with a street fair. Live music, kids' activities, crafts and food.

There's more than food at the Montrose Harvest Market.

Montrose Harvest Market
Honolulu & Ocean View Ave., Montrose
805.637.6635
Sun. 9 a.m.-2 p.m.
One of the showiest markets around, with a bounce house, pony rides, live music, antiques vendors and monthly special events, in addition to the expected food and flowers. Honolulu's shops and cafés do a brisk business, too.

Pasadena – Victory Park
N. Sierra Madre Blvd. & Paloma St., East Pasadena
626.449.0179
Sat. 8:30 a.m.-1 p.m.
A certified farmer's market, with flowers, organic produce and prepared foods.

Pasadena – Villa Park
363 E. Villa, Pasadena
626.449.0179
Tues. 9 a.m.-1 p.m.
A small certified farmer's market, with the customary fresh and organic produce and prepared foods.

South Pasadena Farmer's Market
El Centro St. & Meridian Ave., South Pasadena
818.786.6612
Thurs. 4-8 p.m.
A neighborly, charm-packed market with good street food in addition to the usual farm-fresh offerings. The Gold Line station is here, and shops and restaurants offer market-night specials. It's a social outing for lots of locals.

14 Coffeehouses That Aren't Starbucks

Bean Town Coffee Bar
45 N. Baldwin Ave., Sierra Madre
626.355.1596
Open daily from 5:30 a.m.
We'd live in Sierra Madre just for Bean Town —
it's the perfect coffeehouse. The coffee is robust,
the furniture funky but comfortable, and the
crowd diverse: book clubs, retired guys, moms 'n'
strollers, teens, dogs. Extras include bluegrass
and folk on weekends, WiFi, board games,
sidewalk tables and homemade baked goods.

Buster's Ice Cream & Coffee Shop
1006 Mission St., South Pasadena
626.441.0744
Open daily from 7 a.m.
From a sidewalk table in front of Buster's, with
a scoop of Fosselman's mint chip ice cream or
a blended mocha in front of you and the South
Pas street scene passing by, life is mighty fine.
This colorful, funky neighborhood hub also
showcases local musicians on weekend nights.

Café Alibi
84 S. Fair Oaks Ave., Pasadena
626.577.5779
Open daily from 7 a.m. (but not always)
Located on the back side of the Castle Green,
Café Alibi has free WiFi, a cute little patio
southside, a great, big picture window for
people-watching, friendly service and comfy
chairs for laptop lads and lassies. Hours can be
a little inconsistent.

Buster's in South Pasadena

The sidewalk tables at Bean Town are prized.

Café Culture
1359 N. Altadena Dr., Pasadena
626.398.8654
We shouldn't even tell you about this great
neighborhood secret, but here we go: These
folks steam an excellent mocha. The flaky
apple turnover is from Euro Pane, so what they
don't make themselves they procure from the
best. It's a regulars' kind of place; one laptop-
sporting regular says he knows Café Culture
has been here almost nine years because his
daughter just turned 9 and he first brought her
here in a stroller. Yeah, we like places where the
customers tell time by their children.

The Coffee Gallery
2029 N. Lake St., Altadena
626.398.7917
Open Mon.-Fri. from 6 a.m., Sat.-Sun. from 7 a.m.
So the coffee's not the best in town, and the
service is often bizarrely slow. But we like
this appealingly scruffy place anyway. The
live music in the separate concert room can
be terrific, and the private room is great for a
committee meeting.

Flintridge Bookstore & Coffeehouse
964 Foothill Blvd., La Cañada
818.790.0717, flintridgebooks.com
Open daily from 9 a.m.
Part of the sophisticated new bookstore on
Foothill, this coffeehouse occupies a side patio
with umbrella-shaded tables. It's not terribly
scenic, but the bookstore's great, the coffee is
good, and the atmosphere is easygoing.

Jones Coffee
537 S. Raymond Ave., Pasadena
626.564.9291, thebestcoffee.com
Open Mon.-Fri. from 7:30 a.m., Sat.-Sun. from
9 a.m.
Originally a roaster and wholesaler, Jones has
gradually morphed into a coffeehouse and
community center. It's still primarily a wholesaler

Hometown Pasadena

and roaster, sending the intense smell of almost-burning beans throughout the neighborhood, especially and most amusingly into the parking lot at the Starbucks behind it on Fair Oaks. The baristas make the best and most beautiful espressos and lattes in town; cappuccinos, however, aren't foamy enough. Owner Mireya Jones starts her morning by picking up croissants and pastries at Euro Pane, so get here early if you hope to snag a good one. Free WiFi, good jazz on the stereo and low prices help compensate for the lack of parking.

Kaldi
1019 El Centro St., South Pasadena
626.403.5951
Open Mon.-Fri. from 7 a.m., Sat.-Sun. from 7:30 a.m.
In a handsome old brick building next to the library, this South Pas coffeehouse is one of the best in town, with well-made espresso drinks, a welcoming vibe and sunny sidewalk tables.

Peet's Coffee & Tea
605 S. Lake Ave., Pasadena
626.795.7413
Open Mon.-Fri. from 5:30 a.m., Sat.-Sun. from 6 a.m.
Yeah, it's a chain, but you can't discuss Pasadena coffeehouses without mentioning Peet's. It's one of the most popular meeting spots in town, either on the outdoor terrace or inside, where the aroma of coffee can make you almost woozy. Its robust coffee, coffee drinks and teas are better than at the competing chains. Adjoining Noah's makes a fine bagel.

Perry's Joint
2051 Lincoln Ave., Northwest Pasadena
626.798.4700
Open Mon.-Fri. from 7:30 a.m., Sat. from 10 a.m.
A sophisticated, spacious spot with great jazz on the stereo, Perry's is a terrific place to hold small business meetings or to work on your laptop (free WiFi). Good coffee, tasty sandwiches and a full range of Dreyer's ice cream.

Red Door Café
Caltech, 1200 E. California Blvd., Pasadena
626.395.6158
Open Mon.-Fri. from 7:45 a.m.
Located next to the campus bookstore, this is a secret spot for good coffee and peaceful reading, writing or laptopping (free WiFi), and you don't have to be a student to come here. Beautiful outdoor patio under the trees, and lots of smart people around you.

Coffee as art at Jones Coffee

Swork
2160 Colorado Blvd., Eagle Rock
323.258.5600
2140 Verdugo Blvd., Montrose
818.248.3700
Open daily from 6 a.m.
When this hip, Ikea-ish place opened in 2000, it was the sign that Eagle Rock was finally gelling as a community. Swork went on to become the community's hub, thanks to its kids' play area (and kids' drinks like the Princess Potion), free WiFi, sidewalk tables, good coffee and smoothies and a loyal cadre of locals. The Montrose branch is a hit, too.

Zephyr Coffee House & Art Gallery
2419 E. Colorado Blvd., East Pasadena
626.793.7330
Open Mon.-Fri. from 7:30 a.m., Sat. from 8 a.m.
A hidden gem, Zephyr is a Craftsman cottage suffused with Zen-like beauty and calm. All the rooms have comfy sofas, and the patios have tree-shaded tables; regulars settle in for a few hours with a laptop or a newspaper. There's often-worthwhile live music on weekend nights. Tasty crepes, panini, salads and baked goods make it a good place for breakfast and lunch.

Zona Rosa
15 S. El Molino Ave., Pasadena
626.793.2334
Open Mon.-Sat. from 7:30 a.m., Sun. from 9 a.m.
Tiny and vividly colorful, this coffeehouse next to the Pasadena Playhouse has a Mexican flair, from the music to the decor to the heavenly Mexican hot chocolate. It often showcases really interesting local art with a Latin perspective. The upstairs room is the place to be.

Tea Time

Don't get your coffee filter in a twist – there won't likely be a transfer of caffeine power from java to tea any time soon. But when you're ready for a break from coffee, the tea party awaits. Often frilly and crowded with hen parties, tea shops redefine refreshment with pots of black, oolong, green or white tea and little snacks, both sweet and savory. In our multicultural junction, Pasadena provides ample opportunity for formal English tea or casual Asian tea drinks.

Aloha Boba Tea House
666 W. Huntington Ave., Monrovia
626.303.2283
At this shopping-mall tea joint, you'll trade in your china cup for to-go paper or plastic. Lots of moms and school kids zip in for a 3 p.m. boba fix; whether you want your boba hot or cold, the friendly counter girl will talk you through choosing the chewy blobs.

Au 79 Tea Spirit
1635 S San Gabriel Blvd., San Gabriel
626.569.9768
Come to this noisy café for a huge selection of tea drinks, including a delicious lavender infusion, half-sweet bobas and sweet milk toast (which is an acquired taste), plus Taiwanese hipsters in animated conversations all around.

Chado Tea Room
79 N. Raymond Ave., Old Pasadena
626.431.2832, chadotea.com
This lovely shop stocks more than 200 teas to sip here or to take home. You will want to lie down in the yellow coconut cake, it is so hypnotically sweet and moist.

Four Seasons Tea Room
75 N. Baldwin Ave., Sierra Madre
626.355.0045
Closed Sun.-Mon.
Inside a picturesque Craftsman house, Four Seasons has several rooms plus a spacious back patio. The tea is hot and frequently refreshed, the muffins are great, and all the baked goods are housemade. Except for the glissando music mix, this is a perfect spot for weekday tea. It even has free WiFi.

Huntington Rose Garden Tea Room
Huntington Gardens, 1151 Oxford Rd.,
San Marino
626.405.2100, huntington.org
Closed Tues.
Keep in mind that you must first pay admission to the Huntington, then pony up the $25 price for tea. But this plentiful buffet has six kinds of finger sandwiches, fresh fruit, salads, spreads and little cakes, so you won't go wanting. The two daily selections of hot tea are nothing to write home about, but the servers are friendly, and there's a happy vibe. Reservations essential.

Langham Huntington Hotel
1401 S. Oak Knoll Ave., Pasadena
626. 568.3900, pasadena.langhamhotels.com
The swankest afternoon tea in Pasadena is served all week in the lobby lounge. White linens, silver service, tiered trays of scones, jam, sandwiches, pastries plus champagne. The price – $59 per person, $39 without the bubbly – will sober you up, but what a way to go!

Favorite Place Tea Room
115 W. Wilson, Glendale
818. 507.7409
Closed Sun.-Mon.
This welcoming, chic little lunch shop serves a full "tea party" or a la carte afternoon tea. Great sliced chicken sandwiches on chewy rye bread, excellent salads and lovely rose lemonade.

Scarlet Tea Room
18 W Green St., Old Pasadena
626.577.0051, scarlettearoom.com
In this gilt-trimmed parlor, the scones are delectable, served with the best strawberry jam we've had. We also like the finger sandwiches and lunch specials for heartier appetites.

Tea Rose Garden
28 S. Raymond Ave., Old Pasadena
626.578.1144, trosegarden.com
This is a flower shop, too, and it's the most casual of the porcelain-cup shops. It pours more than 30 varieties of tea daily and offers themed service: English with scones, French with croissants and, yum, Hawaiian with pork buns.

T Room Montrose
2405 Honolulu Ave., Montrose
818.249.6677
Grab a table on the back patio if you can, but inside's plenty nice, too. T Room makes the absolute best egg salad sandwiches anywhere, with a wide array of teas and sweets.

The Drinking Life

In addition to the watering holes we recommend below, you'll find more drink-serving nightspots, including music bars, dance venues and jazz clubs, in the Entertaining chapter.

The Bar & the Lobby Lounge
Langham Huntington Hotel
1401 S. Oak Knoll Ave., Pasadena
626.568.3900
A recent remodel means there are now two bars here: The Bar, a dark, clubby spot known for its live jazz on Fridays and its superb live blues and R&B on Saturdays, and the larger, brighter Lobby Lounge, where a subdued jazz duo entertains. The Lobby Lounge, curiously, attracts a younger crowd, including swarms of college kids when they're back home in Pasadena for vacations. Both bars are resplendent with an aura of old-Pasadena, old-money entitlement and elegance. The Bar sells cigars, which aficionados smoke outside on the lovely terrace.

Bodega Wine Bar
Paseo Colorado, 260 E. Colorado Blvd., Pasadena
626.793.4300, bodegawinebar.com
This sleek, modern Paseo bôite (hiding behind P.F. Chang's) is bright by day and dark by night, with flickering candles providing not quite enough light to read the appealing menu. It's a fine spot for a drink and a bite before a movie, and it's a fun place to try lesser-known wines from around the world. They're all the same price – $5 during happy hour, $8 otherwise – which encourages trying something new. Boomers aren't shunned, but it's a young crowd, especially after 10 p.m., when the dance-beat music gets cranked up.

The Chalet
1630 Colorado Blvd., Eagle Rock
323.258.8800
On the outside, it still looks like the dive bar it once was (Topper's). On the inside, it's a seductive tribute to the ski-lodge watering hole, with a rock-walled bar, low leather banquettes, hokey thrift-store Alpine oil paintings, the dimmest of candlelight and a stone fireplace. The CD-stocked jukebox mixes everything from the Jackson 5 to the Shins with flair, the crowd is hip without being insufferable, and the vibe is conducive to conversation, especially in the early hours (7 to 10 p.m.). After 10 on weekends it's more of a scene.

Sleek style at Vertical Wine Bistro

The Colorado
2640 E. Colorado Blvd., Pasadena
626.449.3485
Think the Chalet is pretentious and wine bars are for posers? Then settle into a vinyl booth at the Colorado, order a Jim Beam or a pitcher of Bud, and put some Allman Brothers on the jukebox. This is a proper bar, where food means pork rinds and peanuts, and real women can play a mean game of pool. No one seems to mind the nose-thumbing at the state's no-smoking-in-bars law. A Pasadena landmark.

Johnny's Bar
5006 York Blvd., Highland Park
323.551.6959
Modern upholstered seats line one wall, sitting under coordinated mirrors. There's one pool table in back, so take turns and play nice, and a flat-screen TV playing movies from the '80s. Stylin' vatos and slouchy gringos mix freely at the capacious bar, where you'll find a cool water dispenser filled with absinthe. It's $14 for a glass, but after all, it is 75 percent alcohol. Bartenders make honest drinks and pour decent wines, a good selection of beers and cider, too, in case your mum's with you.

Little Cave
5922 N. Figueroa St., Highland Park
323.255.6871
This retro-hip bar is frequented by 20- and 30somethings, but the bartender is most friendly

Magnolia's hidden outdoor bar

to oldtimers, too. We went on Drunk Tuesday, where drinks are $1 off, but didn't stay to see how Hangover Wednesday would work out. This brick-front neighborhood bar used to be a German social club, complete with bowling alley, but there's no trace of the pins anymore. Instead it's a relaxing little place with bats projected on the ceiling, red lanterns casting a moody glow and, for your amusement, Pac Man tables and a lively 1980s jukebox.

Lucky Baldwin's Pub
17 S. Raymond Ave., Old Pasadena
626.795.0652
Its nooks and crannies filled with little wooden tables, English beer signs and old kegs, this rabbit warren of a pub has 63 brews on tap. On warm evenings people sit on the alley patio, sip British and Belgian beers and locally brewed Craftsman ales, and talk for hours. The jukebox is stuffed with '70s and '80s rock, and the clientele – students, beer lovers, JPL scientists, date-nighters – is more interested in conversation and beer than the singles scene. The English food is, well, English food.

Magnolia Lounge
492 S. Lake Ave., Pasadena
626.584.1126
The red flocked wallpaper, crystal light fixtures and low velvet couches pay tribute to the speakeasy (Pasadena's first) that purportedly thrived here during Prohibition. In this more

licentious age, 30something patrons freely enter the candlelit walkway that leads from the South Lake storefronts to the hidden world behind: an outdoor bar around a massive old tree trunk, with candles and heaters aplenty, and inside nooks that combine dimly lit plushness with Philippe Starck's Lucite chairs. The music is good, if too loud, the bartenders make a proper drink, the wine list is worthy, and most nights have an interesting happy hour – on Monday, beer is discounted and the bar menu (good salads, snacks, a burger) is half-price. A Pasadena hot spot.

Madeleine's Wine Bistro
1030 E. Green St., Pasadena
626.440.7087
Closed Mon.-Tues.
Part of an upscale restaurant, Madeleine's has a separate wine bar and another full-bar room, and both are romantic spots for a drink and quiet conversation. They take wine seriously here, and the by-the-glass list isn't cheap, but it's good stuff. You can order an elegant appetizer or two (perhaps an onion and olive tart or smoked salmon with shaved fennel) to go with your glasses of Shiraz.

Parkway Grill
510 S. Arroyo Pkwy., Pasadena
626.795.1001
The bar itself is a carved 1920s wooden classic, and the booze is top-notch: single-malt scotches, high-end martinis, good wines by the glass. Add comfortable seating, superb live jazz (mostly piano) and a diverse crowd of local power people and special-occasion celebrants, and you've got one of the best upscale bars in town.

Rancho Bar
2485 N. Lake Ave., Altadena
626.798.7634
High up on Lake sits this funky little (and we mean little) neighborhood bar with an interesting mix of regulars, including young bohos and middle-aged barflies, many of whom smoke despite the ban on indoor smoking. The jukebox is filled with jazz and classic rock, and the pool table sees some good action. It's not easy to find a seat inside, but there's usually room on the patio.

Stoney Point
1460 W. Colorado Blvd., Pasadena
626.449.9715
This old-school continental restaurant on the west edge of Pasadena has a welcoming bar that attracts neighbors from the posh San Rafael

'hood who are looking for a good cocktail and a place to relax and discuss tax cuts. Nice bartenders, pleasant piano music and, if you get hungry, acceptable food.

Vertical Wine Bistro
70 N. Raymond Ave., Old Pasadena
626.795.3999
This swank bôite is on the second floor of an Old Town building, giving it the feel of a secret speakeasy. The people here take wine seriously, offering some 100 choices by the glass from every winemaking region of note in the world. To accompany the wines is a collection of chic small dishes not unlike the ones served at L.A.'s A.O.C. wine bar. If you're careful, you can eat and drink well for a reasonable tab; if you're not careful, the sky's the limit.

The Yard House
Paseo Colorado, 330 E. Colorado Blvd., Pasadena
626.577.9273
Okay, so it's kinda corporate, but we like this huge pub/restaurant anyway. It has the most diverse crowd of any Pasadena bar – all ages, all ethnicities, all social strata – and some 150 beers on tap (and a full bar). It also has much better food (Korean BBQ beef, ahi salad, excellent burgers, a yummy onion-ring "tower") than the typical beer bar. Expect a mob on weekends; waits for dinner can reach an hour. But while you wait you'll have fun trying the Pyramid Hefenweizen, Rogue Dead Guy Ale and Hobgoblin English Ale. We just wish they'd move beyond the classic-rock music – even aging boomers get tired of the Eagles eventually.

The York
5018 York Blvd., Highland Park
323.255.9675, theyorkonyork.com
For proof of Highland Park's increasing hipness, head to this newish gastropub, a high-ceilinged, brick-walled bar with very good food. The draft selection is swell – Newcastle Brown, Craftsman 1903 Lager, Kronenbourg 1664 and more – the wine by the glass is affordable and tasty, and the cocktails are well made. Some folks come just to drink and chat with their friends, but lots also have something to eat, perhaps a very good bowl of soup, some delicious bruschetta, a Cheddar burger or great fish and chips. Come with a gang or come alone with your novel to read (or write) – either way, you'll feel at home.

5 Great Happy Hours

Bar Celona
46 E. Colorado Blvd., Old Pasadena
626.405.1000, barcelonapasadena.com
Happy hour Mon.-Fri. 3-6:30 p.m.
So maybe it's not the most authentic tapas in the world, but the happy hour is a good one and the location is prime. Cocktails and sangria are half-price, beer is $3, and a decent list of Spanish appetizers is half-price. It's a good-looking place and a lively scene.

La Grande Orange
260 S. Raymond Ave., Pasadena
626.356.4444
Happy hour Mon.-Fri. 5-7 p.m.
Pasadena's newest hangout is in the restored 1925 Santa Fe Depot, and the bar is relaxed and friendly, a great place to meet friends after work. All cocktails, beer and wine by the glass are 50 percent off during happy hour.

McCormick & Schmick's
111 N. Los Robles Ave., Pasadena
626.405.0064
Happy hour Mon.-Fri. 3:30-6:30 p.m. & 9:30-11 p.m., Sat. 9:30-11 p.m.
Its woodwork and plants give it an '80s, *Cheers* kind of look, and its bargain happy-hour menu gives it a steady clientele of business people and friends meeting after work or after a movie. Dishes range from a $1.95 cheeseburger to a $4.95 blackened-shrimp pizza. Some drinks are discounted, too.

Mijares
145 Palmetto Dr., Pasadena
626.792.2763
Happy hour Mon.-Thurs. 4-7 p.m.
This 90-year-old Pasadena Mexican restaurant has one of the best happy hours around. Fine free food – nachos, enchiladas – help absorb the tequila in the potent margaritas, which are $1 off. The large bar is convivial, with an eclectic crowd. The restaurant serves workaday Cal-Mex fare.

Twin Palms
101 W. Green St., Old Pasadena
626.577.2567
Happy hour Sun.-Fri. 3-7 p.m.
On a warm summer evening, head for this lively outdoor bar inside the popular restaurant. During happy hour many drinks (house wines, martinis, basic beers) are discounted, and the excellent bar menu – calamari, mussels, sashimi, wood-fired chicken pizza – is half-price.

Wine Shops We've Known & Loved

Pasadena has a few semi-serious vintners, including homeowners scattered along the banks of the Arroyo, but if you can't get a truly local appellation, plenty of wine merchants will help you celebrate the delights of the vine. Here are some of our local favorites.

Jennifer and John Nugent at the Colorado Wine Company

Bev-Mo
885 S. Arroyo Pkwy., Pasadena
626.356.9462
It's a national chain, and of course we should all be supporting our local merchants. We do indeed shop at the independents – but every now and then, like during the get-a-second-bottle-for-a-nickel sales, we spy our neighbors here, surreptitiously stocking up. Service is minimal, but if you know what you like, you can get good deals.

Chronicle Wine Shop
919 E. California Blvd., Pasadena
626.577.2549, cwcellar.com
No credit cards
A remnant of the late lamented Chronicle restaurant, this wine shop is a quirky world away from the high-end tasting rooms. When the flag is up on California Boulevard, the staff is in. The redolent atmosphere is reminiscent of a French *cave* – though the actual location is an old motel room behing Pie 'n Burger. No tastings, but well worth a trip, thanks to its often-remarkable bargains. Caterers shop here for parties, relying on the advice of the savvy sommelier.

Colorado Wine Company
2114 Colorado Blvd., Eagle Rock
323.478.1985, cowineco.com
Closed Mon.
Newcomer Colorado Wine Company in Eagle Rock has proven a big success, thanks to its fun tastings and events and its large selection of bottles for less than $25. The slogan at Jennifer and John Nugent's store is "Wine for everyone." In that spirit, for just $12 they offer generous pours of four wines (served with artisanal cheeses from Auntie Em's) on Sunday afternoons in a snug back room that looks like a tiny slice of New York. The same tasting happens on Friday night for $15, and it's always full. Wednesday nights bring wine-cellar tastings, when customers buy bottles and drink them on site, often sharing with old and new friends; bring in a pizza from next door's Brownstone, and you've got yourself a party.

Gerlach's
1075 S. Fair Oaks Ave., Pasadena
626.799.1166
So imagine you are planning your wedding, and there is unbelievable deadline pressure coming at you from all sides, and sure, you love your mother-in-law-to-be – but could she maybe just lay off for a couple of days? And suddenly the wedding happens, and it is great and everyone is happy and love is in bloom and then it hits you – you forgot to invite your second cousin, whom you love like a brother – but sheesh, somehow in all the craziness you just forgot to put him on the list.

Well, change the wedding to a book and your beloved second cousin to Gerlach's and there you have it: We goofed and forgot to put this Pasadena landmark in the first edition. Fred Fedail is the driving force behind the wine operation, but Gerlach's without his brother Lewy, is, as untold numbers of Pasadenans would tell you, unimaginable. Gerlach's maintains a top-flight wine room, and Fred's love of port, sherry and dessert wine add value to a standout wine selection. Look for great bargains just outside the temperature-controlled room.

Heritage Wine Shop
155 N. Raymond Ave., Old Pasadena
626.844.9333
This woodsy, open-beamed Old Town space stocks a good selection from around the world (and premium liquors, too). The bar serves wines by the glass, or you can drink a bottle you purchased there for a $10 corkage fee.

Mission Wines
1114 Mission St., South Pasadena
626.403.9463, missionwines.com
A pioneer of the increasingly foodie South Pas scene, this great shop hosts six-wine tastings on Saturday afternoons and individual pours the rest of the week. The staff suggestions – from

that "I'm sorry" bottle to a case for a festive birthday party – are always perfect. And it's not all high-end stuff – we've found great choices in the $10-and-under area.

Nose Wine Cellar
696 E. Colorado Blvd., Pasadena
626.666.6991, thenosewinecellar.com
Closed Sun.-Mon.
While Nose Wine Cellar has a smaller selection than many local wine shops, it packs a lot into a small space. Flights of wine paired with a small but good menu of Spanish, French and Italian dishes. Located between the Laemmle Playhouse 7 movie theaters and the Pasadena Playhouse, it makes a fine place for a drink or a casual dinner.

Red Carpet Liquor
400 E. Glenoaks Blvd., Glendale
818.247.5544
If Red Carpet doesn't have it, you may have to head to the westside to find it. It stocks a particularly impressive collection of Californians, but also wine from around the world, as well as spirits, beers, cigars and stemware. Tastings offered on Tuesday evenings and weekends.

Mission Liquor
1801 E. Washington Blvd., Pasadena
626.794.7026, missonliquor.com
Closed Sun.
Mission Liquor improbably anchors a street in Pasadena's Armenian Row with an imposing stone front and an equally impressive collection of wine, beer, liqueurs, and spirits (and cigarettes and cigars). A bright, welcoming layout, good selection of mixers, competitive prices, occasional wine tastings and expert advice make this high-end neighborhood liquor store, in business for nearly 60 years, a gem.

Rosso Wine Shop
3459 N. Verdugo Rd., Glendale
818.330.9130, rossowineshop.com
Closed Mon.
Next door to Bashan restaurant, Rosso specializes in "everyday" wines from Italy, France, Spain and California. But everyday does not mean ordinary. The prices are reasonable (you can find bottles from $10 and up – way up if you'd like), and the selection is interesting, with some well-known vintners mixed with small producers, and great choices from overseas. Part of a Sparr Heights revival, Rosso hosts weekend wine tastings (example: one white and two reds from Spain, $10 for all three) and food-pairing events; you can also buy wine here for Bashan and pay a mere $5 corkage.

Rosso Wine Shop

Topline Wine & Spirits
556 Riverdale Dr., Glendale
818.500.9670
If you're an oenophile who knows what you're looking for, head here. It has a good selection and very good prices, but the slightly frosty staff can be intimidating to the uninitiated. Don't miss the collection of spirits.

Trader Joe's
345 S. Lake Ave. (enter on Del Mar), Pasadena
626.395.9553, traderjoes.com
Many other locations
There's a lot more than Two Buck Chuck here – why, you can spend as much as $6 for a bottle of French wine! It takes tasting effort to find the diamonds in this sea of bargain wines, but many of us have proved up to the challenge.

Q & A: Nicole Grandjean

Nicole Grandjean (pronounced *grahnzsahn*), proprietress of Nicole's Gourmet Foods in South Pasadena, came to us by way of France. With a background of supplying the hotel and restaurant industry with quality products, Nicole and her son Steven opened their first tiny retail location in Pasadena in 1996 and moved to their current larger and lovely location in 2001. Jill and Nicole spoke over coffee on a beautiful winter morning at one of her sidewalk tables.

Tell me a little about growing up in France.
I grew up in the center of France in the countryside. I had my parents and three brothers, and my father loved cooking – he worked in the kitchen of a hotel restaurant. On Sundays, we would cook and bake at home, and we would go to the forest and gather chanterelles and chestnuts. On the first of May I would gather lily of the valley. You would smell their beautiful scent before you would even see them.

What brought you here?
I had traveled all over the U. S. with friends when I was young. Before that I thought it was all big cities, but how wrong I was. Utah, Colorado . . . everywhere it was very beautiful. I came to California in 1987, before Starbucks and La Brea Bakery, so there was no good coffee and no good bread – and, of course, no cheese! I started with a company that was the first to import mainly French products, and my job was to sell cheese to supermarkets – and their people would look at my cheeses and say, no, no, no, people want cheddar. It was no easy job. But I knew the day would come, and here it is. Some of my customers know as much as I do and have very sophisticated palates.

Do you especially enjoy anything from the typical American kitchen?
The hamburger that you cook on the barbecue outside in the garden – I enjoy that very much. And I have broadened my horizons, because now also I love good Mexican food and sushi.

Do you think you will ever return to France to live?
I think I might have a hard time getting used to living there again. By now I have rooted myself here – I have my habits and my way of living. I think maybe someday I will buy a little house in Santa Barbara.

You are closed on Sundays. What do you do on your day off?
I love to drive along the coast, maybe up to Santa Barbara. I love the fresh sea air.

Have you ever gone to the Rose Parade, and what do you think of it?
I love it. Of course, I love flowers. My first time, maybe ten years ago, people were so kind to me. I went early to the corner of Colorado and Orange Grove, and already there were so many people. A policeman began to talk to me and saw it was my first time there, and he helped me to climb up on a fire truck. I had the best seat and the best time ever.

Pasadena is...

Entertaining

In its formative years, Pasadena melded a highbrow cultural sophistication imported from the East Coast with a more free-spirited Western sensibility centered around the Arroyo arts scene – and that dynamic blend continues today. From chamber music in an elegant gallery to alt-rock in a down-and-dirty bar, from challenging theater to family-friendly stagings of *The Nutcracker*, this town has something – actually, lots of things – to entertain everyone.

Outdoor Summer Festivals 178

The Gig Guide 180

On Stage & Screen 184

Classical Music & Dance 187

Q & A: Sheldon Epps 188

Outdoor Summer Festivals

Twilight at the Celebration on the Colorado Street Bridge

California Philharmonic Festival on the Green

Los Angeles County Arboretum
301 N. Baldwin Ave., Arcadia
626.821.3222, 626.300.8200 (tickets), calphil.org
Concerts every other Sat. night, July-early Sept.;
admission charge
The brainchild of L.A. County Parks and Rec and the Cal Phil conductor, Victor Vener, this summertime series has been selling out to al fresco music lovers since its inception. Indy and series tickets are available on the Great Lawn for table seating or BYO lawn chair; picnicking is encouraged, beginning at 5:30 p.m., with the performances (highlighted by Vener's witty running commentary) starting at 7:30.

Celebration on the Colorado Street Bridge

Colorado Blvd. between Orange Grove & San Rafael, Pasadena
626.441.6333, pasadenaheritage.org
Sat. in mid-July; admission charge
Seemingly all of Pasadena turns out to enjoy this lovely summer-evening happening sponsored by Pasadena Heritage. The bridge is closed to automobiles and filled with food booths,

children's activities, antique-car displays and stages for live bands. Everyone eats, drinks, dances and mingles with their neighbors. A must-attend.

Levitt Pavilion

87 N. Raymond Ave., Old Pasadena
626.683.3230, levittpavilionpasadena.org
Concerts Wed.-Sun. nights, June-Sept.; free
Stroll, drive or step off the Metro Gold Line to an evening of free music at the Memorial Park band shell. The nights are themed, from children's performances and world music to Latin beats and jazz. Concerts are held five nights a week all summer long – bring your picnic and a blanket, and thank your lucky stars for this amazing gift to Pasadenans.

Monrovia Free Concerts in the Park

Library Park, Myrtle Ave. & Palm Ave., Monrovia
626.256.8246, ci.monrovia.ca.us
Concerts Sun. nights, June-Aug.; free
Brought to you, courtesy of the Department of Community Services, from June through August on Sunday evenings. A picnic-friendly family affair for lovers of all kinds of music.

One Colorado Summer Film & Blues Series

One Colorado, Colorado Blvd. & DeLacey, Old Pasadena
626.564.1066, onecolorado.net
Movies & concerts Fri.-Sat. nights, July-Aug.; free
On weekend evenings in July, the wall above Crate & Barrel becomes a movie screen, and the courtyard fills with people out to see such classic films as *High Society* or *The Sting*. In August, the courtyard becomes a music club – fun blues bands play at 9 p.m., and everyone dances, from date-night couples to grandpas with their grandkids. It's all free, and it's lots of fun.

Pasadena Jazz Institute – Jazz on the Terrace

Pasadena Museum of California Art
260 E. Colorado Blvd. Ste. 206, Pasadena
626.398.3344, pasjazz.org
Concerts Thurs.-Sat. nights, June-Sept.; admission charge
Jazz fans gather on the museum's third-floor terrace to listen to themed jazz shows by many of L.A.'s finest players. All this, while gazing out at the dramatically lit dome of Pasadena's historic City Hall. For an urban jazz experience, it doesn't get much better than this.

Pasadena Pops Orchestra

Descanso Gardens
1418 Descanso Dr., La Cañada
626.792.7677, pasadenapops.org
Concerts Fri.-Sat. nights monthly, June-Sept.; admission charge

Maestro Rachael Worby brings you four programs a season, each performed one weekend a month at gorgeous Descanso Gardens. Concerts begin at 7:30, but the gates open at 5:30, and you can order meals prepared by Joachim Splichal's Patina Group up to four days ahead – or bring your own picnic, and don't forget your favorite wine.

South Pasadena Concerts in the Park

Garfield Park
Mission St. & Marengo, South Pasadena
626.403.7360
Concerts Sun. nights, June-Aug.; free
This free, family-oriented summer series turns lovely Garfield Park into a concert space on Sundays at 5 p.m. Bring your own picnic or purchase food from vendors at the show. Musical choices range from Latin jazz to swing to country.

Southwest Chamber Music Summer Festival

Huntington Art Gallery
1151 Oxford Rd., San Marino
800.726.7147, swmusic.org
Concerts some Fri. & Sat., July-August; admission charge
One of the most civilized of pleasures is to sit in the Huntington Art Gallery on a summer evening and listen to a soul-stirring performance by the acclaimed Southwest Chamber ensemble. A series of four concerts, each held on a Friday and Saturday night, are held on scattered weekends in July and August. These performances often sell out, so get tickets early.

Movie night in One Colorado's courtyard

The Gig Guide

We cover all sorts of gigs in the pages that follow: folk music at coffeehouses and concert halls, rock and blues bands at pubs, jazz at cafés, DJ spins at bars, salsa music at a dance club. Besides the spots discussed below, you'll find plenty of bars, pubs and wine bars in the Hungry & Thirsty chapter.

Dancing

Erin Stevens and Scott Price swing at the Pasadena Ballroom Dance Association.

The Granada

17 S. 1st St., Alhambra
626.227.2572, letsdancela.com
Salsa dancing Fri.-Sat. 8 p.m.-4 a.m.;
cover $10-$15
This fabulous old building in Alhambra's recently dolled-up Old Town is a dance school by day (salsa, swing and ballroom) and a salsa-dancing paradise by night. The centerpiece of the four-story building is a wooden dance floor (from an old bowling alley) in a vast ballroom with soaring, molded ceilings. You can nosh on tapas on the mezzanine, get drinks from one of two bars and have fun watching the tremendously diverse crowd (all ages and races, from all across the valley and L.A.) on the floor; a dress code helps keep out the riffraff. Sunday evenings are devoted to ballroom dancing.

Pasadena Ballroom Dance Association

Fellowship Hall
997 E. Walnut, Pasadena
626.799.5689, pasadenaballroomdance.com
Swing dancing Sat. 7:30-11:30 p.m.;
cover $12-$15
Tired of the same old thing? Then it's time to go swing dancing. Every Saturday night, the Pasadena Ballroom Dance Association rents a church hall to put on a convivial swing dance. Free lessons are offered from 7:30 to 8, and at 8 p.m., a hot band (perhaps the Jumpin' Joz

Caltech Performances

Caltech Ticket Office
332 S. Michigan Ave., Pasadena
626.395.4652, 888.222.5832,
events.caltech.edu

We Pasadenans are incredibly fortunate to have Caltech, whose several excellent venues offer a range of performances that are open to the public. In addition to Coleman Chamber Music (see page 165), you can see music and dance from such world-renowned acts as Ladysmith Black Mambazo, the Eroica Trio and Les Ballets Trockadero de Monte Carlo. Lectures and terrific kids' events are also on the performance calendar, which runs from September through June.

Beckman Auditorium is Caltech's premier performance venue.

Band or Stompy Jones) takes the stage, and the swinging begins. Ballroom dances (to DJ music) are offered the third Friday of the month. If you want to bone up before a dance, the PBDA has all sorts of classes, from the lindy hop to the shim sham to the freestyle fox-trot.

Paseo Colorado: Dancing under the Stars
280 E. Colorado Blvd., Pasadena
626.795.8891, paseocoloradopasadena.com
Dancing Fri.-Sat. 6-9:30 p.m., July-Aug.; free
On Friday nights in summer, the Pasadena Ballroom Dance Association sets up at the Paseo and offers free dance lessons at 6 p.m.; at 6:30, a swing band kicks into gear, and everyone dances. On Saturday nights the same thing happens, except then the Pasadena Jazz Institute brings in a Latin band, and the dancing continues. It's all free – the dance floor awaits!

Twin Palms
101 W. Green St., Old Pasadena
626.577.2567, twin-palms.com
Live dance music Fri.-Sat. 10 p.m.-1 a.m.; no cover
In the early evening, this is an upscale California restaurant. But on Friday and Saturday nights after 10 p.m., it turns into a party. First-rate cover bands (Stone Soul, MVP, Tango Nato) take the open-air stage near the bar, and the crowd takes to the dance floor.

Jazz

Buster's Ice Cream & Coffee Shop
1006 Mission St., South Pasadena
626.441.0744
Music Sun. evenings
It's hard to go wrong with a walk or a ride on the Gold Line to Buster's for ice cream and the Nairobi Jazz Trio on a Sunday. They start at 4:30 and play until closing at 7. Yum.

Café 322
322 W. Sierra Madre Blvd., Sierra Madre
626.836.5414, cafe322.com
Music Wed.-Sun.; closed Mon.
Café 322 likes to serve its jazz with a nice antipasto, or maybe a little pasta. Sundays are opera nights; Tuesdays are the only nights there's a cover ($10), to help pay for the twenty-piece big band; Wednesdays are for jazz jams; and you take your chances with blues, world music or maybe a jazz trio on Thursdays, Fridays and Saturdays.

John and Gerald Clayton play at a Pasadena Jazz Institute concert.

Jazzing Up Pasadena

Jill talked to Paul Lines, founder and executive director of the Pasadena Jazz Institute, and here's what he had to say about our hometown jazz scene:

"The leading citizens of Pasadena in the 1920s had a vision for their city as the 'Athens of the West.' They saw this as a place where all the arts and music and dance and architecture and literature were meant to flourish, and they were right! We have the museums, the ballet, the institutes of higher learning, the visual arts and the symphony – and my goal is to provide the missing piece of the cultural puzzle by providing a thriving jazz scene for a city that I know will support it."

Holly Street Bar & Grill
175 E. Holly St., Old Pasadena
626.440.1421, hollystreetbarandgrill.com
Music nightly; closed Mon.
Holly Street is getting a real solid rep for its Wednesday B-Jam Jazz nights. Highly regarded bassist Byron Miller starts things off, and great L.A. players sit in for the second and third sets. You never know who will show up, but the evening is always fun. Thursdays feature vocalists, Fridays are hot Latin jazz, Saturdays are usually blues and R&B, and Sunday brunch showcases a guitarist out on the terrace. Make a dinner reservation and stay for the music, or join the scene later for drinks – but note that seats are first come, first served.

Jax Bar & Grill

339 N. Brand Blvd., Glendale
818.500.1604, jaxbarandgrill.com
Music nightly
This is a club committed to its jazz. A jazz act – a trio or more – plays every night of the week starting between 8:30 and 9. Thursday nights are packed for L.A. trumpeter Jack Sheldon, so you might want to make a dinner reservation and stay to enjoy the show. Jax is your typical cozy, low-light-and-brass neighborhood bar, if your neighborhood bar dishes up a side of great jazz with every drink. The meters on Brand are free after 6 p.m., so settle back and enjoy the show.

Parkway Grill

510 S. Arroyo Pkwy., Pasadena
626.795.1001, theparkwaygrill.com
Music nightly
The bar at this destination restaurant is a hands-down favorite for a Friday-night jazz outing, when piano/bass duos play. Whether seated at the bar, a table or on one of the comfy couches, you'll be able to hear world-class jazz at a volume that doesn't overwhelm conversation. Partake of the award-winning wine list or savor a cappuccino and dessert. Skilled solo pianists play all other nights (except Sunday and Monday). A class joint.

David Arnay and Nedra Wheeler at the Parkway Grill

redwhite + bluezz

70 S. Raymond Ave., Old Pasadena
626.792.4441, redwhitebluezz.com
Nightly live jazz is the draw here – Sunday through Wednesday, three sets a night and one at Sunday brunch happen in the front room; on other nights, music lovers head to the Bluezz room behind the restaurant in the alley off Green Street for white-linen service and live jazz. Both rooms serve a full menu (of what they call "cutting-edge American"), as well as sampler flights of wine, cheese, chocolate and charcuterie.

South Pasadena Music Center & Conservatory

1509 Mission St., South Pasadena
626.403.2300, southpasadenamusic.com
One or two evening events happen at this music mecca each week, and get this – they're always free. Concerts, from chamber music and jazz to singer-songwriters and experimental electronica, attract crowds from 20 to 200. Owner and musician Walter Zooi is all about community, and it shows. He sells and rents quality musical instruments and offers a broad range of lessons with expert teachers in classical, jazz, rock and modern music.

Rock, Pop & Folk

The Bar

Langham Huntington Hotel
1401 S. Oak Knoll Ave., Pasadena
626.568.3900
Music Fri.-Sat.; no cover
Staid and formal this hotel may be, but on Saturday nights, its elegant, wood-paneled bar gets down with some of the best blues and R&B bands in Southern California. Friday nights are devoted to jazz combos. Drinks aren't cheap, but there's no cover, and the setting is swell.

Caltech Folk Music Society

California Institute of Technology, Pasadena
626.395.4652, folkmusic.caltech.edu
Tickets $10-$25
About a dozen times a year, this group brings some of the finest folk musicians alive to either Dabney Hall or Beckman Auditorium. Both venues are excellent places to hear the likes of Scotland's Old Blind Dogs, Cape Breton's Natalie MacMaster and America's Chris Proctor.

The Coffee Gallery Backstage

2029 N. Lake Ave., Altadena
626.398.7917, coffeegallery.com
Shows Thurs.-Sun. nights; cover $15-$20
Hidden behind this folksy coffeehouse is a 50-seat performance space with a colorful mural and a friendly vibe. The cover charge ain't cheap for such a funky venue, but the quality of music is often surprisingly high: the Western swing band the Lucky Stars, doo-woppers the Alley

Kelly McCune and Border Radio at the Coffee Gallery Backstage

Cats, virtuoso guitarist Robby Longley, singer-songwriter Peter Case and first-rate bluegrass bands passing through town.

McMurphy's Tavern
72 N. Fair Oaks Ave., Old Pasadena
626.666.1445, mcmurphystavern.com
Music Wed.-Fri.; DJ music Sat.-Sun.; no cover
Every night is different at this popular Irish-style tavern, where the crowd is young, frat-like and often rowdy. Monday is karaoke night, Tuesday is open-mike night, Wednesday brings blues bands, Thursday showcases alternative bands, and Saturday and Sunday are DJ nights. Perhaps the most fun is Friday night, which welcomes tribute bands: Led Zepagain, Cubensis (Grateful Dead), Kick (INXS), Sticky Fingers (the Stones), even Cash'd Out (that's right, Johnny Cash). If you're over 35 and/or don't like it loud, this place is not for you.

Mr. T's Bowl
5621 1/2 N. Figueroa Blvd., Highland Park
323.256.7561, mrtsbowl.tripod.com
Music nightly; cover $5 on Sat.
Located right off the Highland Park Gold Line station, this old bowling alley is the hipster's dive of choice. The drinks are cheap, the food is cheaper, the crowd is either eclectic or strange, depending on your point of view, and the music is inventive and fun. Tuesday is open-mike night, Wednesday through Friday brings local bands, and Saturday is headliner night, with such acts as the Motorcycle Black Madonnas and Hell on Heels.

Old Towne Pub
66 N. Fair Oaks Ave., Old Pasadena
626.577.6583
Nightly 4 p.m.-2 a.m.; cover Fri. & Sat.
The early crowd runs toward middle-aged men watching and talking sports, but later they cede the place to young, music-savvy people coming for the often-interesting live music: power punk to jazz, folk to alt-country. DJs spin when bands aren't playing. Hidden behind the Container Store (enter on Holly), Old Towne Pub is a no-frills place serving mostly tap and bottled beer.

The Scene Bar
806 E. Colorado Blvd., Glendale
818.241.7029, thescenebar.com
Nightly 8 p.m.-2 a.m.; cover $5-$15
Calling itself a "low-down dirty rock bar," the Scene looks on the outside like the old East Glendale dive bar it once was. And though the inside isn't exactly posh – red leatherette, cheap paneling, a pool table – it's got scenester style. At this writing, the Scene is the hottest music spot in town, serving up everything from neo-punk to roots country-blues, catchy indie pop to retro metal; when the bands aren't playing, music is still in the air, either from the great jukebox (particularly strong on alt-rock from the '80s and '90s) or a DJ. It's an over-21 spot, and while middle-aged music lovers do make this scene, the regulars are closer to 21 than 51.

On Stage & Screen

On Stage

While writers and artists created our Arroyo culture, the lively arts were percolating, too. Pasadena had an opera house, San Gabriel built the Mission Playhouse, Glendale was home to a vaudeville theater, Altadena boasted a playhouse for original Theatrica Americana productions, and somebody was always bailing Upton Sinclair out of jail. (But that was a whole other kind of live entertainment, we suppose.) Today, the stage and screen remain integral threads in Pasadena's fabric, and, honey, the cloth is getting larger and finer with every passing moment. Here's a swatch.

The Alex Theatre
216 N. Brand Blvd., Glendale
818.243.2539, alextheatre.org
Glendale's performing-arts hub was built in 1925 for vaudeville and motion-picture shows, and it hosted big Hollywood premieres from the '20s to the '50s. The city purchased the Greek- and Egyptian-themed structure in 1992 and restored her to her former splendor, and today, resident companies include the Gay Men's Chorus of L.A., the Glendale Symphony and the fun Alex Film Society, which showcases old-timey newsreels, cartoons and moving pictures from back in the day. International touring companies are featured with music, dance and comedy. Look for busloads of schoolchildren during matinee performances. Free public tours.

Fremont Centre Theatre
1000 Fremont Ave., South Pasadena
626.441.5977, fremontcentretheatre.com
Artistic directors Lissa Layng Reynolds and James Reynolds (yes, THAT James Reynolds! Commander Abe Carver on "Days of Our Lives!") produce, direct, frequently write and star in many productions at this Equity-waiver theater. Isn't this how Shakespeare started? The roster includes original dramas and comedies, obscure plays and some old favorites. It's been making South Pas theater happen since 1997. And the tiny neighboring restaurant, Bistro K, is swell.

Furious Theatre Company
39 S. El Molino Ave., Pasadena
626.356.7529, furioustheatre.org
Who knew? Upstairs at the Pasadena Playhouse, this intimate venue sparks original plays starring a core of whip-smart resident actors. If the play's not your thing and your mom will let you stay out late, come for the late, late improv show for hilarious audience participation; reservations suggested.

The historic Alex Theatre retains the glamour of Hollywood's golden age.

Glendale Centre Theatre
324 N. Orange St., Glendale
818.244.8481, glendalecentretheatre.com
Now in its third generation of family ownership, the Glendale Centre Theatre opened in 1947 in a converted dance studio with an audience of six. Word spread and before long the Hale family was building its own performing house, the current 440-seat New Orleans–style theater. "Uplifting" family-friendly musicals and dramas take us to a kinder, gentler time, when blond hair and blue eyes were good things.

The Ice House

24 N. Mentor, Pasadena
626.577.1894, icehousecomedy.com
Headliners and emerging comics are showcased in this Playhouse District place, which really did use to be an ice warehouse. Plus comedy workshops (yes, for you, Ms. and Mr. Life of the Party!) and comedy traffic school (no drink minimum for traffic school). Call first for reservations.

A Noise Within Theatre

234 S. Brand Blvd., Glendale
818.240.0910, anoisewithin.org
Home to critically acclaimed stagings of classics from Shakespeare, Molière, Chekhov, Miller, Shaw and Lorca, among others, this fine group is one of the few California resident companies of classically trained actors to produce year-round plays in repertory – and that's nothing to sneeze at. We've seen two Shaw plays here, and he's a lot funnier on stage than when you're reading him in college. A Noise Within is infused with life – you just have to sit back and let it happen.

Pasadena Playhouse

39 E. Molino Ave., Pasadena
626.356.7529, pasadenaplayhouse.org
This 1925 jewel was built by actor and producer Gilmor Brown, who also founded a renowned theater-arts school here in 1928. In 1937, the Playhouse was named the official state theater of California, and over the years such notables as Robert Preston, Raymond Burr, Gig Young, Eve Arden, John Barrymore Jr., Margaret O'Brien, Dustin Hoffman and Elaine May trod its boards. Competition from emerging theater schools forced the closing of the Playhouse and its school in 1969, and a group of concerned citizens saved the building from demolition in 1979. In the last few years it has been reinvigorated by its talented artistic director, Sheldon Epps (see Q & A, page 188), its Broadway-bound plays and its world premieres featuring A-list actors on Hollywood hiatus. The Spanish Revival building, with gilt interiors and velvet upholstery, harks back to an earlier time, and intermission sparkles with twinkly lights in the courtyard, maybe under the watchful eye of the ghost of Gilmor Brown, who is rumored to walk around his old office on the second floor.

The courtyard at the landmark Pasadena Playhouse

San Gabriel Civic Auditorium

320 S. Mission Dr., San Gabriel
626.308.2868, sgcivic.org
Built in 1927, the San Gabriel Mission Playhouse's sole purpose was to house John Steven McGroarty's famed *Mission Play*. (At four and one-half hours, the play was almost as long as the Mission period itself.) The theater was shuttered after the Depression, and the city of San Gabriel bought it in 1945 and renamed it to signify its new multipurpose identity. Local schools perform graduation ceremonies, touring theater companies stage productions, and the Pasadena Dance Theatre produces *The Nutcracker* every December. Its ornate Spanish-Moorish architecture reflects Mexican and Native American influences – McGroarty modeled it after his favorite mission, San Antonio de Padua in Monterey County.

Sierra Madre Playhouse

87 W. Sierra Madre Blvd., Sierra Madre
626.256.3809, sierramadreplayhouse.org
One mark of a nice hometown is a community-theater playhouse. And with a big light-up marquee, wowzer, Sierra Madre has hit the jackpot! Intimate enough that every seat's a good one for the annual mainstage productions, the venue is also large enough to hold a second stage, featuring original works by new-to-you writers. Extras include concerts, musicals from resident Southern California Lyric Theater and workshops for adults and kids.

The Theatre at Boston Court

70 N. Mentor Ave., Pasadena
626.683.6883, bostoncourt.com
This snazzy, state-of-the-art building holds two performance spaces: a 99-seat Equity-waiver theater for BC's four play offerings per season, plus a 60-seat acoustically perfecto concert hall for live music. A great off-Broadway, artist-driven venue in the Playhouse District.

Cheap Tix

Check in often with goldstarevents.com, which offers discounts on tickets for concerts, plays and all sorts of events.

On Screen

Where do cows go on a Saturday night? To the moooovies. The rest of us don't wait till the weekend, though, because there are so many terrific movie theaters around town. Here's the roundup:

There's not a bad seat at the Paseo, the sound quality's clear, and there are clean restrooms galore – but sometimes the crowds and those noisy kids – *basta!* For quiet, the Laemmle Old Pasadena is pin-drop perfect, insulated from the Old Town hustle-bustle outside. The Laemmle Playhouse 7, next to Vroman's, is the spot for independent films. The Academy 6 is a super second-run house, cheap enough that we don't mind that the floors haven't been cleaned since the Carter administration. Monrovia's Krikorian is dandy if you want lots of show times plus a walkable Main Street without the crowds and chain stores of Old Pas. Both of Glendale's Mann multiplexes are located in wonderful pedestrian stretches near scads of restaurants and window-shopping. Alhambra's Edwards 14 has free parking, a dazzling mosaic courtyard and plush seating.

Pasadena/South Pasadena

The Academy 6
1003 E. Colorado Blvd., 626.229.9400

Laemmle's One Colorado 8
42 Miller Alley (Union at Fair Oaks), Old Pasadena, 626.744.1224

Laemmle's Playhouse 7
673 E. Colorado Blvd., 626.844.6500

Pacific Paseo Stadium 14
Paseo Colorado, 336 E. Colorado Blvd., 626.568.8888

Alhambra

Alhambra Edwards Atlantic Palace 10
700 W. Main St., 626.458.8663

Alhambra Edwards Renaissance Stadium 14
1 E. Main St. (at Garfield), 626.300.0107

Arcadia

Arcadia AMC Santa Anita 16
Westfield Santa Anita Mall, 400 S. Baldwin Ave., 626.321.4270

Glendale

Mann Glendale Exchange 10
128 N. Maryland Ave., 818.549.0045

Mann Glendale Marketplace 4
144 S. Brand Blvd., 818.547.3352

Pacific 18 Theatres
Americana at Brand, 322 Americana Way, 866.722.9790

Highland Park

Akarakian Theatres Highland 3
5604 N. Figueroa St., 323.256.6383

La Cañada

UA La Cañada Flintridge
1919 Verdugo Blvd., 818.952.1940

Monrovia

Krikorian Cinema 12
410 S. Myrtle Ave., 626.305.7469

Classical Music & Dance

Arte Flamenco Dance Theatre & Center of World Dance
230 W. Main St., Alhambra
626.458.1234, clarita-arteflamenco.com
Happily, this dance school, which is dedicated to the study of flamenco, Spanish classical and regional folk dance, offers performances at its studio and at La Luna Negra restaurant in Old Town.

California Philharmonic Orchestra
1120 Huntington Dr., San Marino
626.300.8200, calphil.org
Cal Phil does an exceptional job of being a community resource that involves young musicians, while operating at a standard that attracts excellent soloists. This world-class ensemble performs in both full orchestral splendor and in more intimate chamber settings. Its venues include the acoustically perfect Ambassador Auditorium, the historic Castle Green and the even more historic Old Mill in San Marino; see page 156 for its Festival on the Green Series at the L.A. Arboretum.

Coleman Chamber Music Association
Beckman Auditorium, Caltech
332 S. Michigan Ave., Pasadena
626.395.4652, coleman.caltech.edu
Founded in 1904 by Alice Coleman, this group presents six concerts a year to devoted audiences, many of whom would sooner miss a sibling's wedding than miss one of these live performances. All concerts are held on Sunday afternoons in Beckman Auditorium.

Pasadena Civic Ballet
253 N. Vinedo Ave., East Pasadena
626.792.0873, pcballet.com
This ballet company provides instruction for children as young as 4 and adults who have studied dance for decades. Large, elaborately staged recitals are performed at the San Gabriel Civic in alternating years.

Pasadena Community Orchestra
First Church of the Nazarene
3700 E. Sierra Madre Blvd., East Pasadena
626.445.6708
Founded in 1983 by conductor Wayne Reinecke, who still conducts today, the PCO is a full symphonic orchestra made up of gifted instrumentalists who volunteer their time to this wonderful nonprofit, one of Pasadena's treasures.

Pasadena Dance Theatre
1985 E. Locust St., Pasadena
626.683.3459, pasadenadance.org
Performances throughout the year are offered at the historic San Gabriel Civic, including its well-loved and beautifully danced version of Tchaikovsky's *Nutcracker Suite,* performed by a cast of more than 90 dancers.

Pasadena Pro Musica
Neighborhood Church
301 N. Orange Grove Blvd., Pasadena
626.628.2144, pasadenapromusica.org
Pasadena Pro Musica was founded in 1964 by conductor Edward Low. Current director Stephen Grimm has continued to highlight less frequently heard works for chamber chorus and orchestra, as well as new works from contemporary American composers.

Pasadena Symphony
Pasadena Civic Auditorium
300 E. Green St., Pasadena
626.584.8833,
pasadenasymphony.org
How's this for longevity: Since its founding in 1928, the Pasadena Symphony has had only four musical directors. Maestro Jorge Mester has been on the podium for more than twenty years, and he has distinguished himself by enhancing the orchestra's repertoire with rarely heard selections. All performances take place in Pasadena's elegant Civic Auditorium. There is nothing like sitting in a room with a symphony orchestra. Try it, you'll like it.

Jorge Mester, musical director of the Pasadena Symphony

Southwest Chamber Music
2500 E. Colorado Blvd., Pasadena
626.685.4455, 800.726.7147, swmusic.org
This two-time Grammy-winning ensemble takes its name from the Southwest Museum, L.A.'s oldest cultural institution. It offers a six-concert series at Pasadena's Norton Simon Museum. (See page 157 for information on its summer concerts at the Huntington.)

Q & A: Sheldon Epps

Sheldon Epps already had distinguished himself in both theater and television before becoming artistic director of the Pasadena Playhouse in 1997 – he conceived and directed the Duke Ellington musical *Play On!*, which was nominated for three Tony Awards, and conceived and directed the musical review *Blues in the Night*, which was nominated for a Tony Award and two Lawrence Olivier Awards. He's also directed many episodes of hit TV shows, most notably "Frasier." Jill and Sheldon met at the Playhouse on a gorgeous February morning.

What does it feel like to give up the gypsy life of the theater and settle into an artistic home?

I was living just outside New York City and directing five or six shows a year out of town. And even though my work took me to some of America's finest theaters, I was getting tired of the gypsy life. Also, I'm an L.A. boy. I was born in Compton and lived there until I was 11, so I'm really coming home. Many people think I've made this up, but I saw my first professional production at the Pasadena Playhouse. It was Member of the Wedding with Ethel Waters, and I was about 8 years old.

Can you tell me about your vision for this theater?

It's an opportunity to really build an institution. I am working to make this a vital, diverse place where we are always reaching for a higher aesthetic quality. I'm most proud that the audience is more diverse in every way. Theaters everywhere face the problem of an aging audience, and if we don't rebuild our audience base, theaters are going to die.

Do you miss directing?

I still direct television, and I do one production a year here at the theater. This job can be pretty overwhelming. Choosing and staffing the plays, marketing, raising the money and communicating with the national theater community… it takes a lot of time. By continuing to direct television, I can do my work in the theater but not have to worry about paying the bills. And I build relationships that serve the theater.

Did you have any misconceptions about Pasadena?

Like the song said, I thought it was all about the little old ladies, but then I saw a very different picture: younger, hipper and much more diverse. When I took this job, I was often the only person of color and the only one under 60 in the courtyard waiting to see a play. I wanted to shake things up and make sure the theater – onstage and off – would reflect the diversity I knew existed here.

Okay – a final question: How do you feel about the Rose Parade?

As a kid it was a real holiday treat… get in the car at 4 a.m. and make the long trek to Pasadena. Last year Dave Davis, who used to be president of the Tournament of Roses, invited my wife and me. It's a great theatrical event – fabulous design concepts, music and choreography. You watch 300 people in a band turn a corner in synch and you are seeing something!

Outdoorsy

The looming, awe-inspiring presence of the San Gabriel Mountains never ceases to remind valley folk to get outdoors and enjoy the fresh air (believe it not, we have more fresh air than we used to). And get outside they do, whether it's to walk around the Rose Bowl or hike a Sierra Madre trail, ski a Mt. Baldy powder run or cycle down a canyon single-track.

Great Hikes in the San Gabriels	190
4 Walks Around Town	196
Sally & Otto Walk Pasadena	198
Snow Play	199
On 2 Wheels & 4 Legs: Bicycling & Horseback Riding	200
Q & A: Doug Christiansen	202

Great Hikes in the San Gabriels

The most notable feature of the San Gabriel Mountains is their sharp, almost astonishing vertical rise, from a base at some 800 feet above sea level to peaks ranging from 5,000 to 10,000 feet. Said John Muir of the San Gabriels, "Not even in the Sierra [Nevada] have I ever made the acquaintance of mountains more rigidly inaccessible." And yet over the centuries many adventurers, from 17th-century Tongva Indians, to 19th-century American resort builders, to modern Sierra Club hikers, have forged 775 miles of trails coursing through 693,000 acres. And though they look bare and forbidding from the valley floor, the San Gabriels are in fact rich with life and beauty: canyon live oaks and Jeffrey pine, waterfalls and spring wildflowers, mule deer and black bears, owls and red-tail hawks. Watch for rattlesnakes in summer, and be on alert for mountain lions, which have been known (if rarely) to attack humans. Western ticks (not usually a risk for Lyme disease) can be plentiful, so if you're hiking with your dog, consider a preventive tick treatment.

Here are our favorite San Gabriel front-range day hikes, going west to east – but these are just the beginning. For details on the embarrassment of riches, get the essential *Trails of the Angeles* (Wilderness Press).

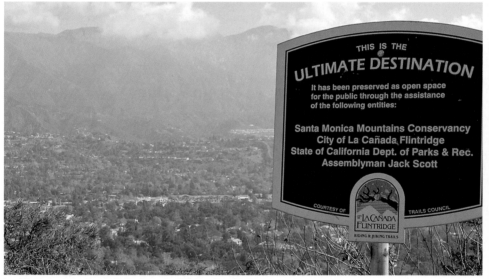

Looking toward the San Gabriels from the Ultimate Destination

Cherry Canyon, La Cañada
2 to 8 miles round-trip; easy to moderate
Alternate: Liz's Loop and others
This isn't actually a San Gabriels hike – it's a little-known series of trails through the chaparral of the San Rafael Hills on the south side of La Cañada, and it's ideal for hikers who don't have more than an hour. A new part of the Santa Monica Mountains Conservancy, the hillside swath of land sits between housing developments and Descanso Gardens, and it's covered with well-marked trails and a fire road. From the parking area, head into Cherry Canyon via Owl Trail, a lovely half-mile path shaded by oaks. This pops out onto the fire road; head left (uphill) and look for a sign sending you downhill to the "Ultimate Destination" – really just a

picnic table on a barren plateau with a sweeping view of the Crescenta and San Gabriel valleys. If you're training for a big hike and just want a workout, power up the fire road, which goes for four miles. Or take the fire road to Descanso Gardens or explore some of the small loop trails, particularly Liz's Loop and the Cerro Negro Trail.

Driving directions: From the northbound 210 Freeway, exit at Berkshire and turn left. Follow Berkshire (past some honkin' mansions) and veer right at the Chevy Chase Drive stop sign. Turn left on Hampstead Drive, right at Cherry Canyon sign, and park on the shoulder.

Hiking directions: From the parking area you'll see the Owl Trail sign. Walk down that trail, which emerges onto the fire road; turn left. Hike uphill on the dirt road until you see a sign for the Ultimate Destination, which you can see below. Go down for a look and perhaps a picnic at the table, then head back up to the fire road. Take the road downhill, passing the Owl Trail sign; if you have time, take the Liz's Loop detour, about a mile and a half.

Upper Arroyo Seco, Pasadena
5 miles round-trip; easy
Alternate: El Prieto Trail

Often called "the JPL Trail" by locals (JPL is next door), this is an ideal hike for hot summer months, following the Arroyo Seco stream under shady cover of bay, willow, sycamore and oak. Tongva villages thrived here in the good ol' days, and in the 19th century, resort cabins lined the Arroyo. This much-loved route is used by JPL lunch-breakers, equestrians, dog walkers, mountain bikers, trail runners, hikers, school groups and scouts, some of whom camp at Gould Mesa. Kids love rock-jumping and fooling around in the stream. Depending on the water levels, be prepared to cross the stream and get your shoes wet.

We typically walk as far as we have time for, then head back. Usually we'll pass the Forest Service residences and the campground (complete with outhouse and water) and stop after 2.5 miles at the Paul Little Picnic Area and turn around. The ambitious can hike another couple of miles to Oakwilde, site of a once-thriving resort camp. If you don't mind the risk of speeding mountain bikes, consider the alternate El Prieto Trail, a lovely single-track climb along a creek in a green, shady canyon up to Brown Mountain Road; it takes about an hour, round-trip.

The Arroyo Seco isn't so "seco" (dry) after all.

Driving directions: Most people park just south of JPL, but we prefer to skip the first, hot-asphalt-road part of the walk. We drive north on Lincoln, turn left on Altadena Drive and park where the street dead-ends.

Hiking directions: From the end of Altadena Drive, take the downhill trail a short distance and turn right onto the asphalt road; stay left when it splits and becomes a dirt road. Stay on this for as far as you care to go. If you want a quick side workout, turn left on the fire road just after Gould Mesa Campground and climb up a spell to get a view. To take the El Prieto alternate, take the right split at the end of the asphalt section and look for the trailhead sign. The trail splits many times, but don't worry, they all reconnect or land in the same place.

Sunset Ridge to Cape of Good Hope, Altadena

6 miles round-trip; moderately strenuous
Alternates: Dawn Mine & Millard Canyon Falls

For a hike that combines beauty, history and exercise, walk up Chaney Trail and follow the Sunset Ridge Trail, which hugs the side of steep Millard Canyon. You enjoy views of the dramatic canyon (look for waterfalls), lots of trees and plant life and, in a few spots, great city views. The single-track trail eventually pops out back on Chaney Trail, a wide dirt road, and a short uphill walk leads to the Cape of Good Hope. On your right you'll see a trail (actually the old railway bed) leading to Echo Mountain.

If you have another hour, walk a little farther up Chaney Trail to find the signposted Dawn Mine Trail and take this steep, one-mile route down into the canyon; at the bottom, keep an eagle eye out for two steel beams set into a rock wall – they mark the entrance to the 1895 gold mine. It's tempting to explore inside, but the timbers are rotting and the mine is not safe. Return the way you came. For yet another alternate, park at Millard Campground and take the easy half-mile trail to the 50-foot Millard Falls. Kids love this outing.

Driving directions: Drive north from Pasadena on Lincoln or Fair Oaks. At Loma Alta, turn right if you're on Lincoln or left if you're on Fair Oaks, then go toward the mountains on Chaney Trail. Wind uphill until you see a gate on the right, and park on the side of the road. (You must have the $30 annual National Forest Adventure Pass, available at Sport Chalet or Jay's Shell in La Cañada, in your car window.) If you want to do the Millard Falls hike instead, stay left on the paved road and drive down to the Millard Campground parking lot.

Hiking directions: Walk through the gate onto the dirt road. This is a rare case where *Trails of the Angeles* is wrong. It directs hikers to take the first trail that splits off to the left, but in fact you take the second trail to the left, about another 300 yards ahead. Follow this canyon-side trail; after a mile the trail splits near a fetching old cabin; follow the sign to stay on Sunset Ridge. You'll emerge on a wide dirt road. Turn left and walk uphill a short distance to the signposted Cape of Good Hope. If you have time and legs, continue up the old railway-bed road a short distance to Dawn Station, then take the trail on the left leading to Dawn Mine. Return via either the Sunset Ridge Trail or Chaney Trail.

An old cabin along the Sunset Ridge Trail

The Sam Merrill Trail switchbacks up the hill in the background.

Sam Merrill Trail to Echo Mountain, Altadena

5 miles round-trip; moderately strenuous
Alternate: Inspiration Point

Named for one of the great trail volunteers of local history, this route is popular with hikers seeking a good workout and a great view. It starts at the gates of the long-gone Cobb Estate, crosses over Las Flores Canyon and then climbs up a sunny, two-mile switchback (home to lovely spring wildflowers if the rainy season was decent) to the top of Echo Mountain, site of a thriving 19th-century tourist resort. Called the White City, the resort was fed by the Mt. Lowe incline railway and comprised two hotels, a small zoo, a reservoir and the Mt. Lowe Observatory. In the early 20th century, fires destroyed most everything; you'll see remnants of the railway and old foundation. The clear-day views are superb, and there are pine-shaded tables for a picnic.

If time, energy and water allow, look for the sign atop Echo Mountain pointing to the Castle Canyon trail to Inspiration Point, and continue on for an additional two miles to this awesome view spot, where an old stone viewing pavilion has been restored. Head back the way you came.

Driving directions: Exit Lake from the 210 Freeway in Pasadena. Drive north on Lake until the very top; park near the gated area on the right.

Hiking directions: Enter through the gate and head up the battered asphalt road until you see a stone water fountain, trailhead sign and sign-in sheet. Follow the trail to the left, which heads downhill, across the dry streambed, and then uphill until you reach the summit at the top.

Mt. Wilson Toll Road to Henninger Flats, Altadena

5.4 miles round-trip; moderate
Alternate: Eaton Canyon Falls Trails

One of the San Gabriels' best local hikes has been compromised since a huge slide occurred during the rainy season of 2004-'05; at this writing, it still remains impassable, but hope springs eternal. If it's fixed by the time you try it, enter Eaton Canyon through the Pinecrest gate, walk down into the canyon and head up the clearly visible dirt road. If the road is still closed, go to the Eaton Canyon Nature Center (see directions below) and take the Walnut Canyon Horse Trail, a fairly short but steep climb that puts you on the Mt. Wilson road at the one-mile mark. From here head on up to Henninger Flats, site of the L.A. County Experimental Forestry Nursery. The nursery produces tree seedlings (Monterey pine, cedar, Sequoia, knobcone pine) to reforest the San Gabriels after fires. There's a visitor's center, campground, water and picnic areas set among fine old trees. This is a fire-road hike, not a trail, and it gets a lot of sun, so it's best in the cooler months or early on summer mornings. On a clear day, you'll see forever!

For an easier alternate, stay on the Eaton Canyon trail, following the sign for Eaton Canyon Falls. This is a kid-friendly 1.5-mile walk to a high, narrow waterfall that is particularly robust in winter and spring.

Driving directions: Go north on Altadena Drive from either the 210 Freeway or your Pasadena location. Turn right on Crescent. Turn right again on Pinecrest. You'll see the gate to the trail entrance on the right; park on a side street. If the gate is locked, that means the lower trail is still impassable. Get back in your car, head south on Altadena Drive, and park at Eaton Canyon Nature Center, 1750 N. Altadena Dr.

Hiking directions: From the Pinecrest gate, walk down into the canyon, across the bridge, and up the Mt. Wilson Toll Road 2.7 miles to Henninger Flats. From Eaton Canyon Nature Center, walk north on the path, cross the creek, and stay left to follow the north bank of the creek, turning right up the Walnut Canyon Horse Trail. Then head uphill on the Mt. Wilson Toll Road.

Mt. Wilson Trail to Orchard Camp, Sierra Madre

7 to 8 miles round-trip; moderately strenuous
Alternate: Continue on to Mt. Wilson

You get it all on this hike: a sunny climb up the face of the San Gabriels, views to the ocean on clear days and a back-side forest hike through ferns, shady glens and little waterfalls.

You're following the historic Mt. Wilson Trail, built by Benjamin "Don Benito" Wilson in 1864, and your final destination is the shady (often buggy) site of Orchard Camp, a trail resort that once drew as many as 40,000 people a year. Only the foundation remains, but if the gnats aren't bad, it's a serene spot for a picnic lunch before either heading back or, if you're really ambitious, continuing up another three miles and 2,500 vertical feet to the summit of Mt. Wilson.

Driving Directions: Exit Baldwin from the 210 Freeway in Sierra Madre. Drive north on Baldwin; it jogs to the left at Foothill. At almost the very top of Baldwin, turn right on Mira Monte. You'll see Mt. Wilson Trail on the left; park wherever you can.

Hiking Directions: This is a straight shot up the Mt. Wilson Trail. When the trail splits, a sign marks the very short detour to First Water, whose waterfalls and pools make for a great rest stop. Orchard Camp is 3.5 to 4.5 miles up the trail, depending on whether you believe the Forest Service signs (3.5 miles) or *Trails of the Angeles* (4.5 miles). It seems on the shorter end to us.

En route to Mt. Wilson

Chantry Flat, Sierra Madre

Several superb hikes are accessed via Chantry Flat Road, which is located off Santa Anita Avenue in Sierra Madre. We're happy to say that the road has been open for a while now after being closed off and on for several years, but don't be surprised if mud slides lead to another closure if you're looking to hike in winter or spring. So we're not including these hikes because of their potential inaccessibility. If the road is open, by all means head up there to explore – the hiking is great – and don't forget to stop for a cool drink at Adams' Pack Station, the only year-round pack station in the United States (people live in some of the cabins up here, and the only way to get supplies in is via pack mule!). To check on the road, call the pack station at 626.447.7356 or the Sierra Madre Police Department at 626.355.1414.

Ben Overturff Trail, Monrovia
7 miles round-trip; moderate
Alternate: Falls Trail

Perhaps the prettiest hike in the region, this trail goes along Sawpit and Sycamore canyons. Up high are views, chaparral and cactus; in the midranges are wildflowers and a green meadow; and on the lower elevations are a creek, waterfalls, oak and sycamore groves and lush fern gardens. (Poison oak is also plentiful, so watch out.) The first leg of the hike is up a steep road shared by cyclists and the occasional car, but once you're on the Overturff Trail, the path is quiet, green and little-traveled. About 1.5 miles up the trail, you'll be in Twin Springs Canyon – pay attention so you'll notice when you walk over the natural rock bridge over a spring. Natural bridges are quite rare, and this is the only known one in Southern California. The trail ends at Deer Park, where you'll see the ruins of a resort lodge built by Ben Overturff. You can return on the Overturff Trail, or take the easier Sawpit Canyon Road back.

For a shorter hike with a more spectacular destination, drive up to the Nature Center and take the .75-mile Falls Trail to the impressive 30-foot-tall Monrovia Canyon Waterfall. This trail is typically packed with people on weekends.

Along the Ben Overturff Trail

Note that the whole park is closed on Tuesdays, and both the Overturff and Sawpit Canyon routes are closed on Wednesdays, when the Monrovia P.D. practices at the firing range off Sawpit Canyon Road.

Driving Directions: Exit Myrtle from the 210 Freeway in Monrovia. Drive north (toward the mountains) on Myrtle, turn right on Hillcrest and then left on Canyon, following the sign to stay on Canyon when the road splits. Park in the lot just before the ranger station. There's a $5 parking fee.

Hiking Directions: Walk up the paved road a short distance and turn right on the road marked "Trask Scout Reservation." Walk up this steep road about 1.5 miles and turn left onto the marked Ben Overturff Trailhead. The two-mile trail ends at Deer Park; you can either return the way you came or walk back on the dirt road.

4 Walks Around Town

Rose Bowl

360 N. Arroyo Blvd., Pasadena
Route: Marked 5K route along the road
circling Brookside Park
Parking available around the south end of
Brookside Park

Pasadena's great uniter, this paved 5K (3.1-mile) loop around the Rose Bowl and Brookside's golf course is home to a glorious array of life, mostly of the human and dog varieties, but also of the squirrel, duck and red-tail hawk varieties. The crowd changes with the hour – early morning sees runners and power walkers with dogs; 9ish sees retirees and stroller-pushers; midday sees a few locals taking a break from work and chores to skate, cycle or walk; and the early evening sees everyone from office workers still in business attire to kids on scooters to buzzing swarms of cyclists training for road races. Rich and poor, young and old, abled and disabled, black, white, Latin and Asian... sooner or later, everybody goes for a spin around the Rose Bowl.

Lower Arroyo Trails

Off S. Arroyo Blvd. between Arbor St.
& California Blvd., Pasadena
Route: Clearly visible trails in the Arroyo
Parking available at the end of the dirt road
leading down into the Arroyo

A lovely swath of nature in the city, the Lower Arroyo has benefited from considerable restoration in recent years. Although the main Arroyo Seco watershed remains concreted, feeder streams now meander in their natural state, and trails meander alongside them. Red-tail hawks soar overhead, San Rafael's mansions perch atop the western hillside, and dogs romp off-leash. (We ourselves choose this path of civil disobedience – but we keep a leash on hand in case we encounter horses, dogs on leash or animal-control officers, who will write tickets.)

You can walk for 15 minutes or more than an hour. Our favorite route is about four miles: From the parking area head north, either on the trail across the dirt road or alongside the concrete streambed. Cross the stream when you reach the footbridge and continue north to the Colorado Bridge. Double back and walk along the west bank of the stream almost to South Pasadena; cross back via the footbridge just north of the equestrian center. Head back on the east side of the stream, feeling free to take the trails to the right – they either reconnect with the main trail or head directly to the Casting Pond.

Caltech Ramble

Starting point at San Pasqual
& Lake, Pasadena
Route: A go-your-own-way exploration
Park on Lake or San Pasqual

Pasadena's best-kept secret playground for small children, the Caltech campus is a wonderful place for a stroll, power walk or child outing, especially on weekends, when the campus is bizarrely deserted. (Where do all those budding young astrophysicists go on Sundays?) We park near Lake and San Pasqual and walk east on San Pasqual, just to see the fabulous '60s-pink garden-

Gargoyles on Caltech's Winnett Building

apartment complex. From there, enter the campus on the San Pasqual Walk and wander at will. You'll discover peaceful little gardens, kid-thrilling fountains and ponds (look for the pond filled with turtles), graceful architecture and intriguing sculptures, reliefs and historic plaques. Two of our favorite spots are the Gene Pool, whose tiled floor looks like a strand of DNA, and the goofy gargoyles next to the bookstore depicting Amelia Earhart, Einstein, Ben Franklin and other pioneers in science and exploration. For details on the buildings, go to caltech.edu and search for the "Along the Olive Walk" walking-tour guide.

Altadena Hill Climb

1456 E. Mendocino St., Altadena
Route: A zigzag of residential streets
Park on the street in front of the Altadena Golf Course, or in the parking lot

Few residential neighborhoods are blessed with such handsome homes, mature trees and awesome mountains. This walk is great for house junkies and those looking for an uphill workout.

Start in front of the Altadena Golf Course and head east on Mendocino. Turn left on Porter and right on Homewood, a particularly beautiful street. Turn right on Morslay and head downhill back to Mendocino. Turn left on Mendocino, cross Allen, and veer left onto Mendocino Lane, passing the Italian Revival Balian Mansion, famed for its over-the-top Christmas lights each December and its Bush-loving signs the rest of the year. Turn left onto Altadena Drive and right on Pinecrest, climbing uphill, and turn left onto Loma Alta. Wind uphill along Loma Alta, where the houses are '60s modern and the occasional glimpses of city views are superb. A bridge will take you across rocky Rubio Canyon, and then Loma Alta curves left and becomes Rubio Canyon Road. Head down this cool, shady street, which becomes Maiden Lane, turn left on Palm and, in a few blocks, turn right on Holliston. Turn left on La Solana to see a lovely one-block stretch of classic '20s Spanish Revival homes. Turn right at the end of La Solana, and you'll be back on Mendocino in front of the golf course.

That route is 4.5 miles, and it's a good workout. If you want a shorter walk, just park anywhere in this neighborhood and go for a wander. You can't go wrong.

Sally Miller and Otto

Sally & Otto Walk Pasadena

Sally Miller is a professional organizer by trade, so when she does something, she does it in a terribly organized fashion. In 2005, she decided that her regular dog-walking route through her Southwest Pasadena neighborhood had become boring – so she got a map and set out to walk every single block in the city of Pasadena. "I love having a project, and I love Pasadena," she says. "I'd lived here twenty years but felt like I didn't really know it." Ten months and some 530 miles later, Sally and Otto, her stubby-legged, walk-loving dog, ended their journey with a walk to City Hall with Mayor Bill Bogaard.

Sally had a system, of course, tracking each walk by color-coding her routes on a map and keeping a journal of every outing. Friends or her husband went along for some of the walks, but mostly it was just Sally 'n' Otto.

"I loved every street," she says. "There are nice gardens in every neighborhood, and there's a run-down house in every neighborhood, too. I never felt afraid, even in the so-called bad neighborhoods, except sometimes I was afraid of dogs." They found blocks of Craftsman houses just waiting to be restored, little restaurants to return to and hidden pockets of the '60s ranch houses that she loves.

As for Sally's walking discoveries, two stood out:

1. Arroyo Terrace, on the east flank of the Rose Bowl. "You have this incredible collection of Greene & Greene houses next to this amazing Buff & Hensman condo building, with the bonus of views of the Rose Bowl and the Arroyo. I'd lived here all these years and never knew about this."

2. Glen Oaks, on the hillside above Linda Vista. "It's kind of tricky – you have to wiggle your way up San Rafael north of Colorado, and you might hit a few dead ends. But when you get to the top, past a new development of me-gamansions so ugly that you want to burn them down, you'll find the most amazing 330-degree view, from Glendale across Los Angeles to Pasadena and beyond."

Since then, Sally & Otto went on to walk every single street in Altadena, where many of her friends live; La Cañada, where her son attends school; and Sierra Madre, which is just so darn beautiful. Next up: South Pasadena. And then it's back to walking her own neighborhood.

Snow Play

A few times each winter, a storm gets cold enough to frost even the front range of the San Gabriels with snow. And that's when locals grab their skis, boards or sleds and head for higher ground.

Angeles Crest Highway

Angeles Crest Hwy. (Hwy. 2), north of
La Cañada
When there's snow in them thar hills and you just want to connect with it, point your car north on Angeles Crest Highway and drive until you find a spot to sled, snowshoe or have a snowball fight. Sometimes it takes no more than twenty minutes of driving.

Mountain High

24510 Hwy. 2, Wrightwood
888.754.7878, mthigh.com
This booming resort on the back side of the San Gabriels is an easy 80-minute drive from Pasadena. If you're a 14-year-old snowboarder who likes to cut loose, skills be damned, then by all means go to Mountain High on a weekend. Otherwise, think twice. During the week, however, it can be swell. Sixteen lifts service 59 trails, and snowmaking covers almost all of it. The area called West Resort is home to the rails, pipes and jumps ("Dude! Check out my air!"); East Resort is for more traditional skiers and boarders; and the new North Resort has an innertubing/snow-play area. Cabins can be rented in the fetchingly rustic town of Wrightwood for a snow-season getaway.

Mt. Baldy

6700 Mt. Baldy Rd., Upland
909.981.3344, mtbaldy.com
The lifts don't actually go to the 10,064-foot-high summit of this grand old mountain on the east edge of the San Gabriels (named Mt. San Antonio, but commonly called Baldy); they ascend two of its ridges. This is the ski mountain that time forgot, with four rickety wooden chairs and a ramshackle lodge – and we adore it all. The snowmaking is as spotty as the grooming, but when there's fresh snow and blue skies (with views seemingly to Mexico), there's no place better in Southern California to be than atop Chair 4. Baldy gets almost one-tenth the number of visitors as Mountain High, and it has the most terrain and vertical feet of any SoCal ski mountain.

Mt. Baldy after a dump

From Pasadena, Baldy is a mere one-hour drive. Don't expect luxuries, and be warned that this is not a good place for beginners. If you want to stay a spell, book a fireplace-warmed cabin at Mt. Baldy Lodge (mtbaldylodge.com).

Mt. Waterman

Angeles Crest Hwy., 34 miles north of the 210 Freeway, La Cañada
818.952.7676, skiwaterman.com
We're happy to report that after being closed for a few years, our favorite SoCal mountain is back in business. A group of longtime locals bought it, repaired neglected equipment, and got everything running by Presidents Day 2008. It has just three chairs and no snowmaking gear, but when the snow is good, these are the least-crowded, most enjoyable runs around, and they're just a one-hour drive from Pasadena. Long live Waterman!

On 2 Wheels & 4 Legs:
Cycling & Horseback Riding

Increasing traffic and a scarcity of bike lanes mean that Pasadena and its neighbor towns aren't ideal for in-town riding, although there are exceptions, particularly in San Marino and Sierra Madre. But cyclists will be happiest either on established road routes or on one of the many trails in the San Gabriel Mountains.

As for traveling by horse, the west/central valley lacks a stable that rents horses for guided outings; this is a shame, because there's no end of beautiful potential routes in the San Gabriels. But we do have a few fine centers that offer lessons and boarding.

Road Cycling

Diehard cyclists start many a Sunday morning by climbing to the top of 5,715-foot Mt. Wilson, a nineteen-mile ride from La Cañada up Angeles Crest Highway to Mt. Wilson Observatory Road. It's a big ol' workout going up and a screaming-fun ride going down – but watch out for cars. A much, much easier and more protected route is the 5K around Brookside Park and the Rose Bowl. Serious cyclists meet here on Tuesdays and Thursdays at 6 p.m. (during daylight saving time) for a ten-lap, high-speed workout, sometimes including 100 or more riders. Call Open Road Bicycles (626.683.9986) for more information. For a completely protected paved route, head for the San Gabriel River Trail, which runs for 38 to 47 miles (no one seems to know for sure), from the ranger station at Azusa and San Gabriel Canyon Road in Azusa to the ocean at Seal Beach.

Mountain Biking

We can only introduce you to the wealth of mountain-biking trails in the San Gabriel Mountains; for in-depth information, go to socalmtb.com, pick up *Mountain Biking the San Gabriel Mountains' Best Trails* by Troy & Woten (Fine Edge) or *Mountain Bike! Southern California* by Story & Leman (Menasha Ridge Press), and/or check out the Pasadena Mountain Bike Club (pmbc.org).

That said, we have a few greatest hits to recommend. The classic ride starts on the JPL trail (see Upper Arroyo Seco on page 169), follows the trail split on the right to Brown Mountain Road (do not go up the trail marked El Prieto) and goes uphill to a three-way fork. From here, you can either turn left, go to the top of Brown Mountain and come down the Ken Burton single-track trail; go straight, and end up over at Chaney Trail; or turn right and look for the sign marking the top of El Prieto Canyon, a technical, single-track trail back down to the JPL trail – it's lot of fun if you're a skilled rider.

Also fun is the Mt. Wilson Toll Road, reached via a gate at Pinecrst and Crescent in Altadena (at press time it was closed because of a slide, but it could well be open by the time you read this), and the steep climb up Chaney Trail (off Loma Alta in Altadena), which you can take to Inspiration Point or all the way to Mt. Wilson if you have the quads. Other good mountain rides include Sawpit Canyon Fire Road in Monrovia Canyon, either up to White Saddle, which has killer views, or way up to the top of Monrovia Peak, which has even more amazing views (road closed Tuesday and Wednesday); Chantry Flat Road, reached via Santa Anita in Arcadia; and Angeles Crest Fire Road, found about seven miles up Angeles Crest Highway from La Cañada.

Horseback Riding

Altadena Stables
3064 Ridgeview Dr., Altadena
626.797.2012
Jane Kellogg's friendly place is recommended for lessons and boarding.

Flintridge Riding Club
4625 Oak Grove Dr., La Cañada
818.952.1233, flintridgeridingclub.org
At this elite, membership-only place, the New Rider Program allows for one-year temporary memberships for adults or kids who take lessons. For serious (or seriously ambitious) equestrians with deep pockets.

Rose Bowl Riders
Hahamongna Watershed Park
4480 Oak Grove Dr., Pasadena
818.790.8341, rosebowl-riders.org
Lessons and organized equestrian events are sponsored by this organization.

In the ring at San Pascual Stables

San Pascual Stables
221 San Pasqual Ave., South Pasadena
323.258.3999, sanpascualstables.com
A lovely spot in the lower Arroyo, this facility is known for its English-style lessons, its classes for children and its equestrian summer camp for kids. Nice people, nice horses.

Q & A: Doug Christiansen

For 35 years, the book *Trails of the Angeles* (Wilderness Press) has been the definitive guide to hiking the San Gabriels. (If you don't have it, you must get it.) When author John Robinson retired a few years ago, he chose Doug Christiansen to take over authorship. An airline pilot by trade and hiker by avocation, Doug lives with his family in Sierra Madre, where he can be on the Mt. Wilson Trail in mere minutes. Colleen met Doug at Bean Town in Sierra Madre for a chat.

Have you always been a hiker?
I grew up in Arcadia, and the mountains were always right there. I was fascinated by them. I started hiking them when I was about 12.

How did you meet John Robinson?
I went on a few hikes organized by the Sierra Madre Historical Society about eight years ago, and John was part of those. We hit it off and started hiking together. He was in his 70s then, and I could hardly keep up with him.

Did you ever imagine you'd become a book author?
Not in a million years. But I can't take credit for the book – it's all John. I just keep my eyes and ears open for changes. I did have to do a significant rewrite of Rubio Canyon hike, because mud slides opened up access to the waterfall again.

What's your favorite front-range day hike?
That's easy: the Mt. Wilson Trail in Sierra Madre to Orchard Camp. It's about eight miles round-trip. The first half is hot, on the face of the mountains, but the second half is on the back side, and it's a totally different world back there – dark and shady, with lots of trees and ferns and total quiet. You get a lot of bang for your buck on that hike.

If you don't have time for a big hike, what do you do?
Fortunately I live in Sierra Madre, so I can just go out my front door, head in any direction, and have a nice walk. This is a great walking area.

What's your favorite place for breakfast?
I don't eat much breakfast. But I do drink coffee, and this place (Bean Town) is my favorite. My favorite restaurant is easy – Burger Continental, on Lake in Pasadena. I've been going there since I was a kid.

What do you *really* think of the Rose Parade?
Uh, well, you probably won't like this… but I'm not a parade person. I don't like standing around – I'd rather be hiking or riding a bike. But I like the planes at the beginning.

Pasadena is...

Athletic

Most Americans know Pasadena as the home of the Rose Bowl, and most locals know it as the birthplace of athletes Jackie and Mack Robinson. (Dodger Jackie broke the color barrier in the Major Leagues; his big brother Mack was a silver medalist in the 1936 Olympics.) We have our longtime cross-town high school football rivalry, the Turkey Tussle, played in November at the Rose Bowl, as are UCLA's home games. We have our share of eccentric solitary runners, dedicated coaches and mentors, weekend warriors, kids' sports leagues and current-day Olympic hopefuls, but most of our athletic tradition is personal, passionate and off the beaten track. Here's how to partake in all of it, from golf games to Rose Bowl football.

The Rose Bowl   204

Working Out   206

Playing Around   208
    The Sports Shopper

Horsing Around (A Day at the Races)   212

A Day with the Dodgers   213

Q & A: Jeff Brown   214

The Rose Bowl

The symbol for sports in Pasadena is the Rose Bowl, that stately football stadium sitting proudly in the central Arroyo. Built in 1922 as a horseshoe-shape stadium seating 57,000, the structure was named by a police reporter who anticipated the bowl shape, which came along in 1929 when a remodel enclosed the southern end. Now seating a whopping 92,542, it has hosted five Super Bowls, Olympic and World Cup soccer, rock concerts and religious revivals; the four Fs – Fourth of July, filming, festivals and the flea market (held the second Sunday of each month) – keep the place hopping throughout the year.

Of course the main thing that happens in the Rose Bowl is football – it is the home stadium for UCLA (located across town in Westwood), and since 1923 it has hosted the Rose Bowl college-football game on New Year's Day, a battle between

The Battle for the Bowl's Future

Thus far the Rose Bowl has been impervious to significant change. It was listed on the National Register of Historic Places in 1987 and is an indisputable civic treasure, an icon of not just Pasadena but of Southern California. But the Rose Bowl Operating Company, a nonprofit overseen by the city, has been hard-pressed to keep the place financially afloat and competitive. One strategy has been to woo an NFL team to the stadium, while another has been to keep plenty of other clients, from Billy Graham to the Rolling Stones, paying to rent the stadium throughout the year. The neighbors want to minimize noise and traffic, the merchants want to lure patrons to their shops and restaurants, the city doesn't want to lose more money on operation costs or spend a fortune to woo the NFL, and football fans would love to see pro ball here. Meanwhile, the Rose Bowl maintains her benign, imperturbable visage as the debate ebbs and flows around her thick walls. Stay tuned.

the winners of the Pac-10 and Big-12 conferences. Except now a new arrangement with the Bowl Championship Series (BCS) means that every several years, it will instead host the BCS game, as it did in 2006 and will do again in 2010. This is the big playoff game between the top two teams in the nation.

In the fall, the weekly transformation of Brookside Park for a UCLA football game is dramatic. By Friday night, the portapotties and vendor tents are set up, and on Saturday morning, soccer players vacate Brookside's fields and golfers cede the links so they can be used to park the thousands of cars that arrive in a most orderly fashion. The tailgate parties begin hours before kickoff, and once the game is in progress, the joyful roar after every touchdown can be heard up and down the Arroyo. After everyone leaves, the mess at Brookside is astonishing, with mountains of trash covering the vast green lawns. But by Sunday, it's all cleaned up and back to normal – the golfers are putting again, the joggers are circling the Rose Bowl, and the traffic is gone.

The biggest Bruin game of the year is the one against cross-town rival, USC; if the game is held at the Bowl, that's the one to try to get tickets for. (Some years it's held at the Coliseum, USC's home stadium.)

Scoring Tickets

Tickets for UCLA games are available from Ticketmaster (ticketmaster.com, 213.480.3232), which has a window at Macy's in the Eagle Rock Plaza. You can also get tickets at the UCLA Central Ticket Office on the Westwood campus; call 310.825.2946 for details. The big games (especially the SC game) sell out early.

Getting tickets to the New Year's Day Rose Bowl game is more challenging, unless you don't mind brokers' 500% markups. A relatively small number of tickets go on sale through Ticketmaster in December, but the date varies each year, so you need to keep checking. A small block is also set aside for Pasadena residents, and these go on sale at the Pasadena Civic in December; check with the Tournament of Roses (tournamentofroses.com) in late November to find out the date. If you're an out-of-towner hoping to attend both the parade and the game, consider the Tournament of Roses' four-night package, which includes tickets, a stay in a good local hotel and other activities. Finally, because most of the tickets go to the participating colleges, see if you've got a friend who's a member of that school's alumni association. (If all that fails, there's always Craigslist.)

The Rose Bowl is reached on the south end via Rosemont Drive (off of Orange Grove) and on the north end via Washington Boulevard (off of Lincoln); go to rosebowlstadium.com or call 626.577.3101 for general information.

Working Out

Gyms

In Pasadena, though there is certainly California body-consciousness, working out is more about feeling good than looking good. The fit life includes getting outdoors, having fun and staying healthy. We have the usual assortment of chain gyms, and a few notable independents.

Bodies in Motion
900 S. Arroyo Parkway, Pasadena
626.577.2211, bodiesinmotion.com
Kickboxing and spinning are the specialties at this California-based chain gym. It has good basic cardio equipment, from elliptical trainers to recumbent bikes, but you can find those anywhere. The real reason to join is for quality classes in boxing (in a formal ring), kickboxing, a ball-based circuit workout, spinning and dance-based cardio. It also offers yoga and mat Pilates, but serious students will want to look elsewhere. Nice locker rooms, easy parking (an increasing plus in Pasadena) and qualified personal trainers.

Breakthru Fitness
87 Fraser Alley, Old Pasadena
626.396.1700, breakthrufitness.com
For individual training in a supportive atmosphere, Breakthru boasts instructors who are experts at getting to know clients and finding them programs that will bust boredom as well as fat cells. Owners Phil and Michelle Dozois have lots of high-tech goodies, like V02 fitness testing, as well as old-fashioned medicine balls and jump ropes. Breakthru offers small classes, nutrition advice, massage and group outings (rock climbing and rafting) just for fun.

Crescenta-Cañada Family YMCA
1930 Foothill Blvd., La Cañada
818.790.0123, ymcacc.org
Less chi-chi than the area's spa-like gyms but every bit as well-equipped, the La Cañada Y (which is what everyone calls it) is a gem. Excellent workout rooms, a large indoor pool offering everything from kids' swim teams to senior water aerobics, pickup basketball and volleyball games, yoga and Pilates classes, racquetball courts, spinning, childcare, teen programs… it's all here, for a most reasonable monthly fee. Nonmembers pay $15 a day.

Equinox
Paseo Colorado
260 E. Colorado Blvd., Pasadena
626.685.4800, equinoxfitness.com
At Pasadena's high-end boutique club, the bodies are as hard as the classes, which run almost all day. Nonmembers who book a massage can work out at this modernist, spa-like facility at Paseo Colorado, which attracts a well-heeled clientele as sleek as their surroundings.

Sarge's Physical Training
626.797.4882, sargesphysicaltraining.com
Keith Gibbs's recruits meet (as do many other boot camps) at the Rose Bowl. The former Marine and Army trainer begins class, as he puts it, at "oh-five-hundred" three days a week. ("You know you don't have anything to do at five in the morning. You might as well work out!") Guest teachers – tae bo and boxing – liven up the stretching, weights, calisthenics and running. If you reach your goal, you can attend the boot camp once a week, free of charge, for life.

Sierra Fitness
20 N. Baldwin Ave., Sierra Madre
626.836.1236, sierrafit.com
Sierra Fitness is as mellow and friendly as its hometown, but the certified personal trainers are not above teasing you if they see you sneak a cookie after a workout (Bean Town is across the street). Single classes are available at this modern, efficient gym; massage is upstairs; the Pilates studio is down the street. It also sponsors a killer boot camp.

24 Hour Fitness Magic Johnson Club
2180 Lincoln Ave., Altadena
626.296.8700, 24hourfitness.com
Co-owned by Magic Johnson, this huge new kid on the Pasadena fitness block occupies a new building in Northwest Pasadena. It immediately became a vibrant community center in this once-neglected, now-improving neighborhood.

Pilates & Friends

Like much of Southern California, Pasadena embraces alternative forms of exercise; you can see adherents of qigong and tai chi gracing our parks, and some of us favor the movement therapy called Feldenkrais, which was invented by an Israeli physicist. **Diane Park** came to the method through her careers as Balinese dancer, masseuse and mom; her one-on-one work corrects the body's imbalances. She'll even show you how to correctly hike up and down the Mt. Lowe trail.

Pilates strengthens the core of the body through work on specialized machines and on the floor. Zoë Hagler-Marcus, who founded her studio, **Zoë,** more than a decade ago, received her certification from Joseph Pilates's disciple Romania Kryzanowska. The Bauhaus-looking equipment (wooden stirrups, chrome frames) takes up much of the high-ceilinged space. Zoë and her team incorporate mat work with reformer training. At **Balanced Concepts,** a light and airy all-reformer studio in a 1920s bungalow, the emphasis is on technique and injury recovery and prevention. Hana Lauterkranc tailors workouts to her clients' abilities. After you've seen a 78-year-old woman do pull-ups while suspended six feet above the floor, you'll become a believer.

Balanced Concepts
170 S. Oakland Ave., Pasadena
626.792.1036

Feldenkrais by Diane Park
2630 Homepark Ave., Altadena
626.791.1660

Zoë
21 S. El Molino Ave., Pasadena
626.585.8853, zoepilates.com

The serenity of Yoga House

Yoga

Pasadena has been a hotmat of yoga for ages; the Awareness Center was founded in 1974 as an ashram in Altadena. Most of these studios sponsor events and have teacher training.

The Awareness Center
2801 E. Foothill Blvd. (2nd Fl.), East Pasadena
626.796.1567, awarenesscenteryoga.org
A 30-plus-year-old pioneer, the Awareness Center was originally an ashram in an old house in Altadena. These days it's an East Pasadena yoga center specializing in Kundalini and meditation.

Mission Street Yoga
1017 Mission St., South Pasadena
626.441.1144, missionstreetyoga.com
A colorful South Pas studio teaching mainly Iyengar-type yoga with a roster of teachers who conduct small classes in deep alignment. A great place for the fundamentals of any practice, Mission Street also instructs kids and offers pre- and post-natal programs.

Yoga House
11 W. State St., Pasadena
626.403.3961, yogahouse.com
Venerable Yoga House holds classes almost every hour of every day, featuring well-known teachers, solid technique, mommy & me, pre- and post-natal programs, workshops and half-price community classes. Classes are popular, so arrive early.

Yoga Kingdom Sanctuary
553 S. Lake Ave., Pasadena
622.792.7871, yogakingdom.com
This homey place nurtures its diverse clientele (from Caltech students to moms and babies) and emphasizes self-development through Hatha-style classes.

Playing Around

Here we tell you where to get out and play, whether it's tennis or golf, archery or fly-casting, running or skating. For cycling, mountain biking, hiking and skiing, see the Outdoorsy chapter.

Golf

Moneyed Pasadena plays behind the gates of some exclusive enclaves, like Annandale Country Club, but there are places for the rest of us. Public golf is centered on **Brookside,** in the shadow of the Rose Bowl. The two fairly flat 18-hole courses, opened in 1928, are lovely to walk and fun to play; Course #2 is shorter and tighter than #1. Don't plan to play right before or after a football game; the city uses the course as a parking lot. **Scholl Canyon** is a hilly course on a former landfill that requires some skill to negotiate; it's short but challenging. The **Alhambra Municipal Golf Course** features a multistory driving range; the rolling **Santa Anita** course shares the racetrack's vista of the San Gabriels. Two scenic 9-hole courses with spectacular mountain views are **Altadena Golf Course** and **Eaton Canyon Golf Course.** Par-3 fans head to **Arroyo Seco Golf Course** for 18 holes in 2.5 hours. Call for tee times on weekends at all courses, and for daily times at Brookside.

Brookside Golf Course

Alhambra Municipal Golf Course
630 S. Almansor St., Alhambra
626.570.5059

Altadena Golf Course
1456 E. Mendocino St., Altadena
626.797.3821

Arroyo Seco Golf Course
1055 Lohman Lane, South Pasadena
626.255.1506

Brookside Golf Course
1133 Rosemont Ave., Pasadena
626.585.3598

Eaton Canyon Golf Course
1150 Sierra Madre Villa Ave., East Pasadena
626.794.6773

Santa Anita Golf Course
405 S. Santa Anita Ave., Arcadia
626.447.2331

Scholl Canyon Golf Course
3800 E. Glenoaks Blvd., Glendale
818.243.4100

Bowling

All Star Lanes
4459 Eagle Rock Blvd., Eagle Rock
323.254.2579
The hippest bowling alley around, with 22 lanes (still scored by hand), vintage kitschy charm and regular Bowl-A-Ramas, when rockabilly and roots-rock bands play. There's even an adjacent bad Chinese restaurant with full bar and karaoke.

AMF Bahama Lanes
3545 E. Foothill Blvd., East Pasadena
626.351.8858, amf.com/bahamalanes
Your basic AMF bowling alley, popular with teens and families and for kids' birthday parties and leagues. It's lively and well run.

The Lesser-Known Sports

A few athletic endeavors, while not unique to Pasadena, serve to define our eccentric take on the sporting life.

The romantically named **Pasadena Roving Archers** have a sylvan range on the western slopes of the Arroyo Seco south of Suicide Bridge. In existence since 1935, they offer free Saturday-morning lessons (ages 10 and older), six-week classes, and Sunday qualifiers that usually begin at 8 a.m. Nearby is the **Pasadena Casting Club,** founded in 1947. It meets on Sunday afternoons to talk fishing and practice technique around the Casting Pond. The world's first **disc golf** (aka Frisbee golf) course was founded in Pasadena's Hahamongna Park. That's to be expected, since Wham-O was first headquartered in the San Gabriel Valley. The hilly, oak-studded course, sometimes called Oak Grove, attracts players from all over.

While croquet is now played only at private Pasadena homes, **lawn bowling,** another pastime that seems to belong to a bygone era, is thriving. The Central Park clubhouse, designed by Wallace Neff in 1927, sits near an unofficial homeless encampment, but that doesn't bother the doughty players, who range from their late 50s to an unbelievably skilled 96-year-old. The 60 or so club members meet Monday, Wednesday and Friday at 9 a.m. on their manicured greenswards; on Wednesdays, they wear natty whites and give free lessons to newcomers. A subtle game of strategy and skill that has endured since the Middle Ages, it's harder than it looks. There are also clubs in Alhambra and Arcadia.

Wednesday is formal-whites day at the Pasadena Lawn Bowling Club.

Disc Golf
Hahamongna Watershed Park
Oak Grove Dr. & Foothill Blvd., Pasadena
626.744.7275

The Pasadena Casting Club
Lower Arroyo, Pasadena
626.356.7406,
pasadenacastingclub.org
Meets Sun. afternoons

Pasadena Lawn Bowling Club
275 S. Raymond Ave., Old Pasadena
626.578.9165, marion@ glendale.cc.ca.us

Pasadena Roving Archers
626.577.7275,
rovingarchers.com

Running

Running groups meet year-round, often at the Rose Bowl. Many are organized by shops dedicated to the sport, or for specific events like the L.A. Marathon (held in March) and the brand-new fall Pasadena Marathon (pasadenamarathon.org).

Mt. Wilson Trail Race
mtwilsontrailrace.com
One of the oldest trail races in the west, the Mt. Wilson Trail Race was first held in 1908. The 8.6-mile, steep, narrow, scenic trail has been in existence since 1840, and it's a challenge even for hikers. Only 300 runners are allowed to tackle the course, which has an elevation gain of over 2,100 feet in 4.3 miles. The race starts and ends in downtown Sierra Madre in late May, and is celebrated with a pancake breakfast and other festivities.

Pasadena Pacers
pasadenapacers.org
Meeting Saturday mornings near the Rose Bowl Aquatic Center for conditioning runs (all levels), this fun and supportive group promises to take you from couch potato to a 5Ker in twelve weeks. The free group was founded by Steve Smith, a local chiropractor who does great on-the-hoof diagnosing of aches and pains. A specialty is the breakfast run to downtown L.A., returning – after some serious eating – on the Gold Line.

Skating

Bonita Skate Park
2nd & Bonita, Arcadia
626.821.4368
A large, open skate park that's one of the better ones in the SG Valley; helmet rules are enforced.

Moonlight Rollerway
5110 San Fernando Rd., Glendale
818.241.3630, moonlightrollerway.com
One of the last of the old-school roller rinks – it still has the wooden announcer's booth stocked with LPs. Popular for birthday parties, goofy date nights and for retro serious skaters; the music ranges from swing to hip-hop.

Pasadena Ice Skating Center
310 E. Green St., Pasadena
626.578.0801, skatepasadena.com
In 2010, this rink is slated to move to another site in the Civic Center complex. It serves loyal cadres of hockey players, recreational skaters and serious young figure skaters, including 2008 U.S. champion Mirai Nagasu.

Verdugo Skatepark
Verdugo Park,
1621 Cañada Blvd., Glendale
818.548.6420
Considered the best vert skate park in Southern California, this large facility in beautiful Verdugo Park is awesome fun for a good skater.

Soccer

With Pasadena's Latino population booming and the entrenchment of AYSO, soccer is big in the SG Valley. The worldwide popularity of the sport is reflected in the team names of the four-year-old **San Gabriel Valley Men's Soccer League** (sgvmsl. com): the Foreign Legion, the Internationalists, Café Beaujolais, Viet United. This league, which appeals to men who are good players, has two divisions, free subbing and three refs. The **Women's Soccer Organization of the San Gabriel Valley** (eteamz.active.com/wsosgv) runs women's, coed and men's leagues throughout the valley and has small teams and a large schedule.

Swimming

AAF Rose Bowl Aquatic Center
360 N. Arroyo Blvd., Pasadena
626.564.0330, rosebowlaquatics.com
Built for the 1984 L.A. Olympics, this sparkling public facility boasts two Olympic-regulation pools and has a full complement of teams, water aerobics, lap swimming and a therapy pool. The diving program is exceptional; water polo is big from age 8 to Junior Olympics. The pools draw a crowd year-round and are packed on hot days.

Sierra Vista Park Aquatic Center
611 E. Sierra Madre Blvd., Sierra Madre
626.355.7135, cityofsierramadre.com
This small, mellow center serves the summer learn-to-swim crowd. Facilities are bare-bones, but the instruction is good, and the outdoor pool has a pretty setting under the San Gabriels.

Just one of the two Olympic-size pools at the Rose Bowl Aquatic Center

Tennis

The public courts at Loma Alta

The best public courts in Pasadena are at **Brookside Park;** in Altadena, we love the pretty, underused courts at **Loma Alta Park** and the new courts at **Farnsworth Park.** Sierra Madre's parks also feature lightly used courts. The ten lighted hilltop courts at **Scholl Canyon** in Glendale are available with a reservation, and the **San Marino Tennis Club** at Lacy Park (six good courts) is open to the public for a $5 to $7 fee. **Rose Bowl Tennis** offers lessons, practice sessions and tournaments at Brookside Park and other park courts. The excellent instruction at **Altadena Town & Country Club** is open to non-members for a modest extra fee.

Altadena Town & Country Club
2290 Country Club Dr., Altadena
626.794.7163

Pasadena City Parks
626.744.7275

Rose Bowl Tennis
323.258.4178, rosebowltennis.com

San Marino Tennis Club
Lacy Park
1196 St. Albans Rd., San Marino
626.793.1622

Scholl Canyon Tennis
3800 E. Glenoaks Blvd., Glendale
818.243.4100

Sierra Madre Parks
626.355.5278

The Sports Shopper

Billy's Ski & Sport
2031 Verdugo Blvd., Montrose
818.249.3600
At this full-service shop for board and snow sports, the 'tude is minimal and the staff knowledgeable – they're particularly good at fitting ski and snowboard boots. Watch for the sales.

Chilloutla.com
This web site offers some great deals for spas and yoga studios around Los Angeles.

REI
214 N. Santa Anita Ave., Arcadia
626.447.1062, rei.com/stores/arcadia
This outdoorsy heaven identifies its location on its web site by its GPS coordinates, which gives you a clue to the sensibility here. You'll find everything for climbing, camping, hiking, biking, snowshoeing and exploring, sold by a staff of aficionados. We also love the outdoorsy clothing. The 25-foot climbing wall is a big draw, too.

Run With Us
235 N. Lake Ave., Pasadena
626.568.3331
A complete resource for runners, walkers and marathoners, with gear, connections to training and classes and expert advice.

Sport Chalet
2 Sport Chalet Lane, La Cañada
818.790.9800
400 S. Baldwin Ave., Arcadia
626.446.8955, sportchalet.com
Now a publicly traded chain of 45 stores, Sport Chalet began in La Cañada in 1959. Norbert Olberz and his wife, Irene, put their life savings into a tiny ski shop and slept in the back for a year, taking showers with a garden hose. In the early '60s, they expanded into then-new sports like SCUBA and mountaineering, and today Sport Chalet serves athletes throughout California, Nevada and Arizona. The La Cañada operation, once spread over four buildings, has been consolidated into a single store anchoring a new shopping center at the corner of Foothill Boulevard and Angeles Crest Highway.

Walt Butler Sports Shoes
1376 N. Lake Ave., Pasadena
626.794.6476
An independent shoe shop run by the eponymous Walt, who fits kids and adults with cleats and basketball shoes with a practiced, patient eye. Funky clothes too.

Horsing Around
(A Day at the Races)

Even if you've seen *Seabiscuit*, you haven't experienced Santa Anita Park until you've spent a postcard-worthy winter day there. The view of the San Gabriels is breathtaking, the architecture grand, the gardens lovely, the people-watching superb, and the horse (and jockey!) flesh divine.

Though the web site touts daily racing in season, the track is actually dark on Tuesdays and Wednesdays. The 1934 art deco grandstand holds 26,000, and 50,000 can visit the infield (open weekends only). The infield has a kids' playground, since only the most horse-crazy youngsters can bear the half-hour wait between races. Early risers can watch workouts every racing day starting at 5:30 a.m. and have breakfast at Clockers' Corner. It's a thrill to watch the horses thunder around the track as the sun rises.

Though general admission is a modest $5, the $20 Turf Club admission (note the dress code) is worth it for those who want to explore everything from the betting rooms and concourse on the ground floor (done in Early Fla-

Off and running at Santa Anita

Santa Anita Park
285 W. Huntington Dr., Arcadia
626.574.RACE, santaanita.com
Season runs Dec. 26-late April, plus a fall meeting in Oct. & Nov. Satellite wagering year-round. Closed Mon. (except holidays) & Tues. First race 1 p.m. weekdays, 12:30 p.m. weekends. Admission $5 (senior discounts), Club House $8.50, box seats $7.50 plus Club House admission, Turf Club $20.
Morning workouts every racing day 5-10 a.m.; Clockers' Corner serves continental breakfast from 5:30 a.m., full breakfast from 7:30 a.m.

mingo), to the second-story Club House, with its art deco and hacienda-style rooms, to the high-up Turf Club, complete with crystal chandeliers and an elegant bar. Take a peek inside the Directors' Lounge – the woodwork was imported from an English country house. It's like ascending to heaven, with ever-more-beautiful settings (and spectators) as you move to the higher levels. Food ranges from hot dogs to the trendy Frontrunner Restaurant, high above the track. Perks for Turf Club diners include the post-horn bugler playing their favorite songs, as well as racing-knowledgeable waiters – even the busboys keep track of their picks.

And, of course, it's really about the picks. Santa Anita provides big purses and top horses each season, and it makes races easy to understand and to watch – video feeds are everywhere. The Saddling Barn and Walking Ring are nice spots to check the condition of "your" horses. The excitement is palpable as the horses enter the gate, and every race elicits yells and groans from the crowd. There's nothing like standing by the rail with a ticket to a long shot in your hand as the pack thunders by, your horse in the lead by a nose.

A Day with the Dodgers

While it's true that Dodger Stadium is not located in the San Gabriel Valley, it is found right off the Pasadena Freeway a mere seven miles south of Pasadena, so we consider going to a Dodger game an essential part of experiencing our corner of the world. Besides, Pasadena's own Jackie Robinson was a Dodger (even if the Dodgers were in Brooklyn at the time) – he signed with the team in 1947, becoming the first African-American in the Major Leagues. Not coincidentally, the Dodgers won the National League pennant that season, and Robinson proved to be one of the finest players the game has ever seen.

The team began as the Brooklyn Bridegrooms in 1890 (because several players got married around the same time), was later renamed the Superbas, and finally became the Dodgers in 1913. In 1958, team president Walter O'Malley saw the possibilities for a better stadium and team growth out west, so they moved to L.A. and played at the Coliseum for four years while Dodger Stadium was being built on a view-rich bluff atop Chavez Ravine, between downtown L.A. and Mt. Washington. Although the city was thrilled to get a major national sports team, the development of the stadium was controversial and contentious, as these things usually are.

Nowadays, there is controversy again – the team's performance tanked when new owner Frank McCourt (who made his money in parking lots, not sports) took over in 2005. In 2008 McCourt brought in acclaimed Yankees manager Joe Torre for a vast sum of money, and things started to look up. At press time the Blue Crew still had more losses than wins, but the tide seemed to be turning.

We love going to Dodger Stadium, controversy or not. On a blue-sky day or at twilight, with views from the San Gabriels to downtown L.A., with a Dodger dog and an outrageously priced beer on our laps and 56,000 of the most wonderfully diverse and lively Southern Californians you'd ever hope to meet surrounding us, waiting for the crack of the bat and a possible home run... well, California living doesn't get much better than that. The stadium may be an antique by modern standards, but it's a thing of beauty and an L.A. treasure.

Dodger Stadium
1000 Elysian Park Ave.
Los Angeles
323.224.1500,
866.363.4377 (tickets),
dodgers.com
Tickets $6-$80, parking $10

A summer's day at Dodger Stadium

Q & A: Jeff Brown

Jeff Brown is the energetic, charismatic director of Pasadena YES (Youth Education and Sports), a year-round sports league for girls and boys ages 5 to 15. Formed as a response to the 1993 "Halloween murders" of three local boys, YES emphasizes instruction, teamwork, sportsmanship and inclusion. A New Orleans native, Jeff came to Pasadena in 1978; he first coached when his son, now an adult in the TV business, was 7. When Jeff's mom had to flee New Orleans during Hurricane Katrina, YES's parents and kids helped her rebuild a life near her son.

Jeff met Mel at a Starbucks between his job at YES and his duties as basketball coach for Weizmann Day School. A gorgeous woman jumped up, hugged him and cried, "I love this guy. He's fantastic!" Jeff says that's one of the perks, when parents and kids remember him, thank him and return to YES as coaches or referees.

What's the philosophy behind YES?
To bring Pasadena together. To let kids have fun and learn sports without pressure, to make new friends and to be allowed to make mistakes and learn from them. We don't let kids wear baggy pants or curse, we ask them to do their best, and we get them exercising. Every kid participates; I put kids of all shapes, colors, sizes and abilities on each team. I've told kids who think they won't like a sport, "Try it, and I'll pay you to leave if you don't like it after three weeks." I've never had to pay up.

Do you like your job?
When I worked in computers, I could hardly get up in time for work. Now I get up two or three hours early – I can't wait to get to work. When you work with kids, they keep you young.

What do you like most about Pasadena?
We really are a community. I can't name one white person I knew in New Orleans. I am Creole, and I only knew Creoles. Here I've met and worked with Hispanics, whites, blacks, Asians, Armenians – it's great. And I love the mountains, how they make me feel how truly insignificant we all are. I'll never leave.

How's your French?
It's terrible, but I sometimes tell the kids they are being a "chee-kee" – that's Creole for "ball hog."

What's your favorite place for breakfast?
My mom's house, then IHOP. For dinner, Cajun Way in Monrovia – it's a great family place.

What do you really think of the Rose Parade?
It's beautiful – much prettier than Mardi Gras, which is just floats made out of cardboard. I like to look up close at the floats after the parade.

What would you do if you were mayor?
I'd open every gym, classroom and playing field so kids and parents could get skills and have fun after school and on weekends. And I'd have just twenty kids in a classroom all the way through high school.

Materialistic

Pasadena and its satellite towns are famed for their flea markets, antiques stores and small-town, pedestrian-friendly main streets. But that's just the beginning. You'll also find quality outdoor and indoor malls and lots of one-of-a-kind sources for clever gifts, fashionable clothing, lovely jewelry, creative stationery, hard-to-find music and home furnishings for both the Craftsman aficionado and the modernist.

An Embarrassment of Riches: Pasadena's Flea Markets   216

The Main Streets That Time Forgot   218

The Old World: Antiques   220

Where the Locals Shop   225

The Goods   227

Q & A: Stephanie Miller   236

An Embarrassment of Riches:
Pasadena's Flea Markets

"I think it's Indian, and I'm pretty sure its old."

"No, I bet it's Chinese. Look at the dragon's nostrils."

"I don't think so, but it could be Turkish – it has a sort of East meets West thing going on."

"I... don't... know... Is it some kind of candelabra?"

"No. Where would you put the candles?"

"Sort of stuck on the tail thingy."

"You're nuts. It would drip wax over everything."

"Well, I like it. It's art. Don't you like it?"

"It's okay, I guess. Do you really like it?"

"I love it."

(The proprietress, who has maintained a discreet distance, moves in.)

"How much?"

"That's an old one. Solid brass. I guess I can give it to you for $70."

"How about $50?"

"$60."

"$55."

"It's yours."

"We'll pick it up before we go. It's too heavy to haul around."

"No problem."

– Conversation overheard at the Rose Bowl Flea Market

Rose Bowl Flea Market

1001 Rose Bowl Dr., Pasadena
323.560.7469, rgcshows.com
Open 2nd Sun. of the month 7 a.m.-4:30 p.m.;
admission $8, $10 between 8 & 9 a.m.,
$15 between 7 & 8 a.m.; kids 12 & under
free with adult

On the second Sunday of every month (rain or shine), tens of thousands of people buy their tickets and take their chances at the Rose Bowl Flea Market, where they are free to wander among five miles of booths selling everything from vintage Jetsons lunch boxes, to 19th-century chandeliers, to midcentury dinettes, to exotic plants, to old watches, to Aunt Sadie's 1907 postcard of earthquake-ravaged San Francisco. ("Wish you were here!" wrote that wicked Sadie 100 years ago.) Preteens and teens love to prowl the mile or so of booths selling new stuff: Indian-print skirts, costume jewelry, candied nuts, goofy toys, pungent incense. The Flea Market (also called the Swap Meet) is a famous tourist destination, and we locals love it – even if we haven't been for years. Many locals are regulars with stories to tell – like the Stickley table and chairs bought in 1980 that sent two kids through college. Movie star sightings galore. Splurge on the early admission if you're looking for something that might get snapped up by 8 a.m.

The Wall Street Journal has ranked it among the top five antiques markets in North America. Tell us something we don't already know.

Pasadena City College Flea Market

Pasadena City College, along Hill St. south of Colorado Blvd.
626.585.7906, pasadena.edu/fleamarket
Open 1st Sun. of the month 8 a.m.-3 p.m.; admission free; free parking in structure on Del Mar

We'll say it right out – this flea market is an earthly paradise for record collectors. Remember records? Hard black vinyl circles, about the size of a pizza (or a personal-pan pizza when we're talking 45s) – you'd spin 'em on a machine and music would come out. Among the cognoscenti, the PCC flea market is said to be one of the best record swaps in Southern California. A first pressing of "A Hard Day's Night" with "I Should Have Known Better" on the B-side – yellow with orange swirl label, and no skips!? Yes, my friend, I speak the truth.

But fear not, ye seekers of all manner of other old and collectible things: 450 vendors sell everything from high-end antiques to *Little Mermaid* pencil cases by the gross, with enough china, 1950s fabric, crystal glasses and tools to rebuild Tara and furnish it for company. And the whole dang thing is free, with free parking to boot. I tell you, life is good on Sundays in Pasadena.

The Main Streets That Time Forgot

Any town with a main street where people park cars like they used to park horses is a main street we like to frequent. The San Gabriel Valley is blessed with several such main streets, all of which have historic appeal and mom-and-pop friendliness. Here are our three faves; even if you've never walked them, you've seen them – they're frequently used as locations for movies and TV shows.

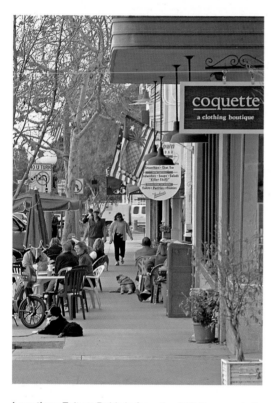

Baldwin Avenue, Sierra Madre

This storybook town has the most compact and appealing main street in the region – it doesn't even have a stoplight. The tiny commercial district centers around the intersection of Baldwin and Sierra Madre Boulevard, and some of the worthwhile businesses, from Lucky Baldwin's pub to the Sierra Madre Playhouse, home to a thriving community theater, are actually around the corner on Sierra Madre. Nothing could be finer on a sunny day than lunch at Restaurant Lozano, followed perhaps by a haircut at Christopher Carole, a look-see at the shops (don't miss Savor the Flavor, a fine gourmet shop, and Iris Intrigue, for womenswear and casual jewelry) and a post-shopping coffee and cookie at Bean Town.

Location: Exit on Baldwin from the 210 Freeway in Arcadia and drive north (toward the mountains); you'll have to jog left to stay on Baldwin. You'll enter the town of Sierra Madre; look to park after the stop sign at Sierra Madre Blvd. The district runs north for two blocks; it also goes three blocks west on Sierra Madre. Parking is free throughout town.

Honolulu Avenue, Montrose

Dating to the 1920s, the Montrose Shopping Park is a tree-lined pedestrian haven stretching along Honolulu Avenue and spilling over onto Ocean View. Kids love Tom's Toys and Once Upon a Time; teens head for the Coffee Bean & Tea Leaf (one of very few chains) and Ocean View Board Sports; crafty types hang out at Paper Rabbit, Needle in a Haystack and Quilt 'n' Things; and the hungry get tables at the Star

Café and Zeke's BBQ. We particularly love the vintage Montrose Bowl, used mostly for kids' birthday parties and filming; the more modern library, on the west end of Honolulu, is also swell. Scattered throughout are all the essential small-town businesses, from a newsstand and bakery to hair salons and dry cleaners.

Every Sunday from 9 a.m. to 2 p.m. the Harvest Market moves in, bringing a farmer's market, live music, kids' activities, antiques and seasonal events, from a haunted house to a classic-car show.

Location: Exit on Ocean View from the 210 Freeway in La Crescenta and drive south (downhill) on Ocean View. Turn right or left onto Honolulu and park where you can; most spots are metered, but there are free lots. The shopping district runs along Honolulu between Verdugo Rd. on the east and Las Palmas on the west; it also runs north and south along Ocean View.

Myrtle Avenue, Monrovia

Of all the SG Valley's main streets, this is the one on which time has most stood still. True, on the north end you'll find a Starbucks, but on the main stretch of Myrtle, the mom-n-pops rule. The eating is great, from swank Restaurant Devon, to romantic Amori, to casual Empanadas Gourmet. Unlike on the other main streets, there's a movie-theater complex (a nice twelve-screen Krikorian), which adds a date-night and teen-hangout appeal. And the shops are personal, quirky and well worth exploring. Don't miss the collectible LPs and old concert posters at A Family Affair, which has been selling records for 50 years; the American antiques at Patty's; and the Arts & Crafts light fixtures at Historic Lighting. Myrtle and its side streets are particularly swell for kids – there's Scoops, a dazzling ice cream and candy store; a few other bakeries and candy vendors; the Comic Cellar; and the sort of gifty boutiques that 12-year-old girls love. The small-town library set in lovely little Library Park was being rebuilt at press time and is scheduled to debut in the spring of 2009; it promises to be a thriving community center. A free trolley runs weekdays from 11 a.m. to 2:30 p.m., Friday and Saturday from 4 p.m. to midnight.

Every Friday from 5 to 9 p.m. from March through December, Myrtle hosts the Monrovia Family Fair, a farmer's market and street fair that's a fun way to kick off the weekend. Besides the usual organic farmer's-market goods, it offers pony rides and bounce houses, as well as live music, street food and craft vendors.

Location: Exit on Myrtle from the 210 Freeway in Monrovia and drive north (toward the mountains). Park anywhere after Olive street; the district runs along Myrtle from Olive to Foothill. Parking is free and abundant throughout town, including in several lots on Myrtle's side streets.

The Old World: Antiques

Pasadena is a fun town for antiquing, to say nothing of "mantiquing" – the art of convincing the fellow of the house that these joints are full of turn-of-the-century tools and sports stuff. Our favorite stores illustrate dual maxims: First, one man's trash is another man's treasure; and second, one man's treasure is another man's treasure, if he can just pony up enough cash. To shop at Pasadena's antiques stores, you'll either need to sell your firstborn for that museum-quality dining table or scootch around the bottom of your purse for change to buy that rhinestone ring.

Limited space precludes including every antiques store in town, but we've placed you in the right neighborhoods for nosing around other shops. And note that we have not included hours of operation, as they can and do change on a dime. Call ahead, and happy hunting.

Pasadena

Bruce Graney & Co. Fine Antiques
By appt. only
626.449.9547, brucegraneyantiques.com
Seeking semi-retirement, the Graneys recently closed their longtime showroom, but are now as busy as ever selling their high-quality 18th- and 19th-century European and English antiques, furnishings, art and reproductions out of their warehouse, which is open by appointment only. This is gawgeous stuff, not for the faint of pocketbook.

While you're in the neighborhood, check out:
Dovetail Antiques
1 W. California Blvd., #412 • 626.792.9410
West World Imports
171 E. California Blvd. • 626.449.8565

F. Suie One Co.
1335 E. Colorado Blvd., Pasadena
626.795.1335
This shop is a descendant of the original F. Suie One in L.A.'s Chinatown (circa 1904). Of Chinese origin, it now specializes in pan-Asian antiques and furnishings.

Pasadena Antique Center & Annex
444 & 480 S. Fair Oaks Ave., Pasadena
626.449.7706, pasadenaantiquecenter.com
For 30 years, 130 dealers have occupied these 40,000 square feet, selling Monterey to midcentury, Orientalia, records, toys, fine furniture, garden furnishings, crystal, silver and vintage you-name-it. One of Pasadena's most fun and fab something-for-everyone antiquing places. Check out the deco jewelry and the 20th-century collectibles, and feel free to bring the kids.

While you're in the neighborhood, check out:
Antiques on Fair Oaks
330 S. Fair Oaks Ave. • 626.449.9590
Rick Kaplan Antiques
450 S. Fair Oaks Ave. • 626.793.6841
Georgene's Antiques
448 S. Fair Oaks Ave. • 626.440.9926
Cable International Fine Art & Antiques
456 S. Fair Oaks Ave. • 626.584.0967

Pasadena Antique Mall
309 E. Green St., Pasadena
626.304.9886
This 12,000-square-foot mall hosts 50 to 60 dealers selling jewelry, American furnishings and decorative arts, '50s kitchenware, a fun book collection organized by topic and dating back to the 1930s, and records.

Pasadena Architectural Salvage
30 S. San Gabriel Blvd., East Pasadena
626.535.9655,
pasadenaarchitecturalsalvage.com
For Craftsman, Victoriana and art deco enthusiasts, this place specializes in 1880 to 1930 hardware, doors, fireplace mantels, gates, plumbing fixtures, stained glass and more. Pray to the antiques gods and you may even find that mint-green midcentury loo you've been pining for.

Revival Antiques
527 S. Fair Oaks Ave., Pasadena
626.405.0024, revivalantiques.com
Two buildings house two distinct collections. One is Spanish Revival and Mediterranean works from 1910 to 1930: stately brass and iron chandeliers that Zorro would be proud to swing from, furnishings, silver, tile and some jewelry. The other is a pristine Arts & Crafts collection, primarily furnishings, art and lighting.

A little bit of everything at Novotny's on East Colorado

Roger Renick Fine Arts & Antiques
696 E. Colorado Blvd., #17, Pasadena
626.304.0008, renickarts.com
Renick's 16th- to 19th-century Spanish,
Mediterranean and Spanish Colonial furnishings
provide a context for the Spanish Revival and
Monterey art and furnishings of the early 20th
century; for fans of religious iconography, the
santos (saints) are not to be missed.

Shibui Japanese Antiques
991 E. Green St., Pasadena
626.578.0908, shibuiantiques.com
A successful dealer for fifteen years, Shibui is
known for developing ongoing relationships with
customers and searching worldwide for quality
pieces, primarily from the 18th through 20th
centuries.

T.L. Gurley Antiques
512 S. Fair Oaks Ave., Pasadena
626.432.4811
The sign says it all: Odd and Unusual –
Bought and Sold. There's a lot more here than
meets the eye from the modest storefront.
The 3,000-square-foot cabinet of curiosities
includes Spanish Revival, Mission, Chinois and
European pieces; California pottery and garden
accessories; stunning urns and garden gnomes;
lighting; and clocks. Love, love, love the horse
portraits covering one wall.

Yoshino Japanese Antiques
1240 E. Colorado Blvd., Pasadena
626.356.0588
A stunning collection – tansu, wall hangings,
screens, porcelain, netsuke, lacquerware, prints,
sculpture – that owner Gary Myers gathers on
annual trips to Japan. Up to the standard of
the serious collector, but also accessible to the
shopper seeking that one exceptional piece.

East Colorado Corridor

New shops and several established
dealers have staked out turf on the east
side of town. From Victorian to art deco
to midcentury, this is destination shopping for antiques lovers. Don't be surprised to see additional pioneers who
opened shop after we went to press.
Park someplace around Colorado and
Sierra Madre and go east, young man
and woman!

East Colorado Antiques
2546 E. Colorado Blvd., East Pasadena
626.796.7989
Two veteran antiques dealers combine forces
to make a great addition to the corridor.
Michelle Beiner's offerings are 1920s lighting
and furnishings. Beiner loves highly carved
wood, so you may find good examples mixed
in among the Spanish Revival furniture that is
her first love. Jack Smith has been collecting art
deco for 35 years. His focus is on lighting, and
he has the sconces, floor lamps, table lamps,
kitchen and bathroom globes, and chandeliers
to prove it. Furnishings are primarily art deco,
with occasional forays into the postwar and
midcentury periods. Collectibles include art,
sculpture, bookends, a bit of pottery and
decorative objects.

Funnel
2540 E. Colorado Blvd., East Pasadena
626.395.0141
Pasadenans are abandoning treks to Melrose
for a quick trip to Funnel. With a focus on 1940s
through '70s furnishings, it features rebuilt and
reupholstered pieces, plus the tables, lamps,
dressers and sideboards you'd swear you saw in
Doris and Rock's apartments when you Netflixed
1959's Pillow Talk. (Okay, so we Netflixed it...
twice.) Owner Ricardo Ramirez will visit your
home for an interior consultation, and he can
design the seating of your midcentury dreams.
Local tidbit: Ricardo is the son of El Portal owner
Abel Ramirez and brother of Yahaira's Armando
Ramirez.

Jason Arnold for Modern
2421 E. Colorado Blvd., East Pasadena
626.440.9663
This is Pasadena's own Hollywood Regency
midcentury destination. The color palette strikes

Just a hint of the depth of antique fixtures carried at Old Pasadena Vintage Lighting

you the moment you walk in: The kidney-shape table, the orange faux-fur chairs – Toto, we are not in Arts & Crafts Land anymore! You may come across pieces by the famous, such as Edward Wormley or Hans Wegner, or simply find the perfect lamp, mirror, table or objet d'art to make your room – and your day.

Novotny's Antique Gallery
2552 E. Colorado Blvd., East Pasadena
626.577.9660, novotnysantiques.com
Many dealers, many deals: The loads of traditional mahogany, Victorian fine furnishings, jewelry, paintings, decorative arts, dolls, books, candelabra, lighting, china and silver just begin to tell the tale. If the script said "antiques store," this is what the location scout would come up with. Retired dealer William Novotny is an accredited member of the International Society of Appraisers (ISA) and will prepare formal appraisals of personal property.

Old Pasadena Vintage Lighting
2569 E. Colorado Blvd., East Pasadena
626.396.0843
Lighting is one of the great design challenges, but this is the place to go when you're looking for that perfect fixture to complete a room. Prices are good, and whether you're seeking vintage or reproduction, you'll find abundant choices, particularly in art deco, Arts & Crafts and Spanish Revival. Owner Jason Mc Farland may even be able to restore your own period fixture.

Pink Plum
2580 E. Colorado Blvd., East Pasadena
626.584.0046
An iron plant stand proudly showing a few of its years out in the garden; a hefty south-of-the-border kitchen cabinet at anything but a hefty price; a glorious Elizabethan-style (teensy pearls galore) cloche hat circa 1950 *with the Saks Fifth Avenue label still attached* – a treasure for your children's dress-up box. Come here for antiques and collectibles, from pottery to kitchen and kitsch, as well as friendly people and friendly prices; dealers like it here.

Sharp Design Works
27 N. Altadena Dr., East Pasadena
626.356.3927
We recall owner Preston Sharp from his work on *Extreme Makeover: Home Edition*, but we appreciate him for his personal interest in, and obvious understanding of, midcentury modern furniture. We were taken with a chair that appeared to be wood, painted with an aluminum-colored finish. It reminded us of an aluminum pigment sometimes used by Richard Neutra for interiors. Turns out, the chair was the Sharp's own work, and it blended seamlessly with many of the other pieces in the store. A fine addition to the corridor, with plenty of parking around the corner on Colorado.

South Pasadena

American Street
1127 Mission St., South Pasadena
626.799.8546, americanstreet.com
Beverly Archer, formerly an actress in several successful sitcoms, is the proprietress of this stronghold of Americana. A longtime collector, Archer welcomes visitors to her saffron-meets-sunshine front room. In space shared with Thomas R. Field, her shop is filled with the industrious, often-quirky toys, quilts, paintings and furniture of an America that clothed, amused and fed itself without benefit of mass production.

Hodgson Antiques
1005 Mission St., South Pasadena
626.799.0229
This is one-stop antiquing, offering postcards, books, toys, paper ephemera that has beaten the odds, costume jewelry, furnishings, collectibles and vintage clothes. The kids will have fun, too, and you can run across the street to Buster's for an ice cream afterward.

Fun old stuff is piled high at Mission Antiques.

Mission Antiques
1018 Mission St., South Pasadena
626.799.1327
A great spot to bring the kids, Mission is small enough to keep an eye on them and carries plenty of fun, funky and affordable items that will hold their interest. If the fabulous folk-art felt pumpkin pillow is gone, we're sorry – we just couldn't help ourselves.

Thomas R. Field American Antiques
1127 Mission St., South Pasadena
626.799.8546, thomasrfieldantiques.com
Something of a rarity for Southern California, this shop has a quality and focus on Americana typically seen in the loveliest Boston antiques shops. Come here for 18th- and 19th-century furniture and folk art, as well as appraisals and estate disposition. Three cheers for the red, white and blue!

yoko
1018 Mission St., South Pasadena
626.441.4758
We'd try a haiku, but we'd just embarrass ourselves. We'll just say this is a lovely shop, with tansu, decorative objects and exquisite fabrics.

Monrovia

Trilco
617 S. Myrtle Ave., Monrovia
626.359.1010
You can visit the great homes of Europe or just walk into Trilco to see large religious statuary and oversize armoires, chests, tables and chairs from the 16th through 19th centuries; some pieces appear European but are in fact American. Fantastic clocks and well-preserved photo albums catch the eye, as do the restoration work and insurance claims. It's located next door to a pawn shop, so you can hock Granny's ring and buy a six-foot-tall 18th-century icon. Beautiful stuff.

While you're in the neighborhood, check out:
Monrovia West Antique Mall
925 W. Foothill Blvd. • 626.357.5235
Patty's Antiques
316 S. Myrtle Ave. • 626.358.0344
Kaleidoscope Antiques
306 S. Myrtle Ave. • 626.303.4042

The Neighborhoods

Strolling on South Lake

South Lake Avenue, between Colorado and California, is Pasadena's business hub, and it's a worthy retail center, too. In the last couple of years, new shops have sprung up at the site of the late, great I. Magnin, one of California's retail grande dames. Macy's occupies the former Bullock's, which, when it came on the scene in 1947 as "the store of tomorrow," put South Lake on the map. Designed to appeal to the carriage trade (shoppers arriving by automobile), it was heavily influenced by the Moderne and International styles. You'll find a smattering of large chains here, including Pottery Barn Kids, Talbot's, Borders and Ann Taylor, along with such smaller chains as Anthropologie and Smith & Hawken. There are even a few independent stores.

Across Lake from Macy's are three fetching arcades, the precursors to the mall: the Burlington Arcade, which looks like it was transplanted from England, the Colonnade and the Commons, which isn't so much an arcade as a courtyard.

As a proper old-fashioned small town should, South Pasadena has a soda fountain at the heart of its shopping district, which is centered around Mission Street and Fair Oaks Avenue. The Fair Oaks Pharmacy and Soda Fountain, located here on Route 66 since 1915, sets the scene for this quaint area, which is particularly rich in antiques stores, cafés and mom-n-pop storefronts selling things like mystery books, wine and children's clothing. And now the new Metro station on Mission and Meridian has added a European feel and inspired more merchants – and visitors – to move in. The hip heart of this retail scene are three women's clothing stores: Rue de Mimo, Koi and Camille's; the funky gift shop, Marz; and riotously colorful Folk Tree, filled with beautiful things from Mexico and Central and South America.

South Pasadena's walkability is celebrated with this sculpture at the Gold Line station.

In San Marino, the shopping scene is positively bucolic. On a tree-lined street, locals stop to chat with neighbors as they come and go from posh little boutiques and high-end beauty salons. The action is on the two-block stretch of Mission Street between El Molino and Euclid. Julienne, where locals come to lunch on the flower-filled patio or take gourmet goodies home, is the heart of the 'hood. Such elegant shops as Asanti Fine Jewelers, DeVelle for womenswear and Paperwhites Fine Stationery are typical of this posh district.

Funky is the operative word for the retail neighborhood around Washington and Hill in Pasadena, known as East Washington Village. With offshoots along Hill and other north/south streets, it includes ethnic cafés, rustic secondhand and antiques shops, great used bookstores (including one for cookbooks and one for theological books) and a couple of upscale florists and gift shops, including Motif. Given character by an Armenian community that's been here for more than 100 years, the neighborhood boasts places like Sarkis Pastry, KoKo's Bakery and Planet Armenia.

Where the Locals Shop

Besides Old Town Pasadena, San Gabriel Valley shopping is spread far and wide. We locals tend to shop in our own backyards – in Altadena or Sierra Madre or La Cañada – dashing out to South Lake Avenue, South Pasadena, Eagle Rock and beyond when the needs arise. We most love the little unexpected pockets: a street here or a block there with clusters of interesting merchants. Here are the basics on the shopping hubs in Pasadena and environs.

The Mallification of Old Pasadena

Old Town Pasadena has come a long way, from a skid row to a creative gentrification district to a posh outdoor mall. This journey is epitomized by the shiny Tiffany & Company. We locals have heard the message loud and clear: Pasadena is a player in the world of big-bucks retail. Just fourteen short years ago, a handful of upscale shops lined Colorado, and you could always find parking. Now Tiffany joins the Apple Store, Abercrombie & Fitch, Banana Republic, Crate & Barrel, Guess, Diesel, J. Crew, Armani Exchange, H&M, Urban Outfitters and Gaps of all kinds. Just about any store a devoted chain shopper hopes to see in an upscale downtown shopping district is now here. Fortunately, chain-store loathers aren't totally neglected – the side streets, especially Union, Green, Raymond and Holly, are home to lots of smaller boutiques with personality, from Lulu Mae (quirky gifts) to Distant Lands (travel books and gear) to Old Focals (vintage eyewear).

Bordered by Pasadena Avenue to the west, Arroyo Parkway to the east, Walnut to the north and Del Mar to the south, Old Pasadena really is old (by L.A. standards), a collection of handsome two-story brick buildings dating from the 19th century, when Pasadena's commercial center was enjoying its first boom period. On New Year's Day, the Rose Parade courses along Colorado Boulevard, Old Pasadena's main drag, but there's a parade pretty much every day and night, most dramatically on weekends. In the warmer months, One Colorado, just west of Fair Oaks, is a focal point – movies are projected on the side of a building, live bands perform, and art shows are staged. (Go to onecolorado. net/cat/events.)

Here in Old Town the proverbial little old ladies from Pasadena (and we mean that fondly) hobnob with teens, boomers, tourists and our own bridge-and-tunnel crowd (coming from Temple City or Sunland), all out to enjoy a day or night of shopping, eating, drinking, moviegoing and people-watching. Pedestrians should watch out for the notorious diagonal street crossings, and cross the street only on "Walk" signs.

One Colorado in Old Town has several sculptures; our favorite is the one our kids call "Big Man with a Hammer."

The Malls

Along the periphery of the San Gabriel Valley are two major malls: Santa Anita in Arcadia and the Glendale Galleria in Glendale. The Paseo Colorado sits in the middle of Pasadena, several blocks east of Old Town (which is also a mall of sorts).

Pasadena's posh outdoor mall, Paseo Colorado

Expanded to the tune of $98 million and 250,000 square feet, **Westfield Santa Anita** has lots of big retailers including Sport Chalet, Borders and American Eagle. Our favorite restaurant is Market City Caffé; also good is the Wood Ranch BBQ. For fun, there's a Dave & Buster's (upscale arcade restaurant) and a sixteen-screen AMC Theatre with wide screens. As with almost any mall, it is quieter on weekdays and crowded (teen alert!) on nights and weekends. The Santa Anita mall (as locals call it) is anchored by Macy's and Nordstrom.

The massive **Glendale Galleria** and the brand-new outdoor "lifestyle center," **Americana at Brand**, dominate downtown Glendale. The $400 million Americana is organized around pedestrian thoroughfares and a town square, and although it has no department stores (they're so 20th century!), it does have such high-end chains as Tiffany, Lacoste, Juicy Couture and Kitson, as well as restaurants like the Cheesecake Factory. For department stores, head to the Galleria. On the third floor near Nordstrom is a teen playground called the Zone, with such stores as the skate-focused Boarders and Goth headquarters Hot Topic. In the rest of the mall you'll find just about every chain there is. Be warned that it's packed with kids on weekends.

At Pasadena's open-air **Paseo Colorado,** high-end shopping meets adolescent hormones. By day, this is a tranquil place for business lunchers and ladies who shop. But on Friday and Saturday afternoons and evenings, it's a teen playground. An example of Pasadena's new multiuse craze, the Paseo has residences, a spa, a fancy gym (Equinox), shops, a movie-theater complex and restaurants (P.F. Chang, Yard House, Islands, Bodega Wine Bar). The Mediterranean architecture attempts to fit in with the Civic Center that surrounds it, although it's no match for the Central Library or City Hall. Still, we love the colorful fountain with tiles by artist Anne Marie Karlsen and the intricate iron grills by Michael Amescua. Instead of the usual mall chains, the Paseo favors smaller, more upscale ones, such as BCBG Max Azria, Max Studio, Tommy Bahama, Lucky Brand Dungarees, Sephora, Jacadi, J. Jill and that popular fashionista bargain store, Loehmann's.

Paseo Colorado

Americana at Brand
889 American Way
Glendale
818.637.8900

Glendale Galleria
Central Ave. & Broadway
Glendale
818.240.9481

Paseo Colorado
280 E. Colorado Blvd.
Pasadena
626.795.9100

Westfield Santa Anita
400 S. Baldwin Ave.
Arcadia
626.445.6255

The Goods

We're not going to waste your time telling you about the mainstream chain stores, every one of which is found in Pasadena and environs – you already know them, and you can find their locations in the phone book or via Google. Instead, we focus on the worthwhile stores you won't find anywhere else, with occasional mention of a chain (but only if there's a very good reason).

Please note that retailers are found elsewhere, too. For bookstores, see Literary. For galleries and museum shops, see Artistic. For sporting goods, see Athletic. For kids' stuff, see Childlike. For nurseries, see Horticultural. For food shops, see Hungry & Thirsty. For practical places like dry cleaners and florists, see Home Away from Home.

Arts & Crafts

Abuelita's Knitting & Needlepoint
1012 B Mission St., South Pasadena
626.799.0355, abuelitasknittingandneedlepoint.com; closed Mon.
This colorful store recently moved to a bigger location down the street from the ever-popular Buster's coffee shop. You'll find a huge array of yarns, needles and hand-painted canvases. Knitting, stitching and kids classes are offered, as well as one-on-one instruction.

The Bead Source
30 E. Huntington Dr., Arcadia
626.445.5145, beadsourcela.com
Reasonable prices and a great selection are the hallmarks of this store which carries semiprecious beads, Swarovski crystal, rhinestones, clasps and chains. Classes are also available.

Blick Art Materials
44 S. Raymond Ave., Old Pasadena
626.795.4985, dickblick.com
Here you'll shop alongside Art Center and PCC students, professional artists, graphic designers and hobbyists – it's the only store in the area offering high-quality art materials for painting, drawing, scrapbooking, kids' projects, graphic design, sculpture, printmaking and calligraphy.

Farrin O'Connor Design Studio
146 W. Bellevue Dr., Pasadena
626.796.5300, farrinoconnordesign.com
Closed Sun. & Mon.
This is the place for jewelry-making supplies – both tools and such raw materials as sterling silver and semiprecious beads and gems. Wannabe jewelry makers can sign up for a class or get expert advice from owner Margo Farrin, a Pasadena treasure.

Sew Joe Stitch Lounge
634 Mission St., South Pasadena
626.799.3739
Closed Sun.
Want to learn to sew? Come here. Owner Jeanie Joe wants to "help people learn to sew fashion apparel, accessories and home decorations while exploring how to think outside the box." Besides offering classes, studio time and one-on-one help, she stocks wonderful fabric, trim and notions, including thousands of buttons, as well as her own handmade items and Brother sewing machines and accessories.

Skein Fine Yarn Store
1101 E. Walnut St., Pasadena
626.577.2035
A knitter's paradise, with the finest yarns from such companies as Amy Blatt, Brown Sheep, Rowan and Jaeger, as well as a large selection of knitting books, magazines and tools.

Stats
120 S. Raymond Ave., Old Pasadena
626.795.9308, statsfloral.com
This Pasadena landmark grew out of a downtown-L.A. flower business started in 1910 by Greek immigrant Dan Stathatos. The regional chain is now a craft, home-decor and floral extravaganza that comes to life in particular during the fall and winter seasons, when the decorations for Halloween, Thanksgiving, Hanukkah and Christmas are staggering. The after-Christmas sales are legendary for getting women out of their beds at 4:30 a.m.

Beads, beads, beads
at Farrin O'Connor

A vinyl paradise at Penny Lane

Audiovisual

La Cañada Camera
930 Foothill Blvd., La Cañada
818.790.6751, lacañadacamera.com
Closed Sun.
In this era of massive chains, we take comfort in kinder, gentler businesses like this one. It has everything the chains have – video and camera sales and repair, digital and film print processing – as well as rentals, photo restoration services and attentive, skilled service.

Old Town Music
42 E. Colorado Blvd., Old Pasadena
626.793.4730
Rooms and rooms of instruments – woodwinds, brass, violins, guitars, cellos, recorders – welcome the music lover at Old Town Music, which also has a great selection of sheet music.

Penny Lane
1661 E. Colorado Blvd., Pasadena
626.535.0949
569 S. Lake Ave., Pasadena
626.568.9999, pennylane.com
Open since 1985, Penny Lane is the oldest independently owned music and video chain in the L.A. area. The Lake store is devoted to used and new DVDs, VHS movies, games and movie memorabilia; the Colorado store is more about music, with new and used CDs, vinyl, DJ gear, books, posters, T-shirts and rarities.

Poo-Bah Record Shop
2636 E. Colorado Blvd., Pasadena
626.449.3359, poobah.com
If you're a serious album and CD collector who doesn't mind a little dust and a very relaxed atmosphere, you want to get yourself to this 30-year-old Pasadena institution.

Samy's Camera
41 E. Walnut St., Old Pasadena
626.796.3300, samys.com
A smaller branch of the famed westside supplier to amateur and professional photographers, this

Samy's has almost everything the aficionado might need in the way of equipment and rentals.

South Pasadena Music Center & Conservatory
1509 Mission St., South Pasadena
626.403.2329, southpasadenamusic.com
Closed Sun.
This store, in a spanking-new space complete with homey brick walls and wood floors, is home to lots and lots of instruments from around the world – guitars, woodwind, brass, percussion, bells and more, as well as accessories and sheet music galore. Rentals and rent-to-own deals are available, and the service is first rate.

Videothèque
1005 Mission St., South Pasadena
626.403.6621, vidtheque.com
When you absolutely must see *Abbott and Costello Meet Frankenstein,* head for Videothèque, the source for independent, foreign, classic, documentary, rare and cult film favorites. It's conveniently located right next to the Mission Street Metro station.

Clothing & Accessories

Anthropologie
340 S. Lake Ave., Pasadena
626.796.5120, anthropologie.com
We know, we know, we said no chains – but we had to make an exception for this collection of whimsical women's clothing, gifts, home decor and accessories. Its flirty feminine style has brought a breath of fresh air to South Lake.

B. Luu
Paseo Colorado, 340 E. Colorado Blvd., Pasadena
626.792.4140, bluustyle.com
Tucked in the bowels of the Paseo, this nice place carries a large selection of fashionable casual wear in a fairly small space. The list of designers represents the latest in women's clothing: AG Jeans, Blue Cult, Hudson, Marc by Marc Jacobs, Velvet, James Perse and more.

Blue Heeler Imports
5058 Eagle Rock Blvd., Eagle Rock
323.982.9111
Closed Mon.
A veritable Aussie wonderland: butter-soft leather wallets, purses and accessories (Bisante), cutting-edge travel, computer and camera bags (Crumpler), all-natural baby toiletries (Aromababy), beautiful lingerie and loungewear

Hometown Boy Makes Good... Really Good

Jerry Kohl is the owner of Brighton, a remarkably successful business that sells accessories: leather belts for men and women, handbags, wallets, luggage, jewelry and watches that coordinate "from head to toe."

Jerry and his wife, Terri, were high school sweethearts in Monterey Park. After school every afternoon, they opened up their little store; when they graduated from Mark Temple High in Alhambra, they opened a bigger shop, and the rest, as they say, is history.

Kohl says he built Brighton "under the radar" with an unconventional business model – a large full-time sales force selling only to small stores – that he utilizes to this day. "All along we sold only to little stores," he says. "I used to joke that we had a $50-million belt company that nobody ever heard of." Today, Brighton does annual wholesale business of about $210 million, and the 97 Brighton retail stores around America do $150 million – and still, he says, his competitors have never heard of him.

So why does Kohl, who could live anywhere he wants to, stay in Pasadena? "I have a friend who left Encino because she got tired of keeping up with the Joneses," he says. "Pasadena people are themselves – there are no Joneses here. It is just the best place to live. You're fifteen minutes from anything, and we couldn't be happier. It gets a little hot in the summer, so you take a vacation."

(Bulb) and the Flat Out Bear, a sheepskin teddy bear that packs flat for traveling tots.

Brighton Collectibles
Paseo Colorado, 340 E. Colorado Blvd., Pasadena
626.577.3849, brighton.com
Normally we wouldn't include a chain, but in this case, the chain is home-grown – Brighton owner Jerry Kohl started out with a tiny shop in Monterey Park in the late '60s, moving to Alhambra in the early '70s. Today, its handbags, Western-influenced belts, ornate silver jewelry, silver-accented shoes and colorful accessories are hugely popular across the nation.

Camille Frances DePedrini
1516 Mission St., South Pasadena
626.441.7868
Known as Camille's, this boutique carries everything you need for an impeccably detailed outfit: dresses, shoes, shawls, jackets and jewelry. DePedrini is best known for her gorgeous wedding dresses (from the classic to the artsy), mother-of-the-bride dresses and her creations for the fanciest of occasions, including the Oscars. Besides her own designs, her lines include Yoana Baraschi, Marianne Kooimans, Chan Luu and Spirithouse.

Wedding dress created by
Camille DePedrini

Carroll & Co.
146 S. Lake Ave., Pasadena
626.396.7060, carrollandco.com
Closed Sun.
In business since 1949, Carroll & Co. is the last of a dying breed: the full-service men's store. Clark Gable and Gary Grant, friends of founder Richard Carroll, used to frequent the Beverly Hills store, and the styles today remain as classic as they were back then. Quality fabrics and tailoring from Europe and the United States.

DeVelle
2537 Mission St., San Marino
626.403.4563
Closed Sun.
With one-on-one customer attention that harkens back to old-school retail, DeVelle offers "finery for the modern woman." Classic but not staid is the look, with great travel-friendly jersey pieces from Yanci Fugel; clothes from Peter Cohen (a favorite of Sharon Stone, Angela Bassett and Anne Heche); and Babette, a line renowned for its pleating, strong colors and geometric shapes inspired by 20th-century modernist architecture.

Distant Lands
56 S. Raymond Ave., Old Pasadena
800.310.3220, distantlands.com
A traveler's best friend, Distant Lands houses everything from an on-site travel agency to a fabulous library of books and maps. The

Color rules at Koi in South Pasadena.

gear includes suitcases and backpacks; such packing aids as compressors, pack-it cubes and shoe sacks; rain gear; travel organizers; adapters and converters; and fashionable, packable and easily washable clothing for men and women by such companies as Columbia and ExOfficio.

Elisa B.
One Colorado, 12 Douglas Alley, Old Pasadena
626.792.4746
From a great selection of Jeanine Payer's inspirational jewelry, to the tiniest Cosabella thongs, to the most current Trina Turk designs, Elisa B. has clothes and accessories for everyone from teens to stylish 60somethings.

Epic Sports
Paseo Colorado, 380 E. Colorado Blvd., Pasadena
626.449.4512, epicsports.com
Roxy, Quicksilver, Ezekial, Ambiguous and every skateboarder style of the moment are represented at this fun and lively coed store decorated in a Hawaiian theme.

Flutter
54 W. Green St., Old Pasadena
626.449.3224, flutteronline.com
Closed Sun.
A new Pasadena institution, Flutter is always ablaze with color and the latest styles in womenswear. Mother-daughter team Jane Popovich and Jennifer Allen have a uncanny knack for finding unusual yet wearable apparel, jewelry and handbags. They comb the country looking for such up-to-date lines as Linq, Beth Bowley, Jon by Teri Jon and One Girl Who, along with jewelry by Becky Kelso and Ray Griffiths and shoes by Beverly Feldman and Rafe.

Frockx
1111 Foothill Blvd., La Cañada
818.949.4429
Closed Sun.
Vine-stenciled columns add to the cottagey feel of this store, which showcases designer women's clothing, accessories and gifts. You'll find an impressive collection of bags from

Bottega Veneta, Gucci, Fendi, Balenciaga and Marc Jacobs, all offered at a discount. (They buy directly from Italy.) Other lines include Michael Stars, Tibi, Walter, Leona and Bishop of 7th. During "Frocktail Fridays," a fifteen-percent discount is offered, along with champagne and wine.

Koi Loungewear
1007 Fair Oaks Ave., South Pasadena
626.441.3254, koiloungewear.com
At this recently expanded store (which locals still call "Sonnie's"), the style is unstructured and comfortable, with soft, flowing jackets, long skirts, pants, T-shirts, jewelry and accessories; the shoes, scarves and handbags are particularly irresistible. Clothing highlights include the Victorian-inspired pieces by Cynthia Ashby; Citron; Jaskar; elegant embroidered silks from URU; and Biya coats. Great sales.

Lily Simone
5022 Eagle Rock Blvd., Eagle Rock
323.254.0530, shoplilysimone.com
Closed Mon.
Owned by former stylist Simone Porter, this Eagle-Rock-chic shop highlights some of L.A.'s newest designers. Displaying housewares as well as clothing and accessories, the space is light, open and very inviting. We love the whisper-soft cotton clothing from St. Grace, jeans from J Brand, clothing from Mike & Chris, candles from Seda France, bags from Foley & Corrina and lots more.

Loehmann's
Paseo Colorado, 248 E. Colorado Blvd., Pasadena
626.795.0067, loehmanns.com
Loehmann's has been deeply discounting high-end clothing since 1921. From Earl Jean to Calvin Klein to every line in between, it is a wonderful source for deals for both men and women. Shipments arrive often, so be prepared to return several times if you're looking for something in particular.

Lucha's Comfort Footwear
921 Fair Oaks Ave., South Pasadena
626.799-6891, comfortfootwear.com
For two decades this store has been supplying clogs and other comfy shoes to chefs, moms, teachers, nurses, walkers and even diabetics with special footwear needs. Carrying shoes from Ecco, Mephisto, Kumfs and Seibel (for kids and adults), Lucha's does not sacrifice style for comfort. The store also employs certified pedorthists – you heard us, pedorthists – who are schooled in fitting shoes to alleviate pain.

Lulu Brandt

26 S. Raymond Ave., Old Pasadena
626.568.8090
Closed Sun.
This elegant boutique showcases more exclusive designers than any other shop in town: Hugo Boss for women, Jean Paul Gaultier, Blumarine and more. The shoes and accessories are great as well. Most importantly, the service is renowned – a saleswoman once insisted on running to the store's nearby warehouse to look for sale items she thought would be perfect for us.

Old Focals

45 W. Green St., Old Pasadena
626.793.7073
If you ever fell in love with a pair of glasses in a period movie, they probably came from Old Focals. Hundreds of vintage, retro, new and refurbished glasses culled from yard sales, antiques stores and the like line the walls of this funky and fun store.

Onesipkim

110 W. Green St., Old Pasadena
626.396.4926, onesipkim.com
It's not often that you know a shop owner's drinking habits before you enter, but Kim Madolora's store is named for hers. This beautiful modern space is rich in the newest names in L.A. fashion – Jenny Han, Voom, LA Made, McKenna, Revolver – as well as Lollia fragrances and candles, bags by Andrea Bruckner and Bulga, jeans by Anlo and Habitual and jewelry by Kimberly Baker and Jessica Elliot. Chic "tween" clothing, for ages 7 to 14 and petite adults, is an added attraction.

Red Shoes

1018 Mission St., South Pasadena
626.799.8615, theredshoes.com
Closed Sun.
For big and little dancers, Red Shoes carries leotards, tights, dance shoes, tutus, hair accessories, dance videotapes and books and a great selection of ballerina dolls.

Regeneration

1649 Colorado Blvd., Eagle Rock
323.344.0430, shopregeneration.com
Closed Mon.
Recyle, repurpose and rethink are the operative words at this one-stop shop for all things green. Most of the products are free trade, organic, recycled, sustainable or a combination thereof. Look for adorable baby tees, books about nature and green living, housewares and candles. Highlights are richly colored recycled bags from India; resin jewelry embedded with leaves and twigs; Brazilian shoes made of partially recycled plastic; and elegant glass bowls from Spain.

Rising Sun & Co.

107 S. Fair Oaks Ave., Old Pasadena
626.793.3479, risingsunjeans.com
Echoes of Levi Strauss in the early days are in the air of this store and studio in an historic building. Much of the merchandise is sewn in the back room on turn-of-the century industrial sewing machines. The specialty is handmade and made-to-order order jeans and other indigo garments, such as skirts, shirts and jackets, as well its own organic-cotton T-shirts, cool vintage leather jackets and carefully restored quilts.

Rue de Mimo

1514 Mission St., South Pasadena
626.441.2690
In its new location on Mission, you'll find colorful, lively womenswear and accessories from an international crowd of designers, including Spain's Skunkfunk, Hoss, and Israel's Sigal Dekel, as well as lots of small designers from Canada. Don't miss handmade shoes from Cydwoq; socks imported from France; and jewelry from Polish, French and local designers.

Therapy

Paseo Colorado, 316 E. Colorado Blvd., Pasadena
626.568.9905
The minimalist decor and natural colors don't distract from the wonderful women's clothing on display here. Therapy is so full of great designs, including Taverniti So jeans, Theory separates and Cristi Conway sweaters, that it's hard for a fashionable woman to walk away empty-handed.

Triangle

637 Foothill Blvd., La Cañada
818.952.0999
Frequented by women of all ages – mothers, daughters, grandmothers – Triangle keeps everyone young, fun and trendy. Tory Burch, Trina Turk, Joie, Splendid Velvet and Liquid are among the clothing lines; Kooba, Tylie Malibu and Botkier are the handbag offerings. Check out the fun events, like the recent prom party.

World Hats
444 E. Colorado Blvd., Pasadena
626.405.9998
Need a fedora? You'll find it at World Hats, along with cowboy hats, yacht-captain hats, newsboy caps, straw boaters and Cat in the Hat hats.

Furniture & Housewares

Bob Smith Restaurant Equipment
1890 E. Walnut St., Pasadena
626.792.1185
Closed Sun.
Serious home cooks and professional chefs frequent this utilitarian store, which sells new and used kitchen appliances as well as pots of all shapes and sizes, chef's clothing, aprons, glassware, dishes, pastry tools and every kitchen tool imaginable. We love the wall of giant whisks, brushes, strainers, peelers, spoons and ladles.

Fedde's Home Furnishings
2350 E. Colorado Blvd., Pasadena
626.796.7103
32 N. Sierra Madre Blvd., East Pasadena
626.844.1160, fedde.com
Since 1937 Fedde has supplied Pasadenans with fine traditional furniture. This once-small family business has grown into two huge stores that carry such lines as Stickley, La-Z-Boy, Drexel Heritage, Maitland-Smith and more.

Historic Lighting
114 E. Lemon Ave., Monrovia
626.303.4899, 888.757.9770
historiclighting.com
Closed Mon.
The headquarters for Craftsman-style lighting in the L.A. area; if you're looking for a period-influenced fixture you saw in a hotel or restaurant, you can probably find it here. The collection includes lighting from E. Bay Sculpture, Johnson Art Studio, Hudson and Mica Lamp, as well as furniture and accessories.

Maude Woods – Artful Living
55 E. Holly St., Old Pasadena
626.577.3400, maudewoods.com
Soon to open at press time, this store in the Raymond Renaissance next to the old Raymond Theater promises to have Pasadena's most interesting collection of home furnishings, from new and restored furniture to accessories. Owner Carrie Davich, a longtime Pasadenan who named the store for her artist grandmother, says everything she carries will be seen nowhere else in town.

Mission Tile West
853 Mission St., South Pasadena
626.799.4595, missiontilewest.com
Closed Sun.
Decorators and homeowners flock to this purveyor of hand-crafted ceramic tile, terra-cotta and stone; it carries fireplace, floor, bath and outdoor tiles in a vast array of styles, shapes and colors, and there's nary an ugly one in the bunch. Lots of tile junkies pass Saturday afternoons here, just to spend time with beautiful things.

Hometown Hardware

Altadena Hardware
849 E. Mariposa St., Altadena
626.794.4393
Don runs the place, as his dad did for decades before him. Altadena Hardware is a good place for advice on fixing that leak, as well as picking up some metal paste and light bulbs when you just can't face another trip to the megastore.

Berg's Hardware
495 N. Altadena Dr., Pasadena
626.793.6161
Berg's is home to the most helpful, knowledge able staff anywhere, bar none. They'll match the bolt you bring in, they'll help you choose the right kind of glue for that craft project, and, if you're a JPL scientist seeking a widget for a secret project, they'll help you with that, too. This place will make you want to run home and do chores.

Crown City Hardware
1047 N. Allen Ave., Pasadena
626.794.0234, crowncityhardware.com
Closed Sun.
A labyrinth of restoration hardware beckons contractors and homeowners at this Bungalow Heaven institution – here since 1916. The staff is crabby, but you can't beat the selection of period doorknobs, hinges, bath fixtures, cabinet hardware, switch plates and other hardware from the principal historic design periods, including Victorian, Craftsman and art deco.

Tritch Hardware
1620 Colorado Blvd., Eagle Rock
323.255.8222
Closed Sun.
Let Eagle Rock gentrify all it wants, as long as it doesn't lose this old-school hardware store, a neighborhood center for generations. Get your keys made, find that metal screw, pick up a hose or a cast-iron skillet, and get advice on every home project you've ever dreamed of doing.

Jewelry & Gifts

Asanti Fine Jewelers
2670 Mission St., San Marino
626.403.0033, asanti.com
Closed Sun. & Mon.
Classic taste and quiet wealth define the San Marino aesthetic, and Asanti Jewelry epitomizes that aesthetic. In a setting of crystal chandeliers and gleaming display cases, this candy store for adults specializes in simple, elegant pieces of its own design, as well as jewelry by Piero Milano, Roberto Coin, Chopard, Hidalgo and Honora.

Dreams of Tibet
20 E.Holly St., Old Pasadena
626.585.8100
Traditional Tibetan music and the aroma of incense make you want to stay a while, and the robust colors of the clothing and art from Tibet and Nepal add to the sensory pleasures. Jewelry, gongs, statues, incense, music for meditation, religious books, tea sets, pillows and more are all offered. Complete the experience with a meal at nearby Tibet-Nepal House.

The Folk Tree
217 S. Fair Oaks Ave., Old Pasadena
626.795.8733, folktree.com
Owner Rocky Behr travels far and wide collecting Latin American folk art and crafts. You'll find Day of the Dead decorations, smiling suns and moons, painted tin, papier mâché, pottery, wood carvings, shadow boxes, masks, lanterns, clay figures, jewelry, toys, holiday decorations and much more.

Gold Bug
22 E. Union St., Old Pasadena
626.744.9963
Everyone's buzzing about Gold Bug, a new shop that's as much an art gallery as a gift shop. Handsome jewelry, fabulous chandeliers, amusing yet beautiful home-decor pieces and great gifts unlike anyone else's fill the vibrant and personal space.

Whimsy is the watchword at Marz

Le Bijou
20 S. Raymond Ave., Old Pasadena
626.796.6886
Small, elegant and understated, this jeweler carries high-end watches (Rolex, Cartier, Chanel) and lots of simple, beautiful diamond and gemstone pieces of its own design. A standout is the flowing yellow-and-white gold jewelry from Italy's Marco Bicego.

Lexington Place
2557 Mission St., San Marino
626.441.5559
Closed Sun. except in Dec.
An eclectic combination of new and vintage wares, Americana, folk art, decorative accessories and jewelry make this store a fun place to explore. Owner Dinah Roberts has a knack for finding the unique: handmade willow furniture from San Diego, Americana paintings from artist Nancy Thomas and jewelry made from whimsical mixes of flea-market finds and modern materials. After the "Hanging of the Green," the store is a holiday wonderland.

The Majestical Roof
88 N. Fair Oaks Ave. (in the courtyard), Old Pasadena
626.844.8886
HIdden in the courtyard behind La Maschera, the Majestical Roof is part art gallery and part purveyor of local clothing, dog apparel, jewelry, cards and accessories, it is home to things you won't find elsewhere. A few of the goods are mass-produced, like the shoes from No Sweat Apparel (a union company), but all the products "have a conscience." Look for Mayan hand-loomed wallets, lotions, soaps and other self-care products made from soy, a peace jewelry line, and DVDs, books and art from local talent.

Marz
1512 Mission St., South Pasadena
626.799.4032
Newly relocated on Mission, Marz has whimsy and wit galore, offering everything from vintage sterling candlesticks to Mexican folk art to kid's bandages with pictures of sushi. The eclectic collection includes books, cards, wrapping paper, pillows, dishes, baby clothes and lots of silly gift items.

Motif
1389 E. Washington Blvd., Pasadena
626.398.5038
Closed Sun.
On a shabby-chic block of old brick storefronts, this high-ceilinged, recently reinvented boutique

emphasizes locally made gifts for the home, table, kitchen and baby, as well as jewelry from California artisans and winning items from international makers like Vietri ceramics. Owner Stephanie Miller (see Q & A) has a great eye for gifts that are both classic and fun. Don't miss the Friday-afternoon wine-and-cheese parties.

Napa Style
146 S. Lake Ave., Pasadena
626.795.8758
It's like going to the wine country when you step into this little bit of Napa in Pasadena. Chef and vintner Michael Chiarello started his small chain in Northern California to encourage people to experiment with food, entertaining, homes and gardens, and the concept works as well in Pasadena as it does in Berkeley. To do: cooking demonstrations, tastings and events. To buy: foods, wines, furniture and gardenware.

Sixty East Fine Jewelry
60 E. Colorado Blvd., Old Pasadena
626.683.2574, sixtyeast.com
A maze of gems, semiprecious stones, gold and silver, this small store is brimming over with goodies. Several fine designers are represented – Xen, Noel, Green Ice – and owner Dennis O'Neill specializes in custom designs using diamonds, other gems and custom heraldry.

Ten Thousand Villages
496 S. Lake Ave., Pasadena
626.229.9892, tenthousandvillages.com
Fair-trade items that help Third World villagers are the center of this nonprofit, but you don't need a social conscience to enjoy the beauty of the bowls, scarves, jewelry, purses, table linens, objets d'art and more. A great gift source, with options ranging from teen-perfect $6 bracelets to bride-worthy $300 serving platters.

Hobbies

The Original Whistlestop
2490 E. Colorado Blvd., East Pasadena
626.796.7791, thewhistlestop.com
Even the most jaded grownup turns into a proverbial kid at Christmas here, all wide eyes and wonder. In business since 1951, the Original Whistlestop is heaven for model train aficionados, as well as parents and grandparents who want to get their child a very special toy. It sells trains and landscaping from all the makers, plus magazines, books and railroad memorabilia.

Personal Care

Davies Gate
815 S. Fair Oaks Ave., South Pasadena
626.338.0608, ext. 701, daviesgate.com
Everything is organic in this store, the first retail outlet for Davies Gate, whose high-end bath and body products have been sold in boutiques for fifteen years; another line, Collective Well Being, is also featured. Lotions, soaps and bath gels come in luscious scents, including sea grass, white clover and lavender. For a fun gift, pick up Perfect Hands, which includes a warming manicure sea-salt scrub and a hand cream.

Lather
17 E. Colorado Blvd., Old Pasadena
626.396.9636, lather.com
What was owner Emilie Davidson Hoyt's bad luck – debilitating childhood migraines – led to our good fortune today. A chance realization that lavender helped her headaches propelled her into the natural soap and body-care business. The products – tea tree shampoo is one of our favorites – are all pure and wonderful. Other standouts: Belgian chocolate body whip, lavender and eucalyptus foot cream and a cranberry-sugar rub.

The Soap Kitchen
43 N. Fair Oaks Ave., Old Pasadena
626.396.9996
The name doesn't lie: This store's own kitchen whips up all of its own delectable vegan and shea-butter soaps. Only essential oils and herbs are used – no synthetic colors, fragrances or preservatives.

Stationery

Carmody & Co.
121 E. Union St., Old Pasadena
626.795.2924, carmodynco.com
Closed Sun.
It seems like it's been there forever, but this classic Pasadena stationer is new. It features Truly Mom personal organizers, Party Girl invitations, and classic stationery from Crane and Co., Kate Spade, Sweet Pea Designs, Vera Wang, William Arthur and more. Carmody prints custom invitations in-house at reasonable prices.

Mimio: The Artistry of Paper
38 S. Raymond Ave., Old Pasadena
626.685.9090, mimiopapers.com
With its clean lines, minimalist look and Asian

aesthetic, this store invites hours of browsing. Mimio has its own line of paper kits, journals, scrapbooks and origami papers, as well as a wide selection of cards, gift wrap, pens and papers. The card-making, bookbinding and box-making workshops are worthwhile.

Paper
2120 Colorado Blvd., Eagle Rock
323.254.0388
Closed Mon.
This small paper emporium carries a great selection of art books, calendars, gifts for children, blank journals, letterpress and handmade cards and wrapping paper.

Paper Source
163 W. Colorado Blvd., Old Pasadena
626.577.3825, paper-source.com
Begun in 1983 from one woman's obsession with paper, Paper Source sells fine handmade papers from around the world: large sheets, pre-cut letter-size sheets, envelopes and accessories in colors developed exclusively for them. Scrapbookers beware – once you enter, you won't want to leave. Classes are offered.

Paperwhites Fine Stationery
2491 Mission St., San Marino
626.441.2196
Paperwhites carries stationery and invitations from Stacey Claire Boyd, Lallie, Blue Mug Designs and Fontaine Maurey, and packaged cards from Lilly Pulitzer and Vera Wang. Candles, date books and gifts round out the collection.

Vroman's Fine Writing, Gifts & Stationery
667 E. Colorado Blvd., Pasadena
626.744.1834
We get our Cranes papers here, and if we were getting married, we'd probably get the invitations printed here, too – the service is excellent, and the quality is high. Lots of gifts as well, from leather desk accessories to gorgeous pens.

Thrift & Resale

Aaardvark's Odd Ark
1285 Colorado Blvd., Pasadena
626.583.9109
Vintage clothes, many from the 1960s and '70s, fill this huge store in an old car showroom, along with some new retro-style things. The selection is narrower but the quality is higher than at many other thrift stores, and everything's clean. Men's vintage suits, Hawaiian and bowling shirts, old jeans and Jackie O dresses are featured, along with the hats, jewelry and scarves to complete the outfits. Before Halloween, it adds wigs, makeup and other paraphernalia to the mix.

Clothes Heaven
111 E. Union St., Old Pasadena
626.440.0929, clothesheaven.com
Closed Mon.
Larayne Brannon says, "We make sure women have fun here – after all, shopping is a recreational sport." And you will indeed have fun exploring this high-end collection of gently worn goods. The best way to negotiate the crowded store is to follow the signs. "Extra Snazzy," for instance, marks suits and dresses from such elite designers as Armani, Chanel and Escada. They're not cheap, but they're in fine shape and cost a fraction of what they would new.

The Huntington Collection
766 S. Fair Oaks Ave., Pasadena
626.535.2468
Closed Sat. & Sun.
The higher end of the clothing at this thrift store benefiting Huntington Hospital is set off – just look for the wedding dresses. You'll find some designer labels (Calvin Klein, I. Magnin), but most of the stock is garden-variety vintage stuff. A good source for glassware, dishware, linens, books and jewelry.

Ritz Resale
46 N. Mentor Ave., Old Pasadena
626.449.3528, ritzresale.com
As its name implies, this place is the crème de la crème of designer resale stores. At any given time the consignment inventory may include Prada, Hermès, Chanel and Gucci. Other lines we've spotted here are Ellen Tracy, Citron, Trina Turk, Eileen Fisher and Nicole Miller.

Wistaria Thrift Shop
550 W. Sierra Madre Blvd., Sierra Madre
626.355.7739
Open Mon., Thurs. & Fri. 10 a.m.-3 p.m.
Behind the Sierra Madre Woman's Club, in an historic 1914 Craftsman bungalow called the Essick House, sits a gem of a thrift shop. It's small, but it delivers, especially during one of its sales; there is a terrific array of clothing, bric-a-brac, jewelry, belts, linens, toys and more.

Q & A: Stephanie Miller

When you're looking for that Pasadena-style gift, chances are you'll find your way to the newly reinvented Motif on funky-hip Washington Boulevard. Owner Stephanie Miller, a Coronado, California native, showcases California jewelry makers, food producers and artisans, and her gifts and home items are now more green and less likely to be found at every chain store in the country. An avid (and very good) tennis player and hiker, she lives in Altadena with her husband and children. Mary Jane Horton met Stephanie at Motif just as she was putting the finishing touches on the renovation of the store.

How did you get into the retail business?
I always wanted a retail store and felt that this area needed a gift store. In 1997 my friend and ex-partner, LeAnn Healy, and I decided to open a store, and after ten good years, we decided to close it. I was amazed at the customer response when I told people we were closing, so I reconsidered and decided to renovate, get new inventory and reopen. With the new store we are emphasizing customer service, which is hard to find nowadays. We're working to make it a fun destination, where people can find help decorating their house or finding a gift. We're also serving wine and cheese on Friday evenings.

What's it like shopping in Pasadena these days?
There are pockets of interesting shopping areas here and there. Washington is really starting to develop. I try to stay away from malls; they make me nuts. I love Old Town during the week. I see a huge change there right now – it is becoming older and more sophisticated, and the teenagers have moved to the Paseo. The antiques and home stores on East Colorado are fun, and Eagle Rock is worth exploring.

Scents are important in a gift store, but what about in the real world? Do you have a favorite Pasadena scent?
The California bay leaves that crunch under my feet when I'm hiking in the foothills. They smell kind of like eucalyptus, but not as minty.

What's your favorite place for breakfast?
The Altadena Golf Course. It is a short-order-grill kind of place. They have great pancakes and omelets, nothing fancy – but you can sit outside and look at the beautiful golf course. It is one of the best-kept secrets around.

What's your favorite thing to do on a Sunday?
To get my family together and hike. We like to go up Chaney Trail and down to Millard Canyon, where there's a waterfall. Above the waterfall is an abandoned gold mine.

What do you *really* think of the Rose Parade?
I think it is fine. I have friends who go every year, but I've only been twice in 25 years. It was magical and I love that it is in my city. I just don't want to get up that early.

Childlike

Pasadena is a great place for families. The wonderful weather and walkable neighborhoods, combined with the nearby mountains and an abundance of beautiful parks and gardens, make it a perfect place to enjoy things outdoors. Indoors, there are wacky conventions, world-class cultural offerings and intimate performance spaces that please all ages. Pedestrian-friendly Old Towns abound in the San Gabriel Valley, providing lovely, leafy places to stroll, shop, nosh and people-watch.

8 Fun Parks	238
Kids & Culture	240
Age to Age: Fun for Little Kids, Bigger Kids & Teens	242
Party Time: Festivals, Parades & Celebrations	245
Eating Like a Kid	248
Shopping Like a Kid	250
Q & A: Jane Kaczmarek	252

8 Fun Parks

Brookside Park, a complex of public facilities enfolding the Rose Bowl Stadium, is Pasadena's great civic park. Set in the northern Arroyo Seco, it features a playground, picnic tables, Jackie Robinson Stadium (baseball), the Rose Bowl Aquatic Center (many kids' lessons, programs and camps), Kidspace (see Age to Age) and Brookside Golf Course, which has junior golf. Soccer and softball fields are nearly always busy in their seasons, and the tennis courts are a hidden gem. The 3.1-mile paved roadway always has walkers, skaters, strollers, dogs, joggers and bikers rounding it in both directions. Hillside hiking paths link Brookside to the wilder sections of the Arroyo (Hahamongna to the north; Lower Arroyo Seco to the south). On weekdays, the large parking lots are great places to learn to ride a bike or drive a car. Remote-controlled cars buzzing around the parking lots on weekends are a hoot. Special events – UCLA football, the swap meet, festivals – take place on many weekends. Though they can snarl traffic, they are fun to attend.

Favorite smaller parks include **Lacy Park** in San Marino, the most beautiful in the region. Parking is tight and costs money on the weekends, but you are rewarded with rolling, well-tended lawns, towering trees, a friendly playground and a round-the-park bike path perfect for taking off training wheels for the very first time. Tennis courts and elderly locals performing elaborate tai ch'i exercises complete the picture. Sierra Madre's **Memorial Park** is a great place to take little ones – or for preteens to use as a base to explore the small-town shops a few blocks to the east. It also hosts a fun concert series in the summer at the bandshell.

Other lovely parks include South Pasadena's **Garfield Park,** west Pasadena's **Singer Park** and central Pasadena's hidden **Tournament Park.** Large playing fields and a gymnasium/community center are found at **Victory Park. Farnsworth Park,**

Brookside Park's vast lawns are always busy in soccer season.

The peaceful playground at Lacy Park

high atop Lake in Altadena, has new lighted tennis courts, a historic rock-built auditorium, an outdoor amphitheater that draws a big crowd for summer concerts, and views to the ocean on a clear day. Many of these parks have such kid-focused activities as summer camps and after-school care; some also field sports teams and offer arts classes.

For more detailed information on kid-friendly outdoor activities, including hiking, biking and sports, see the Athletic and Outdoorsy chapters.

Brookside Park
360 N. Arroyo Blvd., Pasadena
626.744.7275, cityofpasadena.net

AAF Rose Bowl Aquatics Center
Two 50-meter pools, swimming, diving, water polo, family swim
360 N. Arroyo Blvd., Pasadena
626.564.0330, rosebowlaquatics.org
Open to 9 p.m. weekdays, 5 p.m. weekends

Brookside Golf Course
Two 18-hole courses, restaurants, putting greens, driving range
1133 Rosemont Ave., Pasadena
626.585.3598

Charles S. Farnsworth Park
568 E. Mount Curve Ave., Altadena
626.798.6335

Garfield Park
Mission St. & Park Ave., South Pasadena
626.403.7380, ci.south-pasadena.ca.us

Lacy Park
1485 Virginia Rd., San Marino
626.300.0790, ci.san-marino.ca.us
Weekend entrance fee
Tennis 626.793.1622 (fee for court use)

Memorial Park
222 W. Sierra Madre Blvd., Sierra Madre
626.355.5278, cityofsierramadre.com

Singer Park
California Blvd. & St. John Ave., Pasadena
626.744.7275, cityofpasadena.net

Tournament Park
Wilson Ave. & Cornell Rd., Pasadena
626.744.7275, cityofpasadena.net

Victory Park
2575 Paloma St., East Pasadena
626.744.7500. cityofpasadena.net
Community Center open to 8 p.m. weekdays, 3 p.m. Sat.

Kids & Culture

Some of the best things about Pasadena are its cultural offerings, and that goes for kids, too. Summer is a particularly rich season for children. Wonderful free evening concerts are held outdoors at the **Levitt Pavilion** in Memorial Park near Old Pasadena, and one night a week is set aside for kid-friendly performers. Descanso Gardens, the Arboretum and city parks also feature outdoor summer concerts, which make for great family outings. Also in summer, **One Colorado** shows free movies outdoors in the courtyard, and on July and August mornings the **Occidental Children's Theater** – featuring hilarious fractured fairytales and minimal props – is an imagination-stretching, open-air treat for the under-10 crowd. From mid-June through the end of August, the **Center for the Arts, Eagle Rock** presents a series of outdoor performances in the historic (WPA) Sylvan Amphitheater.

Moving indoors, don't miss the kids' programming at Caltech's **Beckman Auditorium,** ranging from goofy concerts to hands-on events like "What's That Noise?" where kids learn how to make sound effects. The grand **Pasadena Civic Auditorium** hosts the Musical Circus on Saturday mornings before the Pasadena Symphony plays, and it also books an occasional holiday-season *Nutcracker*, touring Broadway musicals and the Emmys (great for star-watching). Also be sure to check out the events at the Convention Center: The comic conventions, Invention Convention and others (Star Trek, anyone?) are kid-friendly. Story times, performances and activities are offered at local libraries (see Smart chapter), with Pasadena's enormous yet welcoming Central Library an enchanting place to read, listen to a story or do homework.

Quality instruction in the arts for all ages is offered around the SG Valley. Superb kids' fine-arts classes, for beginners and advanced students, are found at the **Armory** and the **Creative Arts Group,** a nonprofit center in Sierra Madre. Kids who are really motivated will love the **Art Center College of Design's** weekend and after-school classes, for elementary schoolers through high-school seniors, in everything from animation to fine art to creating comic books.

Performing-arts opportunities are many. **Theatre 360** mounts impressive full-scale productions starring and crewed by kids. Week-long camps at **Occidental Children's Theater & Summer Institute of Fun** emphasize movement and improvisation. Good music classes for all levels and instruments are offered at the **Pasadena Conservatory of Music,** a nonprofit that serves more than 1,200 kids from more than 200 schools. Well worth a week are the summertime jazz camps put on by the **Pasadena Jazz Institute,** where kids get to jam with first-rate professional musicians. Quality dance programs are found at **Ballet Petit** in La Cañada, which specializes in serious ballet; **Le Studio,** which offers flamenco, tap, jazz, hip-hop and ballet; and the **Academy of Music and Dance**, a very good new school with classes in musical theater, ballet, hip-hop and modern dance, with music lessons, too.

Dante the drummer at the Pasadena Jazz Institute

Teen actors at Theatre 360 perform a scene from *Legally Blonde* for their musical revue, *Hear My Song*.

Academy of Music and Dance
72 W. Bellevue Dr., Pasadena
626.768.2614, pasadenadanceclasses.com

Armory Center for the Arts
145 N. Raymond Ave., Old Pasadena
626.792.5101, armoryarts.org

Art Center College of Design
South Campus: 950 S. Raymond Ave.,
Pasadena
626.396.2319, artcenter.edu/kids

Ballet Petit
457 Foothill Blvd., La Cañada
818.790.5775, balletpetit.net

Beckman Auditorium
California Institute of Technology
332 S. Michigan Ave., Pasadena
626.395.4652, events.caltech.edu

Center for the Arts, Eagle Rock
2225 Colorado Blvd., Eagle Rock
323.226.1617, centerartseaglerock.org

Creative Arts Group
108 N. Baldwin Ave., Sierra Madre
626.355.8350, creativeartsgroup.org

Le Studio
57 Palmetto Dr., Pasadena
626.792.4616, lestudiodance.com

Levitt Pavilion
Memorial Park
Walnut St. & Raymond Ave., Old Pasadena
626.683.3230, levittpavilionpasadena.org

Occidental Children's Theater & Summer Institute of Fun
Remsen Bird Hillside Amphitheater
1600 Campus Rd., Eagle Rock
323.259.2771, oxy.edu

One Colorado
North side of Colorado Blvd. between Fair Oaks
& DeLacey, Old Pasadena
626.564.1066, onecolorado.net

Pasadena Civic Auditorium & Convention Center
300 E. Green St., Pasadena
Box Office: 626.449.7360
Convention Center: 626.793.2122
pasadenacal.com

Pasadena Conservatory of Music
100 N. Hill St., Pasadena
626.683.3355, pasadenaconservatory.org

Pasadena Jazz Institute
260 E. Colorado Blvd., Suite 206, Pasadena
626.398.3344, pasjazz.org

Theatre 360
75 N. Marengo Ave., Old Pasadena
626.577.5922, theatre360.org

The kaleidoscope entrance at Kidspace

Age to Age: Fun for Little Kids, Bigger Kids & Teens

Little Kids

For young ones, **Kidspace** is the place to be. It began as a labor of love in a makeshift, donated space and is now a state-of-the-art children's museum located in a historic former greenhouse in Brookside Park. Featuring two huge indoor climbing structures, interactive exhibits, live bugs and critters and outdoor play areas (amphitheater, gardens, trike course), Kidspace offers a diverse program of themed activities throughout the day. It really is a kid space, and it can be taken at a kid's pace. But it's comfy for adults, too – there's even a Wolfgang Puck Café.

Other great sites for little ones who like to splash (and what preschooler doesn't?) include the **Arroyo Seco Casting Pond** and its surrounding natural area, and **Eaton Canyon**, especially in the winter and spring, when the stream is running and the waterfall is full (the docent tours are very good). And the best-kept secret for young families is the **Caltech** campus – it's a fabulous place to stroll with little ones, especially on weekends. There are ponds with turtles, sculptures to climb on and endless pathways to wander.

The three great museum-style gardens in the Pasadena area are perfect for young children, or anybody who appreciates being outdoors in a place of groomed natural beauty. These make wonderful outings with grandparents and playgroups, too. All three have admission charges; if you're a local, consider joining your favorite garden as a family – memberships can be a bargain, and they often provide access to special programs.

Huntington Gardens has wide-open grounds, a traditional Japanese house and rock garden, a new Chinese garden, and turtle and koi ponds. The rose and cactus gardens in particular captivate kids. Plenty of activities, plus art galleries and the Huntington Library, make this the most diverse of our museum-style gardens. It is also the most formal, and the food is rather more formal, too – plus, no picnics allowed.

Descanso Gardens is hillier and wilder than the others, with more shade. Descanso boasts spectacular tulip displays, a camellia forest, a choo-choo ride, a picnic area outside the gardens and koi ponds near the Japanese teahouse. It also has the most kid-friendly snack bar and plenty of kids' programming, including a popular performing arts summer camp. And for homesick Easterners, the lilac forest blooms every April.

Los Angeles County Arboretum & Botanic Garden is the sunniest, largest and least intense of the three. Fun small-scale demonstration gardens close to the parking lot are interesting for kids, and the tram ride ($2) takes visitors around the various gardens. Don't miss Baldwin Lake and the Queen Anne Cottage, site of many a movie and TV show ("Da plane, boss, da plane!"). Picnics are allowed (and advisable) – the pricey snack bar is to be avoided, except for drinks.

Best **farmer's markets** for little ones are the ones in Old Town Monrovia (Friday nights) and Montrose (Sunday mornings); both feature bounce houses, petting zoos, etc.

School-Age Kids

Grade-schoolers (and teens) can take advantage of several **skate parks;** in order of preference, they are at Verdugo Park in Glendale, Bonita Park in Arcadia, Recreation Park in Monrovia and Arroyo Park in South Pasadena. Ice skaters head for the shabby but serviceable **Pasadena Ice Skating Center** (which is slated to relocate to snazzier quarters on the other

Water play is part of the fun at the Huntington's Children's Garden.

side of the Civic Center complex in 2010); for roller skating, it's the classic **Moonlight Rollerway** in Glendale. **Altadena Stables** and **San Pascual Stables** in South Pasadena offer riding lessons; the **Blue Angels** ski and board club provides a bus ride to weekend lessons at Mountain High for ages 7 to 16. City parks and rec departments have the usual offerings, and there are sports leagues through AYSO, YES, Brotherhood Crusade and YMCA.

A great outing is the basic but fun 9-hole mini-golf at **Arroyo Seco** ($1.50 per player), with a snack bar that also won't break the bank. Watch out for the "ant hill" – it's reduced many a hardened putt-putter to tears. For high-tech fun, head to **Ultrazone** in Alhambra, a blacklight laser-tag space and arcade.

Junior High & High School Kids

Young teens can happily explore the small **Old Town** districts of Sierra Madre, Montrose and Monrovia on their own. Older teens can take on Old Pasadena – which is considerably larger, often crowded and, late in the evening, sometimes dicey – and Glendale's Exchange theater/mall. At this writing the hot place to congregate is **Paseo Pasadena,** the outdoor mall at Colorado and Euclid where movie theaters, hip fast food and the occasional band attract hordes of 12- to 15-year-olds. (Parents fret about drugs and tough kids, but there are usually plenty of adults and security guards around.) The coolest teens in town never miss the **Rose Bowl Swap Meet** (second Sunday of the month), where they prowl for vintage skateboards, collectible lunchboxes, $5 cashmere sweaters and goofy jewelry and T-shirts. The **PCC Swap Meet** happens on the first Sunday of the month; it's much smaller and more oriented to collectors, including teenage collectors of vinyl LPs, posters, T-shirts and books.

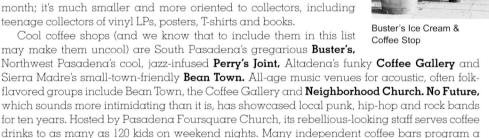

Buster's Ice Cream & Coffee Stop

Cool coffee shops (and we know that to include them in this list may make them uncool) are South Pasadena's gregarious **Buster's,** Northwest Pasadena's cool, jazz-infused **Perry's Joint,** Altadena's funky **Coffee Gallery** and Sierra Madre's small-town-friendly **Bean Town.** All-age music venues for acoustic, often folk-flavored groups include Bean Town, the Coffee Gallery and **Neighborhood Church. No Future,** which sounds more intimidating than it is, has showcased local punk, hip-hop and rock bands for ten years. Hosted by Pasadena Foursquare Church, its rebellious-looking staff serves coffee drinks to as many as 120 kids on weekend nights. Many independent coffee bars program a wide range of music in the evenings.

Also popular are **disc golf** in Hahamongna, **bowling** at Bahama Lanes, Bowling Square or All Star Lanes, and dance lessons through the **Pasadena Ballroom Dance Association.**

The Arts Bus is Pasadena's lifeline for non-drivers. See *the Home Away from Home chapter for bus routes.*

All Star Lanes
4459 Eagle Rock Blvd., Eagle Rock
323.254.2579

Altadena Stables
3064 Ridgeview Dr., Altadena
626.797.2012

AMF Bahama Lanes
3545 E. Foothill Blvd., East Pasadena
626.351.8858, amf.com/bahamalanes

AMF Bowling Square
1020 S. Baldwin Ave., Arcadia
626.445.3160

Arroyo Seco Golf Course
1055 Lohman Ln., South Pasadena
323.255.1506, arroyoseco.com

The ARTS Bus
(Pasadena Area Rapid Transit System)
ci.pasadena.ca.us/trans

Bean Town
45 N. Baldwin Ave., Sierra Madre
626.355.1596, beantowncoffeebar.com

The Blue Angels
blueangelssnow.com

Buster's Ice Cream & Coffee Stop
1006 Mission St., South Pasadena
626.441.0744

Caltech Campus
Wilson & San Pasqual, Pasadena

Coffee Gallery
2029 Lake Ave., Altadena
626.398.7917, coffeegallery.com

Descanso Gardens
1418 Descanso Dr., La Cañada
818.949.4200, descansogardens.org

Eaton Canyon Nature Center
1750 N. Altadena Dr., Pasadena
626.398.5420

Hahamongna Watershed Park
Oak Grove Dr. & Foothill Blvd., Pasadena
626.744.7275

Huntington Library, Art Collections and Botanical Gardens
1151 Oxford Rd., San Marino
626.405.2100, huntington.org
Open at noon on weekdays,
10:30 a.m. weekends;
closed Tues. & major holidays

Kidspace
Brookside Park, 480 N. Arroyo Blvd., Pasadena
626.449.9144, kidspacemuseum.org
Closed Mon.

Los Angeles County Arboretum & Botanic Garden
301 N. Baldwin Ave., Arcadia
626.821.3222, arboretum.org

Moonlight Rollerway
5110 San Fernando Rd., Glendale
818.241.3630, moonlightrollerway.com

Neighborhood Church
301 N. Orange Grove Blvd., Pasadena
626.449.3470, uuneighborhood.org

No Future Café
1500 E. Walnut St., Pasadena
626.627.3424, nofuturecafe.com
Open Fri. 8-11 p.m.

Pasadena Ballroom Dance Association
626.799.5689, pasadenaballroomdance.com

Pasadena Ice Skating Center
310 E. Green St., Pasadena
626.578.0801, skatepasadena.com

PCC Swap Meet
Pasadena City College
1570 E. Colorado Blvd., Pasadena
626.585.7906
1st Sun. of the month; free

Perry's Joint
2501 Lincoln Ave., Pasadena
626.798.4700, perrysjoint.com

Rose Bowl Swap Meet
1001 Rose Bowl Dr., Pasadena
rgcshows.com
2nd Sun. of the month; admission charge

San Pascual Stables
221 San Pasqual Ave., South Pasadena
323.258.3999, sanpascualstables.net

Santa Anita Park
285 W. Huntington Dr., Arcadia
626.574.7223, santaanita.com
Tram tours on weekends: 626.574.6677

Ultrazone
231 E. Main St., Alhambra
626.282.6178, lalasertag.com

Party Time: Festivals, Parades & Celebrations

Experienced parents know that few kids will turn down a festival, fair or anything that offers cotton candy. Part of the small-town appeal of Pasadena and its surrounding towns is the plethora of parades and festivals, where friends bump into one another with charming regularity. Below we list names, locations and/or web sites; dates can vary, so be sure to check for current information.

The name-brand, world-recognized **Tournament of Roses Parade™** – a New Year's Day juggernaut so famous it's trademarked – has a host of events for families surrounding the parade itself. Equestfest is a two-day event at which all those horses and riders who march sedately in the parade get to strut (make that gallop) their stuff. You'll see cavalry units charge around with wagons and shotguns, as well as thrilling gymnastics and dressage – it's great for horse-hungry kids. And the **Rose Bowl** football game usually has a field full of attendant kid-oriented activities to kick off that portion of the party.

Ever popular are pre- and post-parade **float viewing** and pre-parade **float building.** A great place to take little kids with short attention spans is the temporary building barn for South Pasadena's float (at Brent and El Centro); this little float, the oldest "self-built" entry in the parade, is a real community effort, and it often takes home a prize. For those with more endurance, looking at (or helping decorate) the massive floats under construction at Rosemont Pavilion can be an awe-inspiring sight. Night owls prowl the assembly area on South Orange Grove Avenue, where floats line up around 11:30 p.m. on New Year's Eve. This area is well policed, well lit and relatively calm. Spending the night on the parade route requires plenty of warm camping gear (Pasadena gets colder at night than most visitors imagine), thermoses of hot drinks and lots of card games. It can be a convivial time, but as with any large celebration, keep an eye out for misbehavior. And station your group close, but not too close, to the portable cans.

Locals who don't want to buy grandstand seats (the most comfortable but priciest way to see the parade) know to head for the eastern portion of the route, between Allen and Sierra Madre avenues. The parade travels west to east, so the pageant arrives there later; it's also less crowded at this end, and warmer, too. We locals get up at about the time of the flyover (the sonic boom hits about 8:15 a.m., a city-wide alarm clock), park a few blocks north or south of Colorado, dress in layers, bring sunglasses and plan on standing for a few hours. A short stepladder per person also comes in handy.

Every girl's a Rose Queen at the Rosebud Parade.

Alhambra's Chinese New Year Parade

The Rose Parade has inspired two other parades. In the first, Kidspace's November **Rosebud Parade,** the under-7 set decorate their own wagons and bikes with fresh and paper flowers and march down South Lake Avenue. The second is the irreverent and raucous antidote to the serious, sometimes stuffy Rose Parade – the crazy, wide-open, hilarious **Doo Dah Parade.** Connoisseurs of craziness converge on Old Pasadena to cheer on such unique, ragtag units as the Suburban Lawnmower Drill Team and the Prom Queens of the '60s. The date changes, so check the web site.

Chinese New Year occurs in January/February and is celebrated both in Alhambra (at the beginning) and in Monterey Park (with the Lantern Festival, a week later). Pasadena's **Cinco de Mayo** celebration is a long weekend of music, food and booths that commemorates Mexican self-rule. **Altadena's Old Fashioned Days Parade** in late October and occasional street festivals in South Pasadena's Mission District keep things lively. La Cañada has a Memorial Day Parade and festival. In the spring and fall, **Pasadena's Art Night** features free bus rides around town to galleries, Art Center and museums (and all are free). Eagle Rock hosts a Music Festival on the first weekend in October up and down Colorado Boulevard. The **Celebration on the Colorado Street Bridge,** a massive fundraiser for Pasadena Heritage, attracts families who enjoy food, music and being able to stroll "Suicide Bridge" under the stars.

Fourth of July celebrations include daytime parades in South Pasadena and Sierra Madre and fireworks displays at the Rose Bowl, Lacy Park and in South Pasadena. Savvy Pasadenans congregate in the Linda Vista and Prospect Park neighborhoods, on either side of Brookside Park, to see the Rose Bowl show, always a good one. The Altadena Golf Course hosts fireworks the weekend before the 4th, and it can be seen from the surrounding neighborhoods.

Halloween has become something of an adult holiday, but plenty of local commercial haunted houses and theme park takeovers herald the season of spookiness; merchants on South Lake Avenue and in downtown Sierra Madre usually hold daytime trick-or-treat events. Alegria Street in Sierra Madre goes all out with pumpkins; there is a spectacularly scary haunted house each year on Braeburn in Altadena; and such spiffy neighborhoods as Prospect Park, Bungalow Heaven and Milan Street in South Pas get vanloads of trick-or-treaters.

For Christmas lights, cruise down historic **Christmas Tree Lane** (Santa Rosa Avenue in Altadena) with your car lights off, then take in Altadena's over-the-top Balian Mansion (Mendocino and Allen). Travel half a mile further east and drive or stroll the kitschy, spectacular light displays in Pasadena's Hastings Ranch neighborhood (take Sierra Madre Boulevard and go north on Riviera to find the neighborhood). Each street has a theme, and each house, when sold, includes the holiday decorations. Head east on any of the Hastings Ranch streets to Michillinda, take it south a few miles to Huntington Drive, and turn right on St. Albans for San Marino's more tasteful display. You'll compete with tour buses at each location, but it's worth it.

Farther afield, it's fun to take the **Gold Line** to downtown Los Angeles (stops at Southwest Museum, Chinatown and Union Station/Olvera Street). At Christmas time there is La Posada on Olvera Street, and in January/February Chinese New Year takes over Chinatown for a parade with lion dancers and firecrackers. The Gold Line also connects to the Red Line to Hollywood, which has a big Christmas Parade on the Sunday of Thanksgiving weekend. You can easily catch the downtown or Hollywood portions of the L.A. Marathon in March this way as well.

Altadena Old Fashioned Days Parade
altadenarotary.com

Art Night Pasadena
artnightpasadena.org

Celebration on the Bridge
Entrances at Orange Grove & Colorado Blvd. or
Colorado & San Rafael Ave.
Pasadena Heritage
651 S. St. John Ave., Pasadena
626.441.6333 pasadenaheritage.org

Chinese New Year, Alhambra
lunarnewyearparade.com

Chinese New Year, Monterey Park
ci.monterey-park.ca.us

Doo Dah Parade
pasadenadoodahparade.info

Eagle Rock Music Festival
323.226.1617, centerartseaglerock.org

Pasadena Cinco de Mayo Celebration
pasadenacincodemayo.com

Rose Bowl 4th of July Celebration
626.577.3101, rosebowlstadium.com

Rosebud Parade
kidspacemuseum.org

South Pasadena Tournament of Roses
sptor.com

Tournament of Roses Parade
tournamentofroses.com

The Orange Cat

Theorangecat.org is a biweekly newsletter published by Karen Klein, a mom in Temple City. You can subscribe for $12 a year and have it delivered to your e-mail box, or just check in at the web site from time to time. The charming and chatty "Back Fence" column explores what's on moms' minds – it's like you just had coffee with a friend and got some great advice. The bulk of the Orange Cat lists upcoming (and often free) kid-oriented activities throughout the San Gabriel Valley. It's a great source for story times, indoor playgrounds, support and education groups, classes and camps. Check it out: theorangecat.org.

Old-fashioned fare at the Fair Oaks Pharmacy

Eating Like a Kid

The Pasadena area abounds in soda fountains and ice cream parlors, pizza and burger places, rib joints and fun ethnic cafés. Most of these recommendations are based on a solid track record of catering to kids' palates and to, um, their habits in restaurants (i.e., you won't get the evil eye for overturning a water glass or laughing too loudly). These places all offer something for parents, too – sometimes even a full bar! *See the Hungry & Thirsty chapter for lots more family-friendly ideas.*

Afloat Sushi
87 E. Colorado Blvd., Old Pasadena
626.792.9779
Japanese. L & D daily. Beer & wine. $$
Sushi comes in little boats that float past your seat at the bar. Crowded and fun.

Bahooka Ribs & Grog
4501 N. Rosemead Blvd., Rosemead
626.285.1241
American. L & D daily. Full bar. $-$$
Spongebob has nothing on this tiki-and-blowfish-laden restaurant that features aquariums full of fish, a friendly staff and massive portions. Flaming alcoholic drinks for parents and virgin tropical concoctions for the kids.

Domenico's
2411 E. Washington Blvd., East Pasadena
626.797.6459
251 N. Santa Anita Ave., Arcadia
626.574.7433
236 W. Huntington Dr., Monrovia
626.357.7975
Italian. L & D daily; closed Mon. Full bar. $-$$
Always full of families as happy as if they were celebrating simultaneous Little League and AYSO championships, Domenico's serves big portions of classic American-Italian cuisine; the pizza is terrific.

Dona Rosa
577 S. Arroyo Pkwy., Pasadena
626.449.2999, dona-rosa.com
Mexican. B, L & D (open 6 a.m.).
Beer, wine & tequila. $
This fancy taco joint has a more upscale Mexican menu than most, along with kid-friendly portions, non-Mexican dishes and delicious champurrado (Mexican hot chocolate). The case of Mexican pastries is worth checking out, and they even have fruit salads to balance out the pan dulce and breakfast burritos.

Everest Burgers
2314 N. Lake Ave., Altadena
626.797.8204
American/Mexican/Middle Eastern. B, L & D.
No booze. $
This teen fave has something for everyone: good BLTs, chicken gyros, burgers, tostadas, chili fries and more.

Fair Oaks Pharmacy & Soda Fountain
1526 Mission St., South Pasadena
626.799.1414
American. B weekends only, L daily to 5 p.m.
No booze. $
This pocket-size full-service pharmacy features an authentic old-fashioned soda fountain (also serving breakfast, hot dogs, etc.) and some of the best gifts in town for kids and grown-ups. Sit outside to enjoy your phosphate or sundae, or belly up to the marble counter.

Fosselman's
1824 W. Main St., Alhambra
626.282.6533, fosselmans.com
Ice cream. Open daily to 10 p.m. $
Fosselman's makes the premium ice cream that every soda fountain and high-end ice cream store in the SG Valley uses. What is lacking in atmosphere is made up for by authenticity: family-owned since 1919.

From Lorina French lemonade to Izze pop, Galco's has it all.

Galco's Soda Pop Stop
5702 York Blvd., Highland Park
323.255.7115, sodapopstop.com
For underage drinking, no place in the world beats Galco's, which stocks well over 250

kinds of sodas (and a good selection of global beer), as well as freshly made sandwiches. Looking for coffee soda, authentic Kickapoo Joy Juice or Guayaba from Brazil? Galco's is a vast wonderland of fizzy drinks of every conceivable flavor, color and container. And it ships.

Hi Life Burgers
1326 Fair Oaks Ave., South Pasadena
626.799.5401
American. B, L & D. No booze. $
This good, old-fashioned burger stand is always filled with kids from the nearby junior high and high school. In business more than 30 years.

Kansai
36 S. Fair Oaks Ave., Old Pasadena
626.564.1560
Japanese. L & D; closed Mon. No booze. $
Noodles of every description dominate the menu here, and there are also kid-friendly cutlets. You can have your soba or udon in myriad ways, and remember – slurping is considered polite!

Manny's Pizzeria
16 N. Fair Oaks Ave., Old Pasadena
626 795.7330
Italian. L & D daily. Beer & wine. $-$$
Manny's is great to grab a slice while you're walking around Old Town, or you can sit down and have a plate of spaghetti.

The Oinkster
2005 Colorado Blvd., Eagle Rock
323.255.OINK, theoinkster.com
L & D daily. Beer & wine. $
"Slow fast food" is the motto at this remodeled A-frame former burger joint, and while we won't go so far as to call the burgers, pulled-pork sandwiches and hand-cut fries health food, we will say that this is by no means junk food. Excellent rotisserie chicken, fresh salads and killer Valrhona hot-fudge sundaes.

Perry's Joint
2051 Lincoln Ave.,
Pasadena
626.798.4700
American. B & L
Mon.-Fri., L Sat.; closed
Sun. No booze. $
A hub of Northwest
Pasadena's rede-
velopment effort, this
handsome place is
part coffeehouse, part
sandwich shop and part

Waiting for ice cream at Perry's Joint

ice cream parlor, featuring Dreyer's ice cream. A great spot for an afternoon treat.

Shogun
470 N. Halstead St., East Pasadena
626.351.8945
Japanese. L & D daily. Full bar. $$
Make reservations to guarantee a full-on teppan show like the one made famous by the chain Benihana. This is a great place for birthday parties for sword/ninja/anime fanatics or any kid who likes his food set on fire by a professional. It can accommodate up to eighteen at a single grill.

Tibet Nepal House
36 E. Holly St., Old Pasadena
626.585.0955, tibetnepalhouse.com
Tibetan/Nepali. L & D daily; closed Sun. L.
Beer & wine. $
You are allowed (even encouraged) to eat with your hands here – which might entice less-adventurous kids to try some of the wonderful food, cooked by a Nepali mountaineer/chef who trained in Austria and creates silken curries and delicious noodles and dumplings.

Tutti Gelati
One Colorado, 62 W. Union St., Old Pasadena
626.440.9800
Gelato. Open daily.
Delicious and innovative Italian gelato for pre- or post-movies or strolling. Tastes are free; we encourage you to try the more unusual flavors, like fior de latte ("milk flower"), a mild, mothers'-milky sort of creation.

21 Choices
85 W. Colorado Blvd., Old Pasadena
626.304.9521
Ice cream. Open daily to 11 p.m.; closed Mon.
This place is always jammed with eager customers blending yogurt or ice cream with a dazzling array of toppings. From classic and restrained (just a nonfat vanilla for me) to suicidal (raspberry-chocolate swirl with gummy bears, Heath bars and peppermint candy), the choices add up to way more than 21.

Wolfe Burgers
46 N. Lake Ave., Pasadena
626.792.7292, wolfeburgers.com
American. B, L & D daily. Beer & wine. $
Wolfe Burgers offers a delicious and basic burger, a terrific turkey-sausage sandwich, some quick breakfast options and fab onion rings. A few Mexican and Middle Eastern plates fill out the menu. The nice fern-bar-style patio in the back is always full of Caltech students.

Shopping Like a Kid

Kids can find everything in the SG Valley, from old-fashioned penny candy in barrels to sophisticated clothes, vintage comics to quirky collectibles, funky imports to fancy shoes. Parents can find the perfect gift, too, for anyone from a newborn to a college graduate. *More shops are found throughout the book, from sporting-goods stores in Athletic, to bookstores in Literary, to gift shops in Materialistic.*

Whimsical baby gear at Lulu Mae

Comic Cellar
505 S. Myrtle Ave., Monrovia
626.358.1808, comiccellar.com
A huge selection of comic books and graphic novels, and a nice collection of art books, too. Open and airy.

Comic Odyssey
319 S. Arroyo Pkwy., #3, Pasadena
626.577.6696
Hosts tournaments and sells action figures, as well as comics and graphic novels.

Dinosaur Farm
1510 Mission St., South Pasadena
626.441.2767
Specializing in dinosaurs and other animals, with a very good selection of books and toys for the younger elementary and preschool set. Activities and parties, too.

Dreams of Tibet Imports
20 E. Holly St., Old Pasadena
626.585.8100
A teen-girl haven, with tie-dye, incense, CDs, scarves, figurines and bangles. A breath of Kathmandu in Old Town.

Family Fair
810 Meridian Ave., South Pasadena
626.799.6533
Kid heaven: penny candy, kites, stuffed animals, gifts and lots of sweet things.

Folk Tree
217 S. Fair Oaks Ave., Pasadena
626.795.8733, folktree.com
An eye-popping place stuffed with treasures from Mexico and points south, from jewelry to masks, toys, figures, retablos and charms. Don't miss the Day of the Dead, Christmas and other special-event displays in the back room. Fabulous for inexpensive earrings.

La Cañada Books & Toys
653 Foothill Blvd., La Cañada
818.790.1250
In an unassuming shopping mall lives that most essential of hometown amenities – a great store filled with unusual toys and a thoughtful selection of books. In front is the toy section, crowded with a pleasing mix of playthings for all ages and interests, and most do not require batteries! The book section is equally eclectic: new series, the classics, picture and board books, and the La Cañada and Crescenta Valley school-district texts, including lots of titles not to be overlooked by adults (how long has it been since you read *To Kill a Mockingbird* or *Of Mice and Men*?). The staff members all know how to help you pick the perfect present; your kids are welcome to browse and play while you shop. Great sales too!

Lula Mae
100 N. Fair Oaks Ave., Old Pasadena
626.304.9996
A store with wit and charm to spare, Lula Mae has a funky little bit of everything, from jewelry and clothes to stationery and bubble bath. It's girl-oriented, but guys will probably find something that tickles their fancies, too.

Marz
1512 Mission St., South Pasadena
626.799.4032
The psychedelic global aesthetic of Marz features imported tchotchkes, paper goods, books, a few vintage pieces, toys, fragrant things, cards and gag gifts. It's an eclectic collection of stuff from all over the world, perfect for witty birthday gifts for the over-10 set. Don't overlook the adorable baby clothes. Let the teenagers loose here while you browse the delectable clothes at neighboring stores Rue de Mimo (casual) and Camille Frances de Pedrini (event and special-occasion).

Author Kerry Madden with participants in one of the read-a-thons sponsored by Once Upon a Time in Montrose.

Mini-Melt Too

1613 Colorado Blvd., Eagle Rock
323.258.2300, meltcomics.com
A good spot to buy comics, figures and artsy vinyl toys. Nice guys doing business in a tiny storefront.

Once Upon a Time

2207 Honolulu Ave., Montrose
818.248.9668, onceupona.com
Exuding a love of reading and a love of children, Once Upon a Time divides its stock equally between kids and adults. Owner Maureen Palacios does such a wonderful job of choosing her inventory that you'll want to buy every book in the store. Worth going out of your way for.

Rockin Kid Shop

5048 Eagle Rock Blvd., Eagle Rock
888.645.BABY
Born of the attachment parenting movement (also called "baby wearing"), this store first served as the retail outlet for a couple of moms who turned out vintage-fabric baby slings for themselves and their friends.Today it also caters to the littlest rockers, the lover of ugly dolls and the collector of vintage distressed diaper covers. Who can resist teeny-tiny Ramones T-shirts, hipster toys and blankies with attitude? The slings can be ordered through the store, and they're all made in L.A.

San Marino Book & Toy Shoppe

2424 Huntington Dr., San Marino
626.309.0222, toysandbooks.com
Gift wrapping comes with a shiny penny taped to the card at this massive, wonderful emporium of toys and books, featuring a sweet and knowledgeable staff. A family can spend an entire happy afternoon here.

Saturday's Child

2529 Mission St., San Marino
626.441.8888
Lovely togs for rather formal occasions. Dress-up and dressy clothes, good shoes, flannel pajamas and classic togs (i.e., polo shirts) for the well-bred Pasadena tot.

Scoops

120 E. Lemon Ave., Monrovia
626.359.4480
Closed Sun.-Mon.
Candy and ice cream of all kinds, plus a soda fountain and cheap and tasty sandwiches. It's across from the Krikorian movie complex, but we didn't tell you to buy your goodies there before the movie! Good for sugar-fueled little-kid birthday parties, too.

Swanky Blanky

4807 Eagle Rock Blvd., Eagle Rock
323.478.9306
Hipster clothing for babies to about size 10 – wonderful sweaters, adorable accessories and a great family behind the cash register.

Tom's Toys

2281 Honolulu Ave., Montrose
818.249.2178
A huge, old-fashioned toy store (on Montrose's shady, picture-perfect Main Street), Tom's carries everything from the latest high-tech toys to plastic army men. You'll find aisles of board games, fancy dolls, hard-to-find models and craft sets. Better and more fun than a chain store.

The Toy Dept.

255 E. Colorado Blvd., Pasadena
626.396.9487, thetoydept.com
This place specializes in toys from another, simpler era: Erector Sets, yo-yos, dolls, ride-on toys. If it's powered mainly by imagination and kid power, they'll stock it here.

Val Surf

169 W. Colorado Blvd., Old Pasadena
626.796.0668
Pasadena has its quota of surfers, and now there's a shop imported from the Valley that has everything for the surfin' dude/chick (or wannabe). Quality surfboards, skateboards and clothing. A Val Surf sweatshirt is a must-have souvenir for out-of-state tweens and teens.

Vroman's Bookstore

695 E. Colorado Blvd., Pasadena
3729 E. Foothill Blvd., East Pasadena
626.449.5320, vromansbookstore.com
Both stores are terrific, but the original Colorado location is particularly wonderful for kids, with a large upstairs area devoted to children's books, gifts and intelligent toys. Look for storytimes and special events on weekends.

Q & A: Jane Kaczmarek

For seven years, Jane Kaczmarek starred as Lois, the harassed, loving and brutally frank mother of five boys in the TV series *Malcolm in the Middle*, which has been as essential a part of our kids' lives as food. Nominated for six consecutive Emmys, she has also appeared in many films, from *Falling in Love* to *Pleasantville*. On stage, she has played Broadway *(Lost in Yonkers)*, and in Los Angeles, she won an Ovation Award for *Kindertransport*. The Milwaukee native lives in Pasadena with her husband, actor Bradley Whitford, and their three kids. Jane met Mel at a local Starbucks.

Why did you settle here?
We started attending All Saints Church and loved to drive around and look at the wonderful, whimsical architecture. We were living in Los Feliz, and there weren't many multichild families. People actually asked if we were Mormon because we had three kids. We found a neighborhood here where we can walk to school, the grocery store and out to dinner. And we're not immersed in show business. I like it when I ask another mom what she does, and she says she's a physicist. I don't even remember my multiplication tables.

What do you and your family do for fun?
We watch DVDs of old Westerns and musicals, and we go to musicals at the Pasadena Civic and the local high schools. We do Brownies; my son and daughters take ballet at Pasadena Dance Theatre. We ride tandem bikes. We love the Barn Burner BBQ restaurant, because we can be as loud as we want to be.

You founded the Clothes Off Our Back Foundation. Tell me about it.
When Brad and I began getting invited to awards shows, we were staggered by the free stuff – clothes and goodies and all. We knew we were having our fifteen minutes of fame, so we asked friends to join us and donate their clothes for auction. I select three charities each year – like Unicef, Cure Autism Now, Children's Defense Fund and Smile Train – that make a big difference in kids' lives. You'd be amazed – Jennifer Aniston's dress went for $50,000 and paid for 50,000 immunizations in Africa. I steam and fold the clothes, send them to the auction winners and write thank-you notes. We've raised more than two million dollars so far. (Ed. note: go to clothesofourback.org for details.)

What do you do to relax?
I take a music appreciation class at Pasadena Conservatory of Music. I used to drive to UCLA for the class, and then my brilliant teacher, Priscilla Pawlicki, started teaching here – she's from Pasadena. I love to garden: pull out weeds, plant stuff, whatever. I walk my kids around town and quiz them on flowers.

When did you know you were a true Pasadenan?
When I tuned the No. 1 button on my car radio to KPCC.

What do you *really* think of the Rose Parade?
I LOVE parades! I was a baton twirler, and I love to watch the turn at Orange Grove and Colorado. But don't make the mistake I did and buy east-facing seats. My kids spent the entire parade with their heads in their laps because the sun was in their eyes!

On the Train

The arrival of the Metro Gold Line changed life in Pasadena. Just as the Arroyo Parkway provided a state-of-the-art (circa 1940) link from the Arroyo communities to downtown L.A., the Gold Line does the same thing for a new millennium. Schoolchildren take the train to visit Olvera Street or the Southwest Museum, commuters head to downtown's office towers, travelers ride to Union Station to catch the LAX Flyaway bus, and locals hop on to do a little shopping in South Pasadena or a bar crawl in Old Town. Sure, it's slowed traffic on Fremont, Del Mar and California, but we love the Gold Line anyway.

Riding the Rails: Using the Metro   254

Staples Center to Disney Hall: 256
Downtown Culture, Sports & Fun

Best Gold Line Stops   260

Riding the Rails: Using the Metro

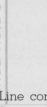

The Gold Line

Completed in 2003, the Gold Line connects downtown L.A.'s Union Station to Pasadena, with stops in Lincoln Heights, Highland Park and South Pasadena. Construction is underway to extend the southern route east from Union Station through Boyle Heights to East L.A.; it should be finished in 2009. The northeastern terminus is currently Sierra Madre Villa in east Pasadena, although there is hope to extend the line all the way to Montclair.

We've ridden the Gold Line (and the Red Line, which connects to Hollywood) many times and have always had a good experience. The compact trains are clean and quiet, and there are usually enough seats, though standing is sometimes necessary at rush hours. In general the passengers are unusually quiet, wearing headphones or reading or staring out the window. The riders reflect the diversity of the city: high school students, service-industry workers, business executives, tourists, school field trips and, of course, the occasional homeless person.

Schedules

Operating times: Gold Line trains run from 4:40 a.m. to roughly midnight. A train generally arrives every fifteen minutes, increasing in frequency during the rush hours (6 to 8:30 a.m. and 3:30 to 6:30 p.m.) and decreasing to about every twenty minutes in the very early and late hours.

Length of ride: Barring the infrequent problem, it takes 34 minutes to ride from Sierra Madre Villa to Union Station. From Memorial Park (Old Town) to Union Station, it's 27 minutes, and from Mission (South Pasadena), it's nineteen minutes.

Express service: During the rush hours, extra express trains skip eight of the stations to make the ride faster from the principal commuter stops. The express trains stop only at Sierra Madre Villa, Del Mar, Mission, Highland Park and Union Station, and the ride is 29 minutes in total, or sixteen minutes from Mission to Union Station.

Updated schedules: Schedules can always change. Go to mta.net for the latest details.

Parking

Parking is not available at all the stations. In Pasadena, your best bet is Del Mar. With an entrance on Raymond, the underground lot charges just $2 a day for Gold Line riders, but you have to show your Metro ticket, so don't toss it! There's pay parking at the Fillmore station.

Buying Tickets

Honor system: Just because there are no turnstiles doesn't mean you don't have to buy a ticket. The Metro is an honor system, so do the honorable thing – besides, L.A. County Sheriffs do come through and check, and if you're caught cheating, you could get fined up to $250 and have to do 48 hours of community service. How does 48 hours of scraping gum off the bottom of train seats sound?

Prices: Even after a few years, a one-way ticket on any Metro train or bus line remains just $1.25 per ride. If you'll be connecting to other lines, consider an all-day pass, which is $5; a weekly pass is $17.

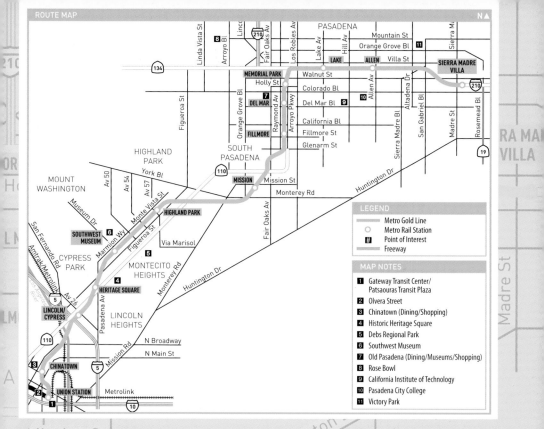

PASADENA

MEMORIAL PARK
DEL MAR
FILLMORE
MISSION

SIERRA MADRE VILLA

LEGEND

Metro Gold Line
○ Metro Rail Station
▦ Point of Interest
▦ Freeway

MAP NOTES

1 Gateway Transit Center/
Patsaouras Transit Plaza
2 Olvera Street
3 Chinatown (Dining/Shopping)
4 Historic Heritage Square
5 Debs Regional Park
6 Southwest Museum
7 Old Pasadena (Dining/Museums/Shopping)
8 Rose Bowl
9 California Institute of Technology
10 Pasadena City College
11 Victory Park

Where to buy tickets: The system is completely automated – you buy tickets from easy-to-operate machines, which take cash only.

Links

Dash Bus: These cute little buses make downtown L.A. accessible for explorers arriving on the Gold Line – and a ride costs only a quarter! On weekdays, catch the B Line from Union Station's front door north to Chinatown or south to the Cathedral of Our Lady of Angels, the Music Center, Disney Hall, the Museum of Contemporary Art, the Central Library and the Financial District. Other lines go to Staples Center, the Convention Center, the Fashion District, Jewelry District and Little Tokyo. Routes change on the weekend – the Downtown Discovery Line runs clockwise from Union Station to Little Tokyo, the Arts District, Grand Central Market, Financial District, Staples Center, Convention Center, MOCA, Disney Hall, the Music Center, Chinatown and back to Union Station. Unfortunately, the DASH does not run in the evening. For details go to ladottransit.com.

Taxis: If you're exploring downtown after 5 p.m. on weekends or 7 p.m. on weeknights, you'll probably need to take a cab to and from Union Station. Cabs wait in front of the station, and they can be found at the obvious downtown places, including Staples Center, the Music Center and hotels.

Red Line: This subway line runs from Union Station west to Wilshire and Normandie in Koreatown, then turns north, ending in North Hollywood at Lankershim and Chandler. Stops of note are Hollywood and Western (Thai Town – lots of good food), Hollywood and Vine (tourist central) and Universal City, home to Universal Studios, Citywalk, the Gibson Amphitheatre and more. An offshoot of the Red Line does not go to Hollywood, but travels a short distance under Wilshire Boulevard, with stops at Normandie and Western.

Blue Line: This line starts at 7th Street/Metro Center, reached from Union Station on the Red Line. It travels due south to the Green Line and then to Long Beach. The final stop, Transit Mall, is in Long Beach's charming old downtown, and is an easy walk from Shoreline Village, home to the Aquarium of the Pacific, the Queen Mary, the Catalina Express and beach paths.

Green Line: This line goes toward LAX, but for some mysterious (shady?) reason doesn't go all the way to the airport. It's mainly a commuter line running from Norwalk to Redondo Beach.

Staples Center to Disney Hall:
Downtown's Culture, Sports & Fun

The Gold Line has delivered you downtown. Now what? Read on to find out.

Arts

One of the many galleries that have sprung up in Chinatown

Chinatown Galleries
It was bound to happen – L.A.'s Chinatown, long ago surpassed culinarily by the vast Chinese communities of the San Gabriel Valley, is hip again, thanks to a burgeoning art scene. Cutting-edge galleries are popping up all over Chinatown, most notably on Chung King Road (west of Hill) and in the Central Plaza. A gallery crawl, followed by a cocktail at Mountain Bar and a Chinese dinner (try Empress Pavilion, Yang Chow or Hop Li) is a great way to spend a downtown Saturday afternoon and evening.

Gallery Row
Downtown lofts started filling up with artists in the 1980s and '90s, so it was just a matter of time until a gallery culture developed. Now an official L.A. district, Gallery Row encompasses Spring and Main streets between 2nd and 9th. A number of worthwhile showrooms live here; perhaps the best way to see them is via the Art Walk, a self-guided tour the second Thursday of every month. MOCA takes part (and is free from 5 to 8 p.m.), as does the Central Library. Most of the galleries stay open until 9 p.m. for Art Walk; go to downtownartwalk.com for information.

Japanese American National Museum
369 E. 1st St.
213.625.0414, janm.org
The only museum in the country devoted to the Japanese-American experience, this modern facility in Little Tokyo displays fine art, historic photos and artifacts and cultural exhibitions. The gift shop is fantastic.

Los Angeles Central Library
630 W. 5th St.
213.228.7000, lapl.org
A California treasure, this Bertram Goodhue–designed library was meticulously restored in 1993 and is worth a day trip all by itself. Artworks litter the place, from the spectacular globe chandelier to the California history murals in the Children's Literature Department. The Annenberg Gallery displays examples from the remarkable special collections, which range from an autograph collection started by then-librarian Charles Lummis, to citrus-label images, to illustrations from children's books. Researchers will go ape for the history, genealogy, patents, science and rare-book collections. We love to have lunch on the cafeteria's terrace, or, if we're feeling flush, under an olive tree at Café Pinot.

Museum of Contemporary Art (MOCA)
250 S. Grand Ave.
213.626.6222, moca.org
As visually dynamic on the outside as it is on the inside, this small museum mounts world-class shows of contemporary art that draw particularly big crowds on Thursdays from 5 to 8 p.m., when admission is free. The gift shop is terrific. Also downtown is the Geffen Contemporary at MOCA (152 North Central Avenue), a Frank Gehry–designed space in Little Tokyo.

The Music Center
Grand Ave. & 1st St.
213.972.7211, musiccenter.org
The cultural heart of Los Angeles, the Music Center comprises four venues. The newest, Walt Disney Concert Hall, is internationally famous for its swooping, soaring design by Frank Gehry and its superb acoustics; it is home to the L.A. Philharmonic and the L.A. Master Chorale, and it hosts a terrific roster of jazz, world music, folk and, in December, holiday music. It also contains a separate venue for Redcat, a showcase for experimental arts performances. Don't miss the gardens, and consider taking a guided tour (information is on the web site). The L.A. Opera and Music Center Dance companies reside at the 1964 Dorothy Chandler Pavilion, named for the L.A. matriarch (known as Buffy) who made the Music Center happen. In the center of the main Music Center plaza sits

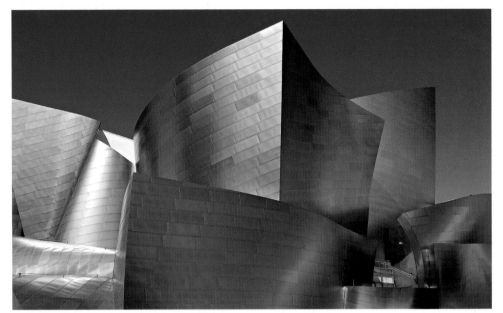
Frank Gehry's Disney Hall

the Mark Taper Forum, an intimate theater-in-the-round. Along with the grander Ahmanson Theatre next door, it is home to the Center Theatre Group, L.A.'s premier stage company. Celebrity chef Joachim Splichal runs the various restaurants, from the ultra-swank Patina at Disney Hall to the casual Pinot Grill on the Music Center plaza. From hands-on kids' workshops to gala opera premieres, something engaging is always going on at the Music Center.

Sports

Dodger Stadium
See Athletic, page 213.

Staples Center
1111 S. Figueroa St.
213.742.7340, staplescenter.com
Home to five teams – Lakers, Clippers and Sparks basketball, Avengers arena football and Kings hockey – this lit-up-like-a-Christmas-tree arena is the cornerstone of a still-developing entertainment and residential community on the south end of downtown. Besides its resident teams, Staples hosts A-list concerts (Madonna, Bruce Springsteen, Garth Brooks), Cirque du Soleil, ice-skating shows and big-ticket boxing matches. It has the expected roster of restaurants (ranging from a private club to the more plebian Fox Sports Sky Box) and fast food.

Food & Drink

Café Pinot
700 W. 5th St.
213.239.6500, patinagroup.com
A fab location in the front yard of the Central Library makes this modern bistro one of downtown's most popular restaurants. Inside it's all clean lines, glass walls and well-dressed business folk; outside are tables under olive trees, our favorite place to sit when the weather's good. Sophisticated food (grilled wild salmon with warm spinach salad, Kobe short ribs osso buco–style) and professional service make the experience a memorable one.

Empress Pavilion
988 N. Hill St.
213.617.9898, empresspavilion.com
Chinatown's best restaurant is found on the north end of the neighborhood. Acclaimed for its lunchtime dim sum (expect a crowd on weekends), it is less known for its dinner menu, which features Hong Kong-style classics, from cod in black-bean sauce to steamed Dungeness crab with flat noodles in garlic sauce.

Langer's Deli
704 S. Alvarado St.
213.483.8050
Just off the MacArthur Park stop on the Red Line, this 1947 landmark is the place in L.A. to get a juicy pastrami on chewy rye, perhaps

topped with coleslaw and cheese or Russian dressing. Its no-frills booths are beloved by everyone from politicians to the working-class Latino folks who live in the neighborhood.

Mountain Bar
473 Gin Ling Way
213.625.7500, themountainbar.com
The former General Lee restaurant is now a happening bar for art lovers prowling Chinatown's galleries. The stylish decor relies on Chinese red, and the atmosphere varies depending on the crowd and the music in the CD player – but generally it's quieter in the early evening and a scene as the night develops.

Patina
Walt Disney Concert Hall
141 S. Grand Ave.
213.972.3331, patinagroup.com
Come prepared to spend, and don't be in too much of a hurry to rush off to your concert – this is a serious restaurant meant for attentive dining. Impeccably trained servers glide through the plushly modern dining room, stopping to discuss such dishes as monkfish with Iberian ham and English peas with diners who either eat like this every day, or wish they could.

Philippe the Original
1001 N. Alameda St.
213.628.3781, philippes.com
We've been coming to Philippe's since we were knee-high to a wooden stool, and there's nothing we love more than sitting on a wooden stool in this 1908 café, eating a deliciously soggy lamb dip sandwich (they claim to have invented the French dip) and watching the most marvelous array of Angelenos: miniature Chinese ladies, strapping cops, big-shot lawyers, down-on-their-luckers who scraped together enough for a sandwich and a cup of the legendary ten-cent coffee. An L.A. treasure.

The Standard
550 S. Flower St.
213.892.8080, standardhotel.com
It's all so preciously '60s that you just might start channeling Austin Powers, which is exactly what some young stockbrokers do here after one too

many Grey Goose martinis. By night the rooftop bar atop the too-hip hotel boasts a swell view, and by day it's an amusing place to get a tuna salad wrap for lunch. Later evening brings a doorman and a line of wannabes, and the drinks cost a lot, but the bar is worth a peek at least once, especially if you arrive unfashionably early.

Tiara Café
127 E. 9th St.
213.623.3663, tiara-cafe.com
At lunch, all the Fashion District cool people are found in this amusingly glam space, noshing on Fred Eric's superb pizzas and organic salads. We love the much quieter evenings, especially before a concert at the Orpheum. Great vegetarian and vegan options.

Traxx
Union Station
800 N. Alameda St.
213.625.1999, traxxrestaurant.com
Owner/chef Tara Thomas has created a spiffy restaurant under the painted beams of Union Station's main room, with an updated streamline moderne look and an appealing upscale-California menu, mostly Mediterranean with Asian and American-comfort influences. We'd come here if the food stunk, just for the setting; luckily, Thomas cooks a mighty fine meal.

Water Grill
544 S. Grand Ave.
213.891.0900, watergrill.com
L.A.'s best seafood restaurant blends first-rate ingredients with snap-to service and a swell setting in an historic office building. The movers and shakers who hang out here wear good suits and carry well-fed Platinum cards.

Yang Chow
819 N. Broadway
213.625.0811, yangchow.com
This friendly Chinatown Szechwan/Mandarin place has been packing 'em in for 30 years. Everyone gets the pan-fried dumplings, slippery shrimp, dry sautéed string beans and cashew chicken, and you should, too.

Zucca
801 S. Figueroa St.
213.614.7800, patinagroup.com
Yet another notch in chef Joachim Splichal's belt, Zucca has one of downtown's dreamiest settings, with rich woodwork, warm tones of Tuscan yellow and masterful lighting. Lunch is packed with business folk, and dinner draws a pre-theater and pre–Staples Center crowd; we

like the happy hour, when drinks and tasty Italian bar dishes are a bargain, given the posh setting.

Fun

Chinatown
This is not L.A.'s original Chinatown – the first one was on the east side of the central L.A. plaza (what is now El Pueblo de Los Angeles Historic Monument). After repeated arson attacks and anti-Chinese movements in the late 1800s, it gradually moved north. Today's Chinatown dates largely from the late 1930s, and it thrived from the '40s through the '70s, until a huge influx of Chinese immigrants began settling in the south San Gabriel Valley. Lately it's been invigorated by the opening of a dozen or so art galleries, a few hip gift shops and the ultra-cool Mountain Bar. Good places to eat include Empress Pavilion, Yang Chow, CBS Seafood and Hop Li; newer Vietnamese immigrants have added some good pho houses, too. Make sure to watch Roman Polanski's great film *Chinatown* before a visit.

Grand Central Market
317 S. Broadway
213.624.2378, grandcentralsquare.com
Dating to 1917, this city-block-size public market isn't fancy, but it's a swell destination for any food lover. You'll find good produce at rock-bottom prices; merchants selling meat, seafood, herbs and every foodstuff imaginable; and wonderful places to eat, everything from pizza to chop-suey at an old Chinese lunch counter; we're partial to the carnitas at Ana Maria's. The parking structure on Hill gives an hour of free parking if you shop.

Los Angeles Conservancy Walking Tours
213.623.2489, laconservancy.org
The Conservancy sponsors a host of guided tours, from single-building ones (the Biltmore Hotel, Union Station and City Hall are favorites)

to neighborhood explorations, including Historic Spring Street, Little Tokyo, the Historic Core and Art Deco. All are led by excellent docents, but if you'd rather do it yourself, you can go to the web site and download your own map. And don't miss the summertime classic-movie evenings in downtown's grand but neglected movie palaces.

Olvera Street

Olvera Street
In 1781, the 44 original Spanish settlers in what would become Los Angeles built a pueblo, and in the 19th century, the city grew around this original hub. The pueblo no longer exists, but many historic buildings and streets do, including the 1818 Avila Adobe and the 1877 Olvera Street, which replaced an older lane called Wine Street (yes, a winery was here). Transformed in 1930 by preservationist Christine Sterling into a traditional Mexican marketplace, the narrow lane is jammed with vendors displaying such essentials as ukuleles, embroidered blouses and painted wood backscratchers; also on the street are restaurants and food stands – the tiniest stand, Juanita's, has the best food, while the fancier restaurants are best for margaritas and mariachis.

Shopping Districts
The hub of the 90-block Fashion District is 9th and Los Angeles streets, home to several large fashion-mart buildings, which are open to the public for sample sales the last Friday of every month. Urban Shopping Adventures (urbanshoppingadventures.com) offers tours, or go to fashiondistrict.org to find your own way around. The Santee Alley area (around Santee between Olympic and 12th), has clothing vendors who sell retail – and who bargain. At 607 South Hill Street is the Jewelry Mart, two buildings packed with some 500 jewelers who sell wholesale and retail. Also worth a visit is the L.A. Flower Market, on Wall Street between 7th and 8th (laflowerdistrict.com). Come early for the best buds.

Best Gold Line Stops

Lake

This stop sits above the 210 Freeway at Lake Avenue, at the north end of Pasadena's increasingly dense business district. It's most convenient for the people who work in the many office buildings, but it's also within walking distance of shopping, dining and culture. Vroman's Bookstore and the Laemmle Playhouse movie theaters are five blocks southwest, at Colorado and El Molino; the Pasadena Playhouse is another block south of that; and the South Lake shopping district (which holds such worthy restaurants as Celestino and Green Street) is a twenty-minute walk south.

Memorial Park

This Old Town station sits at the edge of Memorial Park, home to the Levitt Pavilion and the extraordinary series of free summer-evening concerts. It's also adjacent to the excellent Pasadena Senior Center. From here you can easily cover all of Old Town on foot, from the first-rate restaurants just a block away along Raymond (Yujean Kang's, Mojito's, Vertical Wine Bistro) to all manner of shops, bars and cafés, as well as the Laemmle movie theaters. A ten-minute walk east will take you to the Civic Center: the wonderful Central Library, City Hall, the Paseo Colorado outdoor mall and the Pasadena Civic. Also within a few blocks of the station are two good hotels, the Courtyard by Marriott and the Westin Pasadena.

Del Mar

A massive Archstone apartment complex now surrounds this station, the only one in central Pasadena with plenty of parking ($2 a day for Gold Line riders), so it's popular with commuters to downtown L.A. Designed by new-urbanist architects Elizabeth Moule and Stefanos Polyzoides, this "transit village" centers around the old Santa Fe Depot, built in 1925 and now beautifully restored as the home of a new restaurant/bar called La Grande Orange.

Del Mar is a good stop for antiques lovers. Walk one block west to Fair Oaks to find the huge Pasadena Antiques Center, as well as a number of dealers with their own storefronts.

On California on either side of Fair Oaks are a few high-quality dealers. If you get hungry, have an Italian meal at Gale's (next to the Pasadena Antiques Center), or a tostada at Los Tacos, on the corner of Fair Oaks and California; for coffee, skip the Starbucks and walk east one block to Raymond Avenue for Jones Coffee, which you'll find by following the aroma of roasting beans.

Mission

The most charming stop on the entire route, this station is located in the heart of "old" South Pasadena. Brick storefronts and adorable cottages hold boutiques and bistros, making this a popular stop with the ladies-who-shop-and-lunch. On El Centro you'll find the South Pasadena Library, Kaldi coffeehouse, Firefly restaurant and Nicole's, a French gourmet shop and sidewalk café. On Meridian is the new Heirloom Bakery and Café, as well as a few interesting little shops. Mission is lined with one-of-a-kind businesses: galleries, Buster's Coffee & Ice Cream, three good newish restaurants (Mike & Anne's, Briganti and 750ml), antiques stores and shops. Walk a few blocks east toward Fair Oaks, and you'll discover the historic Fair Oaks Pharmacy and some exceptionally inventive womenswear and gift merchants: Marz, Rue de Mimo, Camille's and, around the corner on Fair Oaks, Koi.

This watering trough, a local historic landmark, is found at the Mission Station.

The old Santa Fe Depot is now a handsome restaurant at the Del Mar Gold Line stop.

Southwest Museum

Used by commuters who live in Mt. Washington and Highland Park, this stop is one pretty block from the Southwest Museum, founded by Arroyo pioneer Charles Lummis, built in 1914 and now run by the Autry National Center. Unfortunately, years of earthquake and water damage and simple old age have taken a toll on the hilltop building that has so long housed this collection of Native American art and artifacts, and the museum is more or less closed until 2010. We say "more or less" because special events are still happening, and parts of it are open on weekends so visitors can watch the conservationists at work restoring both the building and some of the collections. It remains well worth a weekend visit. For information go to autrynationalcenter.org.

Heritage Square

All we can say is that we got lost and wandered Lincoln Heights for 45 minutes trying to find the actual Heritage Square. It's confusing, what with the Pasadena Freeway bisecting this neighborhood. It turns out we went the wrong way – but even if you walk the right way, it's a pretty healthy walk from the station to the wonderful collection of grand houses

The historic Southwest Museum

from L.A.'s 19th-century boom period. The museum comprises eight historic buildings (most of them painstakingly restored) that were moved to this spot at different times. Three hailed from Pasadena: the Longfellow-Hastings Octagon House, an 1893 building that's one of only 500 of these once-faddish houses still remaining in the U.S.; the Queen Anne–style Lincoln Avenue Methodist Church, home to a thriving congregation at the corner of Lincoln and Orange Grove for some 70 years; and the Carriage Barn, a stable house that sat on the land now occupied by Huntington Hospital. The good people who run this place are lobbying the MTA to reinstate the bus line that once connected the Gold Line station to their museum; after getting lost in Lincoln Heights, we're in favor of that effort! Heritage Square is open Friday to Sunday afternoons; hours shorten in winter. Call 323.225.2700 or go to heritagesquare.org for details.

Union Station

Chinatown

As you approach downtown, the train passes the Cornfield, a new state park on open land that was once a Tongva village and then communal farmland for the fledgling pueblo of Los Angeles; most recently, it has hosted art installations. The train then glides along an elevated track above the industrial parts of northern downtown, stopping above Chinatown. Down on the sidewalk level, you'll find a pillar marking the Angels Walk, a self-guided walking tour of historic Chinatown; similar pillars decorated with great stories and images mark other stops along the walk. Along the Angels Walk you'll find plenty of places to eat, shop and explore; don't miss the new art galleries on Chung King Road and in the plazas.

Union Station

The Gold Line terminates at Union Station, which was built in 1939, designed by Donald and John Parkinson and sometimes called "the last of the great railway stations." It's been a location for countless movies and TV shows, and it's one of our very favorite places in California, a gorgeous blend of Spanish Colonial and 1930s streamline moderne. Take some time to admire the tile work, the peaceful outdoor gardens, the painted woodwork on the ceilings and the graceful proportions of the whole place. We love nothing more than to sit with a cup of coffee under the great wooden beams, watching the endlessly fascinating parade of Amtrak and Metro passengers flow past. Directly across Alameda Street from the station is Olvera Street and El Pueblo Historic Monument, where Los Angeles was born.

From this Gold Line terminus you can catch the Red Line to Hollywood and Universal City, other trains to almost anywhere, the zippy Flyaway bus to LAX, or a DASH bus to many downtown destinations.

Home Away from Home

In the pages that follow you'll find everything you need to make Pasadena and the San Gabriel Valley your home away from home: a welcoming hotel, a guide to getting around, a calendar of events and all sorts of useful places to know about, from a dry cleaner to a florist to an emergency vet.

A Comfortable Bed   264

Stuff You Need   268

Getting Around   272

Calendar of Events   274

A Comfortable Bed

The Visitors Bureau would love to see more hotels in the Pasadena area, because every bed sells out for the Rose Parade and Rose Bowl, and overflow visitors stay in hotels as far away as LAX. But for the other 362 days of the year, there are typically plenty of beds to be had in an assortment of upscale hotels and modest motels. Note that most places jack up their rates around New Year's, and rooms book up many months in advance.

At this writing, the city of Pasadena's hotel tax was a whopping 14.5%, so you'll have to add that to your bill at most of the places below. A notable exception are South Pasadena's charming B&Bs, which include taxes in their rates.

The Best of the Rest

Arroyo Vista Inn
335 Monterey Rd., South Pasadena
323.478.7300, 888.927.7696
arroyovistainn.com
$140-$225, including tax
On the western end of South Pasadena sits this serene 1910 home, which Pat Wright spent a year renovating. It's now a fine B&B, with nine rooms (all with private bath) done in soft tones of sage green, sky blue and butter yellow. Although it is furnished with such things as antique armoires and deep, free-standing tubs, the style is clean-lined, not B&B fussy – and you get such hotel amenities as WiFi, robes and iPod players.

Several rooms have balconies and views. Wright cooks a yummy breakfast (and caters events), using ingredients from her own garden, and loves to share wine from the home's original *cave* in the cellar. Good for romance seekers and business travelers alike.

The Artists' Inn & Cottage
1038 Magnolia, South Pasadena
626.799.5668, artistsinns.com
$140-$225, including tax
On a quiet residential street in an old part of South Pasadena sit these two cheerful yellow houses, which have been converted into one ten-room inn. The main house dates from the Victorian era and has a farmhouse look: Roses

Updated Craftsman style — and a proper front porch — at the Arroyo Vista Inn.

spill over the white-picket fence, and white wicker sits on the covered porch. Most of the rooms have queen beds and private bathrooms, and each has some sort of artist theme, from the Van Gogh room, modeled on his famous bedroom painting, to the early-American Grandma Moses room. The rooms have desks and WiFi, making this a fine place for business travelers sick of chain hotels. South Pasadena's business district is a couple of blocks away, and the charming shopping district and Gold Line station (providing access to downtown L.A. and Old Town Pasadena) is an easy four-block walk. Good breakfast, nice people and small-town charm.

The Huntington:
Is There Really Any Place Else to Stay?

Not really. Sadly, most of us don't have the means to stay here whenever we wish, so we offer plenty more fine options. But if you can swing a stay at the Huntington, you should. Here's why.

Langham Huntington Hotel & Spa
1401 S. Oak Knoll Ave., Pasadena
626.568.3900, pasadena.langhamhotels.com
$295-$555, suites $575-$1,250 & more

Pasadena was blessed with a number of posh hotels (none of which survive today) during its first boom period, in the 19th century, but it really arrived with the construction of this place. First built in 1906 as the Hotel Wentworth, it struggled and was finally bought by railroad magnate and local boy Henry Huntington in 1911. He hired architect Myron Hunt to fix the place up, and three years later, the Huntington Hotel opened, becoming the premier winter resort in Southern California. Everyone who was anyone wintered here, strolling the 23 acres of gorgeously landscaped grounds by day and attending formal dinner-dances in the Georgian Room by night. The Huntington's success led to its opening year-round in 1926, when it built California's first Olympic-size swimming pool to refresh summertime guests. It remained Pasadena's swankiest address for decades, though it shut down during World War II, when it was rented to the Army for $3,000 a month.

By the '80s, however, the Huntington (by then a Sheraton) had faded, and its inability to meet earthquake standards led to its closing in 1985. Along came the Ritz-Carlton, which pumped in zillions to bring the place up to modern code and restore it to its 1920s glamour.

And now the Langham, a small, high-end hotel group, has taken over and continues to renovate. Today the Huntington gives guests deeply comfortable rooms, grounds that epitomize gracious Pasadena living, restaurants to rival any in Los Angeles, a luxe spa, solicitous service, a fabled pool, and gobs of period charm, from the Picture Bridge, with its 40 murals depicting California history, to the English-library look of the bar, where jazz and blues bands play on weekends.

You've really made it if you can stay in one of the eight bungalows, most of which were built around the hotel in the '20s and '30s by wealthy regular guests who wanted more comfortable lodgings for a long stay.

If you don't stay at the Huntington, at least come for a sunny-day lunch at the Terrace by the pool, and take time to stroll the grounds. The Dining Room is also a swell place to celebrate an anniversary or unexpected inheritance.

Best Western Eagle Rock Inn

2911 Colorado Blvd., Eagle Rock
323.256.7711, bestwesterncalifornia.com
$88-$150
It's a pretty standard two-story motel, a little closer to the 134/2 freeway interchange than we'd like, but the Eagle Rock Inn is clean and carefully maintained, and most rooms are under $100 if you book online. Internet and a continental breakfast are free, the pool is decent, and there's a hot tub. A mile or so east on Colorado is the oh-so-hip heart of Eagle Rock, home to cafés and funky boutiques.

Bissell House

201 Orange Grove Ave., South Pasadena
626.441.3535, 800.441.3530, bissellhouse.com
$195-$350, including tax
The grand old house is from the Victorian era, but the kind owners were wise enough to eschew oppressive Victoriana for the interior decor. Instead they opted for an appealing mix of dark woodwork and cheerful floral fabrics in the common areas and a not-too-frilly femininity in most of the five bedrooms (the Prince Albert is a bit more masculine). The bedrooms are large, with sitting areas and excellent bathrooms, and the common areas – living room, a wonderful study with dark wood and old books, a pool, lush gardens – are extensive. A delicious, hearty breakfast (scones, fruit, sausage, eggs) is served either on the terrace or in the formal

One of the large rooms at the Bissell House

dining room. The house is located on the south end of stately Orange Grove, making it ideal for an after-breakfast stroll to explore Pasadena's historic Arroyo neighborhoods; the shopping districts of South Pasadena and Old Pasadena are just a few minutes' drive away. The Bissell House is pricey by B&B standards, but you get your money's worth.

Courtyard by Marriott

180 N. Fair Oaks Ave., Old Pasadena
626.403.7600, marriott.com
$149-$219, suites $289
This newish hotel is ugly on the outside but handsome within, especially the modern-Craftsman-furnished lobby and bar. The location is great – it's on the edge of Old Town across Fair Oaks from Parsons, and you can even walk to the Rose Bowl. It's not cheap – we'd rather spend a few bucks more to stay a couple blocks east at the nicer Westin – but if you want to be where the action is, the Marriott is a good choice. Request rooms on the north-facing side of the property if you want a mountain view or facing the pool courtyard if you want quiet.

Embassy Suites Arcadia

211 E. Huntington Dr., Arcadia
626.445.8525, embassysuites.com
$139-$179
This is your basic Embassy Suites: two-room suites with sofa beds, kitchenettes, two TVs and WiFi. Extras include an indoor pool and spa and a lively happy hour every evening, although some guests don't appreciate the happy-hour noise that bounces throughout the seven-story atrium. Several good Arcadia restaurants are an easy walk away; Santa Anita Racetrack and the big mall are just a bit farther; and Pasadena is a ten-minute drive away. The hotel tax is 10% in Arcadia.

Breakfast at the Bissell House

Hilton Pasadena
168 S. Los Robles Ave., Pasadena
626.577.1000, 800.HILTONS, hilton.com
$229-$299
A standard business Hilton, this smallish hotel is well located within walking distance of Paseo Colorado, the Convention Center and the Civic Center. On the down side, the pool and restaurant are basic, the bathrooms are small, and the windows are sealed shut. On the up side, the beds are good, the workout room is well equipped, and the business amenities are all present. Request a higher-up east-facing room for a view of the San Gabriel Mountains.

Quality Inn Pasadena
3321 E. Colorado Blvd., East Pasadena
626.796.9291
$85
The best choice along East Pasadena's motel row, this well-maintained three-story chain is a good value. The furnishings are newer and comfortable, and the continental breakfast (served in a nice kitchen) is more substantial than most, offering things like oatmeal, toaster waffles and fresh fruit. You can hear the nearby 210 Freeway from the rooms, but mostly it's an unobtrusive white noise. Extras include the world's tiniest pool and an indoor spa and sauna.

The peaceful plaza outside the Westin

The Saga sits across from PCC and near Caltech.

The Saga Motor Hotel
1633 E. Colorado Blvd., Pasadena
626.795.0431, 800.793.7242,
thesagamotorhotel.com
$92-$98, family rooms $135
Our favorite budget (i.e., less than $100) hotel in town, the Saga's got it goin' on, midcentury-modern-wise. It's a classic '50s motel, but unlike most in the region, it's been carefully maintained without losing its '50s charm. Heck, there's still real Astroturf around the pool! Located across the street from Pasadena City College, the Saga is popular with Caltech and JPL visitors, and it's central to everything – Old Town and the Rose Bowl are a couple of miles west, Lake Street and the Playhouse District are closer, and Caltech and PCC are an easy walk. The rooms are basic motel, but updated with wooden shutters and cleaner than those of other motels in the neighborhood.

Sheraton Pasadena
303 E. Cordova St., Pasadena
626.449.4000, starwoodhotels.com
$149-$255
Tied to the Convention Center, this low-lying Sheraton has two things going for it: really comfortable beds and a convenient location in the Civic Center hub, near the Paseo and Colorado Boulevard. Otherwise it's nothing special.

The Westin Pasadena
191 N. Los Robles Ave., Pasadena
626.792.2727, 888.625.5144,
starwoodhotels.com/westin
$159-$385
Still called "the Doubletree" by locals, this upscale hotel has been through a few owners and now seems settled into life as a Westin. It is centrally located in downtown Pasadena, a block from City Hall and a short walk to Paseo Colorado; Old Town is several blocks to the west. It has all the bells and whistles of a quality Westin: rooftop pool, small fitness center, in-room internet access, good bed linens and upscale restaurants, including a lovely and quiet outdoor patio where Sunday brunch is served. The insanely driven stay in the "Westin Workout Rooms," which come complete with a spinning cycle, Pilates gear and instructional DVDs.

Stuff You Need

Daily Life

Animal Care – Emergency

Animal Control
Pasadena Humane Society
626.792.7151, phsspca.org
Whether you've found a stray dog or have a troublesome raccoon, these wonderful people will help.

Animal Emergency Clinic
2121 Foothill Blvd., Pasadena
626.564.0704
A fine but expensive night-and-weekend pet clinic.

Eagle Rock Emergency Pet Clinic
4254 Eagle Rock Blvd., Eagle Rock
323.254.7382
We've had to visit this place an unfortunate number of times and have always found the staff to be kind and conscientious.

Florists

Botanicals
1341 Foothill Blvd., La Cañada
818.790.7110, shopbotanicals.com
A great little boutique for home accessories, with a potting shop in the back and floral stop in the main room, Botanicals features not-outrageously priced fresh-cut seasonal flowers. It delivers within a five-mile radius.

Eiji's
4532 Rinetti Lane, La Cañada
818.790.5766, eijisflorist.com
A second-generation family florist, Eiji's is the bouquet stop for both La Cañada's hoi polloi and its Aunt and Uncle Moneybags. Over the years we've received many potted arrangements from here, and they were all consistently lovely.

Jacob Maarse Florists
655 E. Green St., Pasadena
626.449.0246, jacobmaarse.com
Pasadena's A-list florist, with a fabulous space in the Playhouse District. It's pricey, but an arrangement from Maarse means something.

Garden roses are a specialty of San Gabriel Valley florists.

Leonora Moss
9 Kersting Court, Sierra Madre
626.355.1180
The mother-and-daughter owners do lovely arrangements for reasonable prices; they also stock a great supply of gifts, linens and one-of-a-kind jewelry pieces.

Mary Falkingham
1387 E. Washington Blvd., Pasadena
626.794.5443, maryfalkingham.com
Mary does abby fabby custom work, including for big occasions like weddings. This is a small storefront shop, so it's best to call in advance to check available flowers for takeout.

San Gabriel Florist & Nursery
632 S. San Gabriel Blvd., San Gabriel
626.286.3782, sgnursery.com
Plant lovers and folks with a plant's IQ could wander this 1923-vintage nursery day and night and still discover something new each visit. The florist shop, inside the southerly building, has traditional arrangements and single stems to take out. Garden books, seeds, tools, gadgets are located throughout, and members of Descanso, Arbortetum and Huntington get a ten-percent discount.

Silver Birches
650 S. Raymond Ave., Pasadena
626.796.1431, silverbirches.net
We love these guys, always have! Silver Birches does lovely, cutting-edge party and special event design. This is custom work only, so don't drop by for a purty bouquet on your way home.

Tommy Farmer
60 N. Allen Ave., Pasadena
626.403.9151, tommyfarmerflorist.com
Go around to the back of this unassuming brick building to talk to The Man about flowers from simple to jumbo. Farmer specializes in events, and he's known for his elegance and attention to detail.

Libraries
See Smart chapter

Post Offices

La Cañada Post Office
607 Foothill Blvd.
Good parking, rarely crowded.

Pasadena Main Post Office
600 N. Lincoln Ave., Pasadena
An always-busy regional hub. Mail gets processed in remarkable time.

Senior Services

Pasadena Senior Center
85 E. Holly St., Old Pasadena
626.795.4331, pasadenaseniorcenter.org
A wonderful community resource, this modern facility on the edge of Memorial Park houses a fitness center ($40 annual fee), computer lab, coffee bar, kitchens, library, dance studio, meeting rooms and more. Programs include free classes in creative writing, bridge, Spanish, dance, art, computers and more; a terrific roster of college-level lectures by local professors; all sorts of support and discussion groups; and a softball league. The people here can help with anything, whether it's finding nursing care, transportation or help for homebound seniors.

Tickets
Discount ticket services, goldstarevents.com

Health

Emergency Rooms
All of these are large, full-service hospitals with 24-hour emergency rooms.

Glendale Memorial Hospital
1420 S. Central Ave., Glendale
818.502.2344

Huntington Memorial Hospital
100 W. California Blvd. (ER entrance on Fair Oaks), Pasadena
626.397.5112

Methodist Hospital
300 W. Huntington Dr., Arcadia
626.574.3456

Pharmacies

Paseo Pharmacy
Gelson's Market, Paseo Colorado
245 E. Green St., Pasadena
626.564.1000
Personal service and free local delivery.

Sav-On Drugs 24-Hour Pharmacy
1401 S. Baldwin Ave., Arcadia
626.445.1284
2037 Verdugo Blvd., Montrose
818.248.8018
As the name says, prescriptions are filled 24/7.

Personal Care

Churches
See Reaching Out chapter

Dry Cleaners, Alterations & Shoe Repair

Bryan's Cleaners & Laundry
544 S. Arroyo Pkwy., Pasadena
2446 E. Foothill Blvd., Pasadena
2336 N. Lake Ave., Altadena
1461 San Marino Ave., San Marino
626.796.4335 (same phone for all locations)
Good service, high quality, free delivery and pickup… at a price, of course.

Cordial Cleaners
800 Mission St., South Pasadena
626.441.1149
Nice people, good service; pickup and delivery available.

Laurel's Apparel Service
871 N. Baldwin Ave., Sierra Madre
626.355.3280
Laurel Wood is a meticulous seamstress who can do everything from let out a hem to copy a wedding dress.

Susan's Custom Alterations
1400 E. Washington Blvd., Pasadena
626.794.2547
Careful work, reasonable prices.

Zinke's Shoe Repair
592 E. Colorado Blvd., Pasadena
626.793.5790
Look for the neon shoe sign, but be warned that this wonderful landmark building is slated to die so that even more condos can live. It's hoped that the business will survive in the new development.

Nail Care

Han's Beauty Stør
3849 E. Foothill Blvd., East Pasadena
626.351.4776
475 Foothill Blvd., La Cañada
818.952.9588
Manicures, pedicures, skin treatments and more, with a good quality-to-price ratio – and wonderful massage chairs. It's also a full beauty-supply store.

Rex Nails
2667 E. Colorado Blvd., Pasadena
626.793.9192
Experienced nail technicians, a clean and quiet setting and moderate prices.

South Lake Nail Design
350 S. Lake Ave., Pasadena
626.577.9783
A good all-around nail-care emporium that's clean and well run.

Public Restrooms
Sometimes you're out and about and you need to find a disease-free restroom…. quickly. Old Town Pasadena is the trickiest, unless you're eating at one of the restaurants; shockingly, the Starbucks has no facilities. Your best bets are the pay stalls (a quarter) at Equator coffeehouse on Mills Alley. Other good Pasadena facilities are found in Vroman's, Borders on Lake, Macy's on Lake, and at the Paseo on Colorado; if you're in South Pasadena, there's Buster's on Mission, Kaldi on El Centro or Baja Fresh on Fair Oaks.

Salons & Barbers

Ben's Barber Shop
444 Fair Oaks Ave., South Pasadena
626.441.6084
A classic barber shop, with a giant moosehead on the wall and combs in jars of blue stuff. Ben and his crew have been here forever, and they know how to cut a head of hair.

Christopher Carol Designers
122 N. Baldwin Ave., Sierra Madre
626.836.6733
Husband-and-wife team Christopher and Carol left the intensity of the Beverly Hills salon world for the pleasure of quiet Sierra Madre life – so now eastsiders can get a westside haircut at an eastside price. A homey, low-key salon with a devoted clientele.

Ecco Hair Studio
1017 El Centro St., South Pasadena
626.799.6446
A skilled staff in a fetching old South Pas brick building, next to Kaldi coffeehouse and the library. Good colorists.

The Gates Salon
2545 Mission St., San Marino
626.441.1188
This longtime full-service salon has a friendly and experienced staff and a clientele ranging from San Marino matrons to South Pas hipsters. Hair cuts, coloring, straightening, facials, makeup, waxing, massage, manicures, tints… you name it, they'll take care of it. Time your visit so you can have lunch at the neighboring Julienne, our favorite lunch spot in town.

Gene Martin Salon
2479 E. Villa St., Pasadena
626.792.0817, genemartinsalon.com
This quietly hip salon is popular with Pasadena's soccer moms, but teens and grandmas come here, too. It combines small-town warmth with stylists who have big-city skills.

A soak in a seaweed-infused tub at Amadeus Spa

Spas & Facial Care

Amadeus Spa
799 E. Green St., Pasadena
626.578.3404, amadeusspa.com
Paseo Colorado, 260 E. Colorado Blvd.,
Pasadena
626.529.0381
A serene place with the full range of spa services, from deep-tissue massage and salt-glow
treatments to seaweed facials and spa manicures. It's a competitor of Burke Williams, with
similar offerings and a similarly posh setting –
but prices that are, on average, about $10 less
per treatment. The spa pedicure is wonderful.

Burke Williams
39 Mills Pl., Old Pasadena
626.440.1222, burkewilliamsspa.com
Hidden in an alley behind the Apple Store in
Old Town, this spa is grand central for stressed
Pasadena moms and businesswomen; Burke
Williams sell Mother's Day gift certificates by
the truckload. But men also frequent BW – they
get their own spacious quarters, with showers,
whirlpools, sauna and more. We've been
pleased with the massage therapists here – the
shiatsu is particularly good – and the facilities
are excellent. We can't bring ourselves to spend
$40 for a manicure, but the body treatments,
facials and massages are worth it.

Huntington Spa
1401 S. Oak Knoll Ave., Pasadena
626.585.6414
It's the most expensive spa in town ($135 for a
50-minute aromatherapy massage), but if you
can afford it, go for it. The vibe is pampering and
a little less formal than at the neighboring hotel,
and you can spend the day here just wallowing
(including using the fitness center, eucalyptus
steam, whirlpool and more) for the price of a $45
manicure. It's known for its five-color clay-mask
facials, stress-release massages and salon
services.

Tranquility Skin Care & Spa
804 Foothill Blvd., La Cañada
818.790.1076
This quiet, personal salon does a very
fine job, at fair prices, on facials, waxing,
microdermabrasion and the range of skin-care
treatments.

Travel

Foreign Exchange

American Express Travel
269 S. Lake Ave., Pasadena
626.449.2281
You'll get a better rate here than at local banks
or at the airport. All major currencies carried.

Travel Agent

AAA Automobile Club of California
801 E. Union St., Pasadena
626.795.0601, aaa-calif.com/travel
This full-service travel agency is available to
AAA members from anywhere in the United
States. The helpful people will steer you to
member discounts on lodging, cars, cruises and
more. And, of course, they'll help you plan your
driving route.

American Express Travel
269 S. Lake Ave., Pasadena
626.449.2281
If you have an American Express card, these
people will take good care of you, finding you a
flight, hotel, car, cruise or tour. There's a foreign-
exchange window, too.

Visitors Bureau

Pasadena Convention & Visitors Bureau
171 S. Los Robles Ave., Pasadena
626.795.9311, pasadenacal.com

Getting Around

Airports

Burbank-Glendale-Pasadena Airport (BUR)
burbankairport.com
The closest one, and a small one; if you can fly in and out of there, you'll be happiest.

Long Beach Airport (LGB)
longbeach.gov/airport
A JetBlue hub, this charming little terminal 35 to 60 minutes south of Pasadena dates from 1941 and is easy to get in and out of.

Los Angeles International Airport (LAX)
lawa.org/lax
The big one, 30 miles southwest of Pasadena. Allow plenty of time.

Ontario International Airport (ONT)
lawa.org/ont
A medium-size hub 35 miles east of Pasadena.

Airport Shuttles

The Flyaway (bus from Union Station)
metrolinktrains.com

Prime Time
800.733.8267

Super Shuttle
626.443.6600

Car Rental

Avis
626.449.6122, avis.com

Budget
626.449.0226, budget.com

Enterprise
626.568.8445 or 626.432.6688, enterprise.com

Hertz
626.578.0443, hertz.com

Thrifty Car Rental
626.449.0012, thrifty.com

City Bus

Metro Bus System
mta.net or call 800.266.6883

Dial-a-Ride

Dial-a-Ride
626.744.4094
Serves seniors and the disabled in Pasadena, Altadena and San Marino.

Limos & Taxis

BLS Limousine
800.843.5752

Fleetwood Limousine
800.283.5893

People's Taxi
626.577.2227

Yellow Cab
626.796.8294

Metro Gold Line, Metrolink & Amtrak

Amtrak
amtrak.com
America's rail network, departing from L.A.'s Union Station and traveling to Santa Barbara, San Diego and countless other destinations.

Metro Gold Line
mta.net
See the chapter On the Train, on page 251, for in-depth information on the Gold Line, which runs through Pasadena to L.A.'s Union Station, where you can connect to Hollywood's Red Line or other subway lines.

Metrolink
metrolinktrains.com
We know, it's confusing – why is the Gold Line light-rail train part of the Metro system, while the regional trains are part of a completely different system called Metrolink? Couldn't they think of names that aren't so similar? And why is there no link between Metro and Metrolink's web pages? Synergy seems to have eluded our transportation planners. The Metrolink system runs commuter trains on Amtrak rails. From downtown L.A.'s Union Station, reached via Pasadena's Gold Line, you can catch a Metrolink train to Anaheim, San Juan Capistrano, Ventura and many commuter suburbs, or the relatively speedy LAX Flyaway bus to LAX (just $4).

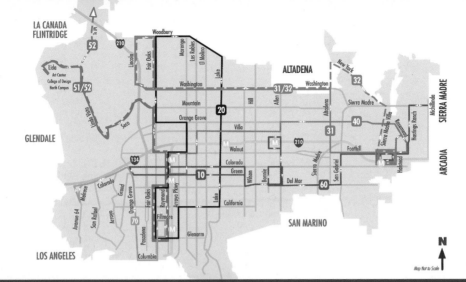

PASADENA
ARTS
Area Rapid Transit System

ROUTES
RT 10
RT 20
RT 31
RT 32
RT 40
RT 51
RT 52
RT 60
RT 70

RAIL
Ⓜ METRO
Gold Line
Station

SYSTEM MAP Effective February 2005

- For ARTS schedule, fare, and route information visit www.cityofpasadena.net or call (626) 398-8973.
- Route schedules and maps are available for downloading from the City website.
- Route schedules are also available at Pasadena libraries, major hotels, community centers, on our buses, and at our office located at 221 E. Walnut, #199.

ARTS Bus

Pasadena Area Rapid Transit System (ARTS)
626.398.8973, cityofpasadena.net/trans

The best deal in town is Pasadena's ARTS Bus – it's only 50 cents, or a quarter for kids, teens, seniors and the disabled, and transfers are free. Of its seven routes (some of which run on limited schedules), most visitors need just one: Route 10, which connects Old Town, the Playhouse District, Lake Street, Caltech, PCC and the Allen Gold Line station. It runs every fifteen minutes (weekdays 6 a.m.-8 p.m., Sat. 11 a.m.-8 p.m., Sun. 11 a.m.-5 p.m.). Another handy route is 20, which runs along Lake from Woodbury to California, over to the Fillmore and Del Mar Gold Line stations and Art Center South, up to Old Town and up Fair Oaks to Northwest Pasadena. That one runs every 30 minutes.

Parking Dos & Don'ts

In all but central Pasadena, parking is not an issue. Here are the basics of downtown Pasadena parking:

Old Pasadena
Keep a pile of quarters with you, and don't think you can cheat the meters in Old Town – the meter maids and misters are vigilant. There are several parking structures. We have a personal aversion to structures and usually manage to score a street spot on Green or Raymond.

Paseo Colorado
God, we hate that parking structure; sometimes we find a spot on Green in front of Gelson's. Otherwise, it's into the bowels of the building you go. Make sure to prepay if you stay longer than the stingy validations allow, so you can exit via the Express Lane.

South Lake
Parking is free on the street and in the lots. There's plenty of free parking behind Ann Taylor and Talbot's; enter those lots from Hudson.

Calendar of Events

For a calendar of every concert, lecture, garden show and happening in Pasadena, go to pasadenacal.com/calendar; for other towns, go to their city web sites.

January
Tournament of Roses Parade; 626.449.4100, tournamentofroses.com
Rose Bowl Game; 626.449.4100, tournamentofroses.com

February
Lunar New Year Parade, San Gabriel & Alhambra; 626.284.1234, lunarnewyearparade.com. A huge Chinese New Year parade and festival on Valley Boulevard; great street food
Black History Parade & Festival, Pasadena; 626.791.7983

March
Spring Home Tour, Pasadena Heritage; 626.441.6333, pasadenaheritage.org
Wistaria Festival, Sierra Madre; 626.355.5111, sierramadrewistariafestival. com. Viewings of the famed vine accompanied by a full-fledged festival

April
Bungalow Heaven Home Tour, Pasadena; 626.585.2172, bungalowheaven.org
Pasadena Showcase House for the Arts; 626.578.8500, pasadenashowcase.org. A Pasadena mansion becomes a decorators' showpiece; hugely popular

May
Cinco de Mayo Celebration, Rose Bowl; pasadenacincodemayo.com. Carnival, soccer, classic cars, children's art and more
Museums of the Arroyo Day; 213.740.TOUR, museumsofthearroyo.com. Free shuttle to the five museums along the Arroyo, including the Southwest Museum of the American Indian, the Gamble House and the Lummis House

Mt. Wilson Trail Race, Sierra Madre; 626.355.5278, mtwilsontrailrace.com. A lively street festival accompanies this historic footrace

June
Levitt Pavilion season opens; 626.683.3230, levittpavilionpasadena.org. A superb summer series of free nightly outdoor concerts in Old Town's Memorial Park
Chalk Street Painting Festival, Paseo Colorado; 626.205.4029, pasadenachalkfestival.com
Pasadena Pops season opens, Descanso Gardens, La Cañada; 626.792.POPS

July
Celebration on the Colorado Street Bridge, Pasadena; 626.441.6333, pasadenaheritage. org. Music, food, art and more on the famed Colorado Street Bridge
Rose Bowl 4th of July Celebration; 626.577.3100, rosebowlstadium.com. Boffo fireworks, inspiring music
Lacy Park 4th of July Fireworks, San Marino; 626.304.9648
Southwest Chamber Music season opens, San Marino; 800.726.7147, swmusic.org. First-rate chamber music at the magnificent Huntington Library

August
Garfield Heights Evening Home Tour, Pasadena; 626.388.2174, garfieldheights.org

September
La Fiesta de San Gabriel; 626.457.3035, sangabrielmission.org. A popular Labor Day–weekend fiesta celebrating the founding of the first mission in the L.A. area
UCLA Bruins Football season opens, Rose Bowl; 626.577.3100,

rosebowlstadium.com
Taste of Old Pasadena; 626.795.2455, pfar.org. A food festival in Old Town

October
Pasadena Symphony season opens; 626.793.7172, pasadenasymphony.org. Excellent music in the stately Pasadena Civic
Wiggle Waggle Walk, Pasadena; 626.792.7151. A fun benefit walk for the Pasadena Humane Society
Craftsman Heritage Weekend, Pasadena; 626.441.6333, pasadenaheritage.org. Home tours, lectures and more at this very popular weekend-long tribute to Pasadena's great architecture

November
Rosebud Parade, Pasadena; 626.449.9144, kidspacemuseum.org. Every kid's a king or queen at this delightful hometown parade for little ones
Doo Dah Parade, Pasadena; 626.205.4029. The anti-Rose Parade, irreverent, chaotic, messy and fun; be warned that it could be moved to another month, just because.

December
Christmas Tree Lane lights up. Turn off your car lights and drive along Christmas Tree Lane (Santa Rosa Ave.) between Woodbury and Altadena Dr. in Altadena; volunteers string 10,000 lights in the massive old deodars
Float Construction Viewing & Decorating and **Tournament of Roses Family Festival,** Pasadena; 626.449.4100, tournamentofroses.com
Racing season opens, Santa Anita Park, Arcadia; 626.574.RACE, santaanita.com. The season begins Dec. 26th

Index

A

AAA Automobile Club 271
Aaardvark's Odd Ark 235
AAF Rose Bowl
Aquatic Center 210, 239
Aarnun Gallery 120
Abuelita's Knitting
& Needlepoint 227
Academy 6 186
Academy of Music
and Dance 240-241
Afloat Sushi 248
AIDS Service Center 126
Airport Shuttles 272
Airports 272
Akarakian Theatres Highland 3 186
Alex Theatre 184
Alexandria II
Metaphysical Bookstore 62
Alhambra Edwards 10 186
Alhambra Edwards 14 186
Alhambra Farmer's Market 167
Alhambra Municipal Golf Course 208
All India Café 146
All Saints Episcopal Church 130
All Star Lanes 208, 243
Aloha Boba Tea House 170
Altadena Community Gardens 96
Altadena Foothills Conservancy 126
Altadena Golf Course 197, 208, 236, 246
Altadena Guild of Huntington
Hospital 126
Altadena Hardware 232
Altadena Homes Tour 86
Altadena Library 55, 65, 72
Altadena Old Fashioned
Days Parade 247
Altadena Public Library 65
Altadena Stables 201, 243
Altadena Town
& Country Club 111, 166, 211
Amadeus Spa 271
American Bungalow 70, 88
American Express Travel 271
American Street 223
Americana at Brand 186, 226
AMF Bahama Lanes 208, 243
AMF Bowling Square 243
Amori 134-135, 219
Amtrak 262, 272
Angelena's Southern Cuisine 135
Angeles Crest Highway 47, 66, 199-201, 211
Animal Care – Emergency 268
Animal Control 129, 268
Animal Emergency Clinic 268
Anthropologie 224, 228
Antiques 220-223,
Arcadia AMC Santa Anita 16 186

Arcadia Public Library 14, 55
Architectural Tours L.A. 86
Archives Bookshop 62
Arlington Garden 96, 104
Armory Center for the Arts 120, 123, 241
Arroyo Arts Collective:
Annual Discovery Tour 86
Arroyo Chop House 134-135, 143
Arroyo Seco Foundation 126
Arroyo Seco Golf Course 208, 244
Arroyo Vista Inn 264
Art Center, South Campus 123
Art Center College of Design 11, 50, 119, 122, 240-241
Art Night Pasadena 247
Arte Flamenco Dance Theatre 187
Artists' Inn & Cottage 264
ARTS Bus 243-244
Artworks Gallery 121
Asanti Fine Jewelers 224, 233
Au 79 Tea Spirit 170
Audiovisual 228
Aun Deli Café 149
Auntie Em's Kitchen 149, 166
Austin, Mary Hunter 58
Avenue 50 Studio 122
Avis 272
Awareness Center 207
Azeen's Afghani Restaurant 146

B

B. Luu 228
Babita Mexicuisine 134-135
Bahooka 135, 248
Bahooka Ribs & Grog 248
Bakeries 162-163
Balanced Concepts 207
Baldwin, Elias "Lucky" 14, 33, 95
Ballet Petit 240-241
Bar & the Lobby Lounge 171, 182
Bar Celona 173
Barbecue 153
Barbecue Man, The 153
Barnes & Noble 62
Bashan 135, 175
Batchelder, Ernest 80, 88
Bead Source 227
Bean Town 25, 65, 168, 202, 206, 218, 243
Beckman Auditorium 45, 48, 180, 182, 187, 240-241
Bellefontaine Nursery 103
Ben's Barber Shop 270
Berg's Hardware 232
Berolina Bakery & Café 162
Berry, Daniel M. 31, 68
Best Western Eagle Rock Inn 266
Big Mama's Rib Shack 153
Bill's Chicken 157

Billy's Deli 149
Billy's Ski & Sport 211
Bissell House 266
Bistro 45 134, 136
Bistro de la Gare 136, 142
Blick Art Materials 227
BLS Limousine 272
Blue Angels 243-244
Blue Heeler Imports 228
Blue Hen 146
Bob Smith Restaurant Equip. 232
Bodega Wine Bar 171, 226
Bodies in Motion 206
Bonita Skate Park 14, 210
Book 'Em Mysteries 62
Book Alley 62
Bookfellows 62
BookHouse 62
Borders Books 63
Botanicals 268
Bowling 208
Brand Library & Art Center 54
Breakthru Fitness 206
Briganti 136, 142, 260
Brighton Collectibles 139, 229
Brinkmann, John 70
Bristol Farms 63, 162
Bronner-Fraser, Marianne 42
Brookside Golf Course 208, 238-239
Brookside Park 98, 107, 196, 200, 205, 211, 238-239, 242, 244, 246
Brown, Jeff 214
Brown, Michael E. 43
Brown, Owen 35
Brownstone Pizza 158
Bruce Graney & Co. 220
Bryan's Cleaners & Laundry 269
Budget 272
Buff & Hensman 198
Bulgarini Gelato 162
Bungalow Heaven
Home Tour 86, 274
Burbank Airport (BUR) 272
Burkard's 102
Burke Williams 271
Busch Gardens 34, 80, 111
Buster's Ice Cream & Coffee 168, 181, 243-244, 260
Butler, Octavia 11, 35, 52, 59, 101

C

Cactus Gallery 122
Café 322 181
Café Alibi 65, 168
Café Beaujolais 136, 152, 210
Café Bizou 134, 136
Café Culture 65, 168
Café Pinot 256-257
Café Santorini 166

Calendar of events 5, 263, 274
California Art Club Gallery 121
California Cactus Center 102
California Philharmonic
Festival on the Green 178
California Philharmonic 187
California School of
Culinary Arts 11, 50
Caltech 10-11, 36-38,
42-49, 56, 65, 72, 74, 86, 96-97, 110
169, 180, 182, 187, 197, 242, 244
Caltech Architectural Tours 86
Caltech Folk Music Society 182
Camille Frances DePedrini 229
Car Rental 272
Carmody & Co. 234
Carniceria La Gardenia 163
Carr, Ezra 34
Carr, Jeanne 27, 32, 34
Carroll & Co. 229
Casa Adobe San Rafael 40
Casa Bianca Pizza Pie 158
Castle Green 33, 65,
68, 81, 85-86, 90, 110,
118, 124, 166, 168, 187
Caterers 166
Cawston Ostrich Farm 26, 39-40
Celebration on the
Colorado Street Bridge 129, 178,
246-247, 274
Celestino 134, 137, 166, 260
Center for the Arts,
Eagle Rock 15, 119, 240-241
Central Park (café) 149
Chado Tea Room 170
Chalet, The 171
Charles S. Farnsworth Park 239
Chilloutla.com 211
Chinatown 256-259, 262
Chinese New Year 247
Chocolate Box Café 162
Christiansen, Doug 202
Christopher Carol Designers 270
Chronicle Wine Shop 174
Chu, Carl 154, 156
Chung King 154, 256, 262
Churches 130-131
City Bus 272
City Hall 72, 76
Claremont Colleges, The 53
Clark, Alson 118
Cliff's Books 63
Clothes Heaven 235
Clothing 228-232
Coffee Gallery 65, 168, 182-183, 243
Coffee Gallery Backstage 182-183
Coffee Tree 65
Coleman Chamber
Music Association 187
Colorado, The 171

Colorado Wine Company 137,
158, 174
Columbo's 137
Comic Cellar 219, 250
Comic Odyssey 250
Connal's 157
Convalescent Aid Society 126
Cook Books by Janet Jarvits 62-63
CORAL Pasadena 127
Cordial Cleaners 269
Courtyard by Marriott 260, 266
Creative Arts Group 123, 240-241
Crepe Vine Bistro & Wine Bar 137
Crescenta-Cañada Family YMCA 206
Crocodile Café 137
Crown Café 154
Crown City Hardware 232
Cuban Bistro 146
curve line space 121
Cycling, mountain 201
Cycling, road 200

D

Daisy Mint 134, 146
Davies Gate 234
Derek's Bistro 134, 137, 166
Descanso Gardens 19, 34,
91-92, 179, 190-191, 240,
242, 244, 274
DeVelle 224, 229
Devon 135, 137-138, 219
Dial-a-Ride 272
Dickenson West Caterers 166
Din Tai Fung 134, 154
Dining Room, The 134, 136,
138, 265-266
Dinosaur Farm 250
Disc Golf 209, 243
Dish 134, 138, 149
Distant Lands 63, 225, 229
Distinguished Speaker Series 45
Dodger Stadium 213, 257
Doerr, Harriet 59, 109
Domenico's 159, 248
Doña Rosa 134, 149, 248
Doo Dah Parade 39,
108, 246-247, 274
Dots Cupcakes 162
Dreams of Tibet 233, 250
Dry cleaners 269
Dumpling Master 134, 154

E

Eagle Rock Pet Clinic 268
Eagle Rock Farmer's Market 167
Eagle Rock Music Festival 247
Earnest C. Watson Lectures 45
East Colorado Antiques 221
Eaton, Benjamin 30
Eaton Canyon Golf Course 208

Eaton Canyon
Nature Center 193-194, 244
Ecco Hair Studio 270
Eclectic Eagle Rock Home Tour 86
Egg Roll Express 160
888 Seafood 154
Eiji's 268
Einstein, Albert 37, 39, 48-49
El Alisal 18, 34, 40, 86-87
El Centro de Accion Social 127
El Metate 159
El Molino Viejo 29, 40, 97
El Portal 138, 221
El Taquito Mexicano #2 159
Elements Kitchen 166
Elisa B. 230
Embassy Suites Arcadia 266
Emergency Rooms 269
Empress Pavilion 256-257, 259
Enterprise 272
Epic Sports 230
Epps, Sheldon 185, 188
Equinox 206, 226
Euro Pane 134, 149, 162-163, 169
Everest Burgers 248

F

F. Suie One Co. 220
Fair Oaks Pharmacy 26, 248
Family Fair 219, 250
Famima 164
Farr, Ellen 118
Farrin O'Connor 123, 227
Fast food 157-158
Fatty's 134, 138
Favorite Place Tea Room 170
Fedde's Home Furnishings 232
Feldenkrais by Diane Park 207
Fenyes Mansion Tours 86
Feynman, Richard 59, 101
Firefly Bistro 138, 142
First Congregational
Church of Pasadena 130
Fish King 163
Five Acres 127, 129
Fleetwood Limousine 272
Flintridge Bookstore 63, 65, 168
Flintridge Foundation 127, 132
Flintridge Riding Club 201
Florists 268
Flutter 230
Flyaway airport bus 272
Folk Tree, The 233
Foothill Creative Arts Group 123
Foothill Family Service 127
Foreign exchange 271
Forest Lawn Memorial Park 16, 100
Fosselman's 168, 248
Four Seasons Tea Room 170
Fox's, The 150

Frank, Scott 59
Frederic Stern Gallery 121
Fredo's Phillys 157
Fremont Centre Theatre 184
Frockx 230
Fu-Shing 139
Fuller Theological Seminary 11, 51
Funnel 221
Furious Theatre Company 184
Furniture 219-223, 232
Futterman, Susan 118
Future Studio 122

G

Galco's Soda Pop Stop 18, 248
Gale's Restaurant 139
Galerie Gabrie 121
Gallery Row 256
Gamble, David and Mary 35, 79, 87
Gamble House 39, 52, 64, 69-71,
    78-79, 82, 87-88, 110, 114, 131, 274
Gamble House Bookstore 64
Garfield Heights Home Tour 87, 274
Garfield Park 26, 179, 238-239
Gates Salon 270
Gaucho's Village 139, 143
Gearhart, Frances 118
Gehry, Frank 50, 74, 81, 116, 256-257
Gene Martin Salon 270
Gerlach's 134, 160, 174
Gerlach's Grill 134, 160
Gifts 233-234
Gilman, Charlotte Perkins 58, 60-61
Glendale Centre Theatre 184
Glendale Community College 53
Glendale Farmer's Market 167
Glendale Galleria 226
Glendale Memorial Hospital 269
Gold Bug 233
Gold Line 10, 38-40, 151,
    167, 178, 181, 183, 209, 224, 247,
    253-256, 260-262, 265, 272-273
Golden Deli 146
Goldstarevents.com 185, 269
Goldstein's Bagel Bakery 162
Golf 208
Good Foods Market 164
Gourmet Cobbler Factory 163
Grace Center 127
Granada, The 180
Grand Central Market 255, 259
Grandjean, Nicole 151, 176
Gray, Harry B. 42
Green Street Restaurant 134, 150
Green Street Tavern 139
Green Village Shanghai 154

Greene & Greene 39, 45, 64,
    69-71, 77-79, 83, 86-88, 114, 198
Grey, Zane 13, 34, 59

Gus's BBQ 153
Gyms 206

H

Habitat for Humanity 128, 131
Hahamongna Park 19, 126,
    201, 209, 244
Hale, George Ellery 37, 39, 47
Happy Trails 166
Harmony Farms 164
Hat World Famous Pastrami, The 157
Hathaway-Sycamores 128
Haus Gallery 121
Heineman, Alfred 71, 78
Heineman, Arthur S. 78, 85, 88
Heirloom Bakery & Café 150, 163
Heritage Wine Shop 174
Hermon 17
Hertz 43, 272
Hi-Life Burgers 157
Highland Park 18
Hillsides 128
Hilton Pasadena 267
Historic Highlands Home Tour 87
Historic Lighting 219, 232
Hodgson Antiques 223
Holly Street Bar & Grill 112, 181
Holy Family Church 130
Horseback riding 200-201
Housewares 230-232
Houston's 139
Howie's Ranch Market 164-165
Huneven, Michelle 57, 59, 66
Hunt, Melany 43
Hunt, Myron 15, 51, 54,
    72, 78, 80, 82, 86, 114, 265
Huntington, Henry 24, 29, 34,
    36, 39, 59, 78, 97, 113-114, 135, 265
Huntington Collection 235
Huntington Library, Art Collections
    and Botanical Gardens 93, 114, 244
Huntington Hospital 86, 126, 269
Huntington Tea Room 170
Huntington Spa 265, 271
Hurd, Gale Anne 112

I

The Ice House 149, 185
Il Fornaio 140
Imix Bookstore 64
In-N-Out Burger 157
Indiana Colony 10, 13, 31, 68

J

Jacob Maarse Florists 268
Japanese American
    National Museum 256
Japon Bistro 140
Jason Arnold for Modern 221
Jax Bar & Grill 182

Jet Propulsion Laboratory (JPL) 38,
    45-48, 72, 74, 97, 109,
    172, 191, 201, 232, 267
Jewelry 233-234
Johnny's Bar 171
Jones, Lucy 56
Jones Coffee 65, 134, 164, 168, 260
Judson Studios 118, 121
Julienne 24, 104, 134, 150, 160, 224
Junior League of Pasadena 128

K

Ka-San Restaurant 147
Kaczmarek, Jane 109, 252
Kaldi 26, 65, 169, 260, 270
Kansai 147, 249
Kaufman, Charlie 59, 109
Kettle's Nursery 103
Kidspace 98, 238, 242, 244, 246
King Taco 134, 159
Kitchen for Exploring Foods 160, 166
Kohl, Jerry 139, 229
Koi Loungewear 230
Krikorian Cinema 12 186
Kristi Engle Gallery 122

L

La Cabanita 134, 140
La Cañada Books & Toys 250
La Cañada Camera 228
La Cañada Farmer's Market 167
La Cañada Post Office 269
La Cañada Presbyterian 130
La Caravana 147
La Casita del Arroyo 80, 166
La Estrella 134, 159
La Grande Orange 140, 173, 260
La Maschera 140, 233
La Pintoresca Library 55
Lacy Park 24, 98, 211,
    238-239, 246, 274
Laemmle's One Colorado 8 186
Laemmle's Playhouse 7 186
Lake Avenue Church 130
Lake Spring 155
Langer's Deli 257
Langham Huntington Hotel 78, 138,
    152, 170-171, 182, 265
Lanterman, Jacob 19, 39
Lanterman House 87
Larkin's 140
Lather 234
Laurel's Apparel Service 269
Le Bijou 233
Le Petit Beaujolais 152
Le Studio 240-241
Lebanese Kitchen 147
LEED 74-76
Leonora Moss 268
Levitt Pavilion 178, 240-241, 260, 274

Lexington Place 233
Libbrecht, Kenneth G. 44
Libraries 54-55, 57, 62, 240, 269
Lily Simone 230
Limos & Taxis 272
Lincoln Avenue Nursery 103
Little Cave 171
Little Flower Candy Co. 163
Loehmann's 226, 230
Lola's Peruvian 161
Long Beach Airport (LGB) 272
Los Angeles Central Library 256
Los Angeles Conservancy
  Walking Tours 259
Los Angeles County Arboretum 95,
  178, 242, 244
Los Angeles International Airport
  (LAX) 272
Los Gringos Locos 134, 141
Los Tacos 134, 160, 260
Lovebirds 134, 150
Lowe, Thaddeus 32-33, 39, 101
Lu Din Gee 156
Lucha's Comfort Footwear 230
Lucky Baldwin's Pub 172, 218
Lucky Boy 134, 157
Lula Mae 250
Lulu Brandt 231
Lummis, Charles 18, 34, 40, 58,
  60-61, 86, 126, 256, 261
Lummis Home 40

M

Madeleine's Wine Bistro 172
Magnolia Lounge 172
Maison Akira 134, 136, 141
Majestical Roof 233
Mamita 147
Mandaloun 147
Mandarin Noodle House 155
Mann Glendale Exchange 10 186
Mann Glendale Marketplace 4 186
Mannheim, Jean 118
Manny's Pizzeria 249
Mantle, Larry 4, 7
Marston, Sylvanus 70, 78-80, 85,
  87, 282
Marston's 104, 151
Mary Falkingham 268
Mary Pat Brandmeyer Catering 166
Mary's Market & Café 151
Marz 224, 233, 250, 260
Masjid Gibrael 130
Maude Woods – Artful Living 232
Mayo, Morrow 60-61
McCormick & Schmick's 173
McKenney, Betty 104
McKenney, Charles 104
McMurphy's Tavern 183
McPherson, Aimee Semple 38, 109

Mei Long Village 134, 155-156
Melody 3, 141
Memorial Park 16, 25, 100,
  178, 238-241, 254, 260, 269, 274
Methodist Hospital 14, 25, 269
Metro Bus System 272
Metro Gold Line 178, 253, 272
Metrolink 272
Metropolitan 65
Mezbaan Indian 147
Mijares 141, 173
Mike & Anne's 26, 141-142, 260
Millard, Alice 58, 79
Miller, Sally 198
Miller, Stephanie 234, 236
Millikan, Robert 37
Mimio: The Artistry of Paper 234
Mini-Melt Too 251
Mission 261 155
Mission Antiques 223
Mission Liquor 175
Mission Museum 40
Mission Nursery 103
Mission San Gabriel 9, 23-24,
  26, 28-29, 39-40, 60, 95, 97, 100, 185
Mission Street Yoga 207
Mission Tile West 26, 232
Mission Wines 134, 174
Mojito's 148, 260
Monrovia Farmer's Market 167
Monrovia Free Concerts 178
Montrose Harvest Market 167
Moonlight Rollerway 210, 243-244
MorYork Gallery 122
Moseley, Jaylene 132
Mother's Day Monrovia
  Home Tour 87
Mothers' Club 128
Motif 224, 233, 236
Mountain Bar 256, 258-259
Mountain High 112, 199, 243
Mountain View Cemetery 13, 35,
  59, 101
Mr. T's Bowl 183
Mt. Baldy 189, 199
Mt. Lowe Railway 33, 35-36
Mt. Waterman 8, 199
Mt. Wilson Observatory 37, 39,
  41, 46-47, 49, 200
Mt. Wilson Trail Race 25, 209, 274
Muir, John 34, 190
Museum of Contemporary Art 256
Music Center 255-257

N

Nail Care 270
Napa Style 234
National Charity League 128
Neff, Wallace 13, 72, 78, 83, 99, 209

Neighborhood Church 79, 131, 187,
  243-244
Nelson, R. Kenton 8, 124, 144
Neutra, Richard 73, 80, 83, 222
NewTown 119
Nicole's Gourmet Foods 151, 164, 176
Night Basketball & Books 128
99 Ranch Market 23, 134, 165
No Future Café 244
Noise Within Theatre 185
Norton Simon Museum 60, 81,
  99, 116, 151, 187
Norton Simon Garden Café 151
Nose Wine Cellar 175
Novotny's Antique Gallery 222
Noyes, Arthur 37
Nuccio's 102

O

Oba Sushi Izakaya 134, 142
Occidental Children's Theater
  & Summer Institute of Fun 240-241
Occidental College 11, 15, 18,
  39, 41, 51, 72, 88, 111, 160
Ocean Star Seafood 134, 155
Oinkster 158, 249
Old Focals 225, 231
Old Pasadena Vintage Lighting 222
Old Town Music 228
Old Towne Pub 183
Olvera Street 247, 253, 259, 262
Once Upon a Time 64, 218, 251
One Colorado 121, 140, 144,
  166, 179, 186, 225, 230, 240-241, 249
One Colorado Film & Blues Series 179
Onesipkim 231
Ontario Airport (ONT) 272
Orange Cat, The 247
Original Whistlestop, The 234
Our Lady of Lourdes West Grotto 99
Outpost for Contemporary Art 122
Owens, Robert 13, 35

P

Pacific 18 Theatres 186
Pacific Asia Museum 82, 117, 119
Pacific Electric Red Cars 39
Pacific Oaks College 11, 52
Pacific Paseo Stadium 14 186
Palacios, Maureen 64, 251
Palate Food & Wine 142
Panda Inn 142
Paper 235
Paper Source 235
Paperwhites Fine Stationery 224, 235
Parking 273
Parkway Grill 134, 142-143, 172, 182
Parsons, Jack 109
Pasadena Antique Center 220
Pasadena Antique Mall 220

Pasadena Architectural Salvage 220
Pasadena ARTS transit 273
Pasadena Art Alliance 10, 119
Pasadena Ballroom Dance
 Association 180-181, 243-244
Pasadena Buddhist Church 131
Pasadena Casting Club 209
Pasadena Central Library 10, 65, 110
Pasadena Church of God 131
Pasadena Cinco de Mayo 247
Pasadena City College 11, 52,
 217, 244, 267
Pasadena City Parks 211
Pasadena Civic Auditorium &
 Convention Center 241
Pasadena Civic Ballet 187
Pasadena Community Orchestra 187
Pasadena Conservatory 240-241, 252
Pasadena Convention & Visitors 271
Pasadena Dance Theatre 185,
 187, 252
Pasadena Educational
 Foundation 129
Pasadena Heritage 38, 84,
 87-88, 129, 178, 246-247, 274
Pasadena Humane Society 129,
 268, 274
Pasadena Ice Skating 210, 242, 244
Pasadena Jazz Inst. 179, 181, 240-241
Pasadena Jewish Temple 131
Pasadena Lawn Bowling Club 209
Pasadena Main Post Office 269
Pasadena Museum of California Art
 113, 117, 179
Pasadena Museum of History 40,
 86-87, 110
Pasadena Pacers 209
Pasadena Playhouse 39, 82, 109,
 117, 138, 169, 175, 184-185, 188, 260
Pasadena Pops Orchestra 179
Pasadena Pro Musica 131, 187
Pasadena Public Library 54-55, 65,
 72, 82, 85
Pasadena Roving Archers 209
Pasadena Sandwich Co. 161
Pasadena Senior Center 260, 269
Pasadena Showcase House
 for the Arts 87, 129, 274
Pasadena Symphony 187, 240, 274
Paseo Colorado 181, 186, 226,
Paseo Colorado:
 Dancing under the Stars 181
Paseo Pharmacy 269
Patina 257-258
Patticakes 163
Patton, George S. Jr. 23-24
PCC Swap Meet 243-244
Peet's Coffee & Tea 11, 169
Penelope's Café 152
Penny Lane 228
People's Taxi 272

Perry's Joint 169, 243-244, 249
Persson's 103
Pharmacies 269
Philippe the Original 258
Pho 79 134, 148
Phoenix Inn 156
Pie 'n Burger 66, 134, 152, 174
Pilates 206
Pink Plum 222
Pizza 158-159
Planetary Society, The 47
Poo-Bah Record Shop 228
Porta Via 152, 161
Porto Alegre 142
Porto's Bakery 163
Post Offices 269
Present Perfect 103, 250
Prime Time 272
Puebla Tacos 134, 160

Q

Quality Inn Pasadena 267

R

Rancho Bar 172
Raymond Hotel, The 33, 39, 68
Raymond Restaurant, The 134, 143
Red Carpet Liquor 175
Red Door Café 65, 169
Red Shoes 231
redwhite + bluezz 166, 182
Regeneration 231
REI 211
Reid, Hiram 32-33
Reid, Hugo 29-30, 95
Reid, Victoria 30
Revival Antiques 220
Rex Nails 270
Rick's Drive-In 134, 158
Rising Sun & Co. 231
Ritz Resale 235
Robin's Wood-Fire BBQ 153
Robinson , Mack 203
Robinson, Jackie 11, 39, 52,
 109, 203, 213, 238
Rockin Kid Shop 251
Roehrig, Frederick 81, 83, 85
Roger Renick Antiques 221
Roma Deli 165
Rose, Guy 118
Rose Bowl 10, 34,
 39, 49, 80, 106, 189, 196, 198,
 200, 203-206, 208-211, 216,
 238-239, 243-247, 264, 266-267, 274
Rose Bowl 4th of July 247, 274
Rose Bowl Riders 201
Rose Bowl Swap Meet 243-244
Rose Bowl Tennis 211

Rose Parade 8, 10, 34, 38, 53, 66,
 101, 104-109, 112, 124, 132, 176, 188,
 202, 214, 225, 236, 246, 252, 264
Rosebud Parade 245-247, 274
Rosso Wine Shop 175
Rubipy 42
Rue de Mimo 224, 231, 250, 260
Run With Us 211
Running 209

S

Saga Motor Hotel 267
Saint Anthony's Church 131
Saladang 134, 143-144
Salons & barbers 270
Salzman, Mark 59
Samy's Camera 228
San Gabriel Cemetery 100-101
San Gabriel Civic 23, 39, 185
San Gabriel Nursery 103, 268
San Gabriel Orange Grove
 Association 31, 68
San Marino Book & Toy 251
San Marino Nursery 103
San Marino Tennis Club 211
San Pascual Stables 201, 243-244
Santa Anita Golf Course 208
Santa Anita Park 212, 244, 274
Sarge's Physical Training 206
Saturday's Child 251
Sav-On Drugs 269
Scarlet Tea Room 170
Scene Bar 183
Scholl Canyon Golf Course 208
Scholl Canyon Tennis 211
Schreiner's Fine Sausages 165
Scoops 219, 251
Sea and Space Explorations 122
Sea Harbour 156
Self-Realization Fellowship 131
Senior services 269
Señor Fish 134, 160
Serra, Junipero 23, 28, 40, 100
750ml 142-143, 260
Sew Joe Stitch Lounge 227
Shamshiri 148
Sharp Design Works 222
Sheraton Pasadena 267
Shibui Japanese Antiques 221
Shiro 135, 143
Shogun 249
Shopping districts 218-219, 224
Shorb, James deBarth 30
Sierra Fitness 206
Sierra Madre Books 64
Sierra Madre Parks 211
Sierra Madre Pioneer Cemetery 101
Sierra Madre Playhouse 25, 185, 218
Sierra Madre Public Library 55
Sierra Vista Park Aquatic Center 210

Silver Birches 268
Sinclair, Upton 35, 38-39, 49, 59, 109, 184
Singer Park 238-239
Sixty East Fine Jewelry 234
Skating 210, 242-244
Skein Fine Yarn Store 227
Smith, Whitney (Whit) 78
Smitty's Grill 143
Soap Kitchen 234
Soccer 210, 238, 270, 274
Social Activism Speaker Series 45
Song 134, 144
SoPas Gallery 122
Soumarelo 161
South Lake 224-225
South Lake Nail Design 270
South Pasadena
  Concerts in the Park 179
South Pasadena Farmer's Market 167
South Pasadena
  Historical Museum 40
South Pas Music Center 182, 228
South Pas Public Library 55, 65
Southwest Chamber 179, 187, 274
Spas & Facial Care 271
Sport Chalet 192, 211, 226
Standard, The 258
Staples Center 255-258
Stationery 234-235
Stats 227
Stoney Point 172
Stratton, Bruce 71
Strobridge, Idah Meacham 58
Super Shuttle 272
Susan's Custom Alterations 270
Sushi Roku 144
Swanky Blanky 251
Swimming 210, 239
Swork 15, 169

T
T.L. Gurley Antiques 221
T Room Montrose 170
Takeout 160-161
Taquerias, Taco Trucks 159, 160
Tarantino's Pizzeria 159
Taxis 255, 272
Taylor's Ol' Fashion Meats 165
Taylor's Steakhouse 134, 144
Tea Rose Garden 170
Temple Sinai of Glendale 131
Ten Thousand Villages 234
Tennis 211
Teri & Yaki 161
Terrace, The 152, 265
Theatre 360 240-241
Theatre at Boston Court 185
Therapy 231
Thomas R. Field Antiques 223

Three Drunken Goats 134, 144
Thrift stores 235
Thrifty Car Rental 272
Tiara Café 258
Tibet Nepal House 134, 148, 249
Tirage Art Gallery 122
Tom's Toys 218, 251
Tommy Farmer 269
Tonny's 144
Top's Burger 158
Topline Wine & Spirits 175
Toros Pottery 122
Tournament of Roses Parade 39, 106, 245, 247, 274
Tournament Park 238-239
Toy Dept. 251
Trader Joe's 26, 39, 165, 175
Tranquility Skin Care & Spa 271
Travel agent 271
Traxx 258
Tre Venezia 145
Triangle 231
Trilco 223
Tritch Hardware 232
Triumphal Palace 155
Tutti Gelati 249
21 Choices 249
24 Hour Fitness
  Magic Johnson Club 206
Twin Palms 134, 145, 152, 173, 181

U
UA La Cañada Flintridge 186
UCLA football 205, 238, 274
Ugo's Italian Deli 152
Ultrazone 243-244
Underground Arts Society 122
Union Station Foundation 129

V
Val Surf 251
Verdugo, Jose Maria 16, 19-20
Verdugo Adobe 40
Verdugo Skatepark 210
Vertical Wine Bistro 112, 145, 171, 173, 260
Victory Park 10, 167, 238-239
Videothèque 228
Village Pizzeria 25, 159
Visitors Bureau 264, 271
Voices of Vision 45
Vroman, Adam Clark 58
Vroman's Bookstore 11, 45, 58, 64, 251, 260
Vroman's Bookstore Author Visits 45
Vroman's Fine Writing,
  Gifts & Stationery 235

W
Wahib's Middle Eastern 148
Walt Butler Sports Shoes 211
Water Grill 258
Weinstein, Cindy 44
Western Asset Plaza 99
Westfield Santa Anita 186, 226
Westin Pasadena 260, 267
Whole Foods 165
Wildflour Baking Co. 163
Williamson Gallery 50, 122
Wilson, Benjamin "Don Benito" 12, 30-31, 40, 101, 194, 282
Wilson, Larry 6
Winter, Robert 67, 77, 88
Wistaria Festival 25, 98, 274
Wistaria Thrift Shop 235
Wolfe Burgers 158, 249
World Hats 232
Wright, Frank Lloyd 58, 69, 79
Wrigley Mansion/Gardens 35, 80
Wrigley, William 35, 80

X
Xi'em Clay Center 123

Y
Yang Chow 145, 256, 258-259
Yard House 173
Yellow Cab 272
Yoga 207
Yoga House 207
Yoga Kingdom Sanctuary 207
yoko 223
York, The 18, 154, 173-174
Yoshino Japanese Antiques 221
Young & Healthy 129
Young Art 122
Yujean Kang's 134, 145, 260

Z
Z Sushi 145
Zankou Chicken 134, 161
Zeke's Smokehouse 20, 153
Zelo Cornmeal Crust Pizzas 159
Zephyr Coffee House 65, 169
Zinke's Shoe Repair 81, 270
Zoë 207
Zona Rosa 65, 169
Zucca 258

Photo credits

Forewords: Larry Mantle by Bill Youngblood; Larry Wilson courtesy of the *Pasadena Star-News*

Historic: San Gabriel Mission painting from Laguna Art Museum, gift of Nancy Dustin Wall Moure; Fr. Serra, Mission San Gabriel by Theresa Kennedy; Indian headstone & Robinson Memorial by Sandy Gillis; Don Benito Wilson courtesy Alhambra Historical Society; first house in Pasadena, Pasadena in 1885, Brown house & Reids courtesy Pasadena Public Library; historic floats courtesy Tournament of Roses Archives; Caltech founders courtesy Caltech; Henry Huntington copyright the Huntington

Smart: Caltech scientists, cannon & Athenaeum courtesy Caltech; Caltech courtyard by Greg Asbury/Pasadena Convention & Visitors Bureau; JPL Rover team courtesy Napa/JPL; Mt. Wilson Observatory courtesy Carnegie Observatories; Art Center South Campus by Steven A. Heller/Vaha Alaverdian, Art Center College of Design; Einstein at blackboard by Brown Brothers Photographers; CSCA Kitchen by Henry Kerker; Occidental College by Kevin Burke; Brand Library courtesy Brand Library & Art Center; Lucy Jones & Pasadena Library by Paul J. Click

Architectural: Castle Green by Robert Landau/Pasadena Convention & Visitors Bureau; Blacker House by Les Nakashima; Gamble House by Alex Vertikoff/Gamble House; Gamble House front door and interior by Tim Street Porter/Gamble House; old City Hall by Frasher's Fotos; new City Hall courtesy of the City of Pasadena; Bullocks courtesy Pasadena Public Library; Castle Green tower by Paul J. Click; Robert Winter and Batchelder House by David Gautreau

Horticultural: Bridge, Mountain View Cemetery & McKenneys by Paul J. Click; Flowering Plum & Descanso train courtesy Descanso Gardens; Japanese Garden, Rose Garden, Huntington Gallery & Aeonium Cyclops copyright The Huntington; Queen Anne Cottage courtesy L.A. County Arboretum; Throop Pond courtesy Caltech; Old Mill garden courtesy Old Mill Foundation; Nuccio's by Zach Shipko; Persson's by Sally Pfeiffer

Famous: Marching Band & White Suiters courtesy Tournament of Roses; the Royal Pains, Count Smokula & Motorized Couch Brigade courtesy Pasadena Doo Dah Parade; Las Encinas by Paul J. Click; 90210 House by Zach Shipko; Gale Anne Hurd courtesy Gale Anne Hurd

Literary: Book Alley and Flintridge Bookstore by Matt Hormann; Michelle Huneven by Paul J. Click

Artistic: Mary Cassatt painting, Pinkie & Ellesmere Manuscript copyright The Huntington; Bergers of Calais & Masterpieces by Degas, Monet & Pisarro copyright Norton Simon Museum; Pacific Asia Museum courtesy Pacific Asia Museum; PMCA courtesy Pasadena Museum of California Art; Fredric Stern Gallery courtesy Frederic Stern; Art Center Wind Tunnel gallery, by Steven A. Heller/Vaha Alaverdian, Art Center College of Design; Center for the Arts Eagle Rock courtesy Center for the Arts Eagle Rock; Kenton Nelson by Paul J. Click

Entertaining: Bridge Party courtesy Pasadena Heritage; One Colorado Movie courtesy One Colorado; Swing Dancers courtesy Pasadena Ballroom Dance Assoc.; John Clayton by Ernest Koberlein; Beckman Auditorium courtesy Caltech; Jorge Mester courtesy Pasadena Symphony/Pasadena Convention and Visitors Bureau; Alex Theatre courtesy Historic Alex Theatre; Pasadena Playhouse by Zach Shipko; Coffee Gallery Backstage by Rob Miller; Sheldon Epps by Paul J. Click

Reaching Out: Stream Team courtesy Arroyo Seco Foundation; Thanksgiving courtesy Union Station; All Saints by Paul J. Click

Hungry & Thirsty: Bistro 45 by David Mendelsohn; Celestino courtesy Celestino; Derek's dish courtesy Derek's Bistro; Akira Hirose courtesy Maison Akira; Three Drunken Goats, Central Park, the Oinkster, Julienne to go, Little Flower Candy Co., Nicole's desserts, Jones Coffee, Rosso Wine Shop & Bulgarini Gelato by Matt Hormann; Bean Town, Dona Rosa tortillas, La Cabanita, Lucky Baldwin's, Nicole Grandjean, Pie 'n Burger, Senor Fish, Monrovia Farmer's Market & Yujean Kang by Paul J. Click; Magnolia Bar by Gina Sabatella; Vertical Wine Bistro courtesy of Vertical Wine Bistro; Karma Bhotia courtesy Tibet-Nepal House

Outdoorsy: Sally Miller by Hana Lauterkranc; Mt. Baldy by Gary Klassen & Tony Crocker; Cyclists, San Pascual Stables & Doug Christiansen by Paul J. Click

Athletic: UCLA Football courtesy UCLA Athletics; Rose Bowl by Long Photography, courtesy Tournament of Roses; Yoga House by Jennifer Cheung & Steven Nilsson; Brookside Golf Course by Tavo Olmos/Pasadena Convention and Visitors Bureau; Lawn Bowlers & Jeff Brown by Paul J. Click; Diver & Aquatic Center courtesy AAF Rose Bowl Aquatic Center; Santa Anita Racetrack courtesy Santa Anita/Pasadena Convention and Visitors Bureau; Dodger Stadium courtesy Los Angeles Dodgers

Materialistic: Montrose, Folk Tree & Stephanie Miller by Paul J. Click; South Lake Shopping by Robert Landau/Pasadena Convention and Visitors Bureau; Novotny's and Old Pasadena Vintage Lighting by Matt Hormann; Paseo Colorado by Zach Shipko

Childlike: Lacy Park, Arroyo Mini-Golf, Sierra Madre & Fair Oaks Pharmacy by Paul J. Click; Theatre 360 by Monique Carroll; Pasadena Jazz drummer by Alan Colville; Rosebud Queen & Kidspace courtesy Kidspace Children's Museum; Chinese New Year float courtesy K & K Communications; Huntington Children's Garden copyright The Huntington; Galco's by Zach Shipko; Jane Kaczmarek courtesy Jane Kaczmarek

On the Train: Southwest Museum courtesy Southwest Museum; Disney Hall & Gold Line train by Paul J. Click; Gold Line map courtesy Metropolitan Transit Authority

Home Away from Home: Arroyo Vista Inn by Suzanna Hayek; Bissell House by Doreen L. Wynja; Huntington Hotel courtesy Huntington Hotel; Amadeus Spa courtesy Amadeus Spa; roses by Matt Hormann; Arts Bus courtesy Pasadena Convention & Visitors Bureau

Most other photos by Colleen Dunn Bates

Thanks to:

The design team: Production director Kate Hillseth, book designer James Barkley, first-edition production designer Sally Pfeiffer, logo designer Pamela Mosher and logo artist Joe Rohde

The artist: Kenton Nelson, creator of the cover painting

The photographers: Paul Click, Colleen Bates, Matt Hormann, Zach Shipko, Les Nakashima, Theresa Kennedy, Sandy Gillis and Sally Miller

The copy queens: Margery Schwartz and Sandy Gillis

The arts and literary advisor: Susan Futterman

The assistant editor: Matt Hormann

The sales team: SCB Distributors, Chris Jansen, Maryanne Herrill and Bored Feet Press

The advisers & photo-providers: Linda Bustos and Paula DiConti (Caltech), Lisa Blackburn (The Huntington), Leann Lampe (Pasadena Convention and Visitors Bureau), Lisa Montano (Pasadena Heritage), Dan McLaughlin (Pasadena Public Library), Judith Carter (San Marino Historical Society), Kathleen Tuttle, and everyone at Balanced Concepts Pilates, Sequoyah School and Flintridge Preparatory School

The bankers/cheerleaders: Joe and Ellie Dunn

The husbands: David Arnay, Darryl Bates, Tom Gammill, Joe Rohde and Stuart Shipko

The kids: Erin, Emily, Miles, Henry, Alice, Kellan, Brandt, Zach and Chloe

Further Reading

Altadena: Between Wilderness and City, by Michele Zack (Altadena Historical Society)

American Bungalow Style, by Robert Winter (Simon & Schuster)

An Architectural Guidebook to Los Angeles, by Robert Winter & David Gebhard (Gibbs Smith)

Architecture of Entertainment: L.A. in the Twenties, by Robert Winter (Gibbs Smith)

At Home Pasadena, by Jill Alison Ganon and Sandy Gillis (Prospect Park Books)

Don Benito Wilson: From Mountain Man to Mayor, by Nat. B. Read (Angel City Press)

Downtown Pasadena's Early Architecture, by Ann Scheid (Arcadia Publishing)

Hometown Santa Barbara, by Nancy Ransohoff, Starshine Roshell, Cheryl Crabtree, Leslie Dinaberg and Zak Klobucher (Prospect Park Books)

Hometown Santa Monica, by Jenn Garbee, Nancy Gottesman, Tippy Helpter and Margery L. Schwartz (Prospect Park Books)

Sylvanus Marston: Pasadena's Quintessential Architect, by Kathleen Tuttle (Hennessey + Ingalls)

Trails of the Angeles: 100 Hikes in the San Gabriels, by John W. Robinson & Doug Christiansen (Wilderness Press)